PRAISE FOR *UNLIKELY ALLIANCES*

"*Unlikely Alliances* offers a prescription about how cooperation between rural Native and non-Native communities and environmental organizers can be extended and encouraged. It is intended as a roadmap for the future, based on past experience."

—**David Rich Lewis**, author of *Neither Wolf nor Dog: American Indians, Environment, and Agrarian Change*

"A broadly comparative work that will be helpful for identifying approaches that lead to workable alliances between neighbors, and for highlighting recent successful Native strategies to assert control over significant natural resources."

—**Lisa Blee**, author of *Framing Chief Leschi: Narratives and the Politics of Historical Justice*

"When Indigenous peoples united with ranchers and farmers to stop the Keystone XL pipeline, they blazed an electrifying new path away from climate catastrophe. Such alliances to defend land and water have been taking shape for decades—and they have much more to teach us. Grossman draws out the key lessons from these stories with great skill and care."

—**Naomi Klein**, author of *This Changes Everything* and *The Shock Doctrine*

"*Unlikely Alliances* demonstrates that our ongoing fights for climate justice are not isolated struggles, but are founded upon a legacy of collaborative resistance. This book is an essential read for all organizers, water protectors, and land defenders who wish to build healthier, more sustainable communities and native nations."

—**Dallas Goldtooth**, national organizer, Indigenous Environmental Network

"Tribal nations' fight for treaty rights has always been on the frontlines. We will build bridges with our neighbors to find common ground, but cannot compromise our future. As place-based societies, we can no longer allow business as usual."

—**Brian Cladoosby** (Spee-Pots), chairman, Swinomish Tribe

Indigenous
Confluences

Charlotte Coté and Coll Thrush

Series Editors

UNLIKELY ALLIANCES

Native Nations and White Communities Join to Defend Rural Lands

ZOLTÁN GROSSMAN

Foreword by Winona LaDuke

UNIVERSITY OF WASHINGTON PRESS

Seattle and London

www.tulalipcares.org

Unlikely Alliances was supported by a generous grant from the Tulalip Tribes Charitable Fund, which provides the opportunity for a sustainable and healthy community for all.

University of Washington Press
www.washington.edu/uwpress

Library of Congress Cataloging-in-Publication Data on file

The paper used in this publication is acid-free and meets the minimum requirements of American National Standard for Information Sciences—Permanence of Paper for Printed Library Materials, ANSI Z39.48–1984. ∞

The author's proceeds from sales of this book are being donated to the Seventh Generation Fund for Indigenous Peoples, Inc. (www.7genfund.org).

Cover photo: *Reject and Protect rally of the Cowboy Indian Alliance in Washington, DC, April 22, 2014.* Courtesy Bold Nebraska.
Opposite: *Quileute canoe in the flotilla at the "Shared Waters, Shared Values" rally opposing the Grays Harbor oil terminal in Hoquiam, July 8, 2016.* (Courtesy Emma Cassidy / Survival Media Agency).

"Things of Intrinsic Worth," by Wallace McRae, from *New Cowboy Poetry*, ed. Hal Cannon (Layton, Utah: Gibbs Smith, 1990) used by permission of the poet.

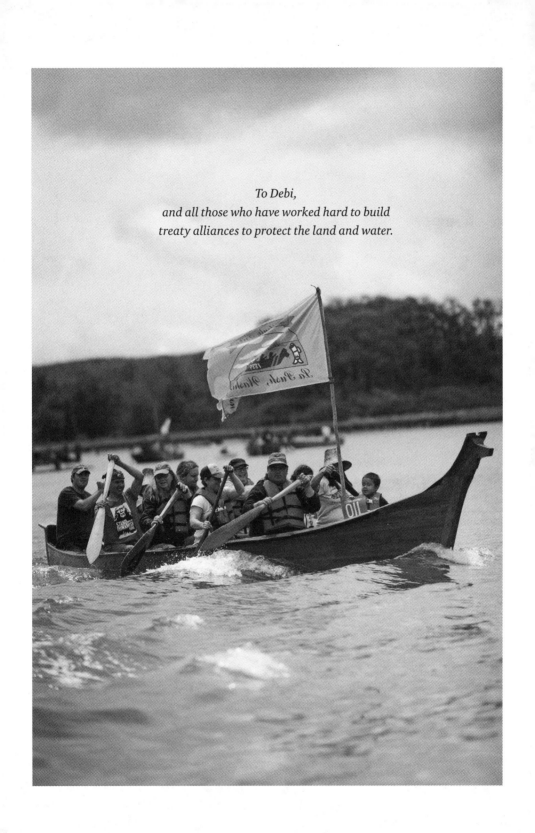

To Debi,
and all those who have worked hard to build
treaty alliances to protect the land and water.

CONTENTS

Foreword by Winona LaDuke   ix

Preface   xi

Acknowledgments   xvii

List of Maps   xxi

List of Interviews   xxiii

INTRODUCTION   3

Part I: RUNNING UPSTREAM   33

CHAPTER 1. Fish Wars and Co-Management:
Western Washington   37

CHAPTER 2. Water Wars and Breaching Dams:
Northwest Plateau   64

Part II: MILITARIZING LANDS AND SKIES   99

CHAPTER 3. Military Projects and Environmental Racism:
Nevada and Southern Wisconsin   103

Part III: KEEPING IT IN THE GROUND   135

CHAPTER 4. Resource Wars and Sharing Sacred Lands:
Montana and South Dakota   139

CHAPTER 5. Fossil Fuel Shipping and Blocking:
Northern Plains and Pacific Northwest   170

Part IV: AGREEING ON THE WATER   205

CHAPTER 6. Fishing and Exclusion: Northern Wisconsin   209

CHAPTER 7. Mining and Inclusion: Northern Wisconsin   239

CONCLUSION   273

Notes   291

Index   347

FOREWORD

Winona LaDuke

*As the Indigenous people, we have watched. We have watched
this thing happen on our hemisphere. We have seen what
has happened. We have seen the community confused and
attacked. We understand that the issue is the land, the issue
is the Earth. We cannot change the political system, we cannot
change the economic system, we cannot change the social
system, until the people control the land, and then we take
it out of the hands of that sick minority that chooses to
pervert the meaning and the intention of humanity.*

—John Trudell

IN THE ANISHINAABE PROPHECIES THIS IS SEEN AS THE TIME OF THE
Seventh Fire. In this time, it's said that our Oshki Anishinaabeg, our people,
who would be aware, conscious human beings, would look about and have a
choice between two paths. One path would be well worn, the other scorched.
It would be our choice.

This book is about that choice. In the time we are in, ecosystems are crash-
ing, our people have become sedated and contaminated, many of us, with the
accoutrements, and, well, poisons of the Predator Economy, the Wasichu
way. . . . Indigenous people have a long history of being oppressed, and sometimes that oppression sticks, and you remain oppressed, and other times it
does not. You wake up and shake off the fog, the accoutrements, and you remember who you are and what are your instructions.

As much as Anishinaabeg and other Indigenous peoples wake and take
action, or deepen and continue the action of the past five hundred years, we
find that there are many who have come to live on this land who understand
and feel the same. This, of course, makes sense, because our Mother Earth,
this land, Anishinaabe Akiing, the land to which we belong, speaks to us and
speaks to those who come to live here. That is, if you are able to listen and hear.

Since I was a very young woman I have worked in this space, between the Native and the non-Native, the Indigenous and the enlightened settler. Because our collective future is tied upon this return to consciousness, return to remembering who we are, and working with the spiritual power that comes from this place to make that future which is good—ji misawaabandaaming. The positive future. In this work, I have allied with many farmers, ranchers, and friends.

My first, and most impressionable, relationship was with Marvin Kammerer, a rancher who came to live in the heart of Lakota territory, in a ranch adjoining the Ellsworth Air Force Base. That was a time when we were facing twenty-six separate uranium-prospecting companies that had come to the sacred Paha Sapa, the Black Hills. There, on his land, he allowed us to gather, in the Black Hills Alliance gatherings of 1979 and 1980, two formative years, in the beginning of times that would mark the cowboys and Indians working together.

This long-standing relationship has marked my life. I am still a good friend of Marv's, and today, thirty-five years later, the same alliance not only has battled off the uranium mining companies but also succeeded in stopping the Keystone XL pipeline. It is that joining of forces, allies, land-based peoples, who will defend our Mother Earth. In that space, I am reminded that I am not a patriot to a flag, but I am a patriot to a land.

Many of us, it turns out, are. In that same space, as an ally and as a friend for over thirty years, is Zoltán Grossman. This book is a prayer, and thanksgiving, and a teaching tool, which tells the story of that relationship, and in telling the stories, we are reminded that we return to our humanity and our greatness as human, spiritual beings. We are reminded that we are able to have agency to make change, because that is how change is made. And we are inspired.

PREFACE

AT A GATHERING IN NORTHERN WISCONSIN ABOUT TWENTY-FIVE years ago, Ojibwe fishers were telling their stories to an invited group of non-Native guests. We were sitting together in a circle in a room on the Lac du Flambeau Reservation, passing an eagle feather from person to person, so each person would speak from the heart and tell the truth. Tribal members of the Wa-Swa-Gon Treaty Association told the non-Native members of the Witness for Nonviolence about growing up on the reservation, fighting for the treaty right to spear fish outside the reservation, and defending that right from violent anti-treaty protesters. They answered questions about how they continue to practice their traditional lifeways, about why they love the lakes and rivers and fish and wild rice, because that is just who they are.

When they were done speaking, Wa-Swa-Gon chairman Tom Maulson turned the questions around. "We've told you who we are, and why we're here today," he said, "now we want to know: What brought *you* here? *Who are you?*" Asking "who are you" was partly a question and partly a challenge, from tribal members tired of the long line of do-gooders coming to reservations to "help," of New Agers attending tribal gatherings to appropriate a Native identity, of academic researchers seeking to extract Indigenous knowledge, or of politicians and activists trying to fit the centuries-long battle for Native nationhood into a temporary political agenda.

In Indigenous nations, the protocol of introducing oneself is the most important first step in building a diplomatic relationship. All of the European American members of Witness for Nonviolence in the room could answer the first question of what motivated them to come, but few could answer the second question of who they are, because they felt too disconnected to their own cultural and spiritual heritage and their extended families. When the eagle feather came to me, I had to think deeply about these two questions, and I have been trying to think about them ever since.

I am the first on both sides of my family to be born and raised in North America. My parents both immigrated as kids from Hungary in the late 1940s and met as teenagers in Buffalo, New York (which made them settlers in Haudenosaunee territory). They never would have met in the Old Country, because my father was a Jewish city boy and my mother was a Catholic farm girl. My dad lost nearly his entire extended family in the Holocaust, except his mom and aunt. When I was a kid, he told me stories of being interned in Budapest, of his many relatives being deported to Auschwitz, of the Nazis executing his father by the Danube on New Year's Eve 1945, and of his mother escaping the Jewish ghetto with him (by pretending to be the widow of a corpse being taken to burial). Today on the banks of the Danube, a moving memorial of bronze shoes marks the spot where my grandpa and other Jews had to remove their shoes before being shot.[1]

From my dad's side, I understood that genocide is not a historically distant, abstract concept, but affects families many decades later. I learned to mistrust cultural pride and difference, because of the horrors it could lead to, and to instead find and appreciate *similarities* among peoples that transcend religious, ethnic, or racial divides.

My late mother was from a small village in western Hungary, where her family still lives today. Many relatives emigrated to work as steelworkers in Pennsylvania, but most returned home before the war. My mom and grandma emigrated after the war to live in Buffalo's large Hungarian community. Grandma worked as a seamstress in Buffalo, lived there until she passed in 1994, and never had to learn English. She baked Hungarian pastries to show her love—stretching the paper-thin strudel dough over her kitchen table to toss on the cherries or poppy seeds—and sent them in perfectly wrapped boxes for my birthday and Christmas. In the conformist 1950s, my mom distanced herself from her culture, and lost her accent, to become more American and "modern." I never adequately learned the (difficult) Hungarian language. When I was seventeen, I visited my mom's birthplace and family with her and my grandma. My first visit will always be a treasured memory, of smelling the fruit trees and hearing the wild stags and boars in the deep forest where my ancestors had lived.

From my mom's side, I understood that cultural assimilation destroys beautiful cultures and languages, homogenizing them into a generic American melting pot. I learned to value ethnic identity, and to find and appreciate the *differences* among peoples, and the importance of cultures having their own space to grow and flourish.

All my life I've been a contradictory mixture, with these two sides of my heart and mind in constant struggle. One side wants people to unite around their universal similarities (such as economic equality or the environment), but the other side wants people to respect each other's particular cultural differences and identities. As one side asks, "Can we all get along?," the other side asks, "Why can't you just leave people alone?" In academic-speak, these two ideas are called "universalism" and "particularism," but I didn't know that until years later. The idea of relating unity and autonomy, of reconciling the teachings from the two sides of my family, has infused almost everything I've done.

I was born in Chicago in 1962 and spent my grade school years in Salt Lake City. My father was a law librarian and chair of the Utah chapter of the American Civil Liberties Union (ACLU). When I was eleven, his was the only ACLU chapter to defend American Indian Movement (AIM) activists arrested by the Federal Bureau of Investigation during the siege of Wounded Knee, at the site of the infamous 1890 massacre. The stories of the outgunned Lakota holding off federal armor on the Pine Ridge Reservation morphed in my young mind with the stories of partisans in the World War II anti-fascist Underground. The Americans who turned a blind eye to repression of Native peoples reminded me of the "good Germans" who just followed orders, and I quietly vowed to be a "bad German" like those who hid out Jews or resisted the Nazis. I personally had a privileged life as a white, straight, male citizen of the United States, but my family history told me not to trust the system and to side with those who challenged the status quo.

We lived in Minneapolis all through the 1970s, at the height of AIM, which was headquartered in the Franklin Avenue neighborhood. After learning how the government "reign of terror" in South Dakota might be linked to uranium mining, I got involved in the Black Hills Alliance, which brought Lakota defending their sacred hills together with environmentalists and ranchers, to defend their water from mining. Only six years after Wounded Knee, some white ranchers began to see the universal similarities they had with the Lakota and also came to appreciate Native treaties and particular cultural differences. Their mutual love of the land united them together, and their diversity gave them the strength to chase off the mining companies. I volunteered to help in organizing the 1980 Black Hills International Survival Gathering, which drew eleven thousand people to the spread of rancher Marvin Kammerer, and my life of activism began.

When I went to college that same year, the best way I could figure out the transformation from conflict to cooperation was through combining geography (the study of change over space) with history (the study of change over time). As I majored in geography and history at the University of Wisconsin–Madison, I studied the relationship between "universalist" working-class movements and "particularist" ethnonational movements. I also visited the Philippines to look at how Filipino leftists fighting the dictatorship of Ferdinand Marcos and class inequalities worked together with Indigenous peoples fighting hydropower dams and other corporate development that threatened their waters and rice terraces.

I worked as a professional cartographer for fourteen years, making curricula and maps for encyclopedias, textbooks, and a state historical atlas. But all along, I learned far more from community organizing and alliance building than from either my schooling or employment. I learned the most from my partner and future wife, Debi McNutt, who had grown up on a Wisconsin dairy farm and had closer ties to the people and the land, as we worked together in all these struggles.

That's how the story comes full circle back to that talking circle, where Debi and I and other non-Native community organizers had gathered with our friends from Lac du Flambeau. In the late 1980s, Ojibwe spearfishing outside the reservations had been recognized in federal courts, and hate groups organized mobs of white sportfishers to harass and attack the Native families at the boat landings. We were among the co-founders of the Midwest Treaty Network, which coordinated with Witness for Nonviolence to train thousands of treaty supporters to deter and monitor anti-Indian violence and harassment. As the anti-treaty groups became more openly racist, and their claims that the Ojibwe were destroying the fishery and tourism industry were discredited, they declined in the early 1990s.

Around that same time, mining companies were trying to open metallic mines in Wisconsin and viewed treaty rights as a potential legal barrier to their plans. We worked with some white sportfishing groups to stop arguing with the tribes over fish and to start joining with the tribes to protect the fish from mining pollution. For ten years we saw the growth of an amazing grassroots alliance of Native peoples, rural environmentalists, and sportfishing groups, which confirmed my previous experience in the Black Hills Alliance and took it to an even higher level. Some of the Native leaders (such as Tom Maulson and Walter Bresette) who had been the most adamant about defending treaty rights from the white sportsmen were the most adamant about urging the so-called rednecks to join them against the mining companies.

Around the same time, I went to graduate school at the University of Wisconsin–Madison to earn my PhD in geography, with a graduate minor (the highest degree available) in American Indian studies. I examined some of these questions of interethnic relations and settler colonialism—whether in Native America, East-central Europe, the Middle East, or U.S. immigrant communities. I wrote my doctoral dissertation in the midst of participating in the anti-mining alliance. After graduating from twenty-second grade, I taught for three years at the University of Wisconsin–Eau Claire, before being hired in 2005 at The Evergreen State College in Olympia, Washington, and becoming a settler in Coast Salish territory. Olympia is near the rivers that had seen a previous fish war and near tribes (such as Nisqually) that had joined with non-Native governments and neighbors to repair and restore fish habitat.

Although I teach in Native American and World Indigenous Peoples Studies, that doesn't mean I teach about Indigenous cultures, a responsibility that is best left to Native peoples themselves. So please don't ask me about Ojibwe ceremonial rituals, your Cherokee great-grandmother, or the latest internal tribal faction dispute. I learn and teach mainly about Native/non-Native relations, including white racism and anti-racism toward Indigenous peoples, and about U.S.-tribal government relations and common-ground issues between reservations and their white "border towns," such as responding to climate change and fossil fuel shipping. As a non-Native academic and activist, my responsibility has been to help remove the obstacles put up by my governments to the sovereignty of Native nations and barriers put up by my communities to Indigenous peoples who are trying to decolonize their own lands and lives.

I'm also writing mostly about the region I know best: the "northern tier" between the Pacific Northwest and the Great Lakes. I've lived and worked as an adult in these states, with my place identity stretched along Interstate 90/94. Most rural counties where I've done my activism and research usually have a white and Native population and not many other groups.

Although I teach about all parts of the country, I don't have adequate knowledge to write about the older colonial processes in the Northeast, or the historically triangulated relationships of whites and Indians in the Southeast (with African Americans), or the Southwest (with Chicanos or Mexican Americans), or U.S. colonialism in Alaska and Hawai'i. Although I follow First Nations politics very closely, this study also doesn't incorporate Canada, which has a vibrant array of local and national alliances—particularly since the advent of the Idle No More movement—but also deeper public awareness of and scholarship on Indigenous politics than in the United States. I'll leave it to better-qualified others to interpret alliances in these places.

I hope this book functions as a type of guide to Native and non-Native community organizers and leaders in the beginning stages of building alliances against new mines, pipelines, or other projects, to see precedents elsewhere in the country and what strategies have worked and not worked. I also hope that the book can stimulate discussion among students, faculty, and researchers studying innovative ways to alleviate racial/ethnic conflict, create populist movements across cultural lines, and roll back the centuries of dispossession and colonization of Indigenous nations.

I hope this preface has first addressed a legitimate question: Why would a Hungarian American secular Jewish-Catholic radical geographer pay attention to Pine Ridge, Lac du Flambeau, or Nisqually, much less write a book about them? My answer: because of who I am. Who are you?

ACKNOWLEDGMENTS

THANKS TO MY WIFE AND PARTNER IN ACTIVISM, DEBI MCNUTT, FOR her love, wisdom, inspiration, and perseverance through this project and through our three decades together.

Thanks to my parents, George and Susanna Grossman, for their love, support, and motivation.

A deeply felt thanks to all the people who agreed to be interviewed, for helping with the project and for teaching us about new ways to respect the land, water, and one another. My profound respect for those whom I interviewed who have since passed on. Rather than mention their passing in the text, I have treated them as living on through their stories and actions.

Thanks to the University of Washington Press and its editors and staff, and particularly to acquisitions editor Ranjit Arab and to Coll Thrush, Charlotte Coté, and Matthew Gilbert of the Indigenous Confluences series for their support and patience, to director Nicole Mitchell, editor-in-chief Larin McLaughlin, assistant editor Whitney Johnson, senior project editor Nancy Cortelyou, senior designer Thomas Eykemans, graphic designer Dustin Kilgore, marketing and sales director Rachael Levay, production manager Margaret Sullivan, intellectual property manager Puja Boyd, communications manager Casey LaVela, and catalog manager Kathleen Pike Jones, as well as Jane Lichty for her edits, Scott Smiley for his indexing, and Julidta Tarver for her encouragement. Thanks to the anonymous reviewers whose comments strengthened my manuscript.

Thanks to my graduate advisor William Cronon, professor of history, geography, and environmental studies at the University of Wisconsin–Madison, for his guidance and insights. Thanks also to all the graduate students who met with Dr. Cronon every Wednesday to exchange research and ideas. Thanks to my other University of Wisconsin faculty advisors Robert Kaiser (Geography), Robert Ostergren (Geography), Gary Sandefur (Sociology and American Indian Studies Program), and Jess Gilbert (Rural Sociology). Thanks to the Morris K. Udall Scholarship and Excellence in National Environmental Policy Foundation and to the University of Wisconsin Foundation for funding my research.

Thanks to the University of Wisconsin–Madison Department of Geography and its faculty for supporting creative research projects. Thanks also to the department's energetic community of graduate students for their support and to the helpful and entertaining Geography Library staff. Thanks to the University of Wisconsin American Indian Studies Program faculty members and students in Madison and Eau Claire, for their inspiration and support. Thanks to other Native and non-Native friends throughout North America who reminded me why this project needed doing and for giving their feedback. Thanks in particular to Winona LaDuke for her support and her foreword to this book.

Thanks to my faculty, staff, and student colleagues at The Evergreen State College in Olympia, Washington, in the Native American and World Indigenous Peoples Studies (NAWIPS) program, the Longhouse Education and Cultural Center, the Tribal Master of Public Administration program, and the Reservation-Based, Community-Determined Program. Thanks to all the cool Evergreen students who have traveled with us to Pacific Northwest Native nations and Maori communities in Aotearoa New Zealand, and to Kristina Ackley for her motivation.

Thanks to the Association of American Geographers (AAG) and its Indigenous Peoples Specialty Group, and the Native American and Indigenous Studies Association (NAISA), for sponsoring presentations based on this study and serving as supportive communities. Thanks also to the University of Wisconsin–Madison Summer Institute on Environmental Justice, Land Tenure Center, Midwest Sociological Society, Wisconsin Department of Public Instruction, Western States Center, Western Mining Activists Network, Center for New Community, Center for Democratic Renewal, Midwest Treaty Network, Wisconsin Geographical Society, Madison Area Technical College, Marquette University, University of Wisconsin campuses in Eau Claire and Stevens Point, Indigenous Environmental Network, Pitzer College, University of Alberta, The Evergreen State College, and others, for inviting presentations on Native/non-Native conflicts and cooperation.

Thanks to the Seventh Generation Fund for Indigenous Peoples for supporting Native environmental organizing. All royalties for this book will be donated to the fund for its ongoing work.

Thanks to the *American Indian Culture and Research Journal* for publishing an overview of this study in 2005 (vol. 29, no. 4). Thanks to Jill Bystydzienski and Steven Schacht for printing a chapter on the northern Wisconsin case study in *Forging Radical Alliances across Difference: Coalition Politics for the*

New Millennium (Rowman and Littlefield, 2001), to *North American Geographer* for printing a similar article in 2000, to *Agricultural History* for printing an article on the Northern Plains case study in 2003, and to Jonathan Clapperton and Liza Piper for printing a chapter on fossil fuel alliances in the forthcoming *Environmentalism on the Ground: Processes and Possibilities of Small Green Organizing.*

Thanks to Suzan Harjo for my interview in the 2014 Smithsonian Press book *Nation to Nation: Treaties between the United States and American Indian Nations* and to Winona LaDuke for my 2014 interview on her KKWE Niijii Radio program. Thanks also to *ColorLines, Cultural Survival Quarterly,* Applied Research Center, and Zed Press for publishing articles or chapters jointly authored with colleagues on alliances, as well as Z, Counterpunch, Indian Country Today, Common Dreams, Portside, Unsettling America, Works in Progress, and other websites for publishing related articles. Complete references to related articles, courses, and presentations are at my website, http://academic.evergreen.edu/g/grossmaz.

Thanks to Oregon State University Press for publishing *Asserting Native Resilience: Pacific Rim Indigenous Nations Face the Climate Crisis,* as a 2012 anthology (co-edited with Alan Parker) on tribal responses to climate change.

Thanks to the kind staff at Cafe Zoma and Electric Earth Cafe in Madison, who smiled when I brought in my laptop day after day and supplied me with the necessary caffeine to complete my work. Thanks also to the staffs of Brigham Park in Blue Mounds, the best spot to write in Dane County, Wisconsin, and of Tumwater Falls Park, the best Wi-Fi–free place to write in Thurston County, Washington.

Finally, thanks to all the water protectors who struggle every day to defend their lands and waters, and to build Indigenous nationhood, whether or not you're recognized in the media limelight. The world is watching, and the future is with you.

For more background and updates on unlikely alliances, visit the book's webpage at https://sites.evergreen.edu/unlikelyalliances/.

MAPS

Examples of Native/Non-Native Environmental Alliances   4

Western Washington Tribes   38

Tribes and Dams of the Columbia Basin   65

Military Projects on Western Shoshone Lands   108

Military Projects on Wisconsin Ho-Chunk Lands   118

Mining in Montana   145

Lakota (Sioux) Treaty Lands   151

Fossil Fuel Basins and Northwest Ports   171

Treaty Rights and Mining in Northern Wisconsin   211

The Proposed Crandon Mine near Wisconsin's Wolf River   242

Proposed Penokees Mine by Wisconsin's Bad River   260

Thanks to Amelia Janes of Earth Illustrated Inc. for revising and updating the maps.

INTERVIEWS

Name	Affiliation of interest at time of interview	Address
Fred Ackley	Mole Lake Ojibwe tribal judge	Crandon, WI
Hadley Akins	Umatilla Basin Project former co-chair	Pendleton, OR
Jennifer Allen	Western Shoshone Defense Project	Crescent Valley, NV
John Anderson	Vilas County zoning administrator	Boulder Junction, WI
Bill Bakke	Native Fish Society director	Portland, OR
Charlotte Black Elk	Cowboy and Indian Alliance; Oglala Lakota	Pine Ridge, SD
Alexis Bonogofsky	National Wildlife Federation Tribal Lands Partnerships Project	Billings, MT
Joye Braun	Camp of the Sacred Stones; Indigenous Environmental Network; Cheyenne River tribal member	Cannon Ball, ND
Walter Bresette	Midwest Treaty Network; Anishinaabe Niijii; Red Cliff Ojibwe	Red Cliff, WI
Faye Brown	Prairie Island Coalition	Minneapolis, MN
Don Bryson	Nez Perce Fisheries biologist	Lostine, OR
Herbert Buettner	Trout Unlimited Wolf River chapter	White Lake, WI
Alaina Buffalo Spirit	Northern Cheyenne; Northern Plains Resource Council	Birney, MT
Lanny Carpenter	Puget Sound Gillnetters Association	Olympia, WA
Roscoe Churchill	Rusk County Citizens Action Group	Ladysmith, WI
Les Clark	Northwest Gillnetters Association former president	Chinook, WA
Patricia Conway	Citizens Against Low-Level Flights	Ontario, WI
Wally Cooper	Rhinelander fishing guide; Wisconsin Resources Protection Council (WRPC)	Rhinelander, WI

Terry Courtney Jr.	Wasco/Tingit Columbia River Inter-Tribal Fish Commission (CRITFC) commissioner	Warm Springs, OR
George Crocker	General Assembly to Stop the Powerline (GASP)	Lake Elmo, MN
Joseph DeLaCruz	Quinault former chairman; Northwest Indian Fisheries Commission (NWIFC) co-founder	Hoquiam, WA
Bruce Ellison	Black Hills Alliance co-founder; attorney	Rapid City, SD
Teresa Erickson	Northern Plains Resource Council	Billings, MT
Michael Farrow	Umatilla Department of Natural Resources director	Umatilla, OR
Karl Fate	WRPC	Rhinelander, WI
Steve Fick	Salmon for All	Astoria, OR
Kenneth Fish	Menominee Treaty Rights and Mining Impacts Office	Keshena, WI
Lea Foushee	GASP / North American Water Office	Lake Elmo, MN
Billy Frank Jr.	NWIFC chairman; Nisqually treaty rights leader	Olympia, WA
Mert Freyholtz	Environmental Rangers	Gildford, MT
Gaiashkibos	Lac Courte Oreilles Ojibwe chair	Hayward, WI
Ona Garvin	Former Ho-Chunk tribal legislator; Citizens Opposed to Range Expansion (CORE)	Pittsville, WI
Al Gedicks	WRPC	La Crosse, WI
Tom Goldtooth	Indigenous Environmental Network executive director	Bemidji, MN
Arthur Grunbaum	Citizens for a Clean Harbor	Aberdeen, WA
Liz Hamilton	Northwest Sportfishing Industry Association	Portland, OR
Corbin Harney	Western Shoshone National Council	Sparks, NV
Jill Hartlev	Bad River Ojibwe mining committee	Odanah, WI
Louis Hawpetoss	Menominee tribal judge	Keshena, WI
Nick Hockings	Wa-Swa-Gon Treaty Association; Lac du Flambeau Ojibwe	Lac du Flambeau, WI
Johnny Jackson	Columbia River Chiefs' Council; Cascade/Klickitat	Underwood, WA

Jewell James	Lummi Sovereignty and Treaty Protection Office	Lummi, WA
Lilias Jones Jarding	Clean Water Alliance executive director	Rapid City, SD
Tyson Johnston	Quinault Indian Nation vice president	Taholah, WA
Marvin Kammerer	Black Hills Alliance; rancher	Box Elder, SD
Philomena Kebec	Bad River tribal staff attorney	Odanah, WI
Rebecca Kemble	*Progressive* magazine correspondent and activist	Madison, WI
Adriann Killsnight	Northern Cheyenne; opponent of Otter Creek coal mine	Lame Deer, MT
Eleanor Kinley	Whatcom County Commercial Fishermen's Association; Lummi	Lummi, WA
Jane Kleeb	Bold Nebraska director / Cowboy Indian Alliance	Hastings, NE
Frank Koehn	The Water's Edge / Penokee Hills Education Project	Herbster, WI
Bill Koenen	Mole Lake Ojibwe environmental officer	Crandon, WI
Anita Koser	Wa-Swa-Gon Treaty Association; Lac du Flambeau Ojibwe	Lac du Flambeau, WI
Phil Lane, Jr.	Ihanktonwan Nakota / Dakota chief	White Rock, BC
Paul Lumley	CRITFC	Portland, OR
Sandy Lyon	Anishinaabe Niijii	Springbrook, WI
James Main Jr.	Red Thunder / Indigenous Environmental Network; Gros Ventre	Fort Belknap, MT
Victor Martino	Skokomish tribal attorney	Bainbridge Island, WA
Tom Maulson	Lac du Flambeau Ojibwe chair; Wa-Swa-Gon chair	Lac du Flambeau, WI
Debra McNutt	Midwest Treaty Network	Madison, WI
Bill Means	International Indian Treaty Council director; Oglala Lakota	Minneapolis, MN
Antone Minthorn	Umatilla Tribes chairman	Umatilla, OR
Ros Nelson	Penokees mine opponent	Washburn, WI
Sandra Palm	Commercial fisher and coal terminal opponent	Bellingham, WA

Carolyn Parker	Environmentally Concerned Citizens of Lakeland Areas (ECCOLA) / Vilas County Board member	Woodruff, WI
Steve Parker	Yakama Fisheries staff	Toppenish, WA
Joseph Pavel	NWIFC staff; former Skokomish chair	Olympia, WA
Allen Pinkham	Nez Perce former chairman, CRITFC commissioner	Lapwai, ID
Manuel Piño	Laguna-Acoma; Indigenous Environmental Network	Acoma, NM
Sylvester Poler	WRPC; Mole Lake Ojibwe	Crandon, WI
Grace Potorti	Rural Alliance for Military Accountability	Reno, NV
Allie Raven	Bad River Ojibwe tribal member	Delta, WI
Cindy Reed	Cowboy and Indian Alliance	Hot Springs, SD
Bill Robinson	Trout Unlimited Washington Council chair; executive director of Washington State Northwest Salmon and Steelhead Council	West Seattle, WA
Steve Robinson	NWIFC	Olympia, WA
George Rock	WRPC	White Lake, WI
Bobbi Rongstad	Bad River Watershed Association	Gurney, WI
Joe Rose Sr.	Professor emeritus, Northland College; Bad River Ojibwe	Odanah, WI
Donald Sampson	CRITFC chairman; former Umatilla chair	Portland, OR
Virginia Sanchez	Citizen Alert Native American Program director; Western Shoshone	Reno, NV
Susana Santos	Tygh fisher, former Greenpeace staffer	Warm Springs, OR
Melvin Schmidtgall	S&M Farming Company	Athena, OR
Robert Schmitz	Wolf River Watershed Alliance	White Lake, WI
Joe Schumacker	Quinault Indian Nation marine resources scientist	Taholah, WA
Paul Seamans	Dakota Rural Action chair	Draper, SD
Chris Sewall	Western Shoshone Defense Project	Crescent Valley, NV

Fawn Sharp | President of Quinault Nation; president of Affiliated Tribes of Northwest Indians | Taholah, WA

Chris Shelley | Salmon Corps director of education/training | Portland, OR

Chuck Sleeter | Nashville town chairman | Pickerel, WI

Joanne Sleeter | Nashville town clerk | Pickerel, WI

Claude Smith, Sr. | Wasco elder/fisher | Warm Springs, OR

Jeff Smith | American Friends Service Committee; Makah | Seattle, WA

Diane Snyder | Wallowa Resources director | Enterprise, OR

Tom Soles | Walleyes for Tomorrow; Sturgeons for Tomorrow | Fond du Lac, WI

Glen Spain | Pacific Coast Federation of Commercial Fishermen | Eugene, OR

Faith Spotted Eagle | Cowboy Indian Alliance; Ihanktonwan (Yankton) Nakota/Dakota | Lake Andes, SD

Tim Stearns | Save Our Wild Salmon director | Seattle, WA

Ted Strong | Former CRITFC director; former Yakama chair | Toppenish, WA

Joanne Tall | Good Road Coalition; Oglala Lakota | Pine Ridge, SD

Larry Thevik | Vice president, Washington Dungeness Crab Fishermen's Association | Ocean Shores, WA

Richard Thieltges | Sweet Grass Hills Protective Association | Helena, MT

Dorothy Thoms | Wa-Swa-Gon Treaty Association; Lac du Flambeau Ojibwe | Lac du Flambeau, WI

Madonna Thunder Hawk | Black Hills Alliance; Oglala Lakota | Pine Ridge, SD

Mark Tilsen | Black Hills Alliance former director | Stillwater, MN

Craig Tucker | Klamath coordinator, Karuk Tribe | Orleans, CA

Krystal Two Bulls | Oglala Lakota; coal opponent at Northern Cheyenne | Missoula, MT

Dorothy Tyra | Pickerel Lake Association | Pickerel, WI

Frank Urabeck | Northwest Marine Trade Association | Federal Way, WA

Frances Van Zile | Mole Lake Ojibwe elder | Crandon, WI

Monica and Mark Vitek	O'Dovero-Flesia Farm, with other family members	Mellen, WI
Rich Wandschneider	Nez Perce Homeland Project	Enterprise, OR
Tom Ward	WRPC	Crandon, WI
Dennis White	Columbia Gorge Audubon	White Salmon, WA
Charmaine White Face	Cowboy and Indian Alliance; Oglala Lakota	Manderson, SD
Mike Wiggins Jr.	Chairman, Bad River Band of Lake Superior Chippewa	Odanah, WI
Dana Wilson	Lummi commercial fisher	Lummi, WA
Jim Wise	ECCOLA / Northwoods Alliance	Tomahawk, WI
Sonny Wreczycki	Rollingstone Lake Association	Ainsworth, WI
Raymond Yowell	Western Shoshone National Council chief	South Fork, NV

UNLIKELY ALLIANCES

Introduction

IN MINNESOTA IN 1978, I COVERED A FARMERS' ENVIRONMENTAL
rally for a high school student newspaper. The white farmers were protesting
against a high-voltage electrical transmission line that crossed their lands.
The farmers had been joined for the first time by Native Americans, who opposed the mining of coal on treaty lands in North Dakota to generate the elec-
tricity in the transmission lines. Next to the rally site, I saw two red pickup
trucks parked side by side. One pickup had the bumper sticker "The West
Wasn't Won with a Registered Gun." The other pickup, more beat-up, sported
a bumper sticker that read "Custer Had It Coming." At the end of the rally, the
white farmer and the Native American drove off in their trucks with these very
different messages attached.

At the same time around the Umatilla Reservation in Oregon, tribal members were in an intense conflict with white farmers and ranchers over their
treaty rights to dwindling water resources. The Umatilla and other Pacific
Northwest tribal nations were also locked in a seemingly life-or-death struggle
with white fishers over their newly recognized treaty rights to harvest fish. Yet
the Umatilla began to cooperate with white farmers and ranchers over improving water flows in order to restore endangered fish runs, with non-Indian
fishing groups to breach hydropower dams and protect fish habitat, and with
state and federal agencies on protecting natural resources from environmental harm.

Just as the Pacific Northwest fishing crises began to be resolved, another
treaty confrontation erupted in northern Wisconsin. In the late 1980s, crowds
of white sportsmen and sportswomen gathered to harass and assault Ojibwe
(Chippewa) exercising their court-recognized treaty rights to spear fish outside
the reservations. Yet by the mid-1990s, tribal members were working together

3

EXAMPLES OF NATIVE/NON-NATIVE ENVIRONMENTAL ALLIANCES

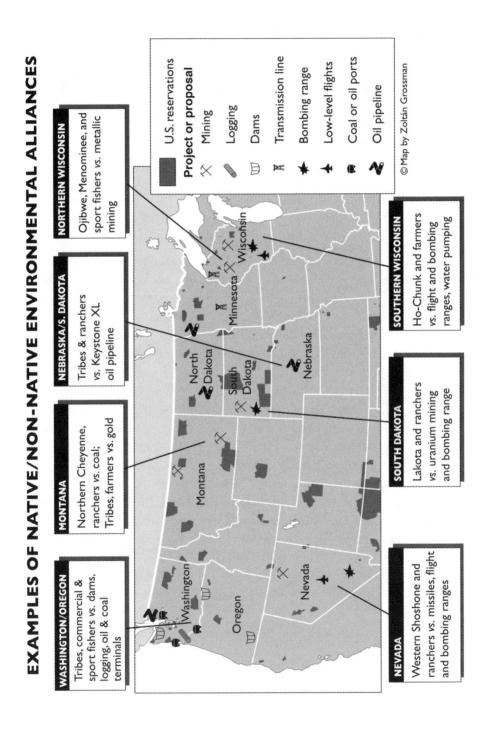

NORTHERN WISCONSIN
Ojibwe, Menominee, and sport fishers vs. metallic mining

NEBRASKA/S. DAKOTA
Tribes & ranchers vs. Keystone XL oil pipeline

MONTANA
Northern Cheyenne, ranchers vs. coal; Tribes, farmers vs. gold

WASHINGTON/OREGON
Tribes, commercial & sport fishers vs. dams, logging, oil & coal terminals

SOUTHERN WISCONSIN
Ho-Chunk and farmers vs. flight and bombing ranges, water pumping

SOUTH DAKOTA
Lakota and ranchers vs. uranium mining and bombing range

NEVADA
Western Shoshone and ranchers vs. missiles, flight and bombing ranges

U.S. reservations

Project or proposal

Mining
Logging
Dams
Transmission line
Bombing range
Low-level flights
Coal or oil ports
Oil pipeline

© Map by Zoltán Grossman

4

with sportfishing groups to protect the same fish from proposed metallic mine projects, using some of the same treaty and sovereign rights that the sportsmen and sportswomen had previously opposed. For the first time, local governments began to cooperate with tribal nations not only to protect the fish but to develop sustainable economies.

Witnessing such "unlikely alliances" drove me to study why Native nations and rural European American residents—archetypal enemies in past and present conflicts—would find common cause to defend their mutual place. In the 1970s to the 2010s, similar alliances brought together Native peoples and rural white resource users in areas of the country where no one would have predicted or even imagined them. Farmers, ranchers, commercial fishers, and sportfishers had been virtually at war with Native nations over the control of land and resources. Yet members of the communities unexpectedly came together to protect the environment from an outside threat. Native/non-Native cooperation has become an important element in the protection of many rural parts of the United States, particularly in the West and Midwest.

The evolution went through four general and often overlapping stages. First, Native peoples asserted their autonomy and renewed nationhood. Second, a right-wing populist backlash from some rural whites created racial conflict over the use of land, water, or natural resources. Third, the racial conflict declined in intensity as the neighbors initiated dialogue over common threats to land and water. Fourth, Native and white neighbors collaborated on the protection of their community livelihood and natural resources using a cross-cultural anticorporate populism. The neighbors felt that if they continued to contest the place, to fight over resources, there may not be any left to fight over.

These Native/non-Native environmental alliances, like the anti-treaty groups before them, began in the Pacific Northwest in the 1970s, grew into the Great Basin and Northern Plains, and gradually reached the Great Lakes. They have included Native/non-Native alliances confronting mines, dams, logging, nuclear waste, military projects, oil pipelines, coal and oil terminals, and other environmental threats. Natives and non-Natives in each area took different paths from conflict to cooperation and experienced varied levels of success in improving relations.

DESCRIPTION OF STUDY

This comparative study is organized around the regions where key, high-profile alliances were born in the West and Midwest and later inspired and nurtured other alliances. The chapters are loosely organized around one or two regions facing a particular threat and responding with cross-cultural alliances. They identify the main flashpoints within each region, where particular local battles were fought, and how the alliances navigated complex challenges and choices as they evolved. The chapters conclude with particular lessons that may help to enrich the internal conversations that any alliance has in its nascent or early stages.

The story begins with the "fish wars" in western Washington, the first source of the "white backlash" against treaty laws and later of tribal co-management of the fishery with state government. It shifts into the Plateau region of eastern Washington and Oregon (and Idaho), where hydroelectric dams have been the main challenge to tribal fishing rights and where farmers and ranchers have long been at odds with tribes over water rights. The story then shifts south into Nevada, where the Western Shoshone first formed alliances in the 1970s to stop military projects, similar to alliances formed by the Ho-Chunk Nation of southern Wisconsin in the 1990s. The narrative switches to the Northern Plains, where the Lakota and Northern Cheyenne formed alliances with ranchers and farmers against coal, gold, and uranium mining in the 1970s. These alliances in Montana and South Dakota formed precedents for new "cowboy-Indian alliances" against fossil fuel extraction in the early twenty-first century, which in turn connected to new alliances in the Pacific Northwest against shipping the oil and coal. Finally, the narrative returns back to a fishing rights struggle, this time in northern Wisconsin in the late 1980s and early 1990s, which evolved into alliances between Ojibwe and white fishers to stop metallic mines that jeopardized the fishery in the 1990s to 2010s.

Each of these chapters seeks to help answer particular questions that face any Native/non-Native alliance and determine its short-term and long-term success:

- First, they address the common "sense of place" of Native and non-Native communities. At what geographic scales can alliances best construct common ground? How do they reconcile different senses of place and notions of sacred space?

- Second, they examine the common purpose of the communities in facing a common enemy. How can alliances anticipate that they may be divided along lines of race and privilege? How can "outsiders" be recast as "insiders" in a common landscape?

- Third, they explore the common sense of understanding that could extend beyond a short-term alliance of convenience to long-term cooperation. How can treaty rights and tribal sovereignty be reframed as protecting both Native and non-Native interests? How can conflicts be resolved from above with better intergovernmental relations or from below with closer people-to-people relationships?

The answers to these key questions give insight into an alliance's success, either in its short-term goal of defeating a harmful project or in its long-term goal of building lasting cross-cultural ties. Some answers to these questions emerge from interviews with key players in the alliances and provide theoretical insights that could be useful to people in other places and eras.

While my study uses many textual sources, the bulk of the sources have been interviews with people on their experiences in building alliances. These individuals served as "primary documents," who speak in their own words about the history of their personal and community transformations. In keeping with Indigenous research ethics guidelines, their voices are prioritized in my study.[1] I correlated their observations with media reports, group newsletters or websites, and other textual sources. Scholarly literature was often scant, perhaps because the alliances were too remote or obscure or scholars studying the environmental issues or intergroup coalitions had not focused on local relationships.

In many cases, the interviewees were the only witnesses to key events and processes. Their own perspectives, however, may have shaped their accounts of the history, just as they shaped the alliances themselves. The case studies explore not only the circumstances that formed the alliances but also the different perspectives that often contested their form and strategies and that can still skew the retelling of stories around them.

From 1997 to 2016, I interviewed 120 members of these Native/non-Native alliances, mostly on research trips in Washington, Oregon, Montana, Nevada, South Dakota, North Dakota, and Wisconsin. Many of the individuals are those who first breached the barriers between the communities and who subsequently served as the initial "bridges" between them. They include sportfishing group leaders and fishing guides, farmer and rancher group leaders, tribal government leadership, Indigenous elders, Native community organizers, and rural white community organizers, schoolteachers, small business owners, and others. They were usually interviewed in the setting where they had carried out their work: in their offices, at environmental gatherings, in public halls, or across their kitchen tables. Some interviews were conducted by phone or e-mail. Other insights came from informal discussions with friends and colleagues in community service and activism.[2]

In the interviews, I posed similar questions covering three areas, revolving around the role of place, the short-term conflict and cooperation, and long-term relations between the communities.

First, how did cultural perceptions of the value of the place, or a "sense of place," affect the outcome? Were members of the other community viewed as "outsiders" who violate social boundaries or as "insiders" in a common, territorially defined "home"?

Second, how and why did Native nations and non-Native communities evolve from confrontation to cooperation and develop a common purpose against common enemies? Did cooperation extend beyond environmental issues and last beyond the environmental victory or defeat?

Third, did the assertion of Native sovereignty weaken or facilitate such alliances? Were attempts made to prevent or mask cooperation? Did the alliances actually lessen divisions or merely gloss over differences? Did the participants develop a common sense of understanding that would outlast temporary environmental threats?

The study focuses narrowly on the alliance formed around environmental issues, rather than on the environmental issues themselves, though some exploration of the location and scope of the threat can shed light on the cooperation. My study does not, for example, review scientific debates over the merits of a development project. The claims that a project is harmful could even be completely false, but the point is that the claims led to the formation of an alliance. The corporate or state threat to the "self-determination" of both Native nations and non-Native communities, not simply the problems with a particular development project, helped to bring together the communities.[3] This study dwells not on laws or the legal status of tribes, which many authors have admirably documented, but on the development of *social movements* that support or challenge that status and organize communities to make change.

The study also focuses narrowly on the history of relationships between Native reservations and rural non-Indian communities that use natural resources, particularly white farmers, ranchers, and fishers. It does not closely examine relations between tribes and urban-based environmental groups, except when they may affect the growth of a rural alliance. Nor does it look closely at relations between urban Indian groups and environmental organizations. Many excellent studies have focused on relations between Indigenous peoples and environmental groups and their similarities or differences within coalitions.[4] A few have studied individual white allies-educators supporting tribal cultural and language revitalization.[5] At least one study has examined common ground with countercultural movements.[6] Others have focused on alliances between Native peoples/nations and non-Native progressive or solidarity campaigns or on non-Native activists becoming "accomplices, not allies" in direct actions.[7]

But this study of environmental alliances is not primarily about organizations; it is about relations between Native and non-Native *neighbors*, between local land-based communities in the rural United States. And it is not a comprehensive study of the entire spectrum of relationships between Native nations and white communities—the good, the bad, and the ugly. In some areas, forming alliances is not yet possible because the two communities do not yet agree on common goals, or the white community is still too anti-environmental and/or racist. This study focuses on places where alliances were formed around common goals despite the continuing occupation of Native lands, as one step toward Native decolonization.

IMPLICATIONS OF THE ALLIANCES

In the United States, non-Native scholars and activists tend to view Native peoples as the smallest and least significant so-called "minority" group, who live on "isolated" reservations and do not affect national politics or the labor market to nearly the same degree as other racial "minorities." This treatment of American Indians and Alaska Natives as merely a demographic afterthought ignores the central role that Native nations have played in U.S. history and the continued existence of their cultures and territorial sovereignty within the boundaries of the occupying power. In some other settler states, such as Canada and Aotearoa New Zealand, Indigenous peoples are viewed more as political players who fundamentally question the settler society's control of the land base.

Native/non-Native environmental alliances may also be viewed as irrelevant or obscure. They could be portrayed as quaint examples of common ground between two allegedly "disappearing" U.S. populations: reservation Indians and rural whites who still value the land and its natural wealth. The popularized image of "cowboys and Indians" has been ingrained in the national (and global) consciousness as a cultural template of irreconcilable enemies.

Yet Hollywood's clichéd, racist stereotype of Indians eternally fighting cowboy "rednecks" belies some contemporary realities. Many white ranchers and farmers see their lifestyle as endangered by corporate globalization, much as tribal members have seen their land-based cultures under siege. Native nations and non-Native rural communities are confronted to different degrees by environmentally damaging projects that would not be tolerated in more populated regions.

Social scientists commonly examine racial or ethnic conflict, but few have studied such examples of cooperation based on common interests and outside threats to survival.[8] Even fewer have looked at mutual community interests based on a common territorial identity or "sense of place."[9] U.S. culture and media sensationalizes disputes between "cowboys and Indians" but rarely publicizes instances when they depart from the norm—even when they go so far as forming a group called the Cowboy Indian Alliance.

Native/non-Native environmental alliances offer an opportunity to go beyond the treatment of ethnic/racial conflict as a natural condition. Many scholars and activists are effectively documenting racism and colonization, but fewer are discussing what to do about it. Many are deconstructing racist institutions and structures, but fewer are discussing how to construct just institutions and structures in their place. Some have studied "geographies of exclusion," or how social boundaries between groups are reflected in place, creating "insiders" and "outsiders."[10] Yet fewer have speculated what "geographies of inclusion" might look like, how different social groups might mutually include each other within a common place. Studying the alliances opens up rarely examined interactions between national sovereignty, racial conflict, and interethnic collaboration— all based at least partly on place. I use the lens of geography, a discipline that was both heavily implicated in the process of colonization and has strong overlap with Native Studies and the place-based process of decolonization.[11]

Most importantly, the alliances offer important insights into the relationship between "particularism" and "universalism."[12] In the modern North American context, "particularism" asserts the particular differences between ethnic/racial groups or other groups based on gender, sexual preference, and other social identities. (In the United States, particularism is often called "identity politics," a clearly inadequate term given that Native *nations* have a distinct relationship to the larger society on the basis of not only their cultural identities but also their particular political and territorial histories.) Conservative and progressive pundits alike have opposed particularist politics as emphasizing group differences over similarities, as "balkanizing" U.S. society into distinct enclaves, or even as dangerously "separatist."

"Universalism" asserts common ground, or the similarities between groups that claim inherent differences. Universalism, which could be called "unity politics," has often been used to describe the common bond of state citizenship that theoretically treats all citizens equally. To socialists, universalism means different ethnic or racial groups uniting around their class consciousness. To feminists, it may mean women from different class or cultural backgrounds uniting around their gender identity. To environmentalists, it means human beings from different backgrounds coming together to defend the Earth.

Universalism usually gets better press than particularism, because it brings together disparate people in a common cause, overcoming insurmountable odds to work in harmony. Yet the glowing media accounts do not explain that even in the midst of the most successful alliances, social inequalities continue to rear their heads. In a geographic sense, as Glen Coulthard points out, appeals to "common ground" accommodation fail to acknowledge that the "commons" has belonged to Indigenous nations.[13]

Most scholars and activists assume that particularist movements asserting identity differences automatically contradict universalist movements emphasizing similarities in human experiences—such as environmental concerns. Scholars and politicians usually portray "particularist" movements around the world as barriers to greater cross-cultural understanding. They ask "minority" groups to subsume their identities within a universalist framework, in the interest of "unity" or the "greater good" of the Earth and humankind. The solution, we are told, is to build "diversity"—to bring together whites and people of color in social institutions so they can better understand each other. This approach is embodied in slogans such as "E pluribus unum," "United We Stand," or "All Lives Matter."

Such appeals or coercion come not only from powerful globalizing institutions, as some progressive scholars would assert.[14] The appeals come also from progressive institutions such as labor unions, political parties, and mainstream environmental organizations. They basically ask, "Can we all get along?" (Rodney King's plea during the 1992 Los Angeles uprising) by simply setting aside our differences.[15]

Two senators who ran for president, for example, discovered that there were issues with their universalist messages. In his 2008 campaign, Barack Obama often referred to the United States as "one nation," yet an anti-Indian group in Oklahoma also called itself One Nation United, reflecting its mission to deny Native sovereignty.[16] Tribal leaders later reminded President Obama that many nations exist within U.S. borders.[17] He addressed racial divisions more in his second term, as police killings and the Black Lives Matter movement made the particularist discussion unavoidable.[18]

During the 2016 campaign, Black Lives Matter activists disrupted Bernie Sanders's rallies, asserting that his economic populist message did not adequately address their concerns. Sanders then intensified his focus on racism in law enforcement and the justice system.[19] He also began to strongly emphasize tribal sovereignty.[20]

As Ta-Nehisi Coates pointed out at the time, white supremacy is "a force in and of itself, a vector often intersecting with class, but also operating independent of it."[21] Ian Haney-López and Heather McGhee urged progressive populists to treat racism "as a political weapon wielded by elites against the 99 percent, nonwhite and white alike," and thereby use an anti-racist message in organizing *white* communities.[22]

The universalist perspective often portrays group conflict as the result of groups floating in a social vacuum, accidentally bumping into the "Other," who we don't like only because they're different. But we don't live within a social vacuum. U.S. society has always been based on a racialized hierarchy, a pecking order of power relations determined by a mixture of class, gender, nationality, and skin color. This institutionalized system is not simply based on people not liking each other, but creates or deepens differences to keep people within their place in the hierarchy. "Diversity" is a laudable goal, but it usually takes the form of adding a few brown or black faces to white majority institutions, legitimizing them as "multicultural," without changing underlying power relations.[23]

Both proponents and opponents of "identity politics" often offer a stark choice between self-determination and unity. Yet particularity and universality are not necessarily in contradiction, nor are they "either-or" propositions. The two are not mutually exclusive; in fact, true "unity" will not work without self-determination, and self-determination will be difficult to win without some connections to the experiences and concerns of at least some whites.[24]

Many universalist movements—such as the global human rights and environmental movements—had their origins in particularist local settings.[25] Some Indigenous movements—such as the Zapatistas in Mexico or anti-corporate protesters in Bolivia—have successfully mixed (particularist) appeals to reverse the colonization of Indigenous peoples, with (universalist) class-based appeals to the non-Native poor.[26] Particularist movements face the risk of local isolation and a failure to confront national or global systems that are the ultimate source of their problems. Universalist movements face the risk of abstracting or homogenizing local differences and locking in inequalities within a "unified" society. But the two concepts can be interwoven to emphasize the strengths and overcome the shortcomings of each.[27]

Real "unity" around larger causes is made possible by a process of equalization. Particularist movements can help level the playing field between the communities, by fighting not only for their own rights but for wider social change.[28] To achieve unity, the majority needs to understand how recognizing and respecting difference can benefit universal values. Native/non-Native environmental alliances are an example of a movement that—consciously or not—has creatively negotiated the tensions between particularity and universality and has attempted to interweave them by *identifying Native self-determination as a way to protect the land and water for everyone.*

The Idle No More movement similarly connected First Nations' sovereignty to the protection of the Earth for all people—Native and non-Native alike. Idle No More emerged from Canada in December 2012, asserting its presence in creative visible ways (such as drum circles in shopping malls), and quickly spread into the United States and beyond.[29] Idle No More co-founder Sylvia McAdam states that "Indigenous sovereignty is all about protecting the land, the water, the animals, and all the environment we share."[30] Blackfeet author, lawyer, and storyteller Gyasi Ross observes that Idle No More "is about protecting the Earth for all people from the carnivorous and capitalistic spirit that wants to exploit and extract every last bit of resources from the land. . . . It's not a Native thing or a white thing, it's an Indigenous worldview thing. It's a 'protect the Earth' thing."[31]

Nishnaabeg writer and academic Leanne Simpson sees Idle No More as "an opportunity for the environmental movement, for social-justice groups, and for mainstream Canadians to stand with us. . . . We have a lot of ideas about how to live gently within our territory in a way where we have separate jurisdictions and separate nations but over a shared territory. I think there's a responsibility on the part of mainstream community and society to figure out a way of living more sustainably and extracting themselves from extractivist thinking."[32]

A debate within Idle No More (later reframed as the Indigenous Nationhood Movement) discussed how the movement can reach and mobilize the non-Native public. In any alliance, the same question always arises at the intersection of unity and autonomy. Should Native partners in the alliance set aside their own distinct concerns in order to build bridges to the white majority over common-ground concerns, such as curbing fossil fuels? Should Native

At the Rosebud Sioux Tribe Spirit Camp near Ideal, South Dakota, set up to protest the Keystone XL oil pipeline, the Cowboy Indian Alliance led "Hands around the Camp," where participants all joined hands in a traditional round dance. (Courtesy: Kermit Grimshaw / Bold Nebraska)

leadership, for example, not as strongly address treaty or human rights abuses, to avoid alienating potential allies among their white neighbors? Conventional wisdom says that we should all get along for the greater good and that different peoples should only talk about universalist similarities that unite them, not particularist differences that divide them. But it's not that simple.

In both my activism and my academic studies, I've often wrestled with this question, and I've spoken with many Native and non-Native activists and scholars who also deal with it. This study will seek to answer the question of whether emphasizing unity over autonomy is helpful or harmful to building deep, lasting alliances between Native nations and non-Native communities. If Native peoples strongly assert their nationhood, will their alliances with their non-Indian neighbors be weaker or stronger?

Much of the discourse about resolving or managing conflict has revolved around the state and using the mechanism of state citizenship to build a common universal identity. But Indigenous nations stake their cultural survival not on state citizenship but on boundaries and institutions that protect their distinctive identities and sovereign nationhood. Most scholars assume a stark choice between national self-determination and a common state citizenship, or try to strike a compromise between the two. Fewer have explored imaginative ways to build common identities *outside* the state-constricted framework, by constructing or using common territorial identities and a "sense of place." Native sovereignty is based not simply on intergovernmental relations but also on the "peoplehood" of Indigenous communities that share language, sacred history, place or territory, and ceremonial cycles.[33]

Indigenous movements prioritize cultural and political distinctiveness, not integration or assimilation into the dominant society. Though they have historically shared a stance with "civil rights" groups against white racism, their goals (as Aileen Moreton-Robinson emphasizes) center on their national sovereignty, including control over their territory.[34] This determination has deep roots in the history of Indigenous-settler relations in North America.

PROCESSES OF COLONIZATION

Studying Native history involves not only exposing the oppression of ethnic groups or a singular racial group but also examining the colonization of diverse Indigenous *nations*. Native history questions not only the decisions of the U.S. government but also the origins of the United States itself. Native history critiques not only federal and state government policies but also the clouded acquisition of the land base on which those policy battles take place. It deals with not only political and economic systems but also the cultural underpinnings of European civilization. Native American history opens a Pandora's box about the settler society that colonized Native nations.[35]

The process of European colonization began centuries ago, not in North America but within Europe itself. Carolyn Merchant has documented how seventeenth-century Western European elites imposed a mechanistic worldview—that studies and manages the natural world by fragmenting it into small pieces—to replace the popular organic worldview that studies and manages holistic interrelationships within the natural world. Merchant has shown how the Scientific Revolution, promoted by the likes of Francis Bacon, intensified the extraction of resources (such as metallic minerals) and labor.[36]

Silvia Federici has documented how the suppression of European Indigenous knowledge, through the mass executions of women healers, for example, was an important element of colonizing European landscapes and minds.[37] E. P. Thompson and Peter Linebaugh have shown how the privatization, enclosure, and division of the "Commons" prompted Robin Hood–style peasant rebel movements in European forestlands and drove many peasants and artisans who lost their lands into urban industries.[38] If this sounds like the colonization and allotment of Native lands, English leaders clearly saw Celtic nations as a testing ground for methods of colonization later used in North America.[39]

English settlers imposed mechanistic landscape management as a central aspect of colonization. William Cronon has demonstrated how the shift from Native to European dominance involved "fundamental reorganizations" in New England's plant and animal communities, including grazing by cattle, sheep, and hogs and the massive felling of timber for wood and charcoal, all increasing erosion and floods.[40] The history becomes all too familiar to Native peoples across North America, who were subjected to land theft, the enclosure and privatization (allotment) of their Commons, the engineering of the landscape for settler/corporate profit, and a degrading of their knowledge systems. The elites' promise of settling "free" (stolen) Native land also became a safety valve to defuse working-class unrest in Europe and on the East Coast, by providing a "dumping ground for a refuse population."[41]

In the meantime, the European encounter with more egalitarian Indigenous societies convinced some scholars, such as Jean-Jacques Rousseau and Lewis Henry Morgan, that class hierarchy was not the natural order, and they in turn influenced many of the social philosophers and rebels of the nineteenth century.[42] Because our history books present settler colonialism as uncontested within non-Native society, we never read about the white Wisconsin settlers who opposed the forced removal of Ho-Chunk and Ojibwe neighbors, the Washington settlers put on trial for collaborating with Coast Salish resistance, the Oklahoma farmers and sharecroppers joining in the Green Corn Rebellion, or other atypical stories of cooperation rather than conflict.[43] Some Europeans and Africans attracted to freer Indigenous societies even became kin to Native families. We never read these dangerous stories of Native/non-Native cooperation in history class, because they undercut the myth of Manifest Destiny as an inevitable, almost natural force. But there were always better paths not followed, even if they were exceptions to the white supremacist rule.[44]

The idea that contemporary Native/non-Native alliances may have deeper roots and precedents in North American history—or even in European history—is a much larger topic that historians are only starting to address. The very existence of the inquiry shows that Indigenous histories stretch farther back in time than the construction of racial identities, into the process of European colonization and settlement.

Mainstream historians sometimes assert that because people in the past didn't know any better, we cannot judge the past by the standards of the present. Yet there have always been vibrant social movements that criticize racist government policies. The leaders, at least, have been fully aware of these objections all along. Some of the poorer settlers may have been unaware of the clouded title of the lands they were colonizing. As Roxanne Dunbar-Ortiz has said, "I have a lot of sympathy for people who were duped, and they don't like to think that they were duped, but they were duped."[45] Some settlers may have been used as government pawns to trigger Native resistance and subsequent cavalry "rescue" to extend the U.S. military occupation zone. Other settlers (mainly women) even sympathized with the plight of their Native neighbors.[46] But the vast majority of settlers clearly understood their role as shock troops for colonization and violently asserted their claims to Indigenous territory.[47]

The brutal realities of settler colonialism should never be forgotten in favor of a "move to innocence" of settlers.[48] The "settler fantasies of easier paths to reconciliation" can indeed divert non-Natives "from the hard, unsettling work of decolonization."[49] Nor should settler colonization be presented as historically inevitable or natural, as a demographic steamroller of "the White Man" that could never have been stopped, with non-Native *governments* never held responsible for implementing and reproducing it.

Federal and state government policies toward Native nations have reflected changes within both Indian and white societies. An understanding of the history of these government policies, and how they have helped construct the identities of Native peoples, is vital to understanding the emergence of Native movements and their relationship to non-Native neighbors.

FEDERAL INDIAN POLICIES

Federal Indian policy is commonly misinterpreted as having "granted" Native peoples new political or territorial rights or as having "accorded special group rights."[50] In the U.S. Constitution (which is decades older than most Indian treaties), Article VI defines treaties as part of the body of law constituting the "supreme Law of the Land." Rather than serving as gifts to the tribes, treaties instead were the major mechanism to steal Native land, as the government coerced or pressured tribes to cede their preexisting rights over land and resources to the United States.[51]

Federal Indian policy in the nineteenth and twentieth centuries is often taught as a series of distinct eras, with policies that swung widely like a "pendulum" between unilateralist policies that sought to assimilate Native people and bilateralist policies that recognized tribes as distinct peoples.[52] Federal policies, however, were only one aspect of the colonization process, which cannot easily be divided into neatly defined eras.[53] Some of the policies that were intended to undermine Native self-rule actually backfired on government policy makers and had the unintended effect of intensifying Native efforts toward self-determination.

Treaties, for example, were meant to weaken Indigenous control over territory, but they also served to recognize collections of peoples as nations and, in doing so, inadvertently helped facilitate Native national consciousness. Early treaty making was a colonial policy to secure alliances with Native peoples before rival colonial powers did, so the treaties generally treated the Indigenous nations as sovereigns.[54] The treaties played a key role in consolidating different Native bands into a single voice in relations with the settler society.

Treaties also defined and set boundaries between Native national territories, where mutual understandings and shifting land-use agreements between Native neighbors had previously existed.[55] Native nations took on the trappings of European sovereign states—with more centralized authority and set boundaries—ironically in preparation for the extinguishment of their land base and forced removal.

Beginning in the Removal era of the 1820s to 1850s, federal troops marched many Native peoples westward to new reservations west of the Mississippi

River. While some forced removals were largely successful, such as the Trail of Tears from the Southeast to Oklahoma, other attempts (notably in the western Great Lakes region) were strongly resisted and elicited a Native determination to stay in or return to their homelands.[56]

Later treaty making evolved into deceptive or coerced land cessions. After the 1850s, the primary concern of U.S. Indian policy was to constrict Native peoples on reservations (through continued removals) and sever their control over their larger homelands, but many Indigenous peoples retained their concept and practice of nationhood in the face of overwhelming odds. Until 1871, the United States signed approximately 371 treaties with Native nations. When the government brazenly broke the treaties, it often stimulated a backlash of even deeper Native resistance.[57]

At the same time, many of the treaties contained clauses for continued use of the ceded lands outside the reservations for cultural or economic sustenance uses—such as religious ceremonies, hunting, gathering, or fishing—in effect maintaining the ceded lands as part of "Indian Country." Even federal officials understood that the tribes could not survive solely on reservation resources. That is why many twentieth-century Native rights battles centered on treaty rights, since those "usufructuary" rights guaranteed continued access to off-reservation resources and contained or implied a larger recognition of Indigenous nationhood.[58]

In the Allotment era of the 1880s to 1920s, a "unilateralist" federal government attacked the cohesion of Indian reservations by privatizing and dividing collectively held reservation lands, then confiscating individual plots for unpaid taxes and selling off large tracts of "surplus" lands to non-Indians.[59] At the same time, many Native youths were moved to boarding schools in a coordinated church-government effort to forcibly assimilate them into mainstream "American" culture. The boarding schools were horrific dens of mistreatment and death, yet inadvertently brought Native youth from different tribes into contact with one another, prompting resistance from students and their families, and educated some of the youths in the skills they later used to fight for tribal sovereignty.[60] Under the 1924 Citizenship Act, all American Indians were made U.S. citizens, in addition to their intact Native national citizenship.[61]

The economic devastation of Allotment led to the 1934 Indian Reorganization Act (IRA), which established federally approved tribal council governments on reservations that voted for the system. Most tribes approved the IRA system, since they had lost most traces of their precolonial forms of government, and some even managed to use the reservation council system to reinforce their tribal identity.[62] Some tribes or factions rejected the IRA as undermining their hereditary chief system or self-organized tribal council. On some reservations, the federally recognized tribal government and the traditional governance system functioned as parallel institutions for decades—sometimes in conflict (such as on South Dakota's Pine Ridge Reservation).[63] The Indian Claims Commission was created in 1946 to review tribal land claims, but could only offer paltry payments as compensation, rather than return the stolen land.[64]

In the 1950s and early 1960s the federal government unilaterally sought to "terminate" federally recognized tribes (such as the Menominee in Wisconsin and the Klamath in Oregon) to quicken their assimilation into U.S. society.[65] Termination triggered a strong counterreaction that brought an end to the policy.[66] Another federal program concurrently sought to assimilate and "advance" Native Americans by relocating them to urban areas. The urban relocation policy met some of its goals of lessening a Native attachment to the reservations, yet it backfired in crucial ways. It brought together members of different tribes in cities (such as Chicago, Minneapolis, Denver, and Los Angeles), leading to increased mutual discussions and action. The urban Indian population was also directly exposed to the civil rights and Black Power movements.[67]

Native activism in the late 1960s and 1970s found a receptive audience among dislocated urban Indians, especially those who had been brought up by "traditionalist" families on the reservations. Diverse tribes became slowly defined (from the outside) as a single pan-Indian "race"—a status that many Native peoples resented as homogenizing different nations but also used in order to strengthen intertribal unity. The Red Power movement pushed U.S. policy and legal decisions toward recognizing tribal governments' political self-determination.[68]

Pro-tribal legislation and court decisions in the 1970s stimulated a counterreaction among some whites on and off the reservations, who founded anti-treaty organizations.[69] This study begins in this period and examines how the modern anti-Indian movement mobilized, sometimes violently, against tribal sovereignty. In the 1990s, the concept of self-determination extended into economic, cultural, and environmental realms. The rise of tribal casinos gave some Native nations (with access to population or tourism centers) economic options they had not had for centuries.[70] The protection of burials, sacred objects, place-names, and cultural images became more widely accepted, and some tribes began to regulate environmental quality both on and off the reservations.

These gains have been matched by ongoing crises of continuing land loss, poverty, pollution, disease, poor diet, crime, divided families, and youth alienation. Although most of the federal court rulings in this study favored treaty laws and sovereignty, others did not, and even some of the favorable rulings placed conditions and limitations on the exercise of these rights.[71] Gaming revenues have given rise to a new popular stereotype of the "rich Indian" that parallels the stereotype of the "welfare Indian."[72] But the trend has been unmistakably toward greater self-determination, at least in contrast to earlier eras. It remains to be seen whether the current trend is just another temporary swing of the "pendulum," with non-Native perceptions of supposedly powerful "rich Indians" soon driving the pendulum back toward hostility.[73]

Federal policies in the United States were intended not simply to exploit people for their labor but to control their land and resources and, according to Elizabeth Cook-Lynn, to promote an ideology of anti-Indianism that "displaces and excludes" Indigenous peoples and cultures.[74] Through these policies, Indigenous peoples were subjected to both physical genocide and cultural genocide, also defined as "ethnocide."[75] As Patrick Wolfe underlined, ethnocidal policies were intended to "eliminate" Native people politically, economically, and culturally, even if they physically survived genocidal extermination.[76] Government and church officials also made sure that settlers did not make common cause with Native peoples or violate the "color bar" by establishing kinship ties with Native families.

Under U.S. Supreme Court rulings, tribes are recognized only as quasi-sovereign "domestic dependent nations," with a territorial base held in federal trust. Tribal membership is ostensibly based on national ancestry but is often defined by "blood quantum" measurements of tribal heritage.[77] Although the federal government originally developed the domestic dependency and blood quantum systems, they have also become largely internalized within the functioning of modern tribal governments.

Many Indigenous people, however, assert their nationhood as preexisting the United States or Canada and therefore not needing the approval of those governments to exercise sovereignty.[78] As the Haudenosaunee leader Oren Lyons has often said, "Sovereignty is the exercise thereof."[79] Indigenous scholars such as Coulthard view Native government attempts to gain official "recognition" from non-Native governments as inherently limiting Indigenous self-recognition.[80] Attempts to seek the acknowledgment of past wrongs, as part of an "apology" process, likewise subordinate Native self-determination to a non-threatening "trite statement of regret," in the words of Mohawk scholar Taiaiake Alfred.[81] Some state governments, for example, have promoted Native/non-Native "reconciliation" programs yet fail to identify the earlier era of "conciliation" that the two peoples should return to.

Nor do Indigenous activists necessarily hold an exclusivist view toward non-Natives, because unlike most nationalists in Europe or Asia, they follow Indigenous knowledge systems that view all human beings as part of the same biological or spiritual family. The problem is rarely posed as the mere presence of non-Natives, but rather is viewed as the institutional restrictions that settler states have placed on Native powers and lifeways. Since most settlers are not going back to Europe or Asia, they have to find ways to live respectfully with the longtime Indigenous residents into the future.

As Alfred asserts, "When we say 'Give it back,' we're talking about Settlers demonstrating respect for what we share—the land and the resources—and making things right by offering the dignity and freedom we are due and returning our power and land enough for us to be self-sufficient."[82] In this way, *alliances-from-below may pose an alternative to recognition-from-above,* as a way to build relationships and partnerships as much outside a state-constricted framework as possible. Native/non-Native environmental alliances represent a model that seeks to extend "bilateralism" beyond government policy into everyday social reality. If Native self-determination can be reframed as serving the common good of Native nations and non-Native communities, perhaps the next "white backlash" will not be as forceful or successful.

COMPLEXITIES OF IDENTITIES

Different perspectives within U.S. society today view Native Americans as a single race, as a collection of ethno-linguistic groups, or as sovereign (or semi-sovereign) nations. These views correspond, respectively, to biological, cultural, and political explanations for differences between peoples. Both "Native Americans" and "whites" are constructed racialized identities rooted in historical developments in North American history. Most Native peoples prefer their distinct national identities, which have themselves been constructed by tribal self-definition and colonial relations.

Before the European arrival, most Indigenous peoples possessed a band-based or clan-based identity. Some bands unified as tribes, and some tribes even unified as confederacies, such as the Haudenosaunee (Iroquois Six Nations

Confederacy) or the Three Fires confederacy around the Great Lakes. Through their interactions with the colonial and settler societies, local identities became territorialized as nations. Their claim to peoplehood became inseparable from territory, which inscribed national identities rather than ethnic or racial identities that do not claim land.[83]

European notions of nations and nationalism are notoriously difficult to apply to Indigenous peoples—particularly those that employ explanations for the emergence of nations as "imagined communities."[84] Without industrialization or strong class stratification, Native peoples developed different paths to nationhood than Europeans did. A Native-focused analysis cannot center on what made "peasants into Frenchmen" but rather can examine what made "Oglalas into Lakotas" —the processes that coalesced diverse peoples into nations. [85] The activation of Native national consciousness can be explained not by labor market roles or a goal of equal political representation but rather by questions of cultural and territorial defense.

Scholars often portray "particularism" as a throwback to preserve consciousness from a past era.[86] Native "nationalists" are often accused of seeking an essentialist return to "premodern" social and political forms. Yet Native "traditional" value systems today are not backward-looking. The contemporary Native movement can instead be viewed as a "resurgence" or "renaissance."[87] Much as the Italian Renaissance adapted Greco-Roman values to a new historical context, the Native Renaissance adapts "traditional" Indigenous values to modern society, without necessarily recreating the old societies.

Native movements seek not a strict reimplementation of previous forms but a "selective revitalization" of elements of an existing culture, adapted to modern society.[88] Their goal is not a simple regression to the tribal past but for modern Native nations to "negate" the colonial "negation" of Indigenous societies and move forward to a decolonized future—on their own terms.[89]

Indigenous nations do not use their treaty rights to romanticize an idyllic vision of a tribal past but use them as "living documents" to safeguard their cultural revitalization and economic livelihood into the future.[90] Indigenous peoples work for protection of natural areas not to become "environmentalists" in the Western sense, interested in protecting nature from human beings, but to maintain access to the natural wealth that had been passed on by their ancestors.[91]

Non-Indian environmentalists often employ images of the "ecological Indian," romanticizing Native peoples of the past as perfectly in harmony with nature and devoid of historical complexity.[92] The white rural neighbors of tribal nations rarely employ this noble "ecological Indian" imagery and so perhaps approach alliance building with different motivations than the environmentalists who do—even if they may possess other inaccurate or racist perceptions of Native people.

Creating a common future on the land for Indians and non-Indians is far more complex than simply building bridges between the two communities. Neither community is monolithic and contains its own diversity and schisms. Non-Indian outsiders attending a powwow may see a singular pan-Indian identity. But to the Native dancers and their families, differences between different tribal identities are always in the foreground, as are band, clan, and family differences within tribes. Class differences affect Native nations, though they are profoundly shaped by Indian-white relations and tribal government structures. Gender, sexuality, and age differences also affect the Native political landscape and interact with cultural and spiritual practices in ways that are often unfamiliar to non-Indians. Native women have gained a particularly powerful voice in narratives on the dispossession of land and water, as can be seen in many of the case studies in this book.[93]

Different tribal perspectives may take different approaches to basic questions of Native rights and land use, particularly when under strong outside pressure. They may address land use with terms so vastly different that it is difficult to tell they are describing the same lands. Tribal officials often take a proprietary or economic approach to land use, tribal attorneys usually stress legal jurisdictional questions, and tribal "traditionalists" emphasize historical and spiritual values attached to land.[94] This is an oversimplified picture, since tribal "factions" often overlap, and Indigenous political survival skills seem to overcome most temporary schisms. But an overly generalized view of "the Native perspective" can gloss over the range of opinion within Native nations.

Much the same can be said of non-Indian communities, including the European American or "white" community. In the same way that a Native American racial identity was constructed over centuries of interaction with European American society, the "white" racial category was constructed during Europeans' encounter with peoples on other continents, to justify and reinforce their enslavement of Africans and colonization of other Indigenous peoples (as discussed further in the chapter on whiteness and military projects). As Theodore W. Allen has documented, the "invention of the white race" turned diverse European ethnic groups in the so-called New World into a single whole, not only to enable the settlers to enslave Africans and control

Native lands but also to suppress class distinctions and rebellion among the settlers.[95]

As David R. Roediger has foregrounded, "whiteness" has historically served as a social control mechanism that turns the economic frustration of poor and working-class whites away from the white elites and governments above them in the racial hierarchy and toward people of color below them in the social pecking order.[96] This history helps explain the contradictory populist impulses of whites in the anti-Indian movement, who are frustrated by socio-economic changes in their communities but take out those frustrations on Native neighbors who had little or nothing to do with those changes and, as Joanne Barker notes, "deploy the discourses of reverse racism to contest the terms of Indigenous legal status, treaty and land rights, and economic self-sufficiency."[97]

Just as Native nations are often torn by internal divisions, "white" communities rarely speak with one voice. Those expressing opinions about Native rights, for example, run the gamut from rightists who reject Native peoples and cultures as inferior to conservatives and moderates who oppose sovereignty but admire tribal "self-reliance" and to liberals and leftists who support Native cultural and environmental distinctiveness, e ven if they do not quite grasp economic autonomy or political sovereignty.

In conflicts over Native rights, media outlets often portray a white anti-sovereignty leader or politician as the sole spokesperson for the white community, counterposed with a tribal government official as the sole spokesperson for the Native community. But the realities of both communities are much more varied and complex, and neither speaks for his or her entire community. In addition, social ties between Native people and whites may be so intertwined that their conflicts are shifted by other loyalties, such as links between families or military veterans. In environmental alliances, as well, identities and opinions vary not only between Native nations and white communities but within each community.

COMPLEXITIES OF NATIVE/NON-NATIVE ALLIANCES

Native/non-Native environmental alliances have not brought together everyone from Indian nations and non-Indian communities. They initially bring together certain parts of each community, particularly Native people who tend to have a more "traditionalist" or pro-sovereignty view and whites who tend to look upward (to corporations and the government) as the sources of their problems. The alliances tend to unite members of both communities who have the strongest bonds to the local landscape, even if those same ties to the land have at times brought them in conflict with each other.

Native leaders have often made parallels between the nineteenth-century dispossession of their lands and the twentieth- and twenty-first-century corporate theft of non-Indian lands and waters. As the Muskogee spiritual leader Philip Deere said in 1981: "The time is coming. Multinational corporations don't care what color you are; they're going to step on you. They're going to slap you in the face like they did the Indians."[98] Taiaiake Alfred writes that when he hears of "a white fisherman or logger or factory worker complain about the pain his family is feeling because of the disruption globalization has caused in their lives," he tries to stifle the recollection of the same white man blaming Native poverty on "lazy Indians" and finds himself thinking, "Looks like we're all Indians now, heh?"[99]

Environmental alliances have not caused rural white and Native neighbors to fundamentally overcome their historic divisions. While some rural white residents may have learned from Native land ethics, and feel imperiled by many of the same corporate pressures that affect Native lands, it is highly doubtful that rural whites have become "new Indians." No matter how their rights have been violated, white rural residents have a position of advantage and have not experienced the same land dispossession, cultural domination, and physical genocide and intergenerational trauma as Native nations have experienced. The alliances do, however, pose a significant challenge to common assumptions about the inevitability of conflict and the impossibility of cooperation. Rural white residents may not be the "new Indians," but as Deere underlined, many are being forced to rethink their relations with Native neighbors when they are both "slapped in the face" by white outsiders.

There have been a few exceptions to the pattern of Native/non-Native environmental alliances, but even these are more complex than they appear at first glance. Three tribal governments in Utah, New Mexico, and Nevada, for example, temporarily planned to welcome radioactive waste storage on their reservations to benefit tribal revenue, pitting them against state officials (and some white environmentalists) who criticized tribal sovereignty as a "loophole" for the nuclear industry.[100] But left out of the media limelight were the efforts of tribal "dissidents," who worked from the inside to stop the nuclear waste projects, with information from other environmental groups that backed tribal sovereignty. Similar dynamics revolve around tribal governments that have promoted coal on the Navajo Reservation or oil fracking on the Fort Berthold Reservation.[101]

In some areas of the Pacific Northwest, tribal loggers have joined with local non-Indian loggers to oppose blanket timber cutting bans promoted by some environmental groups, yet the Northwest tribes have also used their treaty rights to curb environmentally destructive practices of large timber companies. Environmental disputes in Indian Country are rarely as simple as they appear in media accounts that focus only on conflict and not on cooperation.

This study does not cover all the possible examples of Native/non-Native environmental cooperation in North America. Because of different historical and political realities in Canada, it has entirely left out interesting examples of conflict and cooperation between First Nations and white resource users in Quebec, British Columbia, Ontario, the Maritime Provinces, and elsewhere.[102] Also because of very different histories and modern politics, the study has not ventured into Alaska or Hawai'i, both of which offer important lessons on relations between Indigenous peoples and local environmentalists, or the Northeast with its longer period of colonial occupation.[103] Within the forty-eight contiguous states, the study does not examine emerging coalitions against mining companies and military projects in Nevada, New Mexico, Colorado, and elsewhere or groundbreaking cooperation between tribes and labor unions over issues such as uranium miners' radiation exposure.[104] All of these North American examples (as well as similar cases involving Indigenous Australians, Maori in Aotearoa New Zealand, South American *indígenas*, India hill tribes, and other Indigenous peoples[105]) offer fertile ground for future studies of Native/non-Native environmental alliances.

This study attempts to look at some of the best-known examples of U.S. environmental alliances, not merely to document their histories but to point out different possible paths for such movements and to use them to illustrate larger themes of conflict and cooperation. These case studies each appear as examples of alliances that were initially successful but later floundered, of alliances that achieved success in some areas but not others, and of alliances that seemed to meet most of their goals and even began to expand beyond environmental issues.

I hope that some of these lessons not only can be applied to other Native/non-Native environmental alliances but also can open some new directions for rethinking relations between ethnic/racial/national groups in general, even outside an environmental or North American context. Instead of accepting the colonial dictates that Native nations either succumb or become independent states, Native nations and settler states can inhabit a "third space" that accepts the "concurrent sovereignty" of both.[106]

It is remarkable that widely disparate regions of North America experienced Native/non-Native alliances over a rather short period of four decades. The development of the alliances reflected shifts taking place in global politics and economics. As economic globalization makes peoples (and places) more and more similar, and racial/ethnic nationalism seeks to emphasize the particularist differences between peoples (and places), the Native/non-Native alliances recognize difference and similarity as mutually reinforcing conditions.

In the United States, the racist right-wing populism exhibited by the Trump administration resembles the earlier anti-treaty movement in its placing blame on communities of color for economic crisis, and indeed the casino magnate Trump himself has strongly opposed tribal sovereignty.[107] As ethnonational groups around the world face the stark choices between globalization and local reaction, and between harsh conflict and unwanted assimilation, Native/non-Native alliances provide a different direction. In some areas, the racist right-wing populism of the anti-treaty movement was sidelined by the anticorporate populism of alliances that transcended racial and cultural lines, and working-class whites who otherwise may have blamed "minorities" for their lot in life began to redirect their anger toward state and corporate structures. This is one way that identity politics and class-based unity politics can actually be compatible, even in "Trumpland." Defending the places that have been contested between neighbors can become a means to defuse conflict between them.

The state of Indian-white relations in the twentieth century was summed up by Felix S. Cohen's "miner's canary" analogy, in which the limitation of Indian rights "marks the shift from fresh air to poison gas in our political atmosphere."[108] Yet in the twenty-first century, Indigenous nations are in a position to serve as a different sort of precedent for the larger society. They have taken leadership in the fight to halt fossil fuel shipping, from the Lummi and Quinault nations on the Pacific Northwest coast, to Standing Rock on the banks of the Missouri River, and beyond, under the banner of "Water Is Life."

Using a greenhouse analogy, tribal nations can begin to "grow" their own forms of social organization and environmental sustainability, at least partially shielded by treaty laws and sovereignty. Some tribes are starting to use their "traditional" values to solve modern problems, in ways that benefit Indians and non-Indians alike. Reservations can become models or testing grounds for new ways of relating to the land, through land purchases, sustainable agriculture and energy projects, tribal environmental laws that also protect non-

Water protectors blockading and locking down bulldozers that had cut a swath through
North Dakota ranchlands and tribal sacred sites for the Dakota Access Pipeline, north of
the Standing Rock Sioux Reservation, on September 6, 2016. (Photo by the author)

Indian neighbors, climate change resilience, and economic development that
provides jobs to both tribal and non-tribal communities. The growth of Native/
non-Native environmental alliances is only one early sign that can mark a
"shift from poison gas to fresher air" in our political atmosphere.

    The continued existence of Native nationhood today undermines the
claims of settler colonial states to the land.[109] Unlikely alliances can help chip
away at the legitimacy of these colonial structures, *even among the settlers
themselves*. To act in solidarity with Indigenous nations is not just to "support
Native rights" but to strike at the very underpinnings of the Western social
order and begin to free both Native and non-Native peoples. As Harsha Walia
asserts, striving "toward decolonization and walking together toward transformation requires us to challenge a dehumanizing social organization that
perpetuates our isolation from each other and normalizes a lack of responsibility to one another and the Earth."[110]

Scholars and activists have debated the meaning of "allyship" with Indigenous peoples. As I see it, non-Native individuals cannot simply declare themselves to be an "ally" of Indigenous peoples. The only way for settlers to achieve "co-existence" with Native nations, according to Stephanie Irlbacker-Fox, is through "co-resistance" to colonization.[111] As Adam Barker has emphasized, it is ultimately the responsibility of settlers to decolonize themselves.[112] This liberation can be accomplished not merely as an individual "ally" but as *part of a collective alliance*, based on solidarity among its members.[113]

By asserting their treaty rights and sovereignty, Indigenous nations are benefiting not only themselves but also their treaty partners. Since Europeans in North America are more separated in time and place from their indigenous origins, European Americans can respectfully ally with Native nations to help find their own path to what it means to be a human being living on the Earth— without appropriating Native cultures. The most useful role of non-Native scholars may be not to dissect Indigenous cultures but to study Native/non-Native relations and dominant attitudes and policies. My perspective is that non-Native scholars and activists alike have a responsibility to help remove the barriers and obstacles to Native sovereignty in their own governments and communities, whether through their studies or actions.

This book emerges from that perspective, to reverse the gaze of non-Natives' research away from Indigenous peoples and redirect it toward the non-Native communities and governments that have historically been the sources of oppression for Native peoples. It aims to stimulate discussion and action toward disengaging non-Natives from the ongoing project of colonization and engaging them in solidarity with decolonization. As Lilla Watson has reported the opinion of Queensland Aboriginal activists: "If you have come here to help me, then you are wasting your time. . . . But if you have come because your liberation is bound up with mine, then let us work together."[114] Malcolm X suggested, "Let sincere white individuals find all other white people they can who feel as they do . . . to work trying to convert other white people who are thinking and acting so racist. Let sincere whites go and teach non-violence to white people!"[115]

Red Cliff Ojibwe activist Walter (Walt) Bresette once told an audience of non-Indians at a Great Lakes protection gathering: "First premise is that y'all are not gonna go away. You just ain't going back to where you came from." Despite being told numerous times that "this is what you should do, . . . there's no migration home," he said. "It ain't gonna happen! I don't know if y'all have

ADD, I have no idea why you're not getting the message. So you're going to stay . . . and you're multiplying."

Bresette concluded:

> You've got to finally come to that place when you say, "This is my home," but really mean it. . . . "This is the place where I will die, and if necessary to defend, and I have a right, and a duty, to do that." I don't think you've come to that place yet; I think you're still kind of transients: "Well, if I don't live here, I can live there." Well, we can't do that, those of us who've always been here. We can't go back where we came from . . . and the fish can't go back where they came from. . . . Those of you who have come need to make this part of your place. . . . Because you can't defend something unless you really believe in it . . . you have to defend it with your heart and your soul.[116]

As Leanne Simpson writes of the Ojibwe prophecy of the Eighth Fire, it foretells "an eternal fire to be lit by all humans, an everlasting fire of peace, but its existence depends on our actions and our choices today." She explains that "in order for the Eighth Fire to be lit, settler society must also choose to change their ways, to decolonize their relationships with the land and Indigenous Nations, and to join with us in building a sustainable future based on mutual recognition, justice, and respect."[117] Indigenous and non-Indigenous people can allow the "swirling waters of the rapids" of Native knowledge systems "to carry us on a journey of cleansing, renewal, justice, and freedom."[118]

Native/non-Native alliances are just beginning to look ahead to this future. The future would necessitate, as Bresette said, non-Natives beginning to love the land in deeper ways and developing a common sense of place with their Native neighbors who come from the place. It would mean identifying and working together against their common enemies, but not stopping there. A sustainable future also means developing a common sense of understanding that lasts beyond a temporary struggle to defend the land. Non-Native neighbors can begin to look to Native nations for models to make their own communities more socially just, more ecologically resilient, and more hopeful.

PART I

RUNNING UPSTREAM

"Our number-one objective in this life must be to find common ground. . . . It does us no good to forge forward in the struggle to survive if we forget that we must all fit in the same canoe. We share this land. We share these resources. We share a common future. . . . Our customs and traditions may not fit into the same molds that Western society embraces, but that doesn't make them wrong. It makes them different. If we are to paddle the river of life together, we must all learn to understand, appreciate, and, yes, celebrate these differences."

—Billy Frank Jr. (Nisqually)

THE PACIFIC NORTHWEST IS OFTEN CONSIDERED THE PROTOTYPE for conflicts between Native nations and non-Indians over tribal treaty rights to natural resources. Before colonization, tribes along the Pacific coast and Salish Sea had direct access to plentiful salmon, shellfish, and other marine species, and tribes in the semi-arid Plateau region east of the Cascades harvested salmon that migrated into the interior through the Columbia River.

In the 1850s, as full-scale American settlement began in the Pacific Northwest, Washington Territory governor Isaac Stevens negotiated a series of six treaties with the Native nations of what would later become Washington State and parts of Oregon and Idaho. In order to survive on new reservations, and maintain their ancient resource-based cultures, the Native nations signed the treaties only on the condition that they would retain their preexisting rights to fish, hunt, and gather shellfish and plants in their treaty-ceded territories. As the territories were admitted to the Union, state and federal governments restricted tribal fishing in violation of the treaties.

The tribal fishers' reassertion of treaty rights in the 1950s and 1960s set them on a collision course with state government, white sportfishers, and the commercial fishing industry, resulting in numerous violent clashes over two decades. Treaty rights leaders such as Billy Frank Jr. and Joe DeLaCruz repeatedly risked arrest on the rivers in order to fish. Beginning in the 1970s, Northwest anti-treaty movements (and politicians such as Slade Gorton) served as a template for the "white backlash" to Native sovereignty elsewhere in the country. Likewise, federal court decisions to uphold treaty rights (notably the 1974 Boldt Decision), and resulting programs to cooperatively protect fish habitat, have served as a model for other parts of Indian Country.

Since the 1980s, treaties have had profound and lasting implications for landownership and resource politics in the entire region. The tribes have developed their own commercial fishing fleets, sustainable timber and game management, and gaming operations. Non-Indian society has experienced a dramatic transition from an extractive economy based on logging and fishing to a heavily urbanized and high-tech economy. In a dramatic turnaround, a few of the sportfishing and commercial fishing leaders who had opposed treaty rights gradually came to recognize the treaties' power in protecting the fishery from harmful development and in preventing the regional extinction of salmon.

Salmon are not only a delicious food but also a sacred being to Native peoples, an economic keystone for fishing communities, and the key "indicator species" for the health of the entire ecosystem. Salmon survival is affected by the "four H's": harvest of the fish population, hatcheries to enhance the population, hydropower dams that block fish migration, and habitat threatened from logging, agriculture, urbanization, and other development. Simply because of the multifaceted threats to the survival of endangered salmon, protecting fish habitat involves not just a few environmental reforms here and there but a revolutionary overhaul of environmental policies.

The Pacific Northwest case studies examine the Native/non-Native relationship in the harvest and protection of natural wealth and in the common purpose of protecting salmon. But the larger question is how place-based conflict is best managed or resolved. Is it more effective to build a common sense of understanding from the top down, using "government-to-government" cooperation and a common state citizenship as the starting point? Or is it more effective to lessen conflict from the bottom up, using "people-to-people" cooperation and a common sense of belonging to a place? Are these approaches mutually exclusive, or can they somehow be combined or interwoven? If a common "sense of place" can be constructed by an alliance, at what scale is it most effective? Can people wrap their heads around a vast region of river basins and mountains, or is their love for a local watershed the best place to start?

CHAPTER 1

Fish Wars and Co-Management

Western Washington

THE TRIBES OF WESTERN WASHINGTON ARE CLUSTERED AROUND THE mouths of rivers that lead into Puget Sound and the Hood Canal (the southern inlets of the Salish Sea) and the Pacific Ocean.[1] Colonization disrupted their Indigenous cultural and socio-economic systems that had remained resilient for many centuries, through fishing, hunting of game, and gathering of plant foods and medicines in vast territories.[2]

In 1854 and 1855, Washington territorial governor Isaac Stevens, also the superintendent of Indian affairs, negotiated a series of treaties with the Native nations of western Washington and the Columbia Basin, to open the land for American settlement and clear land title for a planned transcontinental railroad to Puget Sound. The treaties extinguished Native claims to 64 million acres of land, in return for the exclusive tribal use of reservations totaling 6 million acres, on some of the region's major rivers.[3] The treaties ceded nearly all the land of the region, limiting the tribes to reservations, but also allowed the tribes to retain access to the rich salmon fisheries of the Pacific Coast and Salish Sea.[4]

The 1854 Treaty of Medicine Creek was typical of these treaties, in stating that the right to fish in "all usual and accustomed fishing grounds and stations, is further secured to said Indians in common with the citizens of the territory . . . together with the privilege of hunting, gathering roots and berries" inside and outside of their new reservations.[5] The treaties defined the relationship between the federal government and up to twenty-two treaty tribes in western Washington, particularly in the "usual and accustomed" areas around the mouths of rivers, where the tribes exercised their "usufruct" (use) rights to harvest the fish even if they no longer owned the land.[6] As Governor Stevens promised the tribal leaders, "This paper secures your fish."[7]

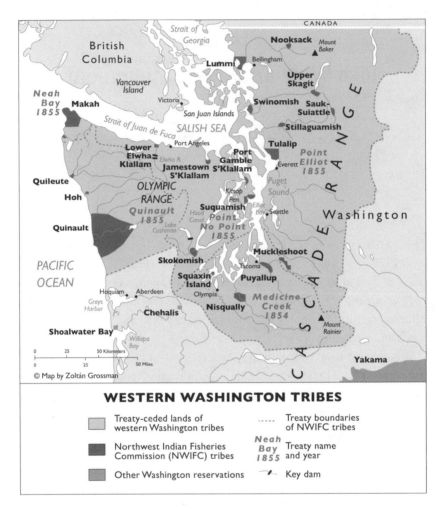

WESTERN WASHINGTON TRIBES

Treaty-ceded lands of western Washington tribes

Northwest Indian Fisheries Commission (NWIFC) tribes

Other Washington reservations

..... Treaty boundaries of NWIFC tribes

Neah Bay 1855 Treaty name and year

Key dam

© Map by Zoltán Grossman

After the treaties were signed, it became clear to the Nisqually, the Puyallup, and some other tribes that the tiny reservations chosen for them by Stevens would constrict their access to their fishing and gathering grounds. They hoped to gain access to larger and better-situated lands, in order to survive. The intransigent Stevens's refusal helped spark the Puget Sound War of 1855–56. Settler vigilantes, backed by Stevens, formed "Volunteer" militias that massacred Native civilians, drawing criticism from other settlers for provoking Native resistance.[8] A notorious 1856 massacre, for example, targeted Nisqually men, women, and children at the confluence of the Nisqually and Mashel Rivers.[9]

A number of settlers around Nisqually, including some who had been employed by the Hudson Bay Company and had become kin to Native families, allegedly gave shelter and supplies to the fighters led by Chief Leschi, a key figure in the revolt. Stevens put five of these settlers (known as the Muck Creek Five) on trial.[10] But the prosecutions were unsuccessful, and in an 1856 agreement the Nisqually and the Puyallup won access to larger reservations on their mainstem rivers, closer to their "usual and accustomed" fishing grounds, as well as prairies for root digging and horse pasture. Chief Leschi was executed in 1858 for the "murder" of a militia officer. Understanding that Leschi's action was legal during the war, the army refused to allow the execution within its fort.[11]

Salmon harvest allocation was not a concern in the rich Puget Sound fishery until the tin can came into common use in the 1880s and the first few canneries opened. Soon after Washington entered the Union in 1889, the new state government began to break provisions of the six treaties. Mechanization and rail access enlarged the commercial fishing industry, and salmon stocks began to become seriously depleted. In the meantime, the exploding non-Indian population took the prime fishing sites, and the state closed them off to tribal members, in the process racializing harvest locations and allocation.[12]

Tribal fishers traditionally harvested salmon with nets at river mouths, but the state government gradually outlawed the nets. Tribes could no longer fish in their "usual and accustomed" places; moreover, the available salmon were harvested by non-Indians before they could return to the treaty fishing grounds. As treaty researcher and activist Hank Adams has observed, "State laws prohibited them from fishing at sites off the reservations, or in the general non-Indian fisheries located any place more distant than five miles away from their particular reservation."[13] State agencies viewed tribal members as subject to state fishing regulations, in the interest of "conservation." Through the early twentieth century, the tribal fishing economy collapsed and the tribes fell into poverty.[14] The ancient fishing cultures struggled to survive, with fishers forced to operate underground for decades.

The tribes finally began to transform the same treaties that had dispossessed their lands into tools for exercising the usufruct rights they had retained to fish and gather. In the 1950s and early 1960s, small groups of tribal fishers took their boats and nets onto the rivers and estuaries of western Washington. State officials described them as "poachers" and "renegades" and blamed them for declining fish numbers, even as the non-Indian sport and commercial harvest levels skyrocketed.[15] Yet even as public controversy raged around treaty fishing, the tribes never took more than 5 percent of the salmon harvest.[16]

THE "FISH-INS"

The first treaty rights cases were brought in the early 1950s by returning Korean War veterans, such as Billy Frank Jr. from Nisqually and Joseph (Joe) DeLaCruz from Quinault. Dissatisfied with negative or limited treaty rights rulings from state courts, tribes and fishing rights activists began to turn to the federal courts in 1954, when Puyallup treaty fishers Robert Satiacum and James Young were cited for steelhead netting in the Puyallup River at Tacoma.[17]

By the early 1960s, the Native activism had stimulated an intense and often violent backlash among non-Native fishers, who cut nets, pushed boats into rivers, and stole fish from tribal nets and traps. Native fishers often came under sniper fire or were threatened with firearms. In 1963, Tulalip treaty rights leader Janet McCloud organized a pro-treaty rally at the state capitol in Olympia, galvanizing the treaty rights movement and gathering non-Indian supporters.[18]

Inspired by the civil rights "sit-ins" of the era, tribal activists organized "fish-ins" and openly fished in front of state police and wardens as a form of nonviolent civil disobedience. Police and wardens would often raid the rivers, using boats and surveillance planes, to confiscate Native boats, equipment, and fish, and fine or jail Native fishers. Police would also ram and confiscate boats and tackle Native fishers.[19]

Among the tribal activists on the Nisqually River were Billy Frank Jr. and Sioux-Assiniboine researcher-organizer Hank Adams.[20] Frank recalled the state police response to the fish-ins by Frank's Landing: "We'd fish at night, get up early in the morning and take our nets out. . . . They'd steal our nets, and steal us, take us to jail. . . . We could get these guys to fight us at the drop of a hat. We'd just put it in the paper that we're gonna have a fish-in down here, and here they come. There'd be hundreds of 'em; just what we wanted. . . . We'd run 'em up and down the river here at nighttime. They didn't know what the hell they were doing; they never knew what they were doing on this river. . . . We beat the hell out of 'em all along this river."[21]

In 1964, the "fish-ins" attracted national attention, particularly when actor Marlon Brando and comedian Dick Gregory were symbolically arrested. In the following years the conflict intensified, with wardens and police beating Native fishers with clubs and flashlights and ramming Native boats. Native fishers fought back, and some began to arm themselves in response to police and vigilante threats. In 1970, a tribal fishing encampment on the Puyallup River

Billy Frank Jr. fishing on the Nisqually River in 1973. (Courtesy: Northwest Indian Fisheries Commission)

was the scene of a violent state raid, in which police used tear gas and clubs to arrest fifty-nine people.[22]

THE BOLDT I DECISION ON FISH ALLOCATION

Soon after the 1970 Puyallup confrontation, the U.S. attorney general brought suit in U.S. District Court on behalf of seven tribes against the state. The tribes asked federal district judge George Boldt to uphold and enforce treaty fishing rights and award damages for loss of fishing rights through destruction of fish habitat.

Judge Boldt, a conservative Eisenhower appointee and Montana sport-fisherman who had earlier sentenced Frank and other tribal fishers, prioritized the harvest question and left the habitat question for a later ruling. In the courtroom and on the reservation, Boldt heard about the treaty history directly from tribal elders.[23]

On February 12, 1974, he issued his famous 203-page decision in *United States v. Washington*. He ruled not only that western Washington tribes have a right to fish under their treaties but that the state can only regulate them if "reasonable and necessary to prevent demonstrable harm to the actual conservation of fish" and all other means to perpetuate fish runs or species had been exhausted.[24]

Boldt interpreted the treaty language "in common" to mean that the tribes had the right to take up to 50 percent of the harvestable fish off the reservation.[25] This "equal sharing formula" meant that the tribes could harvest half the fish left after deducting for spawning escapement (to ensure a healthy continuation of the stocks) and tribal subsistence and ceremonial needs. Furthermore, Boldt ruled that tribes could regulate their own harvests if they met certain structural, staff, and enforcement criteria.

University of Colorado law professor Charles Wilkinson later observed: "Without question, the Boldt decision is among the one, two or three most significant decisions in the history of tribal law. It was that profound."[26] After the Boldt Decision, Frank, DeLaCruz, and other treaty rights leaders formed the Northwest Indian Fisheries Commission (NWIFC), to bring together the western Washington treaty tribes. The intertribal commission named Frank as its chair, offering official legitimacy to a treaty activist who had acted independently of tribal governments. NWIFC assisted in maintaining orderly and biologically sound fisheries and provided a single tribal voice on fisheries. It became a (sometimes contentious) forum to unite tribes with very different histories, economic interests, and fishery policies. Boldt forced these tribes to cooperate with one another and develop joint management strategies.

Recognizing that the state was not interested in enforcing the ruling, the federal court took control of the fishery. The Ninth District Court of Appeals ruled in 1978 that "except for some desegregation cases . . . the district court has faced the most concerted official and private efforts to frustrate a decree of a federal court witnessed in this century."[27] State attorney general Slade

Gorton argued that the Boldt Decision gave an unfair advantage to the tribes based on "race and ancestry." He appealed the Boldt Decision to the U.S. Supreme Court.[28] Besides bringing together the tribes, the Boldt Decision also united opponents of Native sovereignty in the Northwest.

Anti-Treaty Reaction to Boldt I

While individual fishers had been involved in efforts to block Native fishing rights since the early 1960s, the first organized groups opposed to tribal sovereignty were formed in the late 1960s by white property owners who had lived on reservations since the Allotment era. On some reservations, non-Indians formed a majority of the population or owned most of the "checkerboarded" land as residents or absentee landlords. Their opposition was less to treaty rights than to tribal jurisdiction over non-Indians on the reservations, such as Quinault's restricted access to reservation beaches.

Property-owner groups from Quinault, Suquamish, Lummi, and other reservations founded the Interstate Congress for Equal Rights and Responsibilities (ICERR) in 1976.[29] They called for Native Americans to be treated as individual citizens rather than tribal citizens, and they resented what they termed "special rights" based on race.[30] Of course, the irony was that treaty rights and tribal sovereignty were based neither on race nor on ethnicity but on the tribes' status as the former property owners of their ceded territories and the current property owners of reservation lands. ICERR later diversified its anti-tribal message and added a strong dose of an anti–federal government ideology, based on support for "states' rights" and opposition to taxes and the federal banking system. The movement's conspiracy theories over collusion between tribes, federal agencies, and multinational companies dovetailed nicely with a rural right-wing political agenda, which would later be adopted by anti-environmental "wise use" groups, constitutionalist militias, and the Tea Party.

With the Boldt Decision, the movement had a new cause, and the property owners joined forces with the fishermen, who burned Boldt in effigy at their protests through the mid-1970s. Boldt's restrictions on non-Indian fishing were flagrantly violated, leading to dangerous confrontations on the water. Native fishers were commonly targeted with violence, including sniper fire, and had their boats swamped or rammed by commercial vessels.[31] Some of the most intense violence was around the Lummi Nation.[32] The Puget Sound Gillnetters Association and other groups sued the state for enforcing the Boldt Decision, but the "supreme Law of the Land" triumphed in federal court. Non-Indian supporters of treaty rights, coordinated by the American Friends Service Committee, started a witness project to monitor harassment and violence against treaty fishers.[33]

A 1976 *Seattle Times* poll showed that the base of the anti-Indian movement was not necessarily among working-class whites, as had been widely assumed. As Hank Adams described the random sampling, it "showed that the wealthier and better educated among the non-Indian population were the least knowledgeable about the state of the salmon resources and actual causes of the decline—and the most hostile to Indians and Indian rights under the Boldt Decision." He noted that "persons making under $10,000 a year were five times more sympathetic and supportive toward Indians than those making more than $20,000 a year."[34]

The anti-treaty movement gained key support from state Republicans, such as Congressman Jack Cunningham and State Senator Jack Metcalf, and Democrats such as Senator Henry Jackson.[35] Attorney General Gorton, a Republican (of the Gorton's Seafood family), staked his political career on fighting the Boldt Decision, by filing numerous appeals to oppose "special rights" for Native Americans.[36] His appeals were turned down by the U.S. Supreme Court when it finally affirmed the Boldt Decision in 1979.[37]

ICERR and other anti-treaty coalitions grew frustrated in their attempts to overturn treaty rights in the courts. The groups' challenges to the treaties had swelled their movement with new recruits, but the effort was rapidly reaching a dead end. At the same time, salmon runs in Washington waterways began to disappear.[38] By 1988, eight Pacific salmon stocks were listed as threatened and one as endangered.

As Joseph E. Taylor states in his *Making Salmon*: "Many have wanted and do want to save salmon, but few have been willing to accept responsibility and bear the costs of recovery. Instead, they have tried to reframe history to indict rival users of fish, water, and land, and to shift the burden onto less powerful groups. Advocates simplified the past to create scapegoats, and relied on technology to solve social problems."[39]

Anti-treaty groups chose to blame the tribes for endangering the fish runs, but with their focus on harvest allocation they did not address the growing public concern about fishery health. Ultimately, this failure caused moderate non-Indian fishers to begin to disassociate from the militant anti-treaty movement. As the lead tribal attorney in the Boldt case, David Getches, observed, "The number of fish dropped while we were in the courtroom arguing over who got the fish."[40] While Native and non-Native communities clashed over fish harvests, the fish themselves were being threatened with extinction by habitat destruction.

Fish eggs and juvenile fish require clean water, cold temperatures, clean gravel beds, and adequate oxygen levels and water-flow levels. They are threatened by erosion from poor agricultural, logging, dredging, and mining practices and road and real estate development. Silt and sediment blankets the gravel spawning beds and smothers the fish eggs, clogs fish gills, and lowers oxygen levels. High temperatures are caused by organic runoff, industrial discharges, and the harvest of shading trees.[41]

Even if one aspect of fish habitat is damaged, the juvenile salmon will not survive to spawn. Salmon habitat issues in the Northwest carry an "all or nothing" urgency that has revolutionary implications for the entire relationship between human beings and the natural environment in the region.

BOLDT PHASE II ON FISH HABITAT

Boldt's *United States v. Washington* decision had dealt with only one of the four H's of salmon politics: harvest; but the Boldt litigation expanded into a second phase, which dealt with two more H's: habitat and hatcheries. The implications of the Boldt Decision had deepened in 1977 and 1978, when tribes sought to use their treaty rights to place a moratorium on on-reservation tract home development and to stop a proposed off-reservation nuclear plant.[42] A few white fishermen found themselves siding with the tribe in opposing the plant near Swinomish, which they saw as a thermal and radioactive threat to salmon runs.

In 1980, a year after inheriting the case from the retired Judge Boldt, Judge William Orrick ruled in the affirmative on both the hatchery and habitat questions. Orrick wrote in his decision, "If habitat damaging activities reduced fish runs to an extent that jeopardized the tribes' right to a livelihood to fish . . . those activities could be enjoined, just as overfishing by non-Indians had been enjoined." Orrick explained, "Were this trend to continue, the right to take fish would eventually be reduced to the right to dip one's net into the water . . . and bring it out empty."[43]

The Washington State assistant attorney general warned that "the ruling could lead to the tribes' having veto power over real estate projects, logging practices, highway construction, and the use of pesticides in the western half of the state." The Federation of Western Outdoor Clubs responded with its belief that Phase II was "of concern not only to the Indian tribes but to non-

Indian fishermen and conservationists on behalf of the general public's interest in the preservation of the environment." The federation had written an amicus brief to "contribute to changing the widespread misconception of this as a racial conflict" and believed that "the successful outcome of this lawsuit would provide a new source of environmental control of value to the entire community."[44]

Most histories of the Washington "fish wars" focus on the contentious battles over fish harvest that grew out of Boldt Phase I. Yet former Quinault chair Joe DeLaCruz, who also served on the U.S. Commission on Civil Rights, said: "I have a little different perspective. I saw the 'fish wars' as a catalyst to bring people together." He added: "Once Boldt happened, it gave us a unified voice and we pushed . . . to get an Office of Indian Affairs in state government. . . . It took the fish wars to move a lot of this stuff along."[45]

Looking back at the strife, Billy Frank Jr. said he also saw the negative conflict serving as the midwife of a positive relationship: "I can remember when our people . . . were sneaking around digging clams because we weren't able to dig clams out in broad daylight. Today we are managing those clam beds. . . . We don't have to hide anymore. . . . We are only on this earth a short time, walking through this life, to try to make a difference. . . . We have already made a difference."[46]

Boldt II opened up the possibility of tribes using their treaty rights in federal court to force states and private interests to protect or restore fish habitat. After the Orrick Decision, tribes and their allies used the case as a political and legal wedge to defeat proposals that threatened fish habitats, such as the Copper Creek dam proposed on the Skagit River, the Northern Tier pipeline planned to transport Alaskan oil to the Midwest, and a plan to reduce water flows from a dam on the upper Yakima River.[47]

Resource companies were terrified by the implications of Boldt II and anticipated that the tribes would continue their string of federal court victories from harvest issues to habitat issues. But the tribes didn't have to pursue Boldt II in the courts, because industries and agencies were willing to come to the negotiating table with the tribes, out of fear of the long and financially paralyzing lawsuits that would result if they did not.

One example of the impact of treaties on industry was on the timber industry, whose clear-cutting caused erosion and siltation of spawning beds. The Northwest Renewable Resources Center advised timber companies to sit down with the tribes to find common ground around the Timber, Fish, and Wildlife

(TFW) process. The TFW process in 1986–87 used a consensus-based approach that acknowledged tribal co-management authority over natural resources and recognized a "balance of power" among the main players.[48] Despite later setbacks, the TFW process influenced resource managers to take a more locally appropriate approach, and the state created Water Resource Inventory Areas along watershed boundaries rather than political boundaries.

Boldt II / Orrick provided a wedge for tribes to force fish habitat protection without recourse to litigation. The tribes had effectively jumped geographic scales, by gaining federal recognition of their treaty rights and then using that recognition as an opportunity to alter relations with local industries and communities.

Anti-Treaty Reaction to Boldt II

The use of treaties to protect the environment began to cause divisions within the anti-treaty movement in the 1980s. Anacortes commercial gillnetter Bill Lowman, author of the 1978 anti-treaty tract *220 Million Custers*, saw the court affirmation of treaties as a "small part of a more sinister plan" by big oil and described the tribes as "unknowing, but willing pawns" in a "gigantic Federal power drama" that could lead to dismantling hydro dams.[49] On the other side, anti-treaty leader Ted Williams acknowledged that treaties can and should be used to stop projects that could harm a fishery, and he came to support the tribal veto of dams under co-management programs.[50]

Anti-treaty groups were themselves forced to play the environmental card. ICERR's base had stayed narrowly among property owners and did not broaden its appeal to the general public. In 1983, it helped to form a larger alliance, the Steelhead-Salmon Protection Action for Washington Now (S/SPAWN), with its anti-tribal agenda folded into a public appeal for fish and wildlife protection.[51] Discredited by its links to far-right causes, S/SPAWN changed its name in 1989 to the United Property Owners of Washington, which became a key part of the national Citizens Equal Rights Alliance (CERA). CERA claimed up to thirty-five thousand members as the focus of the national anti-treaty alliance shifted to Montana and Wisconsin.[52]

WESTERN WASHINGTON SPORTFISHERS

Parallel to the development of the anti-treaty movement in the early 1980s was a countervailing trend: the first hints of cooperation between tribes and recreational fishers. The success of this growing cooperation isolated the anti-treaty groups, hardened their stances, and shrank their base of support throughout the decade.

The first Washington sportfishing group to formally raise a flag of truce in the treaty wars was Trout Unlimited (TU). According to Bill Robinson, then a TU regional staff director, the anti-Boldt lawsuits were complete failures in the federal courts, with the tribes winning all nineteen cases.[53] The adversarial relationship was gaining nothing for TU, while at the same time the signs were increasing of a decline in the fishery. Robinson said that the more "enlightened" TU leadership decided by 1983 that "enough is enough" and started opening a dialogue with the NWIFC tribes to find agreement.[54]

The relationship between TU and the tribes centered on two pairs of former adversaries. In southern Puget Sound, TU Washington Council executive director Frank Gaffney built bridges to Billy Frank Jr. In the Grays Harbor region along the coast, West Coast TU director Jerry Pavletich opened a dialogue with Joe DeLaCruz. The relationships would form the basis of a détente between TU and NWIFC, which would in turn form the basis of improved relations between tribes and recreational fishers in Washington State.

Frank Urabeck, sportfishing advisor to the Northwest Marine Trade Association, remembered Gaffney as a "facilitator-like individual," who later became project director of the Northwest Renewable Resources Center. A few months before Gaffney died of cancer, NWIFC tribes held a feast to celebrate and honor his life, despite his past as a treaty fighter.[55] Billy Frank Jr. remembered Gaffney and other TU leaders: "These were anti-Indian people. . . . We had to try to work with them now, to understand that we're all one people fighting for the protection of the salmon and the trout and everything else. . . . Trout Unlimited had some great leaders that took it right to them, and said this is the way we're going to go, and that was the policy. And them people died off, and they never were replaced with good people."[56]

DeLaCruz remembered Pavletich as a leader who "started working for solutions" and who told his fellow sportfishers that they had to live with the treaties, because "the law is the law." DeLaCruz eventually joined the Grays Harbor TU chapter and, years later, took the national TU president on a fishing trip on the Quinault River.[57]

Other TU leaders began to see negotiation as a preferable alternative to wasting further resources on fighting treaty rights. The Northwest Renewable Resources Center played the role of facilitator in building bridges between tribal and local governments.[58] Robinson compared the tribal reverence of the natural world with sportfishing's outdoor traditions and believed that both groups hold sacred places in "different places in the heart."[59] He expressed awe at how a small group of "moderate" TU and NWIFC leaders, who were "not environmental radicals," made a breakthrough in relations in the hostile racial atmosphere of the early 1980s. "The suits had tried" (referring not to lawsuits but to bureaucrats' choice attire), "but it hadn't worked." He described Boldt II as the "hammer" and "perceived power" that the tribes possessed to protect the fishery.[60]

But not every TU member supported the new approach. Urabeck recalled that after the TU state council announced the new cooperative policy, some anti-Boldt members started referring to TU as "Tribes Unlimited." Some steelhead chapters began to split off from TU and continued fighting the tribes.[61] Though still critical of tribal harvest numbers, Robinson viewed animosity against the tribes as "counterproductive" and "embarrassing" to the sportfishing community.[62] Urabeck observed that state officials tried to pit sportfishers against the tribes by meeting with them separately without observers from the other party present.[63] Joseph Pavel, a NWIFC staff member, accused TU of being interested more in defending its members' recreational fishing opportunities than in getting salmon numbers up to commercially harvestable levels for tribal and commercial fishers.[64] Tim Stearns, director of Save Our Wild Salmon, observed that the very notion of "harvesting" fish as a family lifestyle is an important commonality between tribal and commercial fishers.[65]

But some of the relationships between sportfishers and the tribes developed not in high-level meetings but at the local watershed level, between a fishing club chapter and a particular tribe. Local TU chapters began to work with Muckleshoot on salmon pens and wild steelhead restoration and enhancement, with Puyallup on restoring fish runs, with Skagit on harvest management, and with Suquamish on habitat restoration. Tribal hatcheries began to release billions of fish, to supplement or restore nearly extinct salmon runs back to a sustainable level of harvest for tribal and non-tribal fishers alike. Sportfisher Jim Swinth commented after fishing near Neah Bay: "I gotta hand it to the tribe. The Makahs have done a good job with this fishery."[66] Steve Robinson, a NWIFC policy analyst, asserted that the only way tribes convinced local communities to protect salmon was to promote a healthy sustainable economy.[67]

DeLaCruz agreed that economic ties between reservations and neighboring communities were a key factor. In the early 1980s, his Quinault tribe convinced two local towns to reverse anti-treaty resolutions they had passed in the heyday of the Boldt conflict, citing the need for closer cooperation between tribal and non-tribal timber industries. DeLaCruz cautioned, "If tribes have an economic base, there's still jealousy." But he concluded: "No matter how a guy has been an enemy, you have to talk. If people start talking, they find a lot more in common." He observed that the Boldt treaty conflict "helped to turn around" the relationship, even going so far as to ask, "Where would the Indians be if it wasn't for [Slade] Gorton?"[68]

Bill Robinson, observing that the developing ties began to extend beyond fishery issues, said: "Some folks have developed personal relationships. You can learn a lot about people across a table, gain insights into people, and gain respect."[69] The legacy of the 1850s treaties began to have profound and long-standing implications for land and resource politics in the Pacific Northwest.[70]

CO-MANAGEMENT AGREEMENTS IN WASHINGTON

The tribal-state co-management of Washington natural resources marched forward through the opposition.[71] Co-management was institutionalized as official state policy in 1989, with the Centennial Accord between the twenty-six federally recognized tribes and the state of Washington. The accord recognized that the "the parties share in their relationship particular respect for the values and culture represented by tribal governments." The tribes committed with the state to strengthen a "collective ability to successfully resolve issues of mutual concern."[72] The accord also included plans for economic development and a commitment to educate all students about tribal rights and cultures.[73] During the state's 1989 centennial, the "Paddle to Seattle" initiated the annual Tribal Canoe Journeys, which grew into a powerful expression of cultural revitalization and connection among coastal Native peoples on both sides of the border.[74]

The accord was affirmed and strengthened ten years later, when the tribes and the state signed the New Millennium Agreement. NWIFC chairman Billy Frank Jr. said: "It is time for the state and the tribes to focus on where we are going, together. The natural resources we all depend upon must be protected for future generations. Water must be protected for fish and wildlife. Rivers must be protected from the onslaught of urban sprawl . . . to bring us to a place where there is a quality of life and where Indians and non-Indians are to understand one another and work together."[75] The Centennial Accord and the New Millennium Agreement hearkened to a new era in state-tribal relations. They were part of a larger trend in tribal and non-tribal governments negotiating settlements (over issues such as land claims and water rights), rather than resorting to litigation, and thereby renewing the original spirit of treaty making.[76]

Obstacles to Co-Management

Co-management met a series of roadblocks in its implementation, especially when it came to fundamental issues of land and water use.[77] The Endangered Species Act (ESA) seemed to be the federal government's solution to restoring "endangered" or "threatened" salmon. But it became clear that the ESA only protected one species at a time, rather than offering comprehensive holistic protection of the watersheds where salmon live. The ESA also provided only enough habitat protection to maintain viable fish populations, rather than healthy, self-sustaining fish resources that can support an economic harvest. Nevertheless, the threat of the ESA's limiting fish harvests forced key parties to begin discussions on habitat protection.

In the 1990s, the movement for salmon recovery became quickly institutionalized, in a structure dominated by federal and state agencies, with participation by tribal governments, business interests, fishing associations, agricultural organizations, and a dizzying array of environmental groups. Endless discussions on Pacific salmon restoration, with little decisive visible action, gave rise to public fears of the emergence of a "salmon recovery industry." Participants in this "industry," as was often proclaimed on barstools throughout the Northwest, were out to build staff numbers and attract funding, rather than restore salmon. Whether or not this negative perception was correct, it became an obstacle to building support for environmental policy changes.

Intertribal relations also grew more complex in the post-Boldt era. The tribes were finally at the table of fishery management, but not all with the same agendas. The treaty tribes began to litigate against each other over harvest boundaries. A few also engaged in conflicts with tribes (such as Chehalis) that had never signed the treaties or others (such as Duwamish) that had not been federally recognized. Elected tribal leaders and Native activists often differed over positions to put forth to the media and the public. In a way, however, these intertribal and intratribal conflicts confirmed that real material and political power was at stake in exercising tribal sovereignty.

NWIFC policy analyst Steve Robinson expressed concern that the "era of cooperation" that started in the mid-1980s had entered a downturn in the late 1990s. He viewed the explosive population growth around Puget Sound as not only endangering salmon habitat but also affecting the non-Indian public's sense of place. Newcomers drawn from the rest of the United States by high-tech industries did not share the attachment to the region and its resource-based economy or remember the treaty rights confrontations, so they did not understand co-management. Robinson felt that relationships needed to be built on the local level, with non-Indian communities drawing on tribal expertise in river history and watershed management.[78] Inherent tensions clearly existed in the co-management framework between federally backed treaty rights and notions of local community involvement and control, which had historically excluded Native people.[79]

Collaborative watershed management is still rare around the United States, but the most favorable factors have appeared in the Pacific Northwest.[80] In the 2000s, Northwest tribes' use of treaty rights to protect fish habitat began to gain real traction in federal courts. A major tribal objection had been the construction of harmful culverts under roads. Salmon would swim up culverts and irrigation ditches into dirty and warm-temperature environments and lose their way to their spawning grounds. Because the state had not fulfilled its co-management commitments to screen existing culverts, or prevent unsafe culverts from being built, the tribes filed a 2001 lawsuit.

In 2007, federal district judge Ricardo Martinez ruled that the state had to fix six hundred fish-blocking culverts and strengthen rules to make new culverts fish-friendly.[81] After the state dragged its feet on the expensive repairs, Judge Martinez ruled in 2013 to affirm the "treaty-based duty that attaches when the state elects to block rather than bridge a salmon-bearing stream."[82] The decisions established a major precedent for tribes using treaty rights to protect habitat from harmful development.[83] In the culverts case, Washington tribes "charted a path for all tribes with reserved fishing rights under the Stevens treaties to force meaningful salmon restoration efforts from the state and federal governments (and even from private parties) that will benefit both Indian and non-Indian salmon fishers."[84]

Despite these advances, treaty rights in Washington are still at risk, due to ongoing destruction of fish habitat and the salmon resource.[85] Tribes face challenges in extending co-management beyond the governmental level to the everyday social level, involving ordinary Native and non-Native residents of endangered watersheds.[86] Cooperation needs to sink roots into local communities to sustain government-to-government relations at the top. Washington tribal experiences in building bridges to sportfishers and commercial fishers demonstrated that this effort had a long way to go.

WESTERN WASHINGTON COMMERCIAL FISHERS

In the tribal/commercial/sports triad of Northwest fishing politics, tribal representatives tend to feel closer to commercial fishers than to sportfishers or environmental groups. Both tribal and commercial fishers look at fish as a resource to be harvested, as the central component of economic livelihood and cultural identity. Native communities and coastal fishing communities have both been "sacrificed" for hydro dams. Both communities feel they are losing the salmon and their way of life.

Both tribal and commercial fishers point to habitat loss, rather than harvest, as the major culprit in the loss of salmon stocks.[87] Swinomish tribal fisheries manager Lorraine Loomis (who became NWIFC chair in 2014) observed: "The commercial harvesters [have] been cutting back their catch of salmon for years, even to closing most of their fisheries down. All these closures have not brought the salmon back, so now it is imperative that we look at habitat."[88]

Lanny Carpenter of the Puget Sound Gillnetters Association began fishing in the Puget Sound in 1992.[89] He asserted that habitat destruction, particularly from real estate sprawl, "just screams at you" and is the main reason for fishery declines.[90] He defined the fishery as a "commons" where no one owns the resources, but different interests try to extract value at the expense of others. Most residents' interaction with the fishery comes at fish markets, which are made possible by commercial fishing.[91] He claimed that the commercial catch and gear use is much more closely monitored by state agencies than the voluntary sports catch reporting is. Yet the area's gillnetters were being "locked out" of large areas of Puget Sound and had their fishing restricted.[92]

Carpenter and Seattle-based association leader Pete Soverel worked closely with NWIFC tribes on habitat and hydropower issues in the 1990s. Carpenter said that anti-treaty groups provide an example of "using a resource to disguise racism" and that "in the Balkans, in Africa, even in this country, people who profit from resources use racism as a tool." He believed that "more than passing relationships" have come out of working with the tribes, pointing to association members who married tribal members. According to Carpenter: "If there hadn't been treaty rights, there wouldn't be a resource. Tribes have 50 percent of the management. Thanks to that, there are fish."[93]

Instead of targeting tribal fishers directly, anti-Indian groups refocused their efforts on the non-tribal commercial fishery as a first step to shutting down the tribal fishery. In 1984, state voters narrowly approved an S/SPAWN ballot measure for the decommercialization of the steelhead fishery.[94] In 1995, the "Save Our Sealife" initiative sought a ban on most commercial harvesting of seafood in state waters, but it garnered only 43 percent of the vote. In 1999, the "Ban All Nets" initiative narrowed in on commercial gillnets, figuratively targeting tribal nets, and won only 40 percent. Up to 80 percent of all Puget Sound netting was by Native fishers. Carpenter expressed the view that the measure was "crafted to pit tribal against non-tribal" and to "get us in a fight with the tribes."[95] Anti-treaty forces were willing to target commercial fishers as surrogates or stand-ins for tribal interests, but such a masked, indirect appeal had no more support than a direct assault on treaty rights.

The complex and shifting relationships among Native and non-Native fishing communities can be clarified by their different opinions about the four H's of Northwest fishery politics. The series of ballot initiatives demonstrate that some non-Native fishing groups, though not all, maintained a state of conflict with the tribes over one of the four H's: harvest. Some of the sportfishing groups also have differed with tribes over another H: hatcheries. Yet both sport and commercial fishing groups cooperated with the tribes in order to work on the two other H's: habitat protection and hydropower dams.

HYDRO DAMS IN WESTERN WASHINGTON

Hydropower dams block the migration of the anadromous (oceangoing) fish and injure or kill migrating fish. They also turn stretches of previously cold, free-flowing oxygenated water into tepid pools of warm, nitrogen-saturated water.[96] River diversions for large hydroelectric projects have also destroyed or prevented tribal access to their "usual and accustomed" fishing spots.

The Cushman Hydropower Project was constructed in the Olympic Peninsula's Skokomish watershed by the city of Tacoma in 1924. The Skokomish Reservation had been located at the mouth of the river on Hood Canal in order to maintain tribal access to abundant fish and shellfish.[97]

As the dam project diverted the river to create Cushman Reservoir in 1929, the tribe filed a lawsuit, with the support of non-Indian landowners. Tacoma was prevented from diverting the South Fork of the river, but diversion of the North Fork into a power plant shrank the river to one-third its historic size. Siltation damaged salmon runs and resulted in severe winter flooding over its banks, affecting Native and non-Native homes downstream.[98]

The Skokomish Tribe sued Tacoma and the Federal Energy Regulatory Commission (FERC) in 1999 to prevent relicensing of the project. The tribe sought $5.8 billion in damages from the loss of salmon, shellfish, hunting grounds, and religious, cultural, and archaeological sites.[99] Skokomish gained strong support for its position among church groups and some fishing groups such as TU and the Puget Sound Gillnetters Association.[100] The tribe also co-operated with a few private landowners on harvesting shellfish.[101]

Skokomish tribal attorney Vic Martino saw local non-Indian opinion going both ways. Some of the "old-timers" had a "strong attachment to the area," said Martino. "They were offered buyouts, but want to fix the problem." Yet around the Cushman Reservoir, more recent white residents formed the group Save the Lakes, to maintain the lake's summer recreational level. Martino called its "newcomer" leader a "racist" who used the dam issue to organize against the tribe. Yet Martino explained, "We made a lot of bridges . . . and are a lot closer to agreeing."[102] NWIFC staff member Joseph Pavel, a former Skokomish tribal chairman, agreed that the "old-timers" had "amicable relations" with the tribal members."[103] The relicensing case was settled in 2008.[104] The tribe began to work with local governments in the Hood Canal Coordinating Council and its Skokomish Watershed Action Team to restore the local watershed.[105]

The country's largest dam removal took place on the Elwha River, farther north on the Olympic Peninsula. For decades, the James River Paper Company had owned and operated the Lower Elwha and Glines Canyon dams, which blocked the annual return of salmon. NWIFC tribes and commercial and rec-reational fishing groups had joined forces with the Lower Elwha Klallam Tribe to call for the dams' removal. In 1998, the tribe brought Secretary of the Inte-rior Bruce Babbitt to sign an agreement to remove them. Bill Robinson, execu-tive director of TU's Washington council, said the Elwha dams' removal "means economic benefits to the local community interests—business, tribal, recre-ation, fisheries and many other interest groups."[106]

The process of removing the dams took place in 2012–14.[107] Salmon soon began to return to the river in large numbers.[108] The release of silt from be-hind the dam even restored a delta at the mouth of the river, giving tribal members access to a sandy beach and shellfish grounds for the first time in generations.[109]

CONTINUING ANTI-TRIBAL SENTIMENT

Despite progress in building ties between tribal governments, state and federal agencies, and both commercial and recreational fishing groups, relations did not significantly improve everywhere. Tensions still remained high in some areas between tribal fishers and sportfishers. During 1991, for example, the Lower Elwha Klallam gave up fishing on remote streams due to verbal and physical harassment. Tribal member Mel Elofson pointed out that vandalism and theft of tribal gear and nets was "usually done by people not from the area, but from over in Seattle or down south—guys who are really into steelhead fishing."[110]

Washington State's Republican leadership continued to take stands against tribal sovereignty. Gorton and Metcalf led the national charge in the 1990s against Native sovereignty. In the 2000 election, tribes around the country gave large donations to Gorton's Democratic opponent Maria Cantwell, who won the election and was appointed to the Senate Indian Affairs Committee.

Although groups opposing tribal fishing rights had lost many of their followers, the same cannot be said of groups opposing Makah whaling. The Makah Nation, on the Pacific coast at the gateway to the Salish Sea, had long played a pivotal role in the marine economy and ecology.[111] The Makah had reserved whaling rights in the 1855 Treaty of Neah Bay, as a crucial part of their cultural traditions and economic livelihood.[112] The Makah proposal to harvest five gray whales a year, out of a migrating herd of twenty thousand, stirred militant opposition from some animal rights groups. These groups saw the plan as a "foot in the door" for commercial whaling, even though the Makah had been allocated an already existing cultural harvest quota from a Siberian Indigenous group and opposed commercial whaling.[113] Other anti-whaling groups such as Greenpeace refused to join the anti-treaty protests, viewing them as a diversion from a focus on larger environmental threats to marine life.[114]

For a brief time, the heated rhetoric of the Boldt days returned. The Sea Shepherd Conservation Society worked closely with Representative Metcalf, despite his openly far-right anti-Indian views. Borrowing a slogan from Wisconsin anti-treaty protests, a banner at one Seattle rally read "Save a Whale, Harpoon a Makah." Makah and other Native families received hate mail and death threats, bomb threats emptied at least one Indian school, and the National Guard was deployed to protect the Makah Days festival. Protests intensified when the Makah finally harvested a single gray whale in 1999.[115] Quinault leader Joe DeLaCruz, however, noted that the Makahs also received moral encouragement from many non-Indian fishers and hunters.[116]

Throughout Washington State, some white reservation residents continued to battle Native legal jurisdiction, such as a 2000 alcohol ban on the Yakama Reservation. White reservation residents formed the Stand Up Committee to oppose the ban, led by CERA president and later Toppenish City Council member Elaine Willman.[117] The same year, the state Republican convention passed a resolution calling for the termination of Indian reservations, much as the federal government attempted in the 1950s.[118] Resolution author John Fleming told the media that if tribes were to fight termination, "then the U.S. Army and the Air Force and the Marines and the National Guard are going to have to battle back."[119] State Republican leaders disassociated themselves from the resolution.[120] The *Seattle Times* editorialized, "Collaboration among tribes, sports fishermen and fishery officials stands in stark contrast to an embarrassing Republican Party resolution calling for an end to tribal governments."[121]

Had the resolution been adopted a decade earlier, it may have caused a serious rift between the tribes and non-Indian governments. Yet co-management had solidified intergovernmental cooperation, giving tribes a policy voice probably greater than in any other state. This cooperation continued largely as a "top-down" process at a statewide policy level. The question is whether "government-to-government" cooperation at the top has translated into cooperation at the grassroots, and the answer is mixed.

In the 1990s and the first decade of the 2000s, some tribal governments began to develop cooperative agreements with neighboring local and county governments, some of which had long been hostile to tribal sovereign jurisdiction. Swinomish, for example, formed joint agreements and committees with Skagit County local governments on issues of transportation, law enforcement, water management, and reservation land-use policies.[122] Some Skagit Valley officials were still influenced by anti-Indian sentiment, however, largely around water rights issues, and continued to battle Swinomish (backed by the state) on in-stream flows for salmon in the 2010s.[123] Tensions festered between the tribe and La Conner over the tax base for the local school.[124] The Puget Sound Anglers also protested Swinomish treaty fishing in 2016.[125]

Other local officials chose to begin to work with Swinomish, turning them from adversaries to potential allies around land and water restoration, especially as climate change intensified flooding in the delta.[126] Swinomish chair Brian Cladoosby, elected president of the National Congress of American Indians in 2013, led the tribal defense of water rights and salmon habitat.[127]

At a local community level, some sportfishing groups and commercial fishing groups have built bridges to tribes, tenuous and fragile as those bridges may be. They have built on local economic relationships forged by casino employment and investment and tribal tourism projects.[128] Significantly, some tribal officials have identified the greatest threats to treaty rights as no longer coming from rural non-Indian neighbors but instead coming from outside interests. At Makah, the outside interests were animal rights groups; at Lower Elwha Klallam, they were urban steelhead sportfishers; at Quinault, they were anti-logging groups. In the 2010s, Washington-based corporations pushed back against state policies to protect Native and other so-called "minority" communities from toxins in fish.[129] Relationships with non-Indians living near the reservations may not be harmonious, but they have developed to enough of an extent to slow the growth of anti-tribal militancy. And a trend toward establishing "watershed councils" increasingly brings together local and tribal interests in a place-based strategy to restore fish habitat.

WATERSHED COUNCILS

The unfolding concept of "watershed councils" includes a role for non-governmental players and thus gives some representation to non-Indian fishing groups, tribal fishers, farmers, and others. Watershed councils are generally made up of individuals, groups, and agencies with a working, day-to-day relationship to the local lakes, rivers, and streams and an intimate knowledge of their natural wealth. Tribes still have legal recourse to use treaty and sovereign rights and may find more allies within their respective watersheds to do so. Since resources such as salmon do not stop at basin boundaries, these partnerships have to work closely with one another and collectively could provide a powerful voice for sustainable management. This collaboration could extend beyond watersheds to adjacent landscapes, foodsheds, and firesheds that are part of the tribal harvesting territory.[130]

Perhaps the most advanced example of a watershed council in the Pacific Northwest, and perhaps in the country, is in the Nisqually watershed, southeast of the Washington capital city of Olympia. The Nisqually River flows seventy-eight miles from Mount Rainier National Park, through private farmlands and local, county, and state government lands, the Nisqually Reservation, and Joint Base Lewis-McChord (JBLM), and empties into Puget Sound at the Nisqually National Wildlife Refuge.

The U.S. Army had removed Billy Frank Jr.'s family from their homestead in 1917, after it took over 70 percent of the reservation to create Fort Lewis. The army coveted the open prairie for an artillery firing range. The family was relocated to a downriver site that was renamed Frank's Landing, and it became the storied site of confrontations during the fish wars. Using the power of the Boldt Decision, Frank pressured the army to allow a tribal fish hatchery to open in 1991 by a natural spring within the base, to limit its training to protect

Logjams on the Mashel River, part of the Nisqually Tribe's salmon habitat restoration program in the Nisqually River watershed of western Washington. (Photo by the author)

salmon habitat from tanks and tribal members from errant shells, and to allow tribal access for limited hunting and gathering.[131] In 2008, the Nisqually started an annual Leschi-Quiemuth Honor Walk within Fort Lewis (renamed JBLM two years later), to visit their former homesteads, intact cemeteries, and other cultural sites on the base.[132]

The Nisqually Tribe had helped to develop a management plan for the Nisqually River in 1987 and began salmon habitat protection efforts three years later, when less than 5 percent of the river and stream banks in the watershed were under protected ownership.[133] The tribe joined with local, state, and federal agencies in placing additional lands under permanent stewardship, and by 2009 about three-quarters of the mainstem Nisqually were in protected ownership, well on the way to the goal of 90 percent.[134]

The Nisqually Tribe was officially recognized as the "lead entity" in creating watershed management plans for local, state, and federal agencies, with the Nisqually River Council deemed as the lead entity's citizen committee.[135]

Private farmland owners, such as Jim Wilcox of the Wilcox Farms, were initially fearful that the tribe would limit or shut down their farm operations. But Wilcox was reassured by speaking with Billy Frank Jr., who cajoled him to cooperate with the tribe in designating the farm operations as "salmon-safe."[136]

Standing in the Nisqually River delta today, one can observe a landscape that is healing, in a process of tribal "environmental repossession."[137] After decades of being diked to create cattle pasture, tidal flows are again allowed to bring saltwater and aquatic species into old restored estuary channels. After decades of being grazed by cattle, riparian vegetation is being brought back to prevent erosion, and sacred springs are protected and returned to tribal control. After decades of being straightened into channels to drain the wetlands, upstream tributaries of the Nisqually River (such as Ohop Creek) are being remeandered, and logjams are being installed to create pools for salmon to rest on their long journey back home from the ocean. After decades of declining runs, the salmon are returning to the Nisqually watershed, because their habitat is finally being restored, and a hatchery is restocking the river. The landscape is slowly being healed, and made more resilient, as part of a larger process of Indigenous decolonization.[138]

The Nisqually Tribe's Cultural Committee headquarters is on the former Braget Farm, the home of a white farming family that refused, along with the tribe and the Nisqually Delta Association, to back an industrial superport (including oil tanks) in the estuary in the 1970s to 1990s.[139] When Ken Braget passed away in 2006, he left the vast property east of the river to the tribe, in order to protect and restore the land damaged by decades of agriculture.[140] The tribe removed the dikes and allowed the tidal flows back into the channels, like the National Wildlife Refuge did on the west side of the river. (In 2016, the National Wildlife Refuge was named after the late Billy Frank Jr.[141]) The Cultural Committee has a canoe shed and hosts a tribal community garden on the property. Garden field technician Grace Ann Byrd said: "We work with our own people, and we have sovereignty to feed our own people. And we do it with love and prayer."[142]

These successes in protecting the Nisqually watershed, and restoring salmon habitat, are usually presented as a triumph of government-to-government relations. But the success would not have been possible without buy-in from local farmers such as Ken Braget and Jim Wilcox, whose cooperation with the Nisqually showed that healing the watershed also involves healing the divisions between Native and non-Native neighbors. Although property owners in most of the western United States resent pressure from government agencies to protect the environment, it can work the other way around when non-Native landowners pressure their government officials to do a better job on watershed protection, if only to protect their own livelihood. In a few cases, these non-Native landowners have even pressured their own government officials to work together with the tribes.

CONFLICT RESOLUTION FROM ABOVE AND BELOW

This complex interplay between "government-to-government" relations and "people-to-people" relations permeates Native/non-Native collaborations in the Pacific Northwest and beyond. On the one hand, government-to-government relations underpin tribal sovereignty, because tribes find their protection from hostile local and state laws in the trust responsibility of the federal government toward the tribes. As former Skokomish chair Joseph Pavel observed of meeting with a non-Indian fishing organization: "They're an interest group—we're a government. We meet with them, but we don't negotiate with a user group."[143] If tribes met with fishing or farming groups as equals, their nationhood would be severely undermined, and they would be relegated to the role of any other "stakeholder." The treaties enshrined the tribes instead as "treaty holders" and "rights holders," former owners of ceded territory who retain rights to use and manage its resources. Non-Indian interest groups did not sign treaties; the federal government did.

But on the other hand, the assertion of Northwest treaty rights in the 1960s and 1970s did not begin with federal officials or judges. It began with grass-roots tribal activists and officials frustrated by centuries of colonization. Their bottom-up activism pressured the reluctant feds to affirm treaty rights, giving the tribes an opportunity to shift power relations at the local level. Some tribes grasped onto the federal hand, confident in the belief that federal recognition would always trump state and local governments' hostility. Other tribes used federal standing as a chance to alter their standing with the state and local scales to expand tribes' local relationships, in the (accurate) belief that the feds would not always have the tribes' best interest at heart.

Creative structures can be found that combine bottom-up grassroots participation with top-down intergovernmental ties, such as the Nisqually River Council. But conflict resolution that is based only on agreements between political elites is increasingly seen as ineffective and even risky. The grassroots bases of each contending group can feel left out of the top-down process, and as the gap grows within each group greater conflict results.[144] To keep the peace, leaders sometimes reign in their more alienated and militant followers.[145]

Elsewhere in the world, a "peace process" between government officials often does not create peace between the communities, as dramatized by the examples of Palestine/Israel, Bosnia, or Ukraine.[146] No matter what kind of peace deals are reached at the top of society, only transforming the issues at the bottom can build a truly lasting resolution.[147] A "paradigmatic shift" toward lasting relationships that promote justice can prevent the regeneration of social tensions.[148] Alliances-from-below can address the sources or roots of the conflict rather than only its effects.[149]

In the Pacific Northwest, natural resource co-management has begun to institutionalize the tribes' role in their ceded territories and to build more respectful relations between Native nations and state and federal agencies. After a quarter century of government-to-government cooperation, some— but not all—of the relationship has trickled down to improve the people-to-people relationship.

Around the country, tribes are encountering obstacles in their dealings with non-Indian local governments. Tribal staff and attorneys may develop a case for environmental or sacred site protection from a strong position— backed by data, federal support, and legal precedent. Yet time and again, local interests portray tribes and federal officials as "outside" interests, and local whites do not gain an understanding of tribal sovereignty or cultures. The result is jurisdictional clashes between tribal and local governments, social conflicts over cultural meanings, and losses in the courts and legislatures. Tribes take an enormous risk when they rely only on political sovereignty and not on local partnerships, because *both* buttress the nation-to-nation relationship. Even in the federal consultation process, a tribal leader backed by substantial public support has a stronger position than a leader who relies solely on federal agencies' trust responsibility.

Sovereignty is more than the strength of tribal government leaders; it is also the ability of a Native *people* to control their own land, economy, and culture.[150] A tribal government can strengthen its political sovereignty by taking its direction from tribal citizens rather than mainly from U.S. or state government officials. Repeated experience has shown that the sovereignty battles are fought not only in the courtrooms and agency boardrooms but also in the hearts and minds of Native and non-Native neighbors.

Tribal public relations and cultural/political education programs can open people-to-people communication channels, especially when Native or non-Native residents do not fully trust their own government leaders. Conversely, people-to-people contact can form a base of support for better relations between tribal and non-tribal political leaders and help construct a "sense of understanding" that defends the interests of both communities and nations.

In some cases, the strongest alliances are those that are set apart from, or even set in opposition to, established governments. Tribes and local non-Indian interests can work together against state (or even federal) policy, as guardians of the local ecosystem. After all, it is the Native and non-Native residents who will have to live together long after the professional negotiators go home.

Building cooperation from the bottom up is a far more difficult task than calling leadership summits that promote "one-size-fits-all" strategies or calling for more state or federal consultation with tribes. It means investigating the unique local character of each conflict. It means respecting grassroots leaders who may not have academic degrees but have an intimate knowledge of a place and its history. It means working with elders who may not have official government titles but possess the respect of their communities. It means opening dialogues with people often left out of formal decision making, especially women and youth.

Building cooperation means extending people-to-people ties beyond a response to short-term threats, into longer-term visions of a mutually respectful future, a "sense of common understanding" that can be adopted into government policy. If they reinforce each other effectively on parallel tracks, both government-to-government relations and people-to-people relations can reinforce the larger nation-to-nation relationship. Working on parallel tracks makes both people and their governments better prepared to face challenges to their communities and natural resources, as can be seen in the mighty struggles over the health of riverways in the vast Plateau interior of the Pacific Northwest.

CHAPTER 2

Water Wars and Breaching Dams

Northwest Plateau

THE SALMON EXTINCTION CRISIS IN THE COLUMBIA RIVER BASIN IN the late twentieth century gave birth to one of the largest Native/non-Native alliances ever seen in North America. Besides tribal governments and Native fishers, the drama involved commercial fishing and sportfishing interests, irrigators (farmers) and ranchers, and an alphabet soup of federal, state, and tribal agencies. Although locked in conflict over salmon harvest levels, these different players were confronted with the overall decline of the salmon and had to navigate new relationships to one another and the regional ecosystem.

The Columbia Basin case studies highlight how geographic scale affects the relationship between Native and non-Native communities. Is it more effective to work at the state or national levels, because altering government policies carry immense weight in influencing local social relations? Or is it more effective to work at the local or regional level, centered in a single watershed or mountain range, which is less impersonal and abstract than larger scales? If place is a potential source of a common identity, what kinds of places, and at what scale, create the strongest identities?

The Columbia Basin is part of the inland Plateau region that is much drier and more open than coastal Washington and Oregon. It encompasses 63 million acres, including the Columbia and Snake Rivers and numerous smaller tributaries. Native peoples of the Plateau cultures have harvested these rich inland waterways for sacred salmon, steelhead, Pacific lamprey, and other migrating fish species for thousands of years. In pre-treaty times, each tributary had a particular "river people" associated with it—such as the Wannapums, the Klickitats, and the Tyghs. Stretches of the mainstem Columbia had larger tribal groups associated with them—such as the Walla Wallas and the Wascos.[1]

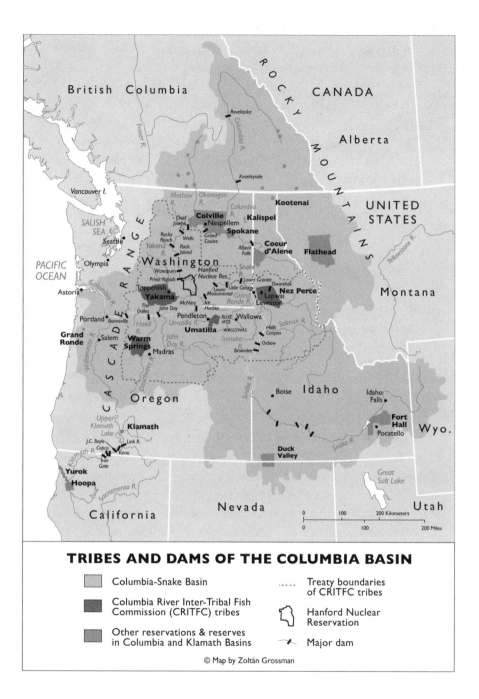

TRIBES AND DAMS OF THE COLUMBIA BASIN

Columbia-Snake Basin

Columbia River Inter-Tribal Fish Commission (CRITFC) tribes

Other reservations & reserves in Columbia and Klamath Basins

..... Treaty boundaries of CRITFC tribes

Hanford Nuclear Reservation

Major dam

© Map by Zoltán Grossman

In the treaty era, Native tribes and bands were consolidated on the Warm Springs Reservation and the Umatilla Reservation in Oregon, the Yakama Reservation in Washington, and the Nez Perce Reservation in Idaho. Tribes that today live on the four reservations together ceded about 41 million acres in the 1855 Treaty of Walla Walla and together retained only about 2.8 million acres, but none of the acreage is on the Columbia or Snake mainstem rivers.

Tribal members continued to seasonally fish for subsistence and commercial purposes on the Columbia in the first half of the twentieth century, particularly at the historic salmon fishing and trading center at Celilo Falls, next to The Dalles, Oregon. Fishing families built large wooden scaffolds and would use thirty-foot-long dip nets and gaffs to catch forty-pound salmon jumping up the falls, under the gaze of amazed tourists.[2]

As commercial fishing and recreational sportfishing grew in the Columbia Basin, they came increasingly into conflict with Native fishing communities, as did non-Indian farmers and ranchers who used water from the rivers. Yet conflicts between Native and non-Native communities paled in comparison to the challenge that both groups began to face from the construction of hydroelectric dams.[3]

HYDROELECTRIC DAMS

The federal government saw hydroelectric dams as one answer to the economic depression that was ravaging the country in the 1930s. The dams could provide power to new industries while, at the same time, providing irrigation water for farmers in the semi-arid interior and making barge traffic possible to new inland ports. The coastal and inland fishing industries, as well as the tribal fishery, were not as highly prioritized; their demise was even considered an acceptable cost of elite-driven industrial development.[4]

World War II accelerated the industrialization of the Columbia, by increasing the demand for aluminum and causing the construction of the Hanford Atomic Works near Richland, Washington.[5] Yet by the 1940s, the reduction in salmon runs had already become apparent. Fish biologists began to warn that dam construction could lead to massive destruction of the basin fishing industries.[6] The two parts of the Columbia's "organic machine"—fishing and energy—could not co-exist in harmony.[7]

In 1957, the worst nightmare of the fishing tribes came true, as Celilo Falls was flooded by construction of The Dalles Dam. In one of the country's greatest cultural tragedies of modern times, the ancient fishery was terminated as

The historic intertribal fishing site of Celilo Falls, inundated by The Dalles Dam in 1957. (Courtesy: Columbia River Inter-Tribal Fish Commission / Wikipedia)

large, tepid pools behind the dams replaced the cold, free-flowing Columbia.[8] Plateau river people struggled for years to obtain tiny "in-lieu" fishing sites that the federal government promised to replace the historic river communities.[9] When all the basin dams would be completed, they would block salmonid species altogether from twenty-eight hundred miles of fish habitat.

Instead of uniting to confront the hydroelectric dam threat to their common livelihoods, non-Native fishers and their state governments intensified their assault on Native fish harvesters. In 1968, fourteen Yakama-affiliated "river people" reacted by filing suit against Oregon in the *Sohappy v. Smith* case.[10] The federal government joined the four reservations in filing *United States v. Oregon*. Both lawsuits were combined under Judge Robert Belloni, who ruled in 1969 that the tribes were entitled to a "fair share" of fish runs.[11]

Compared to Washington, treaty fishing disputes were less confrontational in Oregon, where treaty tribes were far removed from major cities and could work with more moderate lawmakers. The flooding of Celilo Falls visibly conveyed a physical injustice more easily understood than the complex legal injustices around Puget Sound.

As conflicts continued over harvest levels, the U.S. Army Corps of Engineers continued to construct dams. By 1975, it completed the last four dams on the lower Snake, as a severe drought caused large-scale salmon deaths.[12] The Umatilla, Warm Springs, Yakama, and Nez Perce tribes responded in 1977 with the formation of the Columbia River Inter-Tribal Fish Commission (CRITFC), modeled on the Northwest Indian Fisheries Commission (NWIFC) in Washington.[13]

Through the 1980 Northwest Power Act, Congress acknowledged that the hydroelectric system had degraded regional fisheries and in 1982 formed the Northwest Power Planning Council, which for the first time gave the tribes a limited voice in fish management policy.[14] Nevertheless, tribal members continued to face citations and arrests, including the 1982 "Salmonscam" sting operations against David Sohappy Sr. and other river people. The targeting of so-called fish poachers did not restore the fish runs.[15] In 1988, a federal district court approved the Columbia River Fish Management Plan, involving the tribal, state, and federal agencies in a common watershed-based effort to manage the fishery.[16]

The Pacific salmon crisis continued unabated and began to enter the national consciousness and legal policy.[17] In 1991, CRITFC tribes and environmental groups successfully petitioned to place Snake River sockeye and chinook stocks on the Endangered Species Act (ESA) listing.[18] A 1992 American Fisheries Society report documented the extinction of 106 Pacific salmon runs and the imminent risk of extinction of 214 other major runs.[19] By 1995, tribal fishing had collapsed to such an extent that the Warm Springs Reservation had to bring in eight dried Alaska salmon in order to have fish at its annual spring salmon feast.[20] The federal courts began to order changes in the hydroelectric system as a necessary component of salmon stock recovery.[21]

Dam Breaching

The idea of breaching the earthen sections of the four Snake River dams became of a focus of the salmon recovery movement in the 1990s.[22] Dam breaching also became a priority of CRITFC.[23] It was joined by environmental groups such as the National Wildlife Federation and Save Our Wild Salmon and later by federal agencies such as the National Marine Fisheries Service.[24] Pro-dam groups contend that breaching would be an economic disaster for the region.[25] Pro-breaching groups replied that the economic benefits of breaching outweighed the costs.[26] The Bill Clinton administration decided in 2000 to take no action in resolving the controversy.[27]

The blast at the base of Washington's Condit Dam that initiated the 2011 breaching of the century-old dam, the third-largest dam to be decommissioned in the United States. Within an hour, a ninety-two-acre lake was drained and the White Salmon River was allowed to freely flow to the Columbia. (Courtesy: Columbia River Inter-Tribal Fish Commission)

Yet the Northwest movement for dam breaching had created a historic and visible example of cooperation between tribes and non-Indian fishing interests. They joined together to promote the breaching of smaller dams in the basin, such as the 2011 removal of the century-old Condit Dam on Washington's White Salmon River, which was followed by salmon and Pacific lamprey "recolonizing" the river.[28] Even if they could not yet remove the larger Snake River dams, non-Native fishers joined Plateau tribes in a common cause around two of the H's—to breach hydroelectric dams and restore habitat.

TRIBAL RELATIONS WITH FISHING GROUPS

Commercial Fishing Interests

Commercial fishermen had condemned hydropower dams for many decades. When the U.S. Army Corps of Engineers first began constructing the hydroelectric system in the 1930s, Columbia River Fishermen's Protective Union members were horrified.[29] They were on the same side as the tribes, but for different reasons, and without an established relationship. Communication and travel was difficult between the commercial fishing communities on the

lower Columbia and the interior reservations. When commercial fishers won
the construction of fish ladders on some lower dams, they muted their overall
opposition to dams. Some commercial fishermen even cheered the flooding of
Celilo Falls, for eliminating a competing fishery. Cascade/Klickitat chief
Johnny Jackson explained: "Along here they did their best to run us off-river.
When we had Celilo Falls we never gillnetted. But we were forced to gillnet,
then were criticized for it."[30]

When salmonid species were listed under the ESA in the 1990s, commercial
harvests were limited, but the act's listings forced different parties to the table
to discuss the salmon crisis.[31] Some commercial fishing and sportfishing industry representatives began to attend regional salmon summits, where they
met with tribal fish managers and agreed to disagree about harvest levels.
Some commercial fishermen who had seen both the treaties and the ESA as
obstacles began to view them instead as potential levers to protect habitat and
dismantle hydropower dams.

The Pacific Coast Federation of Fishermen's Associations is the largest trade
association of commercial fishermen on the West Coast.[32] It was founded in
opposition to offshore oil leases in California in the 1980s and worked closely
with CRITFC to support dam breaching.[33] Executive director Glen Spain maintained that in fishing battles, the tribes have federal support, the sportfishers
have public and state support, and the dwindling commercial industry has the
least support.[34]

Salmon for All, based in Astoria at the mouth of the Columbia, participated
in lawsuits against treaty rights but began working with the tribes when dam
breaching became an option. Executive director Steve Fick visited with Nez
Perce and Umatilla to share ideas about salmon recovery. He added: "A light
went off in my head as to how similar our communities are. The tribes hold a
ceremony for the first fish caught of the year. Our fishermen take home the
first fish to eat. We have different reasons for doing a similar action."[35]

Donald Sampson, CRITFC executive director in 1999–2003, similarly contended that tribal and commercial fishers have more in common with each
other than either has in common with sportfishers. Sampson added: "Commercial fishermen follow a family tradition. . . . The tribes want abundance,
the tribes want harvestable numbers of salmon, not just salmon recovery. . . .
The *tribes* went to bat for the commercial fishery on the lower Columbia, not
any state agency."[36]

Les Clark, president of the Northwest Gillnetters Association from 1977
to 1990, told a somewhat different story. Although he worked for tribal hatch-

eries, he felt that commercial fishing is being driven out of business by both the tribal and sport fisheries and that state and federal agencies are "good at divide-and-conquer." Clark contended that the government-to-government relationship between the tribes and non-Indian political officials deprived commercial fishers of a voice of their own.[37]

Clark added that in both tribal and non-tribal fish agencies, older fish managers with intimate knowledge of the resource were dying out or being pushed aside by younger technocrats with their main expertise in fishery politics. Clark concluded: "I feel for tribes, in terms of their fishing in the river. All I want to do is continue to fish with these people. Like the Indians, I want clean water and to have fish. If I can't have that, then life is not worth living, as far as being a fisherman is concerned."[38]

River People

Leaders of some small tribes and bands of river people oddly echoed the feelings of exclusion voiced by commercial fishermen. They contended that reservation officials did not always represent their concerns about their river-based homelands in government-to-government negotiations. Some of them rose to positions of tribal authority, and the Warm Springs government formally included hereditary chiefs. Former Umatilla chair Donald Sampson—himself the son of a Wallula chief—acknowledged that tribal councils did not always prioritize the battle to retain a permanent presence on the rivers.[39]

Chief Johnny Jackson, a member of the Columbia River Chiefs' Council, resisted eviction from his in-lieu fishing site at Underwood, Washington, in the 1980s. His Cascade and Klickitat tribes are part of the fourteen tribes and bands of the Yakama Nation. Jackson's work has also included protection of sacred sites from development proposals, such as the 1993 occupation of a Klickitat burial ground at Lyle Point by Native people and non-Indian environmentalists, which prevented construction of a condo subdivision on the site.[40] Chief Jackson also led efforts to curtail recreational windsurfing on the Columbia and to stop the Texas energy giant Enron from building wind turbines on Columbia Hills burial sites.[41]

Jackson complained that recognized tribal governments did not sufficiently back efforts to protect these sacred sites or guarantee fishing rights for the river people. The federal government compensated river people for the loss of their former fishing camps but did not compensate them for the loss of the fish.[42]

Much as Clark contended that modern fish managers lacked a deep knowledge of the resource, Jackson asserted that too many tribal officials lacked knowledge of their history and culture and simply followed the lead of federal agencies. Jackson extended the blame for salmon decline far beyond the Snake River dams to corporate trawlers on the ocean and radioactive wastes from the Hanford Nuclear Reservation.[43]

Susana Santos, part of a Tygh fishing family living at Warm Springs, agreed that opposition to corporate overharvesting should be the main basis of an alliance with non-Indian commercial fishers.[44] Santos, who worked as Greenpeace fisheries liaison in Portland from 1995 to 1997, viewed the attack on Native fishing rights as a diversion from privatization of the ocean fishery. She also connected the 1989 Exxon Valdez oil spill in Alaska to the sudden decline of salmon runs. Santos remembered the days when she and her mother would catch beautiful thirty-pound salmon off their wooden scaffold on the Deschutes River.[45]

Like Jackson, Santos was concerned less about formal government-to-government agreements and more about the people-to-people relationships. A gifted artist, she founded the Sacred Earth Coalition in Portland to educate the non-Indian public—particularly church members—about Native treaty rights and cultures.[46] She viewed the anger of non-Indian fishermen as symptomatic of a deeper economic crisis affecting both communities. "Why are they angry at me?" she asked. "Anger usually masks fear. What are they afraid of? Their livelihood is being destroyed, and they have no way to vent their fear. We need to find out what we have in common and give them a voice."[47]

Sportfishing Interests

While both tribal and commercial fishers share a view of fish as a harvestable food resource, that stance often puts them at odds with recreational fishers concerned with taking an allowable catch. Yet some sportfishers set aside their differences over harvest allocation and methods to work with the tribes for dam breaching.

The Northwest Sportfishing Industry Association represents businesses that serve the recreational fishing industry. Executive director Liz Hamilton said of working with the tribes on dam breaching: "With strange bedfellows is the only way we're going to accomplish our goals. There are still going to be conflicts; we are competing for the same slice of pie, and the pie shrinks. But what we have in common is love for the salmon."[48]

Hamilton credited Ted Strong, a former Yakama chair and CRITFC executive director, for reaching out to commercial fishers, inviting them to a 1995 Salmon Homecoming ceremony and feast, and starting to establish an alliance for dam breaching. She acknowledged that a majority of anglers saw the tribes as short-term adversaries on allocation issues.[49] But she added: "We won't go backwards to the old days [of the treaty wars, because] we still need allies on the environment. Victories are very bonding. . . . We need to disagree in a way that doesn't burn bridges that we need to cross later."[50]

Hamilton's view was shared by many sportfishing group representatives. Yet the cooperation between tribes and sportfishing groups has been much more tenuous and leadership-centered than cooperation between tribal and commercial fishers that share a food harvest lifestyle. The shaky alliance was vulnerable not only to long-standing disagreements over allocation and the use of gill nets but was even more vulnerable to new differences that emerged over cultural values and fish biology. In the early 2000s, a biological debate over the value of wild fish versus hatchery fish erupted into the open and pitted tribes against the Native Fish Society and a few other conservation groups.[51] The intense debate strained relations between tribes that used hatcheries and some sportfishing groups.

Another dispute over fish genetics also rearranged Indian-white relations to include new and sometimes bizarre players. State fish managers would often punish individual landowners for land-use practices that would cause the deaths of a few fish, without curbing hydropower dams or other development that kills thousands of fish. Moreover, the managers would club hundreds of returning hatchery fish, after determining that they do not constitute the correct genetic stock.[52] These policies were strongly opposed by farmers and other landowners affiliated with the "wise use" property rights movement, and they were sometimes joined by tribes defending their own hatchery systems' ability to reconstitute endangered fish runs.[53]

Donald Sampson of CRITFC explained that the tribes needed "strange bedfellows" to stop the state agencies' fish clubbings. He visited agricultural meetings at local Grange halls and told the farmers that the fish should be allowed to spawn. Sampson told the crowd, "Now it's the Indians riding in to save your ass, instead of the cavalry." At one Grange forum, he turned around one property-rights protester by reminding him: "Native people have been in these same shoes for years . . . you took our property. But now we need a sustainable approach." Though the crowd gave him a standing ovation when he left the forum, he reminded himself: "I went to school with these guys . . . there are still Indian bashers within these groups." He concluded, "We'll dance with the devil but not kiss him."[54]

Tribal Plans

Instead of simply complaining about state and federal mismanagement of the fishery, the tribes submitted their own plans for salmon recovery and restoration and gained support in surprising quarters. Ted Strong maintained that the federal approach divisively pit each of the four H's against each other and used the ESA in a "one-species-at-a-time" crisis strategy.[55] Strong described the tribal approach as a comprehensive management plan based on watersheds, or "subbasin planning," incorporating all threats to salmon survival. He partly credited the tribal threat of the "big club" of treaty-based lawsuits as forcing better agency cooperation. Like commercial fisherman Les Clark and Chief Johnny Jackson, he found that elders who had leadership qualities were passing on and that younger leaders were using their "head" rather than their "heart."[56]

In 1995, the four CRITFC tribes released a restoration plan called Wy-Kan-Ush-Mi Wa-Kish-Wit, or Spirit of the Salmon, for integrated action on all four H's.[57] Allen Pinkham, a former Nez Perce chair, summarized the plan by saying, "You've kind of screwed up the earth here a little bit, so let us try it now."[58] The plan stated: "[Fish] need a connected migratory habitat that supports biological functioning throughout their life cycle [and] not just fragments of a good habitat here and there. . . . To return the basin's watersheds to health and productivity, the tribes seek to engage their watershed neighbors in local, collaborative efforts."[59]

CRITFC's approach garnered some support from commercial fishing groups, and its plan won a 2000 award from the American Fisheries Society. But support came most surprisingly from farming and ranching communities, which for years fought the tribes on water rights and watershed protection. Two agricultural newspapers reported strong public support for tribal positions on dams and hatcheries in 1999.[60] Agricultural granges passed resolutions and policies supporting tribal hatcheries.[61] Two regional irrigators' associations backed tribal treaty fishing in the lower Columbia, commenting that "the tribes have a treaty right (property right) that should be honored."[62]

TRIBAL RELATIONS WITH FARMERS AND RANCHERS

Although tribal relationships with fishing organizations slowly progressed through the late twentieth century, a deeper and perhaps more promising relationship began to develop in agricultural areas close to the reservations. Farmers and ranchers had been among the major culprits in degrading salmon habitat through poor agricultural practices. But in cooperation with CRITFC tribes, some started to literally clean up their act and to overcome long standing local tensions.

Conflicts between tribes and white agriculturalists are not like abstract, numerical disputes over allocation of fish that swim under the water's surface, but are immediate and visible disputes over tracts of land and riparian stretches of waterways. Since relations between tribes and white farmers/ranchers tend to have more obstacles to overcome, it is curious why this type of relationship has sunk deeper roots than the ties between tribes and non-Indian fishing groups.

Agricultural degradation of salmon habitat comes from many sources. Poor ranching practices create erosion, with silt and sediment blanketing gravel spawning beds and smothering eggs, clogging gills, and lowering oxygen levels.[63] Flooding damages riparian areas if vegetation is not present to absorb water and anchor the soil. Livestock gather along streams, damaging vegetation and banks, compacting soils, and depositing organic wastes that raise water temperatures. Repair efforts focus on excluding cattle with fences, changing grazing patterns, and managing uplands for the health of the watershed.

Poor farming practices also damage streams with erosion and harm salmon with pesticides. Irrigation systems lose water through evaporation and through leaky pipes, culverts, and canals. Farmers divert water into their ditches, blocking fish passage and reducing flow. These problems can be repaired through screening culverts and eliminating diversions. Erosion repairs focus on planting riparian buffers of native trees and shrubs, instituting contour farming and terraces, practicing crop rotation, and constructing sediment control basins.[64]

Tribes have direct access to salmon recovery funding that local governments lack. The Northwest Power Planning Council directed the Bonneville Power Administration (BPA) to serve as the principal funder for Northwest salmon restoration efforts, to mitigate for damage to fish runs by BPA dam projects. Many collaborative projects would not be possible without this mandated source of funds. Tribal access to federal funds helped to alter the balance of power between tribes and the state and local governments. Yet some critics see the funding as a lesser priority than dismantling harmful dams.[65]

Steve Parker of the Yakama Fisheries Department said: "Scattered damage has occurred incrementally over one hundred years. It is going to take time to undo. . . . We accumulate small successes. We may not see huge benefit in our lifetime, but our children and grandchildren will see it."[66] Many tribal leaders see parallels between the future of the salmon and the future of their youth. One outcome of this philosophy has been a tribally backed program involving young adults in salmon restoration programs.

The Earth Conservation Corps' Salmon Corps program involves mainly Native American young adults, eighteen to twenty-five years old. The Salmon Corps began in 1994 to energize Native young adults to repair the disappearing salmon habitats (often on farms and ranches) with a mission of "reclaiming two of the country's most threatened resources: the environment and disadvantaged young people."[67]

Salmon Corps members have built riparian fencing, planted native trees and vegetation, released salmon eggs, worked in hatcheries, and helped to restore over fifty salmon habitats in the Columbia Basin. Corps members became involved in community service in tribal communities, and their training included a "cultural camp" where members receive Native language and life skills training.[68] Chris Shelley, a Salmon Corps director of education and training, said that farmers and ranchers have tended to be appreciative of Salmon Corps crews working on their land. Corps services were developed to be easily affordable and do not impose government restrictions.[69]

The Salmon Corps has been an example of positive tribal relationships with non-Indian landowners around the reservations. Yet the process of building local relationships was slower in some areas than in others. This lack of uniformity is instructive in the delicate art of building relationships between reservations and neighboring agricultural communities.

WARM SPRINGS RESERVATION

The Confederated Tribes of Warm Springs is a multitribal reservation near Madras, Oregon, consisting of thirty-five hundred members, from the Warm Springs bands of the Walla Walla people, as well as Wasco and Northern Paiute. The Warm Springs and Wasco ceded 10 million acres of their land in the 1855 treaty, but reserved 644,000 acres for their own use.

Many of the "river people" who moved to Warm Springs have continued to fish from off-reservation platforms on the Deschutes.[70] Since the early 1970s, Warm Springs has been building a tourism economy, to mitigate for the loss of the Columbia River fishery. BPA mitigation funds paid for the construction of the Kah-Nee-Tah Resort in 1972.

The reservation had been locked in a conflict with local agriculturalists over water rights. In 1997, the tribes concluded fifteen years of negotiations and reached the Warm Springs Water Rights Settlement Agreement, with the encouragement of Secretary of the Interior Bruce Babbitt. The tribes and the state agreed to maintain minimum in-stream flows in the rivers and streams flowing through and bordering the reservation.[71] Nevertheless, relations between the tribe and local farmers and ranchers were not resolved.

Terry Courtney Jr., a Wasco/Tlingit elder and CRITFC commissioner, remembered periods of drought when the water would be so low in the Deschutes that no fish could be caught. At the same time, fields would be green and pools filled with water in the upstream town of Bend. He said he was so irritated that he wanted to shut the irrigators' gates and "put superglue on them."[72]

Wasco elder Claude Smith Sr., a World War II veteran and past CRITFC commissioner, took a somewhat different view. Raised on a reservation ranch, he remembered good relations between white ranchers and his father, who owned 250 head of cattle. He said that irrigators had met the tribes' request to fence their streams and that spawning areas were "coming back slowly."[73]

Smith's observation that Warm Springs established a cooperative relationship with state agencies is echoed by other observers. Yet the tribes had not established as close a working relationship with local non-Indian landowners. By contrast, the Yakama of Washington State have established ties to individual landowners, but have often been met with antagonism from governmental bodies.

YAKAMA NATION

The Confederated Tribes and Bands of the Yakama Nation are headquartered in Toppenish, Washington, in the fertile Yakima River Valley.[74] The Yakima Valley is an agricultural oasis in the semi-arid region, drawing large-scale farming and a growing Mexican population. About three hundred thousand acres of the reservation within the valley is owned by non-Indians. The Yakima River Basin suffered from overgrazing, overappropriation of water for irrigation, and warm waters from organic waste. Stream flow was so weak at times that the U.S. Bureau of Reclamation suspended all fishing—including treaty-backed tribal fishing—in stretches of the river.

Yakama fisheries staff member Steve Parker admitted that the tribal relationship with farmers was "pretty spotty," with only "pockets of cooperation." Parker, like Republican U.S. senators Dan Evans and Mark Hatfield, placed the blame on local governments and intransigent farming groups.[75]

Parker reported, however, that tribal staff had good success with individual landowners and started habitat improvement projects to assist granges with fencing and revegetation. He reported that some landowners were less skeptical and suspicious of tribal agencies, which were considered more independent and apolitical than state and federal agencies, and that they had a history in the watershed and notably lacked the authority to impose involuntary measures outside the reservation.[76] Despite many obstacles, the Yakama Nation had some large sockeye returns in the 2000s.

By the 2010s, the Yakama teamed up with farmers, ranchers, and environmental groups in a $4.2 billion project to secure adequate water for both fish and agriculture, install fish passages at dams, and protect fifty thousand acres from development.[77] The state and federally funded Yakima Basin Integrated Plan would build new reservoirs and a five-mile tunnel diversion to safeguard waterways against drought. Ellensburg farmer Marc Charlton commented, "In the past we've been at odds, in honest-to-God shouting matches between the two sides." Another Ellensburg farmer, Urban Eberhardt, saw the plan as a "survivability thing," because with climate change, "our snowpack is not materializing and . . . our drought years are increasing."[78]

Yakama staff had grown accustomed to a contentious relationship with local, state, and county governments, resulting in only limited salmon recovery success, until a federally funded project brought them closer. Warm Springs, however, was used to a more cooperative relationship—particularly with state government—and so has not aggressively changed land-use practices outside the reservation. The two approaches were combined on the Umatilla Reservation, which used a creative mixture of confrontational and cooperative tactics to secure treaty rights and restore its watershed.

UMATILLA FISHERIES RESTORATION

The Confederated Tribes of the Umatilla Indian Reservation are just outside the city of Pendleton, in northeastern Oregon. It is home to members of the Umatilla, Walla Walla, and Cayuse tribes and also to some Nez Perce. Under the 1855 treaty, the Umatilla ceded the Umatilla River Basin, where it retained fishing rights.[79]

In the early twentieth century, Pendleton and Umatilla established one of the most interesting cultural relationships anywhere in Indian Country. The annual Pendleton Round-Up rodeo drew tens of thousands of visitors and put Native culture on display in the form of the Happy Canyon powwow.[80] Crowds cheered for Nez Perce cowboy superstar Jackson Sundown and watched parades of hereditary chiefs.[81] The parallel evolution of the modern rodeo and modern powwow—both opening with a "grand entry," invocation, and flag song—can be partly traced to their close relationship at the Pendleton Round-Up.

In the early 1970s, Umatilla proposed legislation returning some tribal lands outside reservation boundaries. Angry white Pendleton residents opposed any new tribal control over off-reservation parcels, forcing the tribes to withdraw the bill. In 1975, white landholders on the reservation fought against tribal zoning ordinances.[82] But a larger battle soon erupted that pitted treaty-reserved water rights against water use by off-reservation farmers and ranchers.

Salmon Extinction in the Umatilla

The Umatilla River originates in the Blue Mountains and flows 115 miles to the Columbia. Meriwether Lewis and William Clark observed one of the largest Columbia fishing settlements when they passed the mouth in 1805.[83] In the 1855 treaty, the federal government implicitly reserved enough water in the river for tribal members to continue their fishing rights. Yet the state also granted water rights to settlers in 1875, and in the 1902 Reclamation Act the feds promised the same water to white farmers.[84]

The U.S. Bureau of Reclamation constructed a dam blocking fish migration on the river in 1914, the first of five irrigation dams. By 1926, salmon were nearly extinct in the Umatilla River.[85] In 1958, three Umatilla fishermen were cited for harvesting some of the few fish left in the river, and they won their treaty rights case three years later.[86]

The Umatilla Tribes saw both the water diversions and erosion of stream banks as a denial of their treaty rights.[87] Under the Winters Doctrine, the tribes possessed an older or "senior" water right that legally would trump the irrigators' water access. The doctrine stems from the *Winters v. United States* case, which protects reservation access to water for economic development.[88]

In the late 1970s, Umatilla threatened a water rights lawsuit against the irrigators. Republican senator Mark Hatfield traveled to Pendleton to "hold a hearing on long-standing water rights in the Umatilla River Basin." He recalled, "These disputes were somewhat typical of other water conflicts . . . in that I was lucky to get out of that hearing room alive."[89] Hatfield claimed that the hearing was "the most argumentative and contentious hearing I have ever attended in my 21 years in the Senate," because "absolutely no one agreed on anything."[90] He felt some sympathy toward the Native perspective, because his mother had been a schoolteacher at Indian schools, and he had visited Celilo Falls as a child.[91]

Former schoolteacher Hadley Akins, then vice president of the U.S. Bank in Pendleton, remembered: "Some irrigators stuck a shovel in the ground and said they won't let the Indians take 'my' water. But they were stealing Indian water too."[92] The chairman of the tribal board of trustees, Elwood "Woody" Patawa, decided to explore negotiation with basin landholders as an alternative to costly and protracted litigation that could shut down farm and ranch operations. Chairman Patawa and Umatilla County commissioner Bill Hansell (a Republican) signed a memorandum of agreement that recognized tribal sovereignty.

Umatilla Basin Project

Between 1981 and 1982, Akins and tribal natural resources consultant Ed Chaney began meeting with irrigation districts and farmers to keep enough water in the river to bring back fish runs. Akins remembered the initial meetings as tense: "If there was a tomahawk on the table, there would have been war. No one knew how to talk to the other guy." But at one of the meetings an irrigator suddenly realized: "We're not each other's enemy. The common enemy is Uncle Sam." Akins explained: "We had to find the common enemy. We were all the enemy of government bureaucracy [that] had given away this water twice."[93]

Yet ironically, it was also "Uncle Sam"—in the form of federal funding, legislation, and treaty recognition—that enabled this local cooperation to develop. The federal government had two roles in the Umatilla Basin conflict: the "outsider" pitting local interests against each other and the conciliator seeking to prevent Native-white conflict that would bring its own resource management into question.

In 1982, the tribes forced the salmon restoration issue by releasing 4 million juvenile fall chinook into a Umatilla tributary. With this assertion of sovereignty, Umatilla could pressure irrigation districts to voluntarily agree to release enough water into the river for the salmon to return in four to five years. Chaney noted the change in "political climate" when the tribes said: "The fish are coming back. What are you going to do about the water?" The negotiations resulted in the Umatilla Basin Project (UBP), run by a steering committee co-chaired by Akins and Patawa and later by their respective replacements Stafford Hansell and Antone Minthorn.

The UBP had to restore enough water to the river during fall and spring migrations. The project steering committee chose the option of a "bucket-for-bucket" water exchange between the Umatilla and the Columbia. Senator Hatfield said the UBP represented "a compromise the likes of which I have seen few times in my public life."[94] He secured $50 million in federal funding—making the project the largest Northwest salmon restoration effort.[95] UBP coordinators agree the funding would not have been forthcoming without long-term cooperation between the tribes and the irrigators.[96] This cooperation was based not only on self-interest but also on mutual recognition of different interests.[97]

Salmon Return to the Umatilla

In 1988, thirteen spring chinook returned to the Umatilla River—the first return of salmon to the river in sixty-five years. By 1990, more than two thousand spring chinook had returned, allowing the first open salmon fishing season on the river since early in the century.[98] Akins observed: "When the fish started to come back, the season was opened for both Indians and non-Indians. Many people figured that the Indians would say, 'Those are our fish,' but they didn't."[99]

A shadow was cast over the implementation of the UBP's second phase in 1991, when a Portland-based environmental group, WaterWatch, threatened to sue irrigators for transporting unused irrigation water outside the basin.[100] The eastern Oregon media treated the WaterWatch accusations as an outside threat, noting repeatedly that the group was founded by a couple from California.[101] Tribal officials viewed the eruption of conflict between irrigators and environmentalists with alarm.[102] Chairman Antone Minthorn felt that "some environmentalists were like the missionaries" in that "they always thought they knew what was best for Indians."[103] He coordinated negotiations between the environmental group and agencies, resulting in a 1992 agreement.[104] Chairman Minthorn had served as a mediator between the white environmentalists and white farmers, demonstrating that tribal leaders had achieved such a political stature that they could referee conflicts among white resource interests.

Umatilla Habitat Enhancement

Habitat enhancement was the part of the fisheries restoration program that brought the Umatilla Tribes into the closest day-to-day contact with white irrigators and resulted in some of the most positive relationships, according to Umatilla Department of Natural Resources director Michael Farrow.[105]

One of the first farmers to work closely with the tribes was Melvin "Bud" Schmidtgall, co-owner of the S&M Farming Company in Athena, north of the reservation. Tribal officials approached him in 1996 to improve an eighty-acre tract along Wildhorse Creek, a tributary of the Umatilla River. The Umatilla Tribes revegetated stream banks, built stream filtration systems, and installed rock berms and cattle fencing—all at tribal expense.[106]

Although Schmidtgall initially got "quite a bit of flak" from his neighbors for "working with the Indians," he reported that the project's success quieted his former critics, who were "falling in line right up the creek." Schmidtgall said that "working it out" with Umatilla was preferable to dealing with federal conservation agencies, which mire landowners in paperwork and strict regulations.[107] He concluded that working with the Umatilla Tribes was "a lot better than working with the government, I'll tell you that."[108]

Chairman Minthorn stated, "A lot of fear between the Indian and non-Indian community has been alleviated . . . there is now peaceful coexistence." But he commented: "While the overall tone of our success in the Umatilla Basin has been cooperation, we did use the Supreme Law of the Land [treaty] to our advantage. . . . The farmers and irrigators always knew that we had a powerful tool backing us up."[109] "If you have sovereignty, you have to assert it," he said. "In order to have freedom, you have to define it on your own terms, or someone will define it for you."[110]

Umatilla as a Model

The success of the UBP was punctuated by the sudden national attention on the salmon extinction crisis.[111] As the *East Oregonian* newspaper editorialized, "It's fortunate that area leaders and others had the foresight to embark on this project before panic set in over salmon."[112] The local salmon population continued to recover in the 1990s and 2000s.[113] For twelve years, from 1992 to 2004, enough spring chinook returned to the river for tribal and non-tribal fishers to have nine fishing seasons.[114] Benton City sportfisher Tom Cossalter said: "This is one of the finest fisheries I've ever been involved in. The Tribes have done a fantastic job. It amazes me."[115] Minthorn declared: "What we have done here in the Umatilla Basin is rare. We restored a river and brought back the salmon. We should all be proud. We have much to celebrate."[116]

The closer working relationship between the reservation and adjacent communities resulted in joint tourism projects. The Wildhorse Casino Resort brought jobs to both communities and helped finance the impressive Tamástslikt Cultural Institute museum on the reservation. The Umatilla Tribes also opened a public golf course; previously, Pendleton only had a private country club golf course. Akins observed, "How much was the influence of the basin project, I don't know, but the fact is we now trust each other."[117]

Other Columbia Basin tribal communities may not have the political backing of a powerful senator, adequate funding, or a history of close cultural contact with their white neighbors. Yet in a nearby area of northeastern Oregon, another tribe had considerable success in cooperative projects with white communities, without the same factors present. The Nez Perce not only built bridges to Wallowa County citizens, but they did so in the same region from which they had been "ethnically cleansed" a century earlier.

NEZ PERCE RETURN TO WALLOWA VALLEY

The Wallowa Valley of northeastern Oregon is a centerpiece of the original homeland of the Nez Perce Indians, who once controlled 13 million acres in Oregon, Idaho, and Washington. The Nez Perce signed the 1855 treaty, which recognized their control over a 1.75 million–acre reservation. With the discovery of gold in the Wallowa Valley, the tribe was forced to negotiate an 1863 treaty that further diminished their reservation to 750,000 acres. The Nez Perce band led by Chief Joseph was offered a reservation in the Wallowa Valley, but local settlers vociferously opposed the offer.[118]

In 1877, land conflicts in the valley led to all-out war between the U.S. Army and those Nez Perce who had refused to sign the treaty. Joseph and other chiefs led eight hundred refugees in a 1,600-mile retreat across three states. His 250 fighters fought a running series of battles that held off the soldiers in more than twenty engagements. Finally, in the Bear Paw Mountains of Montana, only forty miles from safety in Canada, Chief Joseph delivered his famous "I Will Fight No More Forever" speech and was forever forbidden to return to his Wallowa Valley home.[119]

The remnants of Joseph's band were forcibly removed from the region and forced to live in Kansas and Oklahoma. After ten years they were allowed to return to the Pacific Northwest. Joseph returned twice to the valley to resecure land but was rebuffed by white settlers.[120] His band settled instead on the Colville Reservation, where Joseph died in 1904.

Bands that signed the treaty were allowed to form a federally recognized reservation, at Lapwai, Idaho, where they culturally persevered despite losing many of their tribal landholdings during the Allotment era.[121] Today the Nez Perce are still geographically divided among the Lapwai, Colville, and Umatilla reservations, but they increasingly view the Wallowa Valley as a "homeland" that provides a common historical identity. Tourists are drawn to Wallowa County, where each year the Chief Joseph Days celebration is staged, in a town named Joseph, which until recently had no Native residents.

The history of ethnic cleansing in the Wallowa Valley, and the exploitation of Nez Perce culture by the descendants of white settlers who took tribal lands, would seemingly preclude any return of a genuine Nez Perce presence to Wallowa County. But in the 1990s and 2000s, the tribe began to regain a foothold in the valley and even a limited control over land and natural resources. Furthermore, this return of the Nez Perce was supported and even encouraged by Wallowa County residents mindful of their tarnished history.

Wallowa County Fisheries

The return of the Nez Perce presence to the Wallowa Valley emerged, as in so many other Northwest stories, out of the world of resource politics. Around the Nez Perce Reservation in the 1970s, white vigilante groups had tried to block tribal fishing in the Rapid River, leading to the jailing of tribal fishers and the mobilization of the Idaho National Guard.[122] The harassment had lessened after a federal court upheld Nez Perce treaty rights to harvest off-reservation fish in 1982, but the experience had reaffirmed Nez Perce wariness when dealing with white communities.[123]

When Oregon's Grande Ronde and Imnaha Rivers were nominated to become federal wild and scenic rivers in the late 1980s, Wallowa County and the Lapwai-based tribe joined a committee to study the proposed designation. In addition, by 1991 it had become clear that chinook would be listed as under the ESA, and county interests felt threatened by the unknown effects of the listing.[124] Instead of fighting the wild rivers designation, however, county officials decided to work with it. Because the Imnaha Valley was Joseph and his band's wintering area before 1877, the Lapwai tribal government had an interest in developing a resources management plan.

In the course of hammering out the Wallowa Salmon Habitat Recovery Plan, Wallowa County commissioner Pat Wortman met with the head of the Nez Perce fisheries department, Silas Whitman. Wortman was a rancher, a logger, and an official in the county court system. Whitman had previously visited Wallowa County to fish and to play gigs with his band. Whitman and Wortman, with Nez Perce fisheries biologist Don Bryson and timber company operator Bruce Dunn, led the salmon plan committee.

Bryson credited the personal relationship between Whitman and Wortman for the success of the committee in 1993. Unlike some other Nez Perce representatives, Whitman preferred not to dwell on past injustices but to focus on the future benefits of a cooperative relationship. He told committee members: "We know what it's like to be kicked out. We're here to help you keep the valley the way it is."[125] When other tribal officials saw the warm interplay that had developed between Whitman and Wortman, they were "dumbfounded" because "they had never seen anything like it."

Unlike the Umatilla project, the Wallowa County salmon plan had a tiny budget and was based on a voluntary panel of agencies and interests. Nevertheless, a formal Nez Perce government role in the Wallowa Valley had not been seen in over a century.[126] Jaime Pinkham, who formerly headed the tribal natural resources department, said: "When the tribe comes to the table, we bring our attorneys and our biologists and our experts, but we also bring our spirit. And I think a lot of people are starting to use that point of view to reframe their own views of nature."[127]

Wallowa Valley Land Returns

The relationship between Nez Perce tribal members and Wallowa County citizens reached a new stage in 1997, when the tribe took title to 10,300 acres above Joseph Creek, a culturally significant area near the Washington border. The Trust for Public Lands had brokered a deal with the BPA, under which the tribe would manage a "natural area" on the rangeland that would eventually encompass sixteen hundred acres. Because the land was held by the nonprofit trust, the tribe could not put it into federal trust. Yet in a ceremony, the Nez Perce named the site the Precious Lands.[128]

Not all local citizens were happy with the return of Nez Perce landownership to the valley. One woman said at a saloon in Enterprise, "I don't mind 'em coming here, but I don't see why we should have to give any land back."[129] Local governments also feared the loss of tax revenues, but the tribe negotiated a payment in lieu of taxes (PILT) that met the county's economic needs while not compromising tribal sovereignty.

In 1995, in response to tensions between laid-off loggers and environmental groups, County Land Use Planning Committee director Diane Snyder and other community leaders had founded Wallowa Resources, with assistance from Sustainable Northwest in Portland, as a community-based nonprofit that balances the environmental health of the ecosystem with the economic health of the community.[130] Its board included local business leaders, environmentalists, timbermen, and two Nez Perce tribal members. Its Wallowa Ranch Camp brought together Nez Perce and Wallowa Valley youths in summer outings.[131]

The cooperation in Wallowa County stood in contrast to the tensions that grew closer to the Nez Perce Reservation at Lapwai. Many white reservation residents joined with local governments in forming the North Central Idaho Jurisdictional Alliance, which challenged many aspects of Nez Perce sovereignty on and off the reservation. Former Nez Perce chairman Allen Pinkham noted that politicians "are afraid they'll be called Indian lovers."[132]

Yet in one case, in Nez Perce County, the tribe offered a PILT as compensation for a 23,000-acre parcel it took off the county tax rolls, so the county refused to join in challenges to Nez Perce sovereignty. Pinkham pointed out that the tribal settlements with Nez Perce and Wallowa counties have economically benefited local non-Indian citizens—since tribes can more easily attract federal project funds—whereas counties that joined the North Central Idaho Jurisdictional Alliance have lost out by not building a positive relationship.[133]

Nez Perce Homeland Project

At the same time as the return of the Precious Lands in Wallowa County to the Idaho-based Nez Perce Tribe, a more unusual land deal was culminating near the town of Wallowa. Instead of a deal between tribal and federal or state government, the land was purchased by a partnership of Nez Perce and local non-Indian citizens, to begin to fulfill the long-standing dream of a tribal return to the valley.

Since 1946, Chief Joseph Days would draw tourists to the valley every July with a rodeo, a parade, and displays of generic Native culture. In 1991, concerned that Nez Perce culture was being exploited, parade organizers added a small friendship feast and powwow that drew Nez Perce from the three reservations. The powwow was primarily organized by two valley residents: Earl "Taz" Connor (a Nez Perce / Cayuse great-grandson of Chief Joseph's brother Ollokot) and non-Indian history teacher Terry Crenshaw. They envisioned the event as a gesture by local residents to welcome the Nez Perce back to the valley and begin to heal the wounds of the forced expulsion of Joseph's band. The tribal members supplied salmon and venison for the feast, while local residents were exposed to the dancing determined by the Nez Perce themselves.[134]

Connor had envisioned a more permanent site for the powwow, which could also serve as a Nez Perce camping site in the valley and a future site for

Tamkaliks powwow grounds in the Wallowa Valley, the Nez Perce homeland in northeastern Oregon. (Courtesy: Elaine Dickenson, *Wallowa County
Chieftain*)

a cultural interpretive center. The Nez Perce Wallowa Valley Homeland Project
raised enough grants (from the Oregon Trail Sesquicentennial) and private
funds to purchase 160 acres outside the town of Wallowa in 1997. Crenshaw
said, "We want to create a place where the Nez Perce can come back and be
comfortable, a place for them to store and preserve their culture, a place where
they can tell their story—and we're doing it because we think it's right."[135]

The powwow was named the Tamkaliks Celebration in 1998, using the Nez
Perce term for "From where you can see the mountains," and drew thousands

of Indians and non-Indians (and their money) to Wallowa. Connor commented: "It's ironic that they boot us out of there in 1877 because they wanted the land and resources. Now they're asking us to come back and help them with their economic development because they're not surviving."[136]

Rich Wandschneider, director of Wallowa Mountain Engineering and of the Fishtrap writers' institute, was a board member for the Homeland Project. He stressed that the Tamkaliks grounds are a "common ground" for the dispersed and divided Nez Perce bands and so would not be put into trust for any reservation.[137] The Salmon Corps helped build a road and dance arbor, plant native vegetation, and construct a ceremonial lodge.[138]

The implications of the Homeland Project extended beyond the Tamkaliks grounds. The Nez Perce could have posed the reclamation of their homeland as a zero-sum game with the descendants of settlers who stole the valley. But by demonstrating how a Native cultural resurgence can benefit the valley as a whole, they enlisted the support of the local non-Indian community by emphasizing universal values.[139] The ESA later afforded the Nez Perce Tribe leverage in a 2004 settlement of Snake River water rights.[140] The Wallowa case has gone beyond a short-term relationship between government agencies into a longer-term cultural relationship between communities.

The Wallowa Valley can be said to represent a unique case only because of the compelling story of Chief Joseph, and non-Indian encouragement could be viewed as "safe" because of the lack of many local tribal members. Yet other areas with iconic Native histories, such as the Black Hills of South Dakota, are not exactly inviting tribes to reclaim lands or co-manage resources. By inviting the Nez Perce to resettle in their midst, local non-Indians are trying not only to right a historical wrong but also to redefine the valley as inclusive of all who value it as a place.

KLAMATH BASIN

In contrast to the Umatilla and Wallowa stories, probably the most contentious twenty-first-century resource conflict in the Northwest Plateau has been fought in the Klamath River Basin of southern Oregon and northern California.[141] The "water war" pit several tribes, with their allies in environmental and commercial fishing groups, against small and large farmers in the vast 10 million–acre region.[142] The Klamath Basin has for decades been ground zero for conflicts around endangered species, tribal water rights, commercial fishing, and irrigated agriculture.[143]

The bitter conflict concerning the overallocation of water polarized communities whose culture and livelihood were dependent on fishing and farming. Yet even in the midst of this water war, the dispute revealed "the interdependence of economic recovery with ecological restoration, and the urgency for all the communities within the Basin to find common ground."[144]

The Klamath Tribes in the arid, high-elevation upper Klamath Basin of Oregon and the Hoopa, Yurok, Karuk, and Modoc in the lush, forested lower Klamath Basin of California fought hard for in-stream flows and dam removals that would keep fish alive, as part of their historic battle for sovereignty. The Modoc had resisted U.S. troops in the 1872–73 Modoc War, the Klamath had their federal status as a tribe "terminated" in 1954, and the Hoopa and Yurok had won a long court battle for fishing rights from 1971 to 1993. The Klamath had their federal recognition restored in 1986 (with a headquarters near Upper Klamath Lake), but without a restoration of reservation land.[145]

The upper Klamath tributaries flow out of the Cascades into Klamath ceded territory, where the Klamath Tribes' treaty rights retained their access to the sucker fish that are integral to their culture. As in the Umatilla Basin, the Department of the Interior promised and diverted the same water to farmers in 1905, through the Klamath Irrigation Act. Farmers moved in large numbers to the irrigated region in the interwar period to raise cattle and grow crops. In the meantime, a hydroelectric dam blocked fish passage into Oregon in 1918, and three more hydropower dams were built on the river over the following forty-four years, further reducing tribal access to fish and farmers' access to water. The lower Klamath was once the third most productive river system for salmon in the contiguous United States, but the dams, diversions, and pollution reduced salmon population to a tenth of its historic size, threatening downstream Hoopa and Yurok treaty rights and commercial fishing and sportfishing industries.[146]

The 1957 Klamath River Compact recognized the rights of the tribes, power companies, and fish and waterfowl to have sufficient water, but prioritized the competing claim of irrigators to water their crops and have low-cost power rates.[147] Tensions built with the tribes as they asserted their treaty rights in the 1980s, and federal agencies began to use the ESA to list fish species as endangered. In 1988, two species of suckers were listed as endangered in the upper basin, and in 1997 coho salmon were listed as endangered in the lower basin, closing the river to commercial fishers and sportfishers.[148] A 1999 federal circuit court ruling held that irrigators were bound by the ESA and that the dam utility was bound by treaty rights.[149]

The competing claims to water came to head during a severe 2001 drought, when two federal agencies issued biological opinions that required cutting water flows to the farms, to keep the fish alive, and the farmers strongly resisted the move. Farmers lost tens of millions of dollars in crop revenues, and photographs of them standing in dry, dusty fields were splashed on front pages around the country. Their cause was championed by anti-environmental "wise use" groups and anti-Indian sovereignty groups, which depicted the water closure as an outsider attack on rural livelihood. Supporters carried out direct action to open the headgates, and many came from Nevada in a "Convoy of Tears," an insulting reference to the Trail of Tears.[150] The Klamath Bucket Brigade traveled around area communities with a large bucket to symbolize irrigators' rights.[151]

When a 2002 National Research Council report criticized the water closure, the George W. Bush administration reversed course, sending Secretary of the Interior Gale Norton to open the headgates for spring irrigation of farmland. By fall, the low flows in the Klamath devastated the fishery, killing at least thirty-three thousand adult salmon and other species and resonating deeply in Klamath culture.[152] The die-off was one of the largest in recorded history and led four years later to the closure of all salmon fishing in California and Oregon. This time, dead salmon were splashed on the front pages of newspapers, providing a powerful counter to the earlier images. The Pacific Coast Federation of Fishermen's Associations and conservation groups sued the Bureau of Reclamation to keep sufficient water for fish, in a successful three-year lawsuit.[153] The Department of the Interior opened talks with the Klamath Tribes to return terminated reservation lands, to improve the ecosystem and resolve the water rights conflict.[154]

The tribes, farmers, and fishers had all been detrimentally affected by low flows in the Klamath Basin. Part of the responsibility lay with federal agencies, which, because of federal laws such as the ESA, had to choose sides in wild swings of short-term policies, rather than balancing competing claims in a long-term strategy to ensure water for both farms and fish. Part of the responsibility lay with the zero-sum, adversarial process of water rights litigation and adjudication, in which attorneys press legal points and act as intermediaries.[155] Another part of the responsibility could be put on the power companies, whose dams restricted both water flows and fish passage.

The tribal and non-tribal residents of the region began to use listening sessions and negotiations to find collaborative solutions on the dams. For the first time, tribal fishers and irrigators began to connect with each other infor-

Massive fish kill on the Klamath River in Oregon in 2002, after the George W. Bush administration reduced water flows to the river in favor of Klamath Basin farmers. (Courtesy: Bruce Ely)

mally on a human level, without attorneys present. One irrigator from the Yainix Ranch (on former Klamath Reservation lands) even began to work with the Klamath Tribes on a riparian restoration project. Other landowners, conservationists, and tribal representatives came together in the Klamath Watershed Partnership, which recognized treaty rights and the ESA as bases for dialogue.[156] The confidential talks were kept behind closed doors, to keep them out of the media limelight and allow for flexibility. The process was so resented by some irrigators and two environmental groups that the tribes asked them to leave the talks.

As at Skokomish, an opportunity and deadline for collaboration emerged in the process of relicensing the hydropower dams, carried out by the Federal Energy Regulatory Commission (FERC).[157] In 2004, tribes, environmentalists, and fishers began to dialogue over the dams with irrigators and agencies within the Klamath Settlement Group. By 2006, as low salmon returns nearly shut down the coastal fishery, the federal agencies ordered the PacifiCorp utility to remove the dams, and it joined the talks.[158] Yurok tribal member Troy Fletcher described the informal side meetings: "It is very challenging for the irrigation community to start talking about some of their fears, and where there might actually be savings of water, on both sides. Those kinds of discussions where you have to let your guard down are particularly sensitive . . . you're not gaining anything at that moment. . . . But what you are doing is gaining the trust that's going to enable you to get down to that final solution."[159]

Some irrigators even began to view the treaties and federal trust responsibility as a path to shape federal laws (such as the ESA) to the benefit of both communities. The talks between the tribal and irrigator "rights holders" were made possible by the "vertical" relationships of federal laws and court rulings, but they only succeeded because of the "horizontal" communication built between the tribal and irrigator leaders to overcome decades of animosity and hatred and create a "more even playing field."[160]

Craig Tucker, the Klamath coordinator for the Karuk Tribe, indicated that the water crisis created "uncertainty for everybody" and that "risk of uncertainty is what drives people to negotiate deals." He said: "[The irrigators] made a business decision based on the reality that we were creating a lot of economic uncertainty for what they were doing. . . . [Nevertheless,] we would hang out, we'd go have beers . . . and I think people built some relationships that are real and meaningful. . . . I think among the irrigators there's this acknowledgment that, 'what happened to the Indians was a genocide and we need to try to make things right.'"[161]

A solution to the Klamath crisis was reached in 2010 with the Klamath Basin Restoration Agreement, a comprehensive agreement signed by twenty-nine parties to increase water flows for fish, restore habitat (with up to $500 million in funding), make irrigation more reliable, and invest in local economies "to achieve peace on the river and end conflict."[162] Another agreement, the Klamath Hydroelectric Settlement Agreement, would remove the four PacifiCorp dams by 2020, in a process costing up to $450 million.[163] The agreements were approved by the utility, the irrigation district boards, the Klamath Tribes (in a referendum), and the state and county governments. Klamath Tribal Council member Jeff Mitchell observed: "Once we decided to stop fighting and start talking, we realized the opportunities provided by collaboration and coalition building. We haven't seen salmon in our country for 90 years; this Agreement represents our best chance of finally bringing the salmon home to the Upper Basin."[164]

Former Oregon Republican state senator Jason Atkinson produced a film on the agreements, titled *A River between Us,* and this is what he found: "Whenever we have left people out of their own destiny through lawsuits, through dividing communities, the environment has never been healthy. So if you actually let people work together and be neighbors, you can heal these 100-year-old multi-generational problems—and you can heal the river." About his interview with farmer Steve Kandra, Atkinson said: "One of the questions I asked him was, 'You go to church, what are you praying for?' And he said, 'Well for a lot of years I was praying for the wrong thing: I was praying for victory over those Indians.'"[165]

In 2013, the state of Oregon recognized Klamath water rights dated to "time immemorial," making them the most senior rights under the Winters Doctrine. Yet the region was again ravaged by a severe drought, cutting upper basin water flows to 40 percent of normal. Although the agreements protected dry-year water sharing for farmers within the Klamath Irrigation Project, they did not protect upper basin farmers outside the project area. Although the agreements were finally signed in 2014, anti-environmental Republican leaders of the U.S. House Natural Resources Committee stalled funding them, and Klamath County withdrew its endorsement.[166] In 2016, federal and state agencies pressed ahead in their dam removal plans, sidestepping congressional assent, and signed on to a revised Klamath Agreement with three tribes.[167] In a separate action, the FERC also denied permits for a natural-gas pipeline through Klamath territory.[168]

Craig Tucker concluded that grassroots relationship building may not have been enough, comparing the players to Civil War generals who attended West Point together and respected each other but nonetheless waged war against each other. Yet he still believed that "the dams are coming out." "Is it going to take me another twenty years is the question, but I do think they're coming out."[169]

Even though the Klamath Basin agreements still have a long way to go to resolving the water war, for the 2010 agreements to be reached at all among the local rights holders was a significant accomplishment. As noted by two Oregon State University researchers: "While the laws were necessary to force change . . . they were inadequate by themselves for resolving complex social and ecological problems without the right forum to explore socially sustainable ways to implement them. Without local capacity to communicate, strategize and develop place-based, socially sustainable solutions, the settlement agreement could never have been forged." They concluded, "An important part of the Klamath story is the shift from top-down, government-led attempts to resolve water conflict (many of which were ineffective) to bottom-up, locally led solutions involving, importantly, improved tribal/non-tribal social relations."[170]

The crux of Native/non-Native cooperation in the Pacific Northwest, not only in the Klamath Basin, has been about shifting from "top-down" to "bottom-up" solutions.

PEACEMAKING AND PLACE MEMBERSHIP

The recent experiences of Pacific Northwest tribal nations in building bridges to non-Indians, particularly fishers and farmers, have had mixed results. The relative successes in the Nisqually, Umatilla, and Wallowa Valleys have been centered on well-defined watersheds and established bottom-up relationships between tribes and non-Indian neighbors, before federal assistance was secured. Local and county government officials who cooperate with the tribes have tended to bring along their communities, because they have developed social respect for their community leadership, even apart from their political roles.

The less successful cases of cooperation are perhaps even more telling than the successful cases. The Yakama Nation's efforts at watershed restoration were often blocked by local and state governments, but its efforts to work with individual landowners fared better and led to a federally backed watershed restoration project. The Klamath crisis was not resolved, but it led directly to a federally backed local plan to dismantle harmful dams.

Even in less successful cases of cooperation between tribes and farmers/ranchers, the relationships have been deeper and broader than tribal relationships with fishing groups. Tribal members had established some kind of social interaction with local farmers or ranchers—whether positive or negative—by going to the same schools, rodeos, basketball games, or businesses. The more localized the relationships, the stronger their potential to survive inevitable tests and challenges.

Relations between tribes and sportfishing groups rest on a much thinner leadership base, partly given the very different cultural values attached to fishing. This may be changing, as some tribes (such as Umatilla and Nisqually) show fish habitat recovery successes that benefit recreational fishing. Basin tribes and First Nations have proposed new fish passage technologies around the dam to be adopted by 2040, about a century after the dams first blocked passage, and have brought up this goal in the ongoing review of the 1964 United States–Canada Columbia River Treaty.[171]

As discussed in the previous chapter, tribal relations with fishing groups also tend to be subordinate to government-to-government relations with state or federal agencies. That creates resentment and backlash from rank-and-file non-Indian fishing communities, as well as tribal "river people," at being left out of the top-down process. Chief Johnny Jackson and commercial fisher Les Clark asserted that government-to-government relations centralize decision making in political leaders and attorneys. Tim Stearns of Save Our Wild Salmon added that elections too often change the players in government-to-government relations, but "as leaderships change you can institutionalize relationships."[172]

While they have many values and practices in common, tribes and commercial fishing groups have developed cooperation mainly at the leadership level. Lower Columbia fishing communities are still distant from the interior reservations, and the subcontinental Columbia Basin is too large for daily social interaction.

The question of geographic scale permeates many of the Pacific Northwest case studies. If the entire Columbia Basin is too large for establishing strong relationships between communities, can they build ties along the course of the riverway itself? The Voyages of Rediscovery expeditions have included an upstream journey of tribal and non-tribal canoes along the entire Columbia mainstem, to call attention to the need for fish passage around the dams.[173] Another strategy is to treat the larger basins as a patchwork of smaller sub-basins, such as the Umatilla or Yakima, that are at a more manageable scale for overcoming past divisions over subbasins' water and natural resources. The local-scale relationships built in watershed-based models can be stitched together into a larger regional quilt.

Many of the Native sovereignty battles of the past half century have been over different conceptions of geographical scale.[174] As discussed in the western Washington case studies, the top-down, government-to-government approach to resolving conflicts does not always work. The scale of the modern state is not conducive to building ties between peoples, because it is "too large to be known personally."[175] A bottom-up, cross-cultural approach for resolving conflicts uses place at a local scale, such as a watershed, mountain range, or urban neighborhood. It incorporates all the people who live in the place and depend on it for their living. (Some environmentalists use the term *bioregion* to describe a natural region that has a distinct identity for its residents. But this narrow ecological term omits the cultural, economic, and spiritual significance that human beings attach to places and which carve out their territories of belonging.)

Local places are neither simple nor quaint. Quite the opposite: the local scale contains subtle nuances and complex, unanswered questions that are often overlooked in resolving conflicts at national or global scales. The local place is where multiple identities and blurred social boundaries are most apparent. Human relationships are at a scale of experience that can be seen, heard, and felt.[176] Native/non-Native conflicts tend to develop first at the local scale and go on to shape state and federal policies, but solutions to resolve such conflicts have also emerged at the local scale, creating models for other reservations and their neighbors to follow.

A multiethnic local place within a conflict zone (such as Kosovo or Iraq) can ironically be more inclusive of difference than a larger but more exclusive state or ethnic identity.[177] Even in the midst of conflicts between cultural groups at a national level, certain local areas can emerge as enclaves of cooperation.[178] Local environmental projects (such as in Macedonia) can also build cross-cultural bonds by showing common ties to the land and water.[179] By working together to restore fish to a watershed, for example, "people develop their own genuine relationships to nonhumans, expand or adapt their worldviews to others and become able to act together as members of a shared watershed."[180]

Closer community relations are not in contradiction to better government-to-government ties. Better relations at a local scale can provide grassroots pressure for cooperation between political leaders. Better relations at the top can provide an example and direction to relations at the community level. Peace processes (such as in Palestine/Israel) tend to fail when peacemaking is only imposed from above or attempted from below.[181] Instead of being forced into loyalty to a settler state, people can define themselves as members of a place and in so doing construct a territorial identity to counteract social exclusion. I call this strategy "place membership" because it is based on people living in a place rather than within a political boundary.

An environmental alliance is one example of a "place membership" strategy in action: stressing a common bond of residents to a natural ecosystem. "Place members" can and will have a varying depth of membership in a place, with Native peoples claiming a rootedness that is far deeper than white residents' support for environmental quality. Yet the point is that both groups put a strong emphasis on their local identities and include the other group within the place.

The alliances are carving out their own mutual space on the local level, rather than waiting forever for "reconciliation" between their political institutions. The alliances have ironically used place—the main object of contention between Natives and non-Natives—as a tool to lessen conflict. The players effectively turned battles over natural resource allocation into alliances for natural resource protection, using a common defense of the local place as a catalyst to lessen conflict. Native nations do not have to compromise their sovereignty in some feel-good reconciliation scheme with the state. Instead, their sovereignty cements their position as a powerful entity in their own watershed or even (as in the earlier case of Nisqually) as the "lead entity."

A "place membership" at the scale of the Umatilla Basin, Nisqually River watershed, Wallowa Range, or Salish Sea may be more inclusive of Native histories and cultures, and thus more effective as a tool for resolving conflict, than a citizenship-based loyalty to Oregon or Washington or even to the United States. Defending the same lands or resources that have been contested between Native nations and non-Native communities can become a means used to mobilize them in a common purpose. The goal is not simply to defuse conflict, but a "common sense of place" envisions a future of respect, for the land, the water, and each other.

PART II

MILITARIZING LANDS AND SKIES

"The reason we had empathy for those [farmers] was the government policies that the Indian nations always had to follow, that we were always under, which meant the loss of land. [We said] 'now it's . . . the Department of Defense that's taking your land. So we understand where you are.' And that really hit them, it hit all of us, so we decided to try to do something together. . . . That did a lot more for cultural understanding than if we had sat there and talked to them until we were blue in the face."

—Ona Garvin (Ho-Chunk)

THE STORIES OF PACIFIC NORTHWEST ALLIANCES-FROM-ABOVE DIFFER from the stories in Nevada and Wisconsin, where tribal members and white farmers and ranchers joined in alliances-from-below to oppose the U.S. military, as a threat to their peace and livelihood. Rural alliances against military projects have been remarkable and unprecedented, uniting tribal members and whites who saw themselves as "patriotic," in a battle with a military bureaucracy that they felt ran roughshod over democracy. The alliances opened discussions about the best methods of using the lands around military testing ranges and abandoned military sites. Low-level jet flights, bombing ranges, and munitions production and storage profoundly disrupt the fabric of rural life, whether for Native or non-Native people, but their responses sometimes differed in key ways.

The stories of alliances against military projects focus on two nations—the Western Shoshone in Nevada, and the Ho-Chunk in southern Wisconsin. Both tribes have retained strong cultural values and have historically not interacted much with local and state governments. They both possess a powerful connection to their treaty-defined land base, though they control only tiny and scattered parcels of land within their historic territories. They accepted or initiated alliances with white neighbors, without subsuming their differences. Both the Western Shoshone and Ho-Chunk saw their battle against military projects as a continuation of their historic fight to live on their original lands.

It may seem out of place to focus on the Nevada desert, when most of the case studies in this book focus on waterways between the Pacific and the Great Lakes. But Nevada is the place where one of the earliest alliances was formed in the 1970s, against the MX missile system. The federal view of Nevada as a military and nuclear testing site has made both tribes and white ranchers dispensable for the "national security." Nevada also represents a case where a tribal nation has never had its (strong) treaty recognized in the courts (despite tribal fighters such as Mary and Carrie Dann) and where recent alliances with white ranchers have floundered as a result. Rather than only study successful alliances, it is important to study those that have failed to last, and ask why.

As the Nevada and Wisconsin alliances opposed the outside threat of the military, the larger question is whether they helped bridge the gap between the tribal members and their white rural neighbors. This inquiry intersects with the larger questions around "environmental racism" and how white Americans possess relative advantages over their neighbors of color in facing threats to their health and well-being. Although Native/non-Native alliances can challenge white privilege, it can also divide the alliances or render them ineffective, when white "allies" sell out their Native partners.

The ultimate failure of at least some of the Nevada and Wisconsin alliances points toward the need for "environmental justice," which combines the universalist concept of environmental protection with the particularist concept of social justice. The environmental justice movement addresses the disproportionate impacts of toxins on the poor and people of color, including Native peoples, and challenges the racial "blind spot" of mainly white mainstream environmentalists who have ignored social justice.

Native/non-Native alliances are also vulnerable to wedge issues that divide communities that have united against a common adversary, such as the U.S. military. In these cases, is the sense of a common purpose enough to overcome divide-and-conquer strategies? If the white members of the alliance use their relative advantage over the Native members, and have their demands met first, how can "unity" be maintained in the face of inequality? Even if the two sides of the alliance share a sense of place and want to defend a place together, how do they deal with the power relations between them? In short, is mere "unity" enough?

CHAPTER 3

Military Projects and Environmental Racism

Nevada and Southern Wisconsin

IN THE 1980S, U.S. ACTIVISTS AND SCHOLARS BEGAN SERIOUSLY addressing what they first described as "environmental racism," or the disproportionate burden of environmental problems on people of color.[1] The concept was widened to "environmental justice," integrating racial and socio-economic justice into the environmental movement and adding environmental angles into movements for socio-economic and racial justice. In Indian Country, the environmental justice movement could be traced back to 1492—with the arrival of a certain Italian interested in mining gold.

The primary goal of environmental justice scholarship has been to document the correlation between polluting industries and the poor health of so-called "minority" communities, emphasizing that race is a stronger factor than class to predict proximity to environmental health threats.[2] Studies have shown that whites have advantages to move away from polluted neighborhoods and that low-income racial "minorities" have fewer choices.[3]

Native Americans join other communities of color in objecting to environmental racism and questioning (mainly white) mainstream environmental organizations that neglect their issues or try to speak for them.[4] Some mainstream groups have undermined tribal sovereignty by limiting tribes' culturally based use of natural resources. Notions of environmental protection have even been harnessed to exclude Indigenous peoples from "protected" areas (such as national parks).[5] For example, the Sierra Club opposed Havasupai reservation expansion in the Grand Canyon in the 1970s.[6] Greenpeace initially opposed Native whaling and seal hunting in the 1970s and 1980s (although it did not join the later movement against Makah whaling in Washington).[7]

Environmental justice discourse sometimes homogenizes Native peoples as merely part of a larger "minority" racial category. But Native activists tend to look at environmental injustice as a continuation of the historic assault on their control of their national homelands, part of the ongoing "slow violence" of colonialism.[8] In the United States, concepts of race and nature have always been "integrally connected, woven into notions of body, landscape, and nation."[9] Applying environmental justice to Native Nations enables the growth of this discourse beyond race and class, into areas of cultural survival and land-based identities.[10] Environmental sustainability is not a new concept for Indigenous peoples, and Native cultural values challenge the linear thinking of much of Western science.[11]

Whether in Indigenous, African American, or Latino communities, polluting industries take the "path of least resistance" and are more likely to meet the demands of white groups than a community of color to stop or modify a project.[12] Even if a corporate executive possesses no conscious intent to commit environmental racism, various institutional effects combine to create injustices.[13] These structures cause different sets of reactions to environmental problems in different communities.[14]

Environmental justice scholars and activists strongly reject the "not in my backyard" (NIMBY) approach as favoring white communities that do not have polluting industries. Using similar arguments, they advocate a "not in anyone's backyard" approach that seeks to prevent rather than shift contamination.[15] The case studies of low-level flights and bombing ranges are prime examples of the racialized application of NIMBY and the shifting of burdens from whites to Native Nations.

ENVIRONMENTAL "SHELL GAMES"

Companies and agencies use environmental racism not only in the simple geographic placement of toxic wastes or factories in disadvantaged areas. They can also manipulate geography itself, by shifting environmental burdens away from white communities, with the effect of racially dividing environmental alliances.[16] The social-spatial advantage of whites enables them to "vote with their feet," by avoiding or moving away from environmental problems. For example, African American steelworkers in Indiana emphasized cleaning up workplaces and neighborhoods, whereas white steelworkers had a greater ability to move to a safer section of the steel mill or to a less contaminated neighborhood.[17]

The response of white communities and communities of color to the same environmental issue is affected by their social "positionality."[18] In California, Chicanos saw pesticides as a human health issue affecting farmworkers, but white environmentalists viewed pesticides as a scientific ecological concern affecting wildlife and consumers. In New Mexico, Chicano farmers emphasized protection of water in their homeland, whereas white environmentalists emphasized protection of "wilderness" where they could hike on weekends.[19] Struggles over protecting New Mexico forests expose the contentious fault lines of race, culture, and nature that have been constructed in the region.[20]

These observations help explain the very different approaches to environmental issues taken by Native environmental justice activists and predominantly white environmental groups. Many reservations have poor soil and limited access to freshwater, because white settlers had taken the choicest real estate. Although the rural white residents can move away from a polluted landscape to a healthier location, Native residents are less likely to abandon their ancestral homelands and more likely to stand and fight. Tribal members' opposition to the placement of toxic waste dumps on their reservations provided the impetus for the 1990 founding of the Indigenous Environmental Network.[21] The network's motto "We Speak for Ourselves" communicated to other environmental groups that Native people had their own autonomous perspectives and strategies.[22]

A company or governmental agency may respond to pressure from white constituencies to minimize the impacts of a project, without lessening the impacts on Native communities. This "shell game" works best when racial differences happen to coincide with geographic differences, as in the case of reservations and non-Indian border towns. The social/racial effects of such a move are usually justified or masked as the result of neutral geographic or scientific factors.

Examples abound of this geographic shell game in both urban and rural communities. Different industry proposals for new toxic waste dumps or electrical transmission lines may pit one community against another along seemingly geographic lines, but the proposals can quickly become racialized. Even in fixed-site projects such as mines, companies can float different proposals for mine waste management that affect Native lands differently than non-Native lands. In this way, white racial advantages are played out on the landscape. Military projects in Nevada, and the story of the Western Shoshone Nation, serve as an ideal illustration of shell games in action.

WESTERN SHOSHONE NATION IN NEVADA

Nevada forms part of the homeland of the Western Shoshone Nation, or Newe Segobia, while other parts of Nevada are the homeland of Southern Paiute. During the Spanish, Mexican, and American colonial eras, the sparsely populated Great Basin region was at a particularly violent crossroads of trade, slavery, and warfare.[23] In the 1863 Treaty of Ruby Valley, the United States recognized that Western Shoshone retained title to a territory encompassing two-thirds of Nevada.[24] The treaty granted the United States the right to establish military posts, to set rights-of-way for settlement trails and telegraph lines, and to allow settlers to mine and homestead on tribal lands—but the treaty did not cede the tribe's 23.6 million acres to the United States.[25] The Western Shoshone worked for the white-owned mines, ranches, and railroads and lived in towns or scattered ranch colonies and eventually on nine tiny federally recognized reservations established under the Indian Reorganization Act (IRA). Some Western Shoshone continued "traditional" governmental structures through the twentieth century, which at times clashed with the IRA bands and sometimes also worked together with them.

In 1951, five years after the Indian Claims Commission (ICC) was established, an attorney for the Te-Moak Band filed an ICC claim on behalf of all Western Shoshone. Nine years later, the ICC determined that Shoshone title to their treaty lands had been extinguished in 1872 by the "gradual encroachment" of white settlers prior to that date. The Te-Moak Band fired the attorney in 1977 and rejected his agreements with the ICC, which refused to recognize the band's action.[26] In December 1979, the ICC offered $26 million as compensation to the Western Shoshone—using an 1872 land value of $1.05 per acre—and directed that the money be paid to the secretary of the Interior for later disbursement. Some Western Shoshone leaders advocated taking the money to alleviate tribal poverty, while others rejected the payments as an illegal extinguishment of their land claim.[27]

Western Shoshone who refused to accept the land claim settlement united in 1982 as the Western Shoshone National Council, including the federally recognized Te-Moak and Duckwater tribal governments. The council has continued into the twenty-first century to refuse the money and has instead sought affirmation of Western Shoshone sovereignty from the United Nations and the Organization of American States. Some IRA government leaders continued to press for acceptance of the claims money.[28]

The Western Shoshone land claim affects private landowners in a limited way, since only about 13 percent of Nevada is private property, concentrated around Las Vegas and other cities. Most of Nevada is controlled by either the military or the U.S. Bureau of Land Management (BLM). The BLM requires Indian and non-Indian ranchers to pay grazing fees for the privilege of using public rangeland. A key flashpoint of the Western Shoshone land rights dispute since the early 1970s has been Native conflicts with the BLM, particularly in Eureka County's Crescent Valley.[29]

In 1974, the Dann family contested a BLM trespass citation after their cattle were caught grazing without a permit outside their 800-acre Crescent Valley spread.[30] The sisters Carrie and Mary Dann quickly became symbols of the Western Shoshone national movement. Their legal case using the Treaty of Ruby Valley to assert the land claim lost in 1985, when the U.S. Supreme Court upheld the ICC award.[31]

The BLM began a running conflict with the Danns by impounding their cattle and horses in different confrontations stretching over three decades. The sisters and their allies resorted to civil disobedience in 1992, by physically obstructing impoundment crews, risking harm to themselves. The frustrating battle brought millions of dollars in BLM back fees and penalties to the Danns and other defiant Native ranchers, but it also brought international recognition to the Western Shoshone movement.[32] The BLM impoundment of cattle even caused some white ranchers to support the Dann sisters, but without supporting their treaty rights.[33]

The desert landscape of Nevada, and its lack of extensive private property, would seem to present an ideal opportunity for Native/non-Native cooperation. The treaty claim over federal lands also would seem to have been a strong basis for joint tribal/federal co-management of natural resources. Indeed, next door in the California section of Western Shoshone territory, the Timbisha Band reached an accord in 1999 with the National Park Service, which recognized clear tribal title to 7,500 acres in and around Death Valley National Park and a role in co-managing another 750,000 acres of the park.[34]

But the case of Nevada is unique, due to the overwhelming presence of the armed forces in the state—both direct military ownership of vast tracts of land and the military and nuclear-related use of even larger areas. In 1951—the same year that the legal process of extinguishing Western Shoshone land claims began—the military began a twelve-year series of one hundred aboveground nuclear explosions on the tribe's southern treaty lands. More than eight hundred underground nuclear weapons tests were conducted at the Nevada Test Site by 1992, making it the "most bombed place on earth."[35]

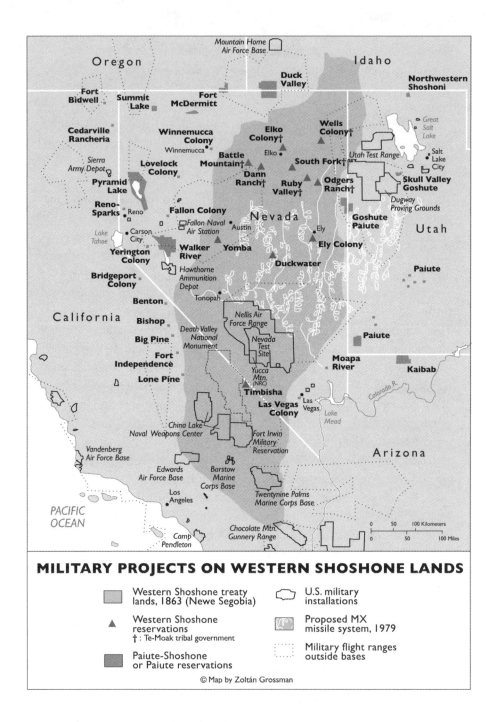

MILITARY PROJECTS ON WESTERN SHOSHONE LANDS

Western Shoshone treaty lands, 1863 (Newe Segobia)

Western Shoshone reservations
†: Te-Moak tribal government

Paiute-Shoshone or Paiute reservations

U.S. military installations

Proposed MX missile system, 1979

Military flight ranges outside bases

© Map by Zoltán Grossman

Many Western Shoshone contend that federal courts have not upheld their treaty rights due to the pervasive military presence in Nevada. National security priorities, they say, also stand in the way of co-management proposals that would protect Nevada's natural resources. They blame the heavy military presence for weakening their sovereignty and weakening their position in legal clashes with non-Indian landowners. Ironically, though, the military presence has also been the catalyst in building alliances between Nevada's Native and non-Native communities, beginning with the infamous MX missile proposal.

The MX Missile System

The Jimmy Carter administration's plan for an MX missile system served to bring rural people in Nevada and western Utah together in a common cause in 1979–81, despite the states' status as two of the most conservative in the country, at the height of the anti-communist hysteria in the late Cold War. Rural citizens resented being set up as a "sponge" for attacking Soviet missiles and feared that the huge mobile system would damage the rangeland.[36] Some Western Shoshone "traditionalist" leaders opposed the system as a violation of their treaty rights and sacred lands. They entered into an alliance with environmental and peace groups, as well as some outspoken ranchers.[37]

The gargantuan MX system proposed in June 1979 would have involved placing two hundred nuclear missiles on a series of huge train-like transport vehicles that would play their own shell game by dashing between forty-six hundred underground shelters. In this way, the Soviet Union's missiles would have to target all the shelters on the MX "race tracks," and the MX would "absorb" the brunt of a Soviet strike.[38]

Western Shoshone leaders, such as former Te-Moak Band chairman Raymond Yowell (himself an Air Force veteran), formed the Western Shoshone Sacred Lands Association to fight the MX. They grew suspicious through 1979 that the MX was preventing any favorable court settlement on their treaty rights, particularly when the Dann trespass case was delayed in the courts.[39] In April 1979, Interior Secretary Cecil Andrus abandoned talks with the Western Shoshone on forming a new 3 million–acre reservation, only two months before Carter's MX announcement. Native suspicions mounted in December when the ICC offered compensation to extinguish tribal land claims, and they concluded that the feds viewed Western Shoshone land rights as a possible obstacle to the MX.[40]

The air force defined the project area as "public lands" under the BLM's domain, but the tribe objected that it had never extinguished its title. The chairman of the House Subcommittee on Public Lands agreed that "if this land belongs to the Shoshone by treaty, then there is no way that the Air Force can get it without agreement of the Shoshone tribe."[41] Tribal leaders also objected to the destructive impact that the project would have on wildlife and springs and in restricting tribal access to sacred sites. Western Shoshone elder Corbin Harney said, "The Air Force probably thinks that no one will care about putting the MX here because no one's here but the coyotes, the jackrabbits, and a few Indians."[42]

In March 1980, the Western Shoshone Sacred Lands Association helped form the Great Basin MX Alliance, "comprised of ranchers, miners, farmers, businessmen, Native Americans, sportsmen, recreationists and conservationists."[43] Yowell remembered that the anti-MX alliance was the "first time we went off the reservation and said something about the land outside the reservation that we still considered ours." Non-Indians in the alliance, Yowell says, "didn't say too much on the treaty but 'let us talk about it.'" He said that the alliance was made up of "everyday people who recognized each other's interests" but that only a few vocal ranchers became visibly involved.[44]

The fate of the MX was sealed in June 1981 when the Mormon Church released a statement opposing the project.[45] In October, the Ronald Reagan administration announced that the MX (renamed Peacekeeper) missiles were to be deployed in fixed underground silos in Wyoming. But the MX controversy had left behind two legacies. It had strengthened the Western Shoshone national movement, even as the tribe's treaty rights were losing in federal courts. As Carrie Dann commented, "When the United States wanted to put the MX in, it opened the eyes of some Western Shoshone people."[46] The MX fight also presented the first example of environmental cooperation between Native Americans and white ranchers in the Great Basin.

Yowell agreed that the MX fight was a key factor in the founding of the Western Shoshone National Council, of which he became chief. He remembered, however, that most non-Indians in the movement did not carry it beyond the MX controversy, adding that "once the MX was done, they were through."[47] The white allies had never viewed tribal land rights as a means to stop the missile system and so did not build a relationship with tribal members beyond the immediate outside threat.

Military Testing Ranges

By 1984, new military plans met opposition from new alliances of the Western Shoshone, Southern Paiute, white ranchers, and environmental and peace groups, though with smaller numbers of participants than the anti-MX alliances. The navy and air force planned the expansion of bombing and gunnery ranges, including the increased use of low-level jet flight training. The training simulates war conditions of flying under radar and has been criticized for its health effects on livestock and wildlife and on its psychological effects on human beings.[48]

Grace Potorti, director of the Rural Alliance for Military Accountability in Reno, said that in Nevada "it used to be that the Pentagon would not be questioned" but that "bloody hell is being raised" about military plans. *Audubon* magazine described Potorti as "reassuring to cowboys, miners, and tribal leaders who may be uncomfortable questioning the military directly."[49]

The disputes centered on two valleys—Walker Valley in the Paiute region of central Nevada and Dixie Valley in the Shoshone region of northern Nevada. Potorti said that the threat of the military operations to the environment and the rural lifestyle affected Native and white ranchers alike.[50] In the Dixie Valley, for example, eighty-six ranchers were relocated to make way for an expansion of the Fallon Naval Air Station, some without full compensation.[51] The navy already owned several bombing ranges and controlled ten thousand square miles of airspace over the state. The navy proposed a withdrawal of hundreds of thousands of acres of public land for expansion of its bases.[52]

Bill Rosse of the Western Shoshone National Council played a key role in mobilizing Native opposition to the overflights and gaining non-Indian support. The bombing ranges and low-level flights had long been opposed by Western Shoshone Resources (affiliated with the Western Shoshone National Council), the Western Shoshone Defense Project, and the Citizen Alert Native American Program. Anita Collins, director of the Nevada Indian Environmental Coalition, documented effects of the bombing around her Walker River Paiute Reservation, where the bombing destroyed twenty-six thousand acres, killed livestock, disturbed wildlife, and accidentally hit buildings, wells, fields, and corrals.[53]

Many non-Indians also opposed the expansion of both bombing ranges and low-level flights, including the sonic booms that crack windows, buildings, and nerves and cause cattle and wildlife to abort their young. Ray Salisbury, chairman of Lander County Public Lands Use Advisory Committee, said: "I'm a former Navy man who served in combat. But I have the right to peace and quiet." Even the anti-environmental "wise use" group People for the West opposed the navy request for more land around Fallon.[54]

Western Shoshone face Nye County sheriff's deputies and federal security at the Nevada Test Site boundary during a 2011 Nevada Desert Experience sacred peace walk. (Courtesy: Chris Nelson)

The alliance had therefore brought together not only Native Americans and non-Indian ranchers but also peace groups and military veterans and even environmentalists and anti-environmentalists. Potorti observes: "It's a very strange alliance . . . we know it will take strange bedfellows. . . . We agreed to leave the shotguns at the door." Potorti saw that alliance participants were "broadening in perspectives, understanding" and that the tribes had the recourse of a federal consultation process.[55]

Virginia Sanchez, director of the Citizen Alert Native American Program, agreed that building bridges around the issue of flights was a positive, if difficult, experience.[56] Since the early 1980s, Native activists and non-Indian anti-nuclear activists had participated together in the Nevada Desert Experience movement's civil disobedience actions at the Nevada Test Site.[57] But Chief Raymond Yowell observed that at all the actions against nuclear testing at "ground zero"—and against proposed nuclear waste storage nearby at Yucca Mountain—he "never saw a non-Indian rancher down there protesting or even watching."[58]

Potorti explained that it was much easier to unite against a threat that comes from outside the geographical area, than to face a problem that emerges from within the local area and affects historic relations between local people. Because military jets come out of the sky, they do not challenge complex local realities such as grazing or water rights. Potorti asserted that "it has to be an alien thing" that brings the different communities together.[59]

Relations with White Ranchers

Although the Western Shoshone worked together with white ranchers to oppose "alien" military aircraft, they largely remained at odds over grazing rights on the ground, particularly in Crescent Valley, where the Dann family confronted the BLM.[60] Next to the Dann ranch, white rancher Maynard Alves purchased a ranch for $1 million in 1988, unaware of the contentious Native land rights case pursued by his new neighbors. He sued the Danns for grazing their cattle on his new ranch and confronted their Western Shoshone Defense Project supporters with a rifle.

When a proposed open-pit gold mine threatened the water table under both the Dann and Alves ranches in 1995, Alves set aside his differences with his tribal adversaries and joined them in legal efforts to protect the wells.[61] Yet within two years, a gold mining company bought Alves's ranch for $15 million and hired his son as mine manager. Western Shoshone activists often protested water pollution from northern Nevada's large gold mines. Jennifer Allen and Chris Sewall of the Western Shoshone Defense Project recalled that they made little headway with white ranchers over these concerns, since some of the ranchers benefited economically from gold mining.[62]

Corbin Harney, a Western Shoshone leader of the anti-nuclear Shundahai Network, grew up working on non-Indian ranches.[63] He remembered Native and non-Native ranchers rounding up cattle together and selling hay to each other around his Duck Valley Reservation. But he also said that "greed" prevented white ranchers from working closely with the Western Shoshone, and "they thought we would take over their land." But he claimed that a few ranchers expressed hope that the Western Shoshone would win their treaty rights case because, as they explained, "then we can deal with you rather than the government." Harney told the ranchers that the two communities can "value the land" if they "have a cooperative deal, tear down the fences, lower the [use of] fertilizer."[64]

Chief Yowell also contended that Western Shoshone sovereignty would provide better grazing rights for Nevada's white ranchers, with lower grazing fees than the BLM or U.S. Forest Service and a larger return of the fees for range improvements. "We have no issue with private landholders," Yowell said. "Our interest is only in the federal public domain lands, and in some lands held by the corporations."[65] He proposed to remap abstract allotment blocks to follow natural land contours and slopes and to increase rotation of grazing areas to allow grass to regrow. Private ranchers "would have no threat from us," he asserted. "The only thing is, they would have a different landlord than the BLM. We think we'll be a better landlord."[66]

Harney agreed with Yowell that some non-Indian ranchers had become more open to meeting with Native people and that a few prefer Native land-use policies to federal land-use policies. "The BLM is not paying attention to them," Harney said, "just like us Indian people." He told the white ranchers that government officials have been "lying to us for five hundred years, now they're lying to your people."[67]

Yet Yowell tempered his co-management vision with the reality of Western Shoshone losses in the federal courts. He believed that only about ten out of the two hundred white ranchers around his South Fork Reservation understood and supported the Treaty of Ruby Valley. When he asked the Nevada Cattlemen's Association's Lands Committee to pass a resolution supporting treaty rights, its chairman replied that the treaty rights were "lost" in the 1985 Supreme Court decision in the *United States v. Dann* case.[68] Carrie Dann predicted that if the treaty were actually upheld in the federal courts, "not much would change" for the white settlers, but "we would have to negotiate all use of the land." She said: "Nukes, nuclear dumping, gold-mining ponds, and the Test Site should be done away with. Wildlife should be protected. But the main thing is water."[69]

The fact that the Western Shoshone treaty has fared poorly in the courts means that the tribe is not on an equal legal footing with non-Indians and is therefore an unequal partner in any potential alliance for change. If Western Shoshones are correct that the heavy military presence prevents the recognition of their treaty rights, they are caught in a vicious cycle. If the treaty is not recognized, tribal legal powers are weakened and non-Indians assume that the tribes have little to offer in a common cause against military projects. Without a common Native/non-Native front, efforts to curb the military presence in Nevada are less likely to succeed. The continuation of the military presence makes treaty recognition less likely, and the vicious cycle starts again.

The Nevada experience perhaps offers some reasons for the successes or failures of Native/non-Native alliances elsewhere in the country. If the Native and white participants in the alliance are on an unequal footing, and if whites look toward preserving their own advantageous position, then the alliance may be too weak to prevail. By not actively supporting Native treaty rights and sovereignty, the non-Indians were in effect guaranteeing the ultimate weakness of their own campaign. The tribal/non-tribal unity alone was not enough to stop the military flight and bombing range expansion.

The absence of meaningful cooperation between the Western Shoshone and white ranchers has left a vacuum in social movement organizing that has since been filled by right-wing libertarian groups that direct ranchers' populist anger at both the federal government and environmentalists. In 2000, Elko County residents led a direct action to reopen a wilderness road that had been closed by the U.S. Fish and Wildlife Service to protect the endangered bull trout habitat from erosion runoff. The Jarbridge Shovel Brigade used shovels to rebuild the washed-out road and destroy a boulder they named "Liberty Rock."[70]

A long-standing dispute over BLM restrictions to protect the threatened desert tortoise erupted in a 2014 armed confrontation between backers of Clark County millionaire rancher Cliven Bundy and federal agents backing BLM attempts to confiscate his cattle. Bundy had claimed that his Mormon family's presence on the land before federal control gave him the right to not pay grazing fees for two decades.[71] Under pressure from Nevada politicians and the media, the BLM backed down, in contrast to its ongoing aggressive confiscations of cattle from nonviolent Western Shoshone ranchers.[72]

As one freelance writer contrasted the two cases: "Unlike Bundy, who claims his ancestors were homesteaders on his ranch in 1877 and never ceded it to the federal government, the Danns, two Western Shoshone sisters, were not trampling over land set aside for sensitive plants and animals. Nor were they getting rich off the land."[73] (In January 2016, Bundy's sons Ammon and Ryan led an armed takeover of the Malheur National Wildlife Refuge headquarters near Burns, Oregon. The militia action was opposed by the Burns Paiute Tribe, the Harney County sheriff, and many local ranchers[74]).

Denied the strong tools of treaty rights, the Western Shoshone have held little sway or influence over their white rancher neighbors, even as they were fighting against the same federal agencies, and so have not been able to connect their social justice fight with environmental protection, including recent concerns about climate change.[75] Alliances opposing low-level flight ranges spread in the 2010s to other Western states, such as New Mexico and Colorado, where the Peaceful Skies Coalition organized "tribal leaders and local governments, ranchers and environmentalists, veterans and pacifists."[76]

HO-CHUNK NATION IN SOUTHERN WISCONSIN

The Western Shoshone case study in Nevada provided an important precedent to the more in-depth case study of the Ho-Chunk Nation in southern Wisconsin. The issues of jet overflights and a bombing range resemble the issues in Nevada, even though Wisconsin has a much less active military presence. The Ho-Chunk believed that they had a strong alliance with local white farmers to stop proposals for overflights and a bombing range expansion in the mid-1990s.

Like the Western Shoshone, the Ho-Chunk (formerly Winnebago) had not had their treaty rights recognized in federal courts, although they had been able to use their sovereign powers and tribal gaming income to reclaim and co-manage some lost lands. In doing so, they began to build a better relationship with white farmers than the Western Shoshone have built with white ranchers—but within limits.

Southern Wisconsin forms most of the homeland of the Ho-Chunk Nation, who see themselves as the descendants of the effigy mound builders that have left their ancient earthworks around the region.[77] Americans invaded southwestern Wisconsin during the 1820s "lead rush," provoking limited armed Ho-Chunk resistance. Ho-Chunk leaders were forced or tricked into treaty cessions in the 1830s and subject to forced removals.[78] Some found refuge in eastern Nebraska, where the Winnebago Reservation still exists today. At each stop along the removal route, many Ho-Chunk walked (or canoed) back to their homeland.[79]

In the meantime, other Ho-Chunk bands hid out in Wisconsin woodlands, refusing to be removed. Soldiers periodically rounded up the holdouts in different waves of ethnic cleansing. The successful holdouts and returnees called themselves the Wazijaci (Dwellers among the Pines) and lived in small impoverished settlements. Their resistance to removal gained support among some non-Indians. Norwegian farmers intimidated soldiers at the Reedsburg train station in 1873 into surrendering a Ho-Chunk family they were attempting to load aboard a westbound train.[80] The following year, the federal government permitted tribal members to purchase private homesteads, but it did not grant reservation status to any of the scattered tribal plots.

The lack of a reservation condemned the Wisconsin tribal members to continued poverty into the twentieth century and the loss of private landholdings to tax forfeiture. In the early 1920s, Ho-Chunk gatherers lost their wild cranberry bogs to white settlers, who established a commercial cranberry industry around Cranmoor. Many became seasonal migrant workers in the bogs they had previously owned, and others wove baskets and danced for tourists in the nearby Wisconsin Dells.[81]

Yet ironically, the lack of federal oversight also enabled the Ho-Chunk population to protect much of its tribal culture and language and continue seasonal economic patterns of hunting, trapping, and planting for decades after reservation-bound tribes were forced to abandon their ways.[82] The Ho-Chunk continued to follow the tribe's strong warrior tradition by enlisting in disproportionate numbers in the U.S. armed forces, and returning veterans led the securing of federal tribal status in 1963. In late-twentieth-century Indian Country, the Ho-Chunk were still widely known for their powerful veterans associations.[83]

In 1994, the tribe renamed itself Ho-Chunk (People of the Big Voice) to replace outsiders' historic name of Winnebago (People of the Dirty Water). Among the Wisconsin public, the name change was closely associated with the concurrent opening of the Ho-Chunk Casino near Wisconsin Dells, rather than with the tribe of over five thousand members. The tribe had built two other large casinos and was well on its way to becoming the largest employer in Sauk and Jackson counties. Yet non-Indians were largely unaware of the strong attachment that tribal members had to their homeland.

Low-Level Flights Proposal

Although the Ho-Chunk have a long history of enlistment in the U.S. armed forces, even tribal veterans did not hesitate to take on the military to defend their people.[84] Tribal members around Black River Falls and Nekoosa had since 1955 lived under a military jet flight path coming west from Minnesota to the Hardwood Bombing and Gunnery Range in Wisconsin's Juneau County. In late 1994, an alliance similar to the Nevada coalition against low-level flights grew suddenly, after the Air National Guard proposed numerous new flight paths for its jets over much of the rest of southwestern Wisconsin and with the concurrent expansion of the Hardwood Bombing Range north into Wood County.[85]

The Air National Guard proposal centered on flights of F-16 fighter jets, which could fly as fast as 615 miles per hour, creating noise levels of 133 decibels, about twice the sound of a loud rock concert.[86] The Guard proposed up to 2,151 sorties a year, some flying as low as two hundred feet to practice flying under radar.[87] Guard spokespersons described the deep coulees of the unglaciated region known as the Driftless Area as resembling the valleys of Bosnia—then embroiled in an interethnic war and U.S. bombing campaign.[88]

MILITARY PROJECTS ON WISCONSIN HO-CHUNK LANDS

Ho-Chunk (Winnebago) treaty-ceded lands	Military installations
Ho-Chunk lands, 2015	Air National Guard flight corridor
Other reservations	Proposed flight corridor, 1994
Ho-Chunk treaty boundary	Kickapoo Valley Reserve
1837 Date of treaty cession	Frac sand mine, 2013
Wisconsin county boundary	

Adapted from *Wisconsin's Past and Present: A Historical Atlas* (University of Wisconsin Press, 1998) by the Wisconsin Cartographers' Guild

© Map by Zoltán Grossman

Negative reaction to the proposal came immediately from long-standing dairy farming families, organic farmers who had settled in the area in the 1970s, and others who saw the shattering noise as an intrusion into their peaceful rural lifestyle. They questioned the health effects of jet fumes on human and livestock health and farm crops, the possibility of disrupted TV and radio reception, restricted small aircraft travel, and the risk of jet crashes and lower property values.[89]

In 1995, 45 percent of the Ho-Chunk Nation's Wisconsin tribal members lived within counties under the existing and proposed flight paths.[90] Tribal legislator Ona Garvin consulted with tribal veterans' groups and the nation's elders' council, which voiced concern that the flights would disrupt spiritual ceremonies and that the sonic vibrations may affect ancient petroglyphs and pictographs. Garvin and Ho-Chunk veterans' leader Bert Funmaker consulted with Air National Guard officials, who agreed to halt flights during tribal ceremonies.[91]

Ho-Chunk concerns about the low-level flights were more muted, however, than the stronger tribal resistance to the Hardwood Range, which directly affected their communities. Although northeastern Juneau County lies just outside Ho-Chunk ceded territory, the bombing range is close to Ho-Chunk villages.

Hardwood Range Expansion Proposal

The Air National Guard's proposed expansion of the Hardwood Range directly affected a much smaller land area than the parallel low-level flight corridor plan, but the two proposals were intimately connected. Its rationale was that "rapidly encroaching development," such as cranberry bogs and summer homes, was making it more difficult for pilots on bombing runs to avoid populated areas.[92] Opponents portrayed the range expansion as a justification for the new flight corridors.

The 8,400-acre Hardwood Air-to-Ground Weapons Range was located near Finley, in Juneau County, and the proposed expansion was to the north into Wood County, into county forest land and private land owned by eighteen families.[93] Landowners feared that the Wisconsin Department of Natural Resources (DNR) would displace them to compensate for the loss of county forest.[94] The Wood County Board of Supervisors objected to the loss of revenue from the withdrawal of county forest land and strongly opposed the expansion.[95]

Environmentalist opponents pointed to the impact of bombing on endangered species. Cranberry growers around Cranmoor, long under environmentalist criticism for flooding wetlands, wanted to continue using ditches located in the expansion zone. Ten miles away, workers at large paper mills (the primary industry of the Wisconsin River Valley) also complained that they might lose sleep and productivity.

Ho-Chunk representatives voiced their key concern over the proximity of the range to tribal homes and facilities.[96] The range boundary was only two miles from the Rainbow Casino, a major source of tribal income, and close to the tribe's Chak-Ha-Chee village. Garvin complained that the Air National Guard "didn't even know that Indians lived under these flights" and observed that "already the schoolchildren hit the floor in panic when the bombers approach the range so low and loud."[97] In addition, the Ho-Chunk Nation expressed alarm over the possible impact of bombing on gathering rights and on sacred burial and effigy mounds.[98]

Opposition to Flight and Bombing Ranges

In 1995 and 1996, opposition grew concurrently to the proposed flight paths, led primarily by white farmers, and to the proposed Hardwood Range expansion, led by Ho-Chunk and joined by other local residents. Ontario resident Pat Conway observed that the flight plan "pivots on the sale of county forest land to the military."[99] Yet for the most part, two separate broad-based opposition alliances developed out of the two issues, at times closely cooperating but at other times reflecting different interests.

The group Citizens United Against Low-Level Flights was founded in 1994, when it purchased full-page newspaper ads proclaiming, "This is our home! Speak up now!" It also secured resolutions from county boards, rural towns, and school districts concerned about student stress and jet crashes.[100]

In April 1995, Amish farmers unexpectedly joined the opposition. A handwritten petition signed by four hundred community members expressed fear that low-level flights would cause horses to rear and buck dangerously, causing buggy and farm accidents.[101] The petition against the "visual symbols of war" attracted heavy media coverage and proved to be a turning point in the battle.[102]

The opposition to the Hardwood Range had drawn together an alliance of local citizens who had lost trust and faith in the Air National Guard and, in the process, had gotten them to know their neighbors for the first time. The alliance brought together Ho-Chunk with white neighbors, environmentalists with cranberry and potato growers, and peace activists with military veterans.

When Ho-Chunk tribal legislator Ona Garvin met with the landowners, she realized that "the common bond was the land" and empathized with the poverty of some landowners in the depressed area.[103] In February 1995, the Ho-Chunk Nation hosted a meeting of range expansion opponents at the Rainbow Casino, where they founded the Citizens Opposed to Range Expansion, or CORE.[104]

"The reason we had empathy for those people was the government policies that the Indian nations always had to follow," Garvin said, "which meant the loss of land." She told the landowners with a "vested interest" in the land: "Now it's the Department of Defense that's taking your land. So we understand where you are." She remembered: "That's what really hit them, it hit all of us, so we decided to do something together. . . . That did a lot more for cultural understanding than if we had sat there and talked to them until we were blue in the face."[105]

Journalist Susan Lampert Smith observed: "A few years ago . . . the tribe was beset with poverty and torn by frequent political upheavals. But the money brought by gaming and the stability brought by a functioning government has made the nation a true political partner to its neighbors." Dale Gray, owner of a farm threatened by the expansion, emphasized that "we don't mean nothing" to the military and that he was "real glad" to see Ho-Chunk focus public attention on the range expansion.[106]

Garvin agreed that the CORE alliance was "a really good experience," because the local white participants "learned about Indians." She pointed out that some of the same local white residents had opposed the tribe's acquiring land for the casino but that the tribe's "good neighbor" revenue-sharing program had smoothed over some of the differences. She saw more conflict between environmentalists and cranberry growers than between Native and white members of CORE. She observed, however, that some members expected the tribe to do most of the fighting and to foot the bill.[107]

While CORE had built bridges between Ho-Chunk and white opponents of the Hardwood Range, it found difficulty in making links to the closely related opposition to the low-level flights. In May 1995, some anti-flight leaders joined CORE in linking the range and corridor expansion issues, but other leaders felt that the Hardwood issue would divert from the flights issue and misrepresent what they saw as a local quality-of-life concern as an anti-military cause.

The inability of the white-led and Native-led alliances to sponsor joint projects prompted organizers to found a larger umbrella alliance that they named the Coalition for Peaceful Skies, which held a large October 1995 prayer rally opposing both the low-level flights and the bombing range. The Ho-Chunk

Nation provided free bus transportation to the state capitol in Madison.[108] This unity, however, proved to be short-lived.

The Military Divides the Opposition

In April 1996, the Air National Guard dropped the plan for new flight corridors, but it retained the existing flight corridor over Ho-Chunk lands and kept intact its plans to expand the Hardwood Range.[109] Local newspapers termed the move a "victory."[110] Some anti-flight leaders sponsored a "victory" barn dance to celebrate the "defeat" of flight range expansion.

The Ho-Chunk and neighboring landowners, however, maintained their opposition to range expansion, and only a few former low-level flight opponents stood with them. "If the [range] land is condemned," said Garvin, "there will be more military flights."[111] Conway said that other anti-flight leaders had "made a promise" to the Guard that accepted bombing range expansion in return for the abandonment of flight range expansion in their own backyard, adding "that's not a victory, that's a segmentation."[112] A leader who stood with the tribe, Deb Schwarze, feared that the Guard "has strategically dropped the low-level flight corridor proposal to weaken public opposition." She said that "their hope is that no one will be watching as they propose their broad-based plan in bits and pieces that requires less stringent public and environmental review."[113]

Anti-flight leaders who did not agree with the decision to disband set up a new group, Citizens United Against Range Expansion, which kept up the opposition through 1997. But without the deep-seated opposition to flights over a large geographical area, the new efforts lacked statewide exposure and legal or financial support. The lack of public input into the state environmental assessment process further marginalized the alliance. The Air National Guard's 2000 final environmental impact statement dismissed Ho-Chunk cultural objections to the range expansion.[114]

In the late 1990s and 2000s, the issues of flight and bombing ranges gradually received less attention from the Wisconsin media and public.[115] In their place, a very different set of land issues affecting the Ho-Chunk Nation began to take a more prominent role in environmental debates. Instead of objecting to military plans, the nation pressed for returns of parcels of its ceded territory. The land return proposals centered on a former dam site in the Kickapoo River Valley and former military munitions plant site on the Sauk Prairie in the Wisconsin River Valley. The response of environmentalists and local residents to these proposals was varied, pointing toward different visions of future coexistence with the Ho-Chunk Nation.[116]

Dam Site in the Kickapoo Valley

The Ho-Chunk experience of land dispossession in the 1820s and 1830s began to be reversed only at the very end of the twentieth century, notably in the Kickapoo Valley of Vernon County, in the same region affected by the low-level flights. In 1961, the U.S. Army Corps of Engineers had proposed a flood control dam on the Kickapoo River near La Farge. The dam proposal jeopardized the picturesque river, popular among canoeists, who transformed the issue into one of the state's first major conservation battles. In 1975, the U.S. Senate withdrew support for the dam, but after local white residents had been displaced for its construction. After the removal of the white landowners from a fourteen-mile stretch of the river, the 8,600-acre evacuated area grew over into an almost wild state.[117]

After years of conflict over the land along the river, the federal government in 1997 agreed to give the land to the state of Wisconsin to establish the Kickapoo Valley Reserve. The state in turn agreed in a memorandum of understanding to give back twelve hundred acres to the Ho-Chunk, who have sacred archeological sites in the area and had a historic presence before their forced removal.[118] Under the 1997 agreement, the state and tribal parcels together would be jointly managed by the Ho-Chunk Nation and the Kickapoo Reserve Management Board (it would directly control an additional seventy-four hundred acres).[119] When it was formed in 2001, the eleven-member board had two Ho-Chunk representatives (at least one a local resident), three appointees of the governor, and six non-Indian residents of adjacent communities or the Kickapoo watershed.

The state-tribal land negotiations aroused both support and resentment among some former white landowners and provided a backdrop to the alliance against low-level flights. Some white valley residents resented the planned return of lands in their area to the Ho-Chunk and viewed the tribe as not "local" to the area. Although only eight Ho-Chunk tribal members lived in Vernon County, tribal members had maintained contact with the ancient rock art sites near the river.[120] Other valley residents, however, backed the return of the former private parcels to their previous Native owners. Some of these local residents approved of direct Ho-Chunk ownership of twelve hundred acres, as a way to prevent all eighty-six hundred acres from falling under jurisdiction of the board, which they viewed as an unwelcome new layer of state bureaucracy.[121]

Ho-Chunk representatives sought dialogue with white residents on both sides of the land dispute, seeking common ground based on historical analogies.

As Susan Lampert Smith noted: "Interestingly, say tribal representatives, today's valley residents and the Ho-Chunk share a bitter story with the federal government. In the 1960s, federal land agents scoured the valley, evicting dozens of farmers from the land for a dam. More than a century earlier, Ho-Chunk . . . were evicted from their Wisconsin homeland, including the valley."[122]

Badger Army Ammunition Plant at Sauk Prairie

The land return agreement in the Kickapoo Valley provided a precedent to a much larger proposed land return in southern Sauk County. It centered on a treeless plain between the Baraboo Hills and the Wisconsin River, known historically as the Sauk Prairie, which had been a prime bison hunting ground, with mounds and other sacred sites. After the 1837 treaty cession, Ho-Chunk villagers were removed to make way for white settlers, who tilled some of the most fertile river valley land in Wisconsin.

After the United States' entry into World War II, the army condemned the rich farmland for what would quickly become the Badger Ordnance Works and removed numerous white farming families, offering limited compensation. The sprawling Badger complex operated throughout World War II and much of the 1950s, transforming the economy of the quiet rural counties. The renamed Badger Army Ammunition Plant also produced fuel and explosives during the Vietnam War, becoming the target of protests. The 7,354-acre complex was put on standby in 1975. In the 1980s, local residents became alarmed at news that nitrates from the underground explosive storage bunkers had leaked into the aquifer, imperiling drinking water wells and the Wisconsin River. Local opponents also defeated plans for a huge "Star Wars" antimissile electromagnetic energy system within the plant.[123]

Even before the army finally closed the "Badger Munitions" plant in 1998, the future of the site had become a major controversy. Though local families remembered their removal from the site, they did not want to return due to the massive groundwater contamination. Industrial interests proposed to use the mothballed buildings for new chemical plants, arousing opposition from many local residents, environmental groups, and the Ho-Chunk Nation, who instead wanted to restore Sauk Prairie in a public nature reserve. Although the groundwater was contaminated, the lack of recent farming had allowed prairie grasses, bird species, and other flora and fauna to flourish.[124]

The Ho-Chunk Nation made a request to the federal General Services Administration for ownership of 3,050 acres of the Badger site, to reintroduce buffalo to the grassland, restore the prairie, and protect sacred sites and cultural resources. The U.S. Department of Agriculture requested seventeen hundred acres for research, and the Wisconsin DNR expressed interest in owning the entire property for park and recreational purposes.[125]

Resistance quickly developed to Ho-Chunk participation in Badger's future. Some Sauk County residents and environmentalists voiced concern that the Ho-Chunk would build a casino on the site, like the Ho-Chunk Casino in the northern part of the county. Tribal officials replied that federal gaming laws would prohibit a casino without state approval, and the groundwater was too contaminated for human use.

To convince skeptical white residents, the Ho-Chunk Nation released a March 1998 land-use plan, in which it stated: "Land is permanent and stable, a source of spiritual origins and sustaining belief. . . . It is possible through a collaborative effort, joint support and mutual assistance to restore the Sauk Prairie [through] the efforts of community, farmers, environmentalists, sportspersons, conservation groups, historians, and local and tribal government." In a December 1998 memorandum of understanding, the tribe and state began to identify shared objectives for agriculture, ecological restoration, environmental cleanup, and economic development.[126]

Despite this tribal stress on common local concerns, some white residents expressed the same opinion as some Kickapoo Valley residents—that the Ho-Chunk were not "local" to the area. Yet Sauk County had the second-highest Ho-Chunk population in the state; tribal members lived mainly in the northern part of the county, but the tribe contributed to the economy of the entire county.[127] Despite this fact, media reports and government officials repeatedly referred to "local residents" (meaning only whites) and the Ho-Chunk as two separate players in the Badger negotiations.[128] Some Madison-based environmental figures expressed support for the Wisconsin DNR's acquiring the full Badger site and attaching it to the adjacent Devil's Lake State Park, using the need for ecological viability to argue for a single intact unit.

The *Shopper Stopper* newspaper in Merrimac, a strong opponent of Badger reindustrialization, conducted a poll presenting Ho-Chunk and Wisconsin DNR control as two separate, mutually exclusive options. Only 4 percent backed exclusive Ho-Chunk ownership, while 72 percent chose a state park, 5 percent chose an industrial park, and 19 percent offered other options (including joint state-tribal control). Some respondents expressed hostile anti-Indian attitudes, such as "Don't give the land that my ancestors died for back to their killers."[129]

Some local environmentalists, however, came to look upon the Ho-Chunk land reclamation as preferable to full DNR control of the site. The Community Conservation Coalition for the Sauk Prairie proposed "collaborative management" of the prairie, even if it was divided into state, federal, and tribal parcels. It felt that contiguous habitats would be better protected by an integrated board of agencies that provide a check-and-balance on each other, rather than by a single agency that could change its land-use priorities.[130] The local relationship began to extend beyond the immediate question of how to use the Badger site and into education about local tribal history.

By 2001, dozens of Wisconsin groups had endorsed the land-use proposal, and the Badger Reuse Committee adopted a similar "vision" for the landscape, suggesting that "uses and activities at the Badger property contribute to the reconciliation and resolution of past conflicts involving the loss and contamination of the natural environment, the displacement of Native Americans and Euro-American farmers, and the effects of war."[131] The final plan envisioned the site being jointly managed by a board representing federal, tribal, state, and local governments.[132]

Environmental groups such as the Community Conservation Coalition for the Sauk Prairie, the Sauk Prairie Conservation Alliance, and Citizens for Safe Water Around Badger (CSWAB) expressed support for the Ho-Chunk bison restoration as a draw for ecotourism.[133] CSWAB executive director Laura Olah viewed the Kickapoo Valley agreement as a precedent for joint management of Badger and backed tribal sovereignty as leverage to force a federal cleanup of the site (which could cost as much as $250 million). Olah wrote of the Ho-Chunk land claim: "What might appear a dilemma, is indeed an extraordinary opportunity for all of us to work together toward a common goal, to create one of the largest prairie and oak savanna restorations in the entire Midwest, while bringing together cultures, resources, and a shared land conservation ethic. Such an endeavor promises to restore more than just the land and waters, it holds the promise of bringing us together as neighbors and residents."[134]

The state and federal governments failed to recognize the Ho-Chunk claim for many years. The state backed site division proposals that would have left the Ho-Chunk with the most polluted sections of the property. The General Services Administration decided in 2003 to grant the Ho-Chunk only 420 acres of land, much less than the tribal claim.[135] The Ho-Chunk Nation negotiated for 1,553 acres in 2007, but the U.S. Bureau of Indian Affairs refused to take possession of the land, citing environmental cleanup costs.[136] It was not until 2014 that congressional action secured the parcel for the Ho-Chunk Nation.[137]

Ho-Chunk Nation hosts a 2015 land transfer ceremony at the Badger Army Ammunition Plant site in Sauk County, Wisconsin. (Courtesy: Jon Greendeer)

The land was finally returned to the tribe in 2015.[138] The outcome had been delayed for seventeen years, partly due to inadequate support from environmentalists and hostility from state and county officials.

Alliances for the Water

In 2000, the Ho-Chunk Nation intervened in another major environmental issue north of the Badger site. It filed a lawsuit against Perrier's plans to pump out springwater from Big Spring in the Adams County township of New Haven, near Wisconsin Dells.[139] Ho-Chunk Nation Department of Historic Preservation researcher Samantha House testified at public hearings that the pumping site was near cultural sites such as burial mounds and an old Ho-Chunk village site. The tribe later filed a lawsuit against the Wisconsin DNR for not consulting with it on cultural resource matters connected to the project, before granting a project permit.[140]

The Ho-Chunk intervention was warmly welcomed by the anti-Perrier alliances Waterkeepers of Wisconsin and Concerned Citizens of Newport, consisting of rural non-Indian residents fearful that their wells would be pumped dry for Perrier's one-million-square-foot Ice Mountain bottling plant.[141] The anti-Perrier alliance drew national media attention to the privatization of public groundwater resources.[142] In 2002, Perrier suspended its operations in Wisconsin. The company instead moved its focus to Michigan's Mecosta County, where it encountered opposition from farmers, environmentalists, and three tribes.[143]

In 2010, a new environmental concern emerged in Ho-Chunk territory. The national boom in hydraulic fracturing (fracking) of bedrock to extract oil and gas resulted in the massive mining of "frac sand" used to keep underground cracks open during the fracking process. Fracking did not directly threaten Wisconsin, but the state quickly became the number one producer of frac sand. Over the space of only three years, eighty-four frac sand mines were started in western Wisconsin, shipping 130,000 tons of sand a day. The mining of the silica sand created health concerns about silica dust, heavy truck traffic, gashes left in the land, and contamination of surface waters and groundwater, and generated grassroots opposition.[144]

The Ho-Chunk Nation passed resolutions against frac sand mine permits and played a leading role in hosting and assisting the citizens' alliances.[145] Local groups such as the Save the Hills Alliance, Jackson County Citizen Voices, the Crawford Stewardship Project, Save Our Unique Lands (SOUL) Wisconsin, and Echo Valley Hope welcomed the tribal involvement. Ho-Chunk Nation president Jon Greendeer testified against "threats to natural resources and waterways" and to mounds and sacred sites.[146] Several county and local governments passed temporary moratoriums on frac sand mining and clashed with Governor Scott Walker, who backed a 2013 bill to limit local government powers to regulate the $1 billion industry.[147] President Greendeer testified against the bill as "bulldozing any community that rejects or questions" the frac sand industry and as threatening "democracy at its most granular level."[148]

At a 2013 gathering in Black River Falls, Ho-Chunk tribal member Bill Greendeer presided over the event's opening ceremony and prayer.[149] On a tour of mine sites around his hometown of Tomah, he said: "The mines have completely torn up the area where I used to play in the woods. Where I saw wolves and mountain lions there are now just piles of sand. It made me feel sick." He added: "Nobody is talking to the Indians. We haven't trusted the government for years. . . . This land is sacred."[150] Although the Ho-Chunk Nation had often been ridden with political and financial schisms, tribal members generally closed ranks on issues of protecting the water and sacred sites.

Migizi Advocates for Turtle Island, led by tribal member Andi Cloud, organized rallies against frac sand mining, including a 2013 rally at Ho-Chunk Nation headquarters. She said, "The only way we're going to be successful is that if we all come together, whether you are a Ho-Chunk, whether you are

Ojibwe, whether you are white, just everybody who cares about Mother Earth."[151] In 2015, the Ho-Chunk Nation became the first U.S. Native nation to amend its tribal constitution to enshrine the rights of nature, including a ban on genetic engineering, fossil fuel extraction, and frac sand mining.[152] The Save the Hills Alliance went beyond the frac sand issue in 2016 when it urged its members to attend a state capitol rally—called by the Ho-Chunk Nation—to oppose a bill permitting burial mound destruction.[153]

Both the alliances against springwater pumping and frac sand mining combined concerns about air and water quality with tribal concerns about sacred site protection, without the divisions with white neighbors that were apparent in the earlier alliances against military projects.

Lessons from Ho-Chunk Case Studies

Native/non-Native opposition to military projects in Nevada and southern Wisconsin provide some important contrasts to environmental alliances in the Pacific Northwest. The relationship was established not between tribal and federal governments but between Native and non-Native opponents of U.S. military plans. Oppositional "alliances from below" can focus attention on the outside threat posed to both communities, without acknowledging local inside barriers to justice, such as obstacles to tribal water rights. The common front to defend the land may not permanently shift opposing perspectives on who should control the land or how to use it.

The fluctuating alliances between Ho-Chunk tribal members and white farmers over military projects and the reclamation of former military and dam sites, like the Nevada alliances, offer resonating insights. Different communities' environmental interests often are exhibited spatially. White interests may emphasize one set of environmental concerns that affect their territory or resources, while Native interests emphasize environmental justice concerns that focus on other places or resources.

In turn, the company or the government agency providing the source of the threat may also act in a spatial manner that just happens to coincide with racial geography. In meeting the demands of rural white residents, but maintaining the threat to Indigenous lands, a company or a government agency can maintain that its decisions only took into account the nature of the physical landscape or technical concerns, even if the decisions disadvantaged the Native community.

In Nevada, when a military plan affected the white communities they generally defended their own interests and failed to incorporate Native concerns.

In Wisconsin, the white communities had the opportunity to have their primary environmental demands met, at the expense of their Native partners,
and had two different responses. The alliance against the military ranges fell
apart when whites did not stick by their Native allies. While no "smoking gun"
memo can prove an intentional Guard strategy to manipulate geography to its
political advantage, the fact that it dropped a flight range affecting predominantly white counties, while retaining a bombing range that was confronted
mainly by a Ho-Chunk-led opposition, was not anticipated by the alliance.

In the Badger Munitions fight, most local farmers and environmentalists
failed to back up the Ho-Chunk land claim. The alliances around the Kickapoo
Valley and Perrier springwater pumping, however, succeeded in their goals
when white farmers stopped standing in the way of the tribe, and a similar
alliance grew around frac sand mining.

The opening of a schism within an alliance is accomplished not simply by
a passive dividing of communities on the basis of their different interests but
by reinforcing the advantages of the community that already possesses the
greatest social, political, or economic clout. A deal that meets white demands
without meeting Native demands deepens the historic inequalities between
white and Indian communities. The key test of any cross-cultural movement
is when the more advantaged group has its primary demands met but the
demands of the less advantaged members have not yet been met. The whites
have the choice of continuing toward the larger victory or expressing satisfac-
tion at the smaller victory and selling out their partners. Any alliance that
hopes to survive needs to anticipate this moment, educate its full membership
in advance, and prepare for the eventuality.

A short-term "victory" for the dominant partner in an alliance may in fact
result in a long-term defeat even for its own interests. The victory may prove
to be not a small step forward but a self-defeating step backward, by accepting
a bombing range expansion that could make low-level flights likely in the future. Similarly, excluding the Ho-Chunk from control over part of the Badger
Munitions site would have left out a player with a legal trust relationship with
the federal government—a relationship that may become legally useful if the
U.S. Army dragged its feet in cleaning up groundwater.

A key organizing tactic at Hardwood, the Kickapoo Valley, Badger Munitions, and Big Springs was the creation of parallels between historic Native
dispossession of the land through federal removal policy and more recent
white farmers' dispossession through federal eminent domain policy or corporate power. Although Ho-Chunk and white farmers' historic priorities could

easily be set against each other (as Native and white interests were in Nevada), the parallels also can help create a common moral community based on a *return of the land to those that respect it the most.*

The Wisconsin land return proposals may not have been possible before casinos, because gaming has enabled the tribes to use legal and public relations resources previously beyond their financial reach. The opposite is true in Nevada, where impoverished tribes have no access to the wealth generated by casino gaming.

The Ho-Chunk cases point to a possible future direction for tribal relations with non-Indian communities. Tribes can build closer ties with rural neighbors not by surrendering their land claims but by asserting these claims in tandem with the environmental/economic concerns of local non-Indians. A successful return of tribal land transforms a temporary environmental alliance into a more permanent and irreversible process of justice, based on the power of land. Joint tribal/non-tribal management of environmentally and culturally sensitive sites demonstrates that their interests need not be mutually exclusive. In a larger sense, joint management prioritizes the place itself and begins to undermine white privilege in the name of place.

"WHITENESS" DIVIDING ALLIANCES

Failed environmental alliances, like those against bombing ranges in Nevada and Wisconsin, bring up larger questions that constantly plague cross-cultural alliances around common concerns. Are so-called "minority" rights of secondary importance to building ties with the white majority around "more pressing" or "larger" issues? By asserting their treaty rights, for example, would Native peoples somehow alienate their white neighbors, making cooperation less likely? By de-emphasizing their differences, are group members helping to build unity on common ground? In short, is "unity" enough?

Native/non-Native alliances have achieved success only where they interweave (particularist) Native rights and (universalist) environmental protection, while at the same time leaving the door open to a larger vision of a common world. As they deconstruct racial hierarchies, Native peoples are constructing new frameworks based on a defense of common values and places. Environmental "unity" between Native nations and white communities is not possible without environmental justice for Native nations, and, conversely, environmental justice may be aided by unity with parts of the white community. Whites can best serve their own interests by merging them with those of the people

whose lands they have settled. Whites who want social change are only hurting their own long-term interests by accepting racial double standards and can
only make deep changes by challenging the institution of "whiteness."

After the "invention of the white race" in seventeenth-century Virginia,
white elites used whiteness not only to repress people of color but to control
English and Irish indentured servants, so they would not join rebellions with
enslaved Africans.[154] Poor whites were offered a niche in the racial pecking
order above other racial groups: they may be poor, but at least they're white.[155]
Due to this history, many whites have a "dual consciousness" of racial and class
loyalties, deflecting them to look downward to so-called minorities as the
source of their problems rather than upward to the state or elites. Their relative
advantage has prevented or frustrated interracial alliances around common
causes ever since.[156] For example, a multiracial strike could be divided when
company management meets the demands of white workers but not other
employees.[157] This "racial bribe" makes it far less likely that whites "would
sustain interracial political alliances aimed at toppling the white elite."[158]

The construction of racial formations has shaped the construction of places
in the United States, even in settings that are seemingly ordinary and race-
neutral.[159] Even if one's European ancestors immigrated to America after the
settlement of Native territories or were themselves ethnically oppressed, they
became "white" through the process of assimilation and racial solidarity.[160]

Downplaying race does not eliminate it as a force within universalist social
movements but merely serves to sweep it under the rug. Directly addressing
and defusing racism helps to level the playing field. This cannot be adequately
done on an individual level, with whites renouncing their personal "white skin
privilege," but "unmaking whiteness" needs to be done *collectively* within larger
social movements that challenge structural hierarchies.[161]

Cross-racial "unity" is not enough if it is applied to unequal partners. A
strong process of equalization (such as through treaty rights) is a necessary
prerequisite to building better ties to whites around common concerns. The
white racial consensus can be broken if even a minority of whites break with
racist ideologies.[162] The critical precondition is clear signals that society is moving toward respecting tribal sovereignty rather than maintaining the status
quo of environmental racism. To prevent interracial unity, governments and
companies keep playing shell games to drive wedges between neighbors.

The military shifting of flight ranges in Nevada and Wisconsin provides a
stark example of a government shell game: how an environmental threat can
be fluidly arranged in the sky to ensure the survival of a controversial program.

Land-based bombing ranges are more difficult to site than air-based flight ranges, as shown by the closure of U.S. Navy bombing ranges in Kahoʻolawe (Hawaiʻi) and Vieques (Puerto Rico) after long, intense local protests.[163] The North Atlantic Treaty Organization (NATO) moved flight ranges from Europe in response to a public outcry, to more sparsely inhabited regions of North America, such as Nevada and Labrador.[164] But even within these regions, the military can move flight ranges around like pieces on a chessboard, to minimize public criticism. The Wisconsin Air National Guard was able to preserve a bombing range expansion by dropping a new flight range, setting white farmers' interests against Native interests, simply by playing the air against the land.

Whether or not Air National Guard leaders intended this outcome is beside the point. The point is that the Guard's decision functioned as a wedge issue between the white farmers and the Ho-Chunk. The white farmers who abandoned the fight against the Hardwood Range, much like the environmentalists who tried to undermine the Ho-Chunk claim to Badger Munitions, assumed that there was a conflict between their environmental interests and Native interests. They accepted a partial victory that met their needs and did not persist in the fight for a larger victory that included Native demands. Holding out for a larger victory for the entire alliance may have better served their own environmental interests.

The white environmentalists or farmers assumed that they were accepting the best deal on behalf of the environment. But by accepting the expansion of Hardwood, they inadvertently kept open the possibility of a later expansion of low-level flights to the enlarged bombing range. Similarly, by accepting full state control over the Badger site, they left out a tribe with a trust relationship to the federal agencies engaged in site cleanup. Recognizing Native demands and persisting in the fight may have helped strengthen rather than weaken the long-term environmental future.

In virtually every cross-cultural environmental alliance, white members have to question their racial loyalties to avoid a split with the Native community. This split can also play out as a division between whites who want to go in different directions. The clash between racial and environmental interests can also play out as dual consciousness within individuals, in which two parts of an individual's brain are working at cross-purposes by emphasizing different interests, resulting in contradictory behavior. A white rural resident may work fervently to stop a military or corporate project, while working just as hard to defeat Native treaties that can form a legal barrier to the project. Another could support Native rights to fish and hunt, while supporting a new industrial plant that would contaminate fish and wildlife. Company or agency policies appeal not only to different social groups but to factions and individuals that hold contradictory values within the groups.[165]

It's not difficult to see white dual consciousness at work within environmental alliances. Whites may offer neutral geographic or scientific reasons for reducing cooperation with Native neighbors, when what they are really thinking is that Native interests will harm their own interests. But on the flip side, whites who oppose Native rights may make "exceptions" to their racist attitudes at critical junctures and unexpectedly cooperate with the tribes.

A cooperative effort that only appeals to universalist values—what the two groups have in common—will fail to dismantle these (usually unspoken) racist assumptions. Whites have the ability to understand the particularist values and strategies of communities of color, even if they do not support them. If Native Nations are homogenized into a "greater" universalist whole, or represented by white allies, they will not be able to make their fullest contribution to the alliance, which is more likely to fail.

Affirming the sovereignty of Native nations is not only a way to correct past injustices toward them but is to the benefit of both Native and non-Native communities and their future together on the land. Even if they stand together with Native peoples in a common environmental purpose, whites who stand in the way of Indigenous political and legal powers are standing in the way of environmental justice. Mere "unity" against a common enemy is not enough to sustain a true alliance.

PART III

KEEPING IT IN THE GROUND

"They say that history is written by the victors. But how can there be a victor when the war isn't over? The battle has only just begun, and Creator is sending his very best warriors. And this time, it isn't Indians versus cowboys. No, this time it is all the beautiful races of humanity together on the same side, and we are fighting to replace our fear with love."

—Lyla June (Diné), "All Nations Rise"

THE NORTHERN PLAINS HAVE LONG PROVIDED AMERICANS WITH A prototypical setting for Native/non-Native relations. Its cultural landscape includes the Native Americans that U.S. schoolchildren have historically viewed as the stereotype of all tribes—living in tipis and hunting bison. The landscape also includes the stereotype for the non-Indian westerner—the "cowboy" riding on horseback across semi-arid rolling hills.

The popular image of "cowboys and Indians" has been ingrained in the national consciousness and serves as a cultural template of two archetypal enemies fighting each other since time immemorial. "Cowboys," or cattle ranchers, have been portrayed in both historic and contemporary times as conquerors of the West. "Indians" have been portrayed as obstacles to this conquest, who resisted the "inevitable" advance of Manifest Destiny until their resistance melted away after the 1890 Wounded Knee Massacre.

The popular image of cowboys and Indians as primordial and eternal enemies belies some important realities. Many Plains Native people have themselves long participated in the ranching economy and culture. Today tribal members wear cowboy hats, listen to country music, drive pickups, and can literally change from their powwow outfits into rodeo gear on a hot summer weekend. Many non-Native ranchers see their land-based lifestyle and culture as endangered by corporate globalization, in much the same way as tribal members have seen their cultures under siege. Both Native nations and non-Native communities are affected by large-scale resource extraction, such as coal, uranium, and gold mining, and the use of the relatively unpopulated regions for bombing ranges, which would not be tolerated in more populated regions.

Native peoples in Montana and South Dakota have very different histories. South Dakota has nine reservations—all of them Sioux (Lakota, Dakota, or

Nakota). Montana has reservations of the Crow, Assiniboine, Gros Ventre, Northern Cheyenne, Salish, Kootenai, Blackfeet, Chippewa Cree, and Sioux. Most non-Indians in the region originally settled for work in ranching, farming, mining, or railroads.

In the Northern Plains, Native peoples continue to clash with anti-Indian racism, which is still harsher and more open than in other areas of the country, perhaps given the region's relatively more recent "Indian wars." Yet the region with the greatest Native-white polarization ironically also has some of the earliest and most successful environmental alliances, with ranchers such as Marvin Kammerer and Lakota activists such as Bill Means building the bridge to form the Black Hills Alliance in the late 1970s.

In the twenty-first century, the Northern Plains have emerged as a major front line in the fossil fuel wars, against plans for new oil pipelines and against coal and uranium mines. The Cowboy Indian Alliance blocked the northern leg of the Keystone XL pipeline, for the first time putting leaders such as Faith Spotted Eagle and Jane Kleeb in the national media limelight. Tribal opposition to the fossil fuel shipping routes from the Northern Plains to the Pacific Northwest powerfully fused the Plains Native struggles to protect sacred places and water and the coastal treaty struggles for fishing rights. These fossil fuel shipping conflicts have been a major test for how Indigenous-led alliances can attract significant non-Native solidarity, growing the movement for climate justice.

For Plains Indigenous peoples, certain places have sacred meaning, whether as the sources of ancient stories or as areas where the aquifers are recharged with water. When mining threatens these sacred places, such as the Black Hills, Sweetgrass Hills, or the Tongue River Valley, Native peoples interpret it as a profound threat to their spirituality. How can white ranchers and farmers join with tribes in a common sense of purpose to protect the water, even if they come with a less deeply rooted historic attachment to the land? How can they find a common sense of understanding if they love the land in a different way than their allies? How might their senses of place overlap and enrich an alliance?

CHAPTER 4

Resource Wars and Sharing Sacred Lands

Montana and South Dakota

MUCH OF THE U.S. SUPPLY OF URANIUM AND LOW-SULFUR STRIPPABLE coal is found in the Northern Plains. Mining companies coveted these deposits in the 1970s, after the 1973 Mideast War and resultant Arab oil embargo of the Western powers. Large-scale mining project proposals imperiled both Native treaty rights and the lifestyle of white ranchers and farmers, by jeopardizing their clean surface waters, heavily draining groundwater, and bringing in large numbers of outside miners.[1]

Mining also threatened sacred sites that are integral to tribal spirituality, just as many of the sites are viewed as culturally and ecologically significant by non-Native settlers. As Peter Iverson asked in *When Indians Became Cowboys*: "Can rural people, white and Indian, see commonality as well as difference? . . . Can they talk to each other about continuity and change—and survival?"[2]

A 1973 National Academy of Sciences report demonstrated how semi-arid landscapes would take centuries to recover from coal mining and suggested that such landscapes be designated as "National Sacrifice Areas" for U.S. energy self-sufficiency.[3] Water had been a primary point of contention between tribes and white agriculturalists, neither of whom wanted to become "national sacrifice people." The resource projects redefined the conflict as one between both groups and outside corporate interests proposing coal and uranium mining in South Dakota and coal and gold mining in Montana.

COAL AND GOLD IN MONTANA

The Powder River Basin coal mines of southeastern Montana and northeastern Wyoming have for decades met the energy needs of Los Angeles, Minneapolis,

Sign posted in the 1970s in Tongue River Valley, Montana. (Courtesy: Terrence Moore / Northern Plains Resource Council)

and many other cities around the country, supplying about 42 percent of all coal mined in the United States.[4] Powder River Basin coal has a lower sulfur pollution content than coal from eastern U.S. shaft mines, yet stripping the coal has resulted in profound environmental damage. Strip-mining machines the size of a twenty-story building ravage the landscape, removing the "over-burden" topsoil and leaving behind a sterile "hardpan" surface where nothing can grow. In coal boomtowns, trailer parks have colonized the hillsides, as the local communities extend their public services for the influx of miners, leading to an inevitable "boom and bust" effect.

The two Native nations in the area have long held divergent views about coal mining. The Crow tribal government welcomed coal development for the economic benefits to the tribe, while the adjacent Northern Cheyenne feared social and environmental consequences. The Cheyenne have a strong attach-ment to their 445,000-acre reservation as a historic refuge from persecution. The tribe was ravaged by a series of U.S. Army massacres and by forced re-moval to Indian Territory in 1877. Some tribal members escaped and fled back to the northern part of their vast homeland, where they were granted a small reservation parcel in 1884.[5] In 1900, the parcel was enlarged into the Tongue

River Valley, where a single coal strip mine operated in the 1920s through the 1950s in the (appropriately named) town of Colstrip.[6]

Coal Wars in Southeastern Montana

In the early 1970s, the Northern Cheyenne found out that the U.S. Bureau of Indian Affairs (BIA) had leased about 64 percent of the reservation's acreage to coal companies. BIA leases gave a royalty to the tribe of only 17.5 cents per ton and contained few if any environmental safeguards for strip-mining operations.[7] The coal leases caused divisions within the Northern Cheyenne Tribe, as well as between Northern Cheyenne and Crow. In 1972, a group of concerned tribal members formed the Northern Cheyenne Landowners Association as a local watchdog group that monitored damage from company operations, worked with local and national environmental groups, and filed a petition with the Department of the Interior.[8] In 1974, Interior Secretary Rogers Morton suspended many leases pending environmental studies and negotiations with the tribe.[9]

In the same year, a group of white ranchers and farmers in the Tongue River Valley outside the reservation formed the Northern Plains Resource Council (NPRC) to fight for their interests against coal companies and particularly against a newly proposed coal-fired power plant near Colstrip.[10] Ranchers and farmers in the area had formed the Rosebud Protective Association to work on coal and agricultural issues around Rosebud Creek, the site of two strip mines and five coal-fired power plants.[11]

The NPRC saw one of its primary tasks as building bridges between agricultural and environmental concerns. Instead of focusing on mainstream environmental issues such as wilderness protection or endangered species, the NPRC strategy reframed ecological issues to fit the "rights of property owners to protect their land and water from negative effects of unsustainable development."[12] Whereas most Western landowners historically had looked at their land as a commodity, the Montana ranchers working against coal development highlighted nonmonetary values for determining the value of land, much like their tribal neighbors.[13]

Ranching families around Rosebud Creek had for decades lived next to the Northern Cheyenne. The village of Birney straddled the Tongue River, the eastern boundary of the reservation. Ranchers lived on the east bank of the river, referred to as "White Birney," and Northern Cheyenne lived on the west bank of the river, referred to as "Indian Birney." Although only a few tribal members were employed by businesses in White Birney, both Indian and white students attended the Colstrip high school. Tribal and white families therefore had personal relationships—for better or worse—that predated any political alliances.[14] As Birney resident Alaina Buffalo Spirit noted, "Our most sacred ceremonial people are buried within the hills and some of our most sacred medicines still grow on the east side of the Tongue River." A few white land-owners would allow her family access to the area.[15]

A key individual in the formation of the anti-coal alliance was the young Northern Cheyenne activist Gail Small, who built a close relationship with young women from local ranching families. She served on a tribal negotiating committee to void the coal leases on the reservation, which threatened the tribal culture and environment. Small observed: "The Cheyenne people, like most Tribes, are waging many battles on many fronts and with few allies. . . . I told the Tribe to request help from the big white environmental organiza-tions. . . . No one responded to our calls for help, except the few white ranchers living in the impacted area."[16]

One of the key white ranchers was Wallace McRae, who co-founded the NPRC and would later become widely known as one of the country's foremost cowboy poets. McRae and his son Clint run a 31,000-acre ranch by Rosebud Creek, where the family has homesteaded for 125 years, and often interacted with Northern Cheyenne families.[17] He saw the growth of the coal mining and agribusiness industries not simply as a threat to smaller ranchers and farmers but as a cultural threat to their rural and cooperative way of life, as one of his poems later illustrated:

> Remember that sandrock on Emmells Crick
> Where Dad carved his name in 'thirteen?
> It's been blasted down into rubble
> And interred by their dragline machine.
> Where Fadhls lived, at the old Milar Place,
> Where us kids stole melons at night?
> They 'dozed it up in a funeral pyre
> Then torched it. It's gone alright.
> The "C" on the hill, and the water tanks
> Are now classified, "reclaimed land."
> They're thinking of building a golf course
> Out there, so I understand.
> The old Egan Homestead's an ash pond
> That they say is eighty feet deep.

The branding corral at the Douglas Camp
Is underneath a spoil heap.
And across the crick is a tipple, now,
Where they load coal onto a train,
The Mae West Rock on Hay Coulee?
Just black and white snapshots remain.
There's a railroad loop and a coal storage shed
Where the bison kill site used to be.
The Guy Place is gone; Ambrose's too.
Beulah Farley's a ranch refugee.

But things are booming. We've got this new school
That's envied across the whole state.
When folks up and ask, "How's things goin' down there?"
I grin like a fool and say, "Great!"
Great God, how we're doin'! We're rollin' in dough,
As they tear and they ravage The Earth.
And nobody knows . . . or nobody cares . . .
About things of intrinsic worth.[18]

Wallace McRae later observed: "I think there are cultural values that are threatened here, and I think there are cultural wars going on, and I don't want to see us lose that cultural war. I don't want to see the Northern Cheyennes losing their cultural war either. I've got some close friends that I went to high school with, and although I don't share the trauma of what they went through . . . both of our cultures are being threatened."[19]

To protect the area's air quality, the Northern Cheyenne Tribe in 1976 redesignated its entire reservation air quality as Class I airspace, pursuant to the federal Clean Air Act's Prevention of Significant Deterioration amendments. The tribe was the first in the United States to redesignate its air quality under the U.S. Environmental Protection Agency's "Treatment as State" provision. Local ranchers backed the move as protecting their own air quality. The Class I status blocked the planned expansion of coal plants in the area, but coal mining outside the reservation continued. The Northern Cheyenne coal fight "changed forever the way that tribes looked at federal environmental laws."[20]

In the mid-1980s, Small founded the group Native Action to organize Northern Cheyenne members. Some tribal officials were tempted to accept new coal leases to overcome a high tribal unemployment rate, and Small was elected to the tribal council to successfully stop tribal lease proposals. The tribal government convinced Congress to finally void the reservation coal leases by 1988.

Through the 1980s, Northern Cheyenne and white rancher communities maintained cooperation around coal mine reclamation issues, but at a reduced level, as the water rights conflict over Rosebud Creek also simmered. Northern Cheyenne leaders did not want more divisions with neighboring communities and chose to settle the legal dispute in the early 1990s.

NPRC staff director Teresa Erickson related the difficulties of maintaining trust and community ties in the face of continuing economic and cultural differences. She said: "It is a constant struggle. . . . It is sometimes hard to understand how it reverts back and forth." She pointed to bitter financial conflicts over the new reservation high school and over banks' "redlining" of loans to tribal members. Yet Erickson also saw positive legacies of the 1970s environmental alliance, such as tribes and smaller ranchers joining forces in taking on big meatpackers, low cattle prices, and farm/ranch foreclosures.[21]

In 1980, the NPRC again brought together white ranchers and Northern Cheyenne against plans for the eighty-nine-mile Tongue River Railroad. The railroad would be used for shipments of coal from Wyoming's Powder River Basin fields, providing rail access to the largest untapped low-sulfur coal reserves in the country. McRae commented then: "When the first trappers showed up on Northern Cheyenne lands, they should have, but weren't, seen as a threat. The same is true of mining."[22] The threat of coal dust pollution again brought together white ranchers and Northern Cheyenne when the railroad plan went ahead in earnest around 1992. Although the railroad would not run on reservation land, tribal members opposed it because they foresaw desecration of ceremonial sites, burial grounds, and collection areas for sacred and medicinal plants. Ranchers and farmers opposed the railroad because they saw it as destroying prime agricultural land next to the river, causing fires and weed growth, and endangering cattle.[23]

In the mid-1990s, the coalfields of southeastern Montana unexpectedly came to figure in a national controversy over a proposed gold mine in southwestern Montana, near Yellowstone National Park. In 1996, President Bill Clinton announced the federal buyout of the New World gold mine from the Noranda corporation. Most national environmental groups hailed the move as protection for national parklands. Yet many Montana environmental, agricultural, and tribal groups later found that Clinton's deal had provided $10 million in federal coal mining rights, to be transferred to Montana. The NPRC

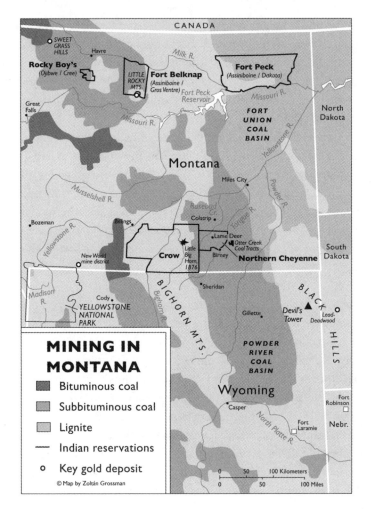

opposed the "coal for gold" deal as shifting the burden of environmental pollution from park goers to Native Americans and ranchers, driving a wedge
between those groups and white environmentalists.[24] Clinton reversed his
position, but too late to stop the deal. In fighting the shift of mining plans from
the Yellowstone area to the Tongue River Valley, tribal and white agricultural
communities were each other's closest allies, both suffering from inadequate
environmentalist support.

The fight to stop the Tongue River Railroad continued into the 2000s. The
alliance built on the previous fight against coal-fired power plants and inter-
sected with the Northern Cheyenne fight against coal-bed methane extraction,
also led by Native Action and the tribal nonprofit Yellow Bird, led by Phillip

Whiteman Jr. and Lynnette Two Bulls. The Bureau of Land Management gave approval to sinking up to seventy-five thousand methane wells in the area, without consulting with the tribe. After a lawsuit was filed by the tribe and the NPRC, a federal judge found in 2005 that the bureau's environmental study was inadequate.[25] A 2006 tribal referendum to promote coal-bed methane development was defeated.[26]

Despite the renewal of tensions between white and Northern Cheyenne communities following the 1970s alliance, the previous model had enabled environmentally minded residents to more easily construct a new alliance. The earlier Native/rancher cooperation in Montana coalfields had taken two steps forward, then one step back. The new alliances against the Tongue River Railroad and coal-bed methane had again taken Native/non-Native cooperation two steps forward, in preparation for new coal mining battles ahead.

Gold Mining in Northern Montana

In the northern part of the state, two other gold mining controversies clearly demonstrated the importance of unity between tribes and white farmers and ranchers. The contrast between the stories of the Little Rocky Mountains and the Sweetgrass Hills affirmed that the two groups may be potentially stronger with each other as allies than they would be with outsiders.

In northeastern Montana, the Little Rocky Mountains on the Fort Belknap Reservation had long been the scene of large-scale gold mining. The Zortman-Landusky mine just outside the reservation served as a national symbol of the dangers of unregulated gold mining. Yet the Gros Ventre and Assiniboine tribes fought the mine and its proposed expansions largely on their own, with some help from environmental groups but little or none from local ranching communities.[27]

The piney Little Rockies had been a center of prayer and fasting, a destination for tribal members on vision quests, and a burial site. The small mountain range dramatically juts out of the surrounding rolling prairie, looking almost like a green oasis or an island in the middle of a rolling sea. It is considered one of the key "island mountain" ranges in the Northern Plains. As a Helena photographer wrote, "Like the Black Hills of South Dakota and the Sweetgrass Hills . . . the Little Rockies are seen as a refuge in these tribes' sacred geography."[28] All these ranges elevate cloud systems and condense moisture over their slopes, and so they recharge the aquifers of the vast surrounding plains.

The mountains became part of the original Fort Belknap Reservation when it was established in 1887. The U.S. Congress ceded forty thousand mineral-rich acres of the reservation to mining companies in 1895. Underground gold mines were dug in the ceded land, yet tribal members continued to use natural resources and water. The mines closed when the high-grade gold ore petered out in the early 1950s. By the mid-1970s, mining companies had found a new technique to extract the low-grade gold remaining in the ore, using cyanide to dissolve out the metal from the rock. Cyanide ore processing has been implicated in massive fish kills and has contaminated water supplies around the world.[29] The mining of low-grade ore also causes enormous physical destruction; on average it takes 100 tons of ore to extract only 1.6 ounces of gold.[30]

In 1979, Pegasus Gold Corporation opened a cyanide heap-leach gold mine complex in the Little Rocky Mountains. Gros Ventre activist James Main Jr. claimed that the twenty-eight hundred tribal members were "guinea pigs in a sacrifice area" and that "most ranchers sold out" in the face of company financial offers.[31] Tribal members were horrified that the mining operation leveled the sacred peak of Spirit Mountain, one of the three major peaks of the range, by about one-third. They were also alarmed when a waste tailings dam released toxins into local streams. They formed a series of tribal environmental groups, including Red Thunder and Island Mountain Protectors, with support from the Fort Belknap Community Council and the tribal government.

In 1996, federal and state officials forced Pegasus to spend up to $32.2 million in fines for pollution of the reservation.[32] The company filed for bankruptcy in 1998, leaving behind an estimated $4 million in cleanup costs.[33] Public outrage at the Zortman-Landusky disaster fueled the 1998 passage of a state ballot initiative to prohibit cyanide ore processing in Montana mines. But for the most part, in the area around the Little Rocky Mountains, the Assiniboine and Gros Ventre had been forced to fight the Zortman-Landusky mine almost alone, without local white ranchers, only winning their fight after the ecological and cultural devastation had been done.

In contrast to the Little Rocky Mountains, ranchers and farmers have joined tribes seeking to prevent gold mining in a similar island mountain range 130 miles to the west: the Sweetgrass Hills. The hills consist of three separate rocky, grassy buttes that rise dramatically out of the plains. At least seven tribes—the Blackfeet, Chippewa Cree, Gros Ventre, Assiniboine, Sioux, Salish, and Kootenai—have used the Sweetgrass Hills as a sacred site for prayer. The hills are also economically significant to local white ranchers and wheat farmers as a key source of water for the semi-arid region.[34]

Some of the white farmers, however, view the hills' value as more than economic. Richard Thieltges, a third-generation wheat farmer descended from

German immigrants, grew up next to the hills. He asserted that the hills are "intrinsically a sacred place" with a "certain mystique."[35] Rancher activist Arlo Scari claimed that "many farmers and ranchers of the area share that sacred respect for the Hills as a vital source of water and unique habitat and landscape offering outstanding scenic and recreational values."[36]

In the 1980s, two companies proposed gold exploration operations in the Sweetgrass Hills, with the aim of building cyanide heap-leach mines. Local ranchers and farmers grew alarmed, particularly as the scope of the Zortman-Landusky disaster unfolded. In 1986, local white agriculturalists and other citizens founded the Sweetgrass Hills Protective Association to fight the mining plans. In the early 1990s, association members became more aware of the sacredness of the hills in Native spiritual beliefs and began to work closely with area tribes.[37] Jim Main Jr. welcomed the involvement of ranchers in the newer struggle, saying, "They use our arguments. . . . They join in our prayers, call it Mother Earth."[38] Congressman Pat Williams observed, "Just as these hills are significant to generations of ranchers and farmers, they have been among the most sacred of places to Great Plains Indian Tribes for thousands of years."[39]

Thieltges described the "natural alliance" of Native Americans, white farmers/ranchers, and environmentalists as a "tripod" that needs all three legs in order to stand. "Farmers-ranchers, Native Americans, and environmentalists are three sides of a natural alliance," he said. "We are the only people who truly have to bear the burden of what's happened to the land. So the mining industry tries to drive wedges between us."[40] In 1996, a 600-mile Native walk to protect the hills was met by support from non-Indian communities along its entire route from South Dakota to Montana. Blackfeet-Lakota march leader Brock Conway was "joined at various times by the great-granddaughter of a homesteader, a grandmother from the Crow tribe, and a cowboy herding cattle on an ATV."[41]

In 1997, Secretary of the Interior Bruce Babbitt visited the Sweetgrass Hills and withdrew the hills from gold mining for twenty years. The tribe and its farmer and environmental allies celebrated the move and observed that the secretary would have never made a supportive visit to the area had it not been for the federal-tribal trust relationship.[42] Main and Thieltges contrasted this federal response, however, to the more lackadaisical government response to protect the Little Rocky Mountains next to Fort Belknap. The exclusively tribal response, without local white support, eventually demonstrated its powers to influence the federal government, but only after the damage had been done. In contrast, the Native/non-Native alliance around the Sweetgrass Hills succeeded in stopping a similar cyanide gold mining operation before it even reached the stage of mineral exploration.

The Sweetgrass Hills victory also left behind a legacy of greater contacts between the communities. Thieltges claimed that an "ongoing relationship" with the tribes taught local white farmers a great deal about Native cultures and "sacred places." He took a strong interest in Indigenous herbal medicines, which he initially only learned of as natural resources to protect against the effects of mining. Thieltges described this process of cultural education as the "most important thing" that has emerged from the Sweetgrass Hills alliance.[43]

Yet in much of the rest of Montana, the lack of cultural contact between Native and non-Native rural communities stayed the norm, and tensions remained high. Montana's anti-Indian movement had emerged in the 1970s among white residents of Montana reservations, who challenged tribal jurisdiction over non-Indians.[44] The All Citizens Equal group grew openly racist by 1990, when a poster advertising an "Indian shoot" was enclosed in one of its newsletters.[45] In 2000, the Montana Human Rights Network reported that the state's anti-Indian movement was thriving.[46] The network and other anti-racist groups sought to shift the agenda with a reconciliation conference, yet ensuing state-tribal discussions were marred by state legislators' racist remarks.[47] The Native/non-Native environmental alliances did not play a central role in this dialogue. A common front against outside corporate interests had not translated into a strong common movement to address racism on social or institutional levels.

Where tribes established relationships with white farmers or ranchers, the alliances were extremely effective in meeting their environmental goals. The local alliances around Northern Cheyenne and the Sweetgrass Hills—in some of the most isolated corners of a sparsely populated state—effectively held off mining company plans, even when they had inadequate support from environmental groups. Where tribes had the backing of urban-based environmental groups but not local white communities, such as in the Little Rocky Mountains, the alliances could not prevent mining. In the case of Clinton's "coal for gold" deal, both tribes and farmers/ranchers were sold out in the name of environmental protection.

Native activists who have been the most vocal in support of Indigenous treaties and cultures—such as Gail Small and Jim and Rose Main—have also been the tribal members seemingly most open to an alliance with white ranchers and farmers. Their openness deftly parallels their unremitting work against anti-Indian racism within local white communities—over schooling, hiring, banking, and other issues. Their attitude brings forth a paradox seen repeatedly in Native/non-Native relations.

The most successful alliances have tended to use a "carrot-and-stick" strategy—using a "stick" to confront racism by white communities and institutions, while dangling a "carrot" that promises a common future based on common land-based values. If the Native groups had practiced only confrontation, they would not have modeled an appropriate set of behaviors and practices for their white neighbors to follow. If they had practiced only cooperation, they would not have begun to overcome centuries of discrimination and would have played a subordinate role in any alliance. A combination of confronting racism, while leaving the door open to cooperation, integrates the ideas of confronting the exclusivist past, while building a more inclusive future. This lesson is even more pronounced in western South Dakota, the scene of some of the most famous battles between the United States and Native nations in the nineteenth and twentieth centuries.

LAKOTA NATION IN WESTERN SOUTH DAKOTA

The Native nation known as the Sioux extends from Montana to Minnesota. Despite their dialect- and band-based divisions, the Sioux had a common origin story, centered on the island mountain range they called Paha Sapa or He Sapa (Black Hills).[48] In their regional dialects, the Sioux call themselves Lakota in their western territory, Nakota in their central territory, and Dakota in their eastern territory. Within their traditional governance structures, the seven main bands are organized into the Oceti Sakowin (Seven Council Fires). Most attention by historians and journalists has focused on the "Teton Sioux" or Lakota bands in present-day western South Dakota.

In 1868, after the U.S. Army lost battles to Lakota forces led by Oglala Lakota leader Mahpiya Luta (Red Cloud), federal officials signed the Second Fort Laramie Treaty (the first being in 1851) to recognize Lakota sovereignty over western South Dakota, with unceded lands extending into a large area between the Missouri, Platte, and Big Horn Rivers. The Black Hills were at the heart of the recognized Great Sioux Reservation.[49]

Six years after the treaty signing, U.S. Army forces led by Colonel George Armstrong Custer discovered gold in the northern Black Hills, unleashing an invasion of gold miners. Custer's intervention led to his 1876 ill-fated battle at Little Big Horn with the Lakota, Arapaho, and Northern Cheyenne. Custer's defeat was followed by detachment of the Black Hills from Lakota territory

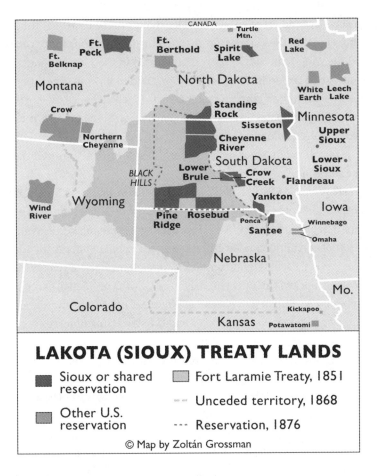

LAKOTA (SIOUX) TREATY LANDS

■ Sioux or shared reservation   ☐ Fort Laramie Treaty, 1851

     ⋯ Unceded territory, 1868

☐ Other U.S. reservation   --- Reservation, 1876

© Map by Zoltán Grossman

and the vengeful government herding of Lakota onto reservations. In the 1880s, the Great Sioux Reservation was broken up into five smaller reservations: Pine Ridge, Rosebud, Lower Brule, Cheyenne River, and Standing Rock. Continuing tension culminated in the 1890 massacre of hundreds of Oglala Lakota at Wounded Knee—a tragedy that most Americans assumed marked the end of the Indian Wars.[50]

Lakota national identity—centered on the 1851 and 1868 treaties, the Black Hills occupation, Little Big Horn, and Wounded Knee—was passed from generation to generation through oral tradition in the twentieth century.[51] Oglala Lakota elder Agnes LaMonte said in 1974 in federal court testimony: "I was raised by my grandparents. My grandfather and other old chiefs would come together and talk about the Treaty since I was knee high to a grasshopper. They wanted to get back the Black Hills."[52]

The Fort Laramie Treaties became a key factor in the rebirth of the Native rights movement in the early 1970s. After young Minneapolis Indian activists founded the American Indian Movement (AIM) in 1969, they made contact with reservation residents in South Dakota, Oklahoma, and other states and combined urban Indian community concerns (such as police violence) with the rural elders' emphasis on culture and treaty rights. In late 1972, after AIM occupied the BIA headquarters in Washington, D.C., it turned its attention to the racist murders of Lakota men in white "border towns" around the Pine Ridge Reservation.[53]

By early 1973, AIM had earned a reputation for militancy in South Dakota, which repelled white citizens but was welcomed by some Pine Ridge tribal members. They accused the BIA-backed tribal government of President Richard Wilson of corruption and of stifling dissent. Tribal members founded the Oglala Sioux Civil Rights Organization (OSCRO) to impeach or remove Wilson. When Wilson blocked this effort in early 1973, OSCRO decided to make a stand in the symbolically important hamlet of Wounded Knee—the most important confrontation between Native peoples and U.S. government forces in the late twentieth century.[54]

The AIM/OSCRO stand at Wounded Knee village on February 27, 1973, was immediately met by heavily armed Federal Bureau of Investigation (FBI) agents and U.S. Marshals in helicopters and armored personnel carriers, pro-Wilson Oglala militiamen, local white rancher gunmen, and Air Force Phantom surveillance jets. Hundreds of Native supporters from around the country streamed into Wounded Knee, where they fought running battles with federal agents for seventy-one days, which left two Native fighters dead. They welcomed Oglala Lakota chiefs to the small village and established a small-scale version of Indigenous self-governance and society for the duration of the siege. The confrontation galvanized public opinion in the United States and Indigenous movements and around the world.[55]

After the Wounded Knee siege ended, Oglala Lakota chiefs negotiated with the White House about federal recognition of the 1868 treaty, but to no avail.[56] However, they also began meeting on a regular basis with chiefs from other reservations and bands and formed the Sioux Nation Council to push for recognition of the treaty. In 1974, the Indian Claims Commission offered a cash payment of $106 million to the Sioux Nation Council to settle the Black Hills treaty claim.

The council rejected the settlement both as financially insufficient—given the billions of dollars in gold and timber extracted from the Black Hills—and as not meeting the Lakota demand to return the stolen land. The chiefs asserted that since the Black Hills were essential for the survival of Lakota culture, and could provide a continuing source of economic sustenance for future generations, the land was "not for sale."[57] The council proposed that state and federal lands be returned to the tribe, while flexibly guaranteeing that local residents would retain their private lands, thereby avoiding a conflict with the white landowners. Since the Indian Claims Commission could not return stolen lands, the federal government placed the treaty payments in an escrow account, where they remained. Lakota tribal government elected leaders and hereditary chiefs have shown remarkable unity (in contrast to the Western Shoshone land claim settlement) in rejecting the claims payments.

In 1974, on the Standing Rock Sioux Reservation, AIM drew on global support for its Wounded Knee stand to form the International Indian Treaty Council, which soon gained non-governmental organization status at the United Nations. For three years after the Wounded Knee siege, the Wilson tribal government and federal agents continued to battle AIM activists and Oglala community members, resulting in dozens of violent deaths.[58] The fighting culminated in the June 26, 1975, Oglala shootout that left two FBI agents and one Lakota AIM member dead. AIM leader Leonard Peltier was convicted the following year for the agents' deaths in a controversial trial.[59] By 1976, new tribal leaders took office on the Pine Ridge Reservation, reducing the level of violence. International human rights groups continued to highlight Peltier's case into the twenty-first century.[60]

Black Hills Alliance

In the mid-1970s, as the Pine Ridge conflict was lessening, the global energy crisis led to a rekindling of the historic conflict over minerals in the Black Hills. Multinational mining companies, such as Union Carbide and Exxon, proposed the development of the Black Hills for energy resources, including coal mines, uranium mines, and coal slurry pipelines. The hills had been mined for gold since Custer's arrival a century before and had also been mined for uranium in the 1950s, resulting in extensive irradiation of the southern Black Hills town of Edgemont.[61]

In the mineral rush of the 1870s, the battle was over gold, and white residents were the enemy of the Lakota. In the mineral rush of the 1970s, the battle was over coal and uranium, and the white residents of the Black Hills became not enemies but allies. This time, the Lakota who feared damage to sacred places were joined by non-Indians who saw the plans as a threat to groundwater. The Lakota treaty rights movement entered a new phase in the late 1970s, when it gained new, strange bedfellows in its fight to save the Black Hills.

The Lakota origin story holds that people emerged from the Earth at Wind Cave, now a national park in the southern Black Hills. Lakota ceremonial cycles and camps also link Black Hills cartography to the arrangement of stars, for example, linking the seven summits of Harney Peak to the "seven sisters" of the Pleiades.[62] Another story holds that an ancient race between four-legged animals and two-legged animals (including human beings) left behind blood, resulting in the red iron-rich soil found today in the "racetrack" that surrounds the sacred Black Hills.[63]

Many Lakota maintain that the Black Hills are the "heart" of the Earth and attribute the presence of uranium and other minerals to sacred forces that were feared and left alone by Lakota. Although some Western historians have expressed skepticism of an ancient Lakota historical presence in the Black Hills, they agree that the American claim to the land is dramatically more tenuous.[64] Lakota identity has long been geographically situated in the sacred space around the Black Hills and was explained as such to the original settlers. As Linea Sundstrom has observed: "Instead of asking why the Lakotas were claiming sacred status for the Black Hills in the 1970s, we might more productively ask how the conventional wisdom of the 1870s—that the Black Hills were the Lakotas' holy land—came to be disputed in the 1970s. The answer seems to lie in the sudden relevance of sacredness to land claims disputes."[65]

The 1970s mineral rush involved twenty-seven corporations exploring more than five thousand claims in the Black Hills.[66] In 1978, a gold miners' group in the northern hills, Miners for Safe Energy, held meetings to educate local citizens about the radioactive dangers of uranium mining. Other groups, including the Sierra Club and the Black Hills Energy Coalition, also began to oppose the mining plans but declined to associate with Native people, because they feared alienating potential white followers. At the same time, some ranchers and farmers concerned about the large-scale diversion of groundwater began to discuss the issue with Lakota community organizers. Lakota elders were concerned that the primary site where Union Carbide had identified uranium deposits was Craven Canyon, where many ancient pictographs were located.[67]

AIM leader and International Indian Treaty Council director Bill Means remembers the delicate process that followed of "building a bridge" between rival communities that had fought over water rights. Means said the first ap-

The 1979 Black Hills National Gathering of the People draws four thousand marchers against mining plans in the sacred hills of western South Dakota. (Courtesy: Dick Bancroft)

proach to the ranching community was to "explore through mutual friends, who get along with Indian people." Their message was that the Lakota "had something in common with ranchers"—the view of water as a "precious commodity" and a desire to keep the land in good condition.[68] Means eventually spoke directly with small groups of ranching families, with the message that if the energy corporations had their way, there would be little water left to fight over. Means recalled that he and other Lakota "didn't push the racism issue" and defined the treaty as covering only state and federal lands, not private lands. He said that he, in turn, also came to understand the concerns of ranchers about low cattle prices and contamination from pesticides and herbicides. Out of these discussions came the 1979 founding of the Black Hills Alliance (BHA), a coalition of Lakota, grassroots environmentalists, Black Hills residents, and about twenty to thirty off-reservation ranchers and farmers opposed to corporate plans for the region.[69]

BHA co-founder Mark Tilsen remembers that before the group formed, the Lakota and white ranchers had only two points of social contact: rodeo and basketball.[70] Some white residents had learned a bit about Native cultures

through attending community powwows.[71] There was also some overlap between the groups, as some Lakota had taken up ranching, although they were
rarely the same Lakota who strongly opposed mining the Black Hills. Tilsen
recalled that it was a "political statement" by white ranchers to simply meet
with the Lakota and that the meetings at times went poorly until the ranching
women stepped in to demand that the Lakota be treated with respect.[72]

BHA co-founder Bruce Ellison remembered the early meetings: "You could
feel the tension in the air . . . ever since white people came [to the region] the
corporations have used ignorance, to keep the people most in common with
each other at each other's throats. We wanted to avoid that being an available
tactic." Yet in a series of community meetings in small Black Hills towns, Ellison
saw local residents' faces change when they examined the extent of mineral
leases on a BHA map, believing that uranium mining "threatened them and
their families' future survival."[73] Oglala Lakota BHA organizer Madonna
Thunder Hawk saw that the white residents came to understand that the treaty
could help to prevent uranium mining: "They realized how helpless they were
in the face of eminent domain. But Indian people had treaty rights—they could
stop things!"[74]

Rancher Marvin Kammerer, whose family has lived east of Rapid City since
the 1880s, first opposed uranium mining because of the use of uranium in
nuclear weapons. He had opposed the expansion of the Ellsworth Air Force
Base onto his land and recalled a day when all the B-52s took off from the base
at once, causing him to fear that a nuclear war had begun. Kammerer was one
of the ranchers who served as a bridge to the Lakota and helped to form the
BHA.[75] In a *New York Times* interview, Kammerer said: "I've read the Fort Laramie Treaty, and it seems pretty simple to me; their claim is justified. There's
no way the Indians are going to get all of that land back, but the state land and
the federal land should be returned to them. Out of respect for those people,
and for their belief that the hills are sacred ground, I don't want to be a part
of this destruction."[76]

Kammerer later said, "The cowboys are now suffering the same fate as the
Indians . . . our way of life is dying."[77] In an era when land values have risen
and property taxes skyrocketed, Kammerer said: "We're being pushed off our
land just as the Native Americans were. It's a way to make a lot of money
quickly, with total disregard for the Native American culture and total disregard for the rancher. . . . But we don't have to sell out to the next carpetbagger
that comes up to the door. That's not what we're made of."[78]

The 1980 Black Hills International Survival Gathering draws eleven thousand participants to the Kammerer ranch next to Ellsworth Air Force Base, near Box Elder, South
Dakota. (Courtesy: Dick Bancroft)

In July 1980, Kammerer's ranch hosted the Black Hills International Survival Gathering, which drew eleven thousand participants from around the
world to learn about Indigenous treaties, energy resource conflicts, and alternative energies.[79] I served as an eighteen-year-old office worker in the BHA's
Rapid City office, living in the "BHA House," and helped to invite and coordinate hundreds of international participants in the Survival Gathering. The
event was a pivotal moment in the safe-energy movement throughout the
Midwest, where many current grassroots groups can trace their origins to the
inspiration and relationships developed at the Survival Gathering.

At the time of the gathering, Kammerer's children were teased in school
for being "Indian lovers," and Bill Means also reported that his children were
likewise teased by fellow Lakota students. Ellison asserted: "[The BHA was]
looked at in the Indian community as a white organization and in the white
community as an Indian organization. We looked at it as both."[80] The alliance
building clearly resulted in tensions within both communities, but it also had
some success in improving community relations. Means credits the success to

the "breaking down of doors" at the grassroots level, asserting that a similar effort to build ties between tribal and local white governments would have met the barrier of entrenched political interests.[81]

In 1980, the U.S. Supreme Court affirmed that the Black Hills had indeed been stolen from the Lakota in 1876 and backed the Indian Claims Commission's cash-based "just compensation" rather than a return of the sacred land.[82] Wounded Knee veteran Russell Means led the establishment of the Yellow Thunder Camp in 1981 to provide a Lakota presence in the Black Hills and dramatize the treaty claim.[83] In 1982, Lakota youth began to commemorate the ancient race between the two-leggeds and the four-leggeds, with an annual 500-mile Sacred Hoop Run around the Black Hills.[84]

Uranium prices had dropped in the wake of the 1979 Three Mile Island nuclear accident, and BHA court victories finally forced the cancellation of uranium mining plans in the Black Hills. The BHA also helped to pass a 1984 statewide initiative to block a low-level radioactive waste dump in the Black Hills.[85] A 1985 bill sponsored by Senator Bill Bradley, Democrat from New Jersey, proposed the return of 1.2 million acres of Black Hills federal lands to the tribe, which would then establish the "Sioux National Park," but the bill could not overcome objections from South Dakota's congressional delegation.[86] The Black Hills remained an area outside of any federal reservation, but it was an area that would become increasingly important in building support for Lakota treaty rights.

Black Hills Gunnery Range and CIA I

In February 1987, the Minneapolis-based Honeywell Corporation announced plans to open a weapons testing range in the southern Black Hills, in Hell Canyon near the Cheyenne River and the town of Hot Springs. The company planned to test gunnery munitions in the 6,200-acre site, including some tipped with depleted uranium—a low-level radioactive substance dense enough to penetrate tank armor. The Hot Springs Chamber of Commerce, some Fall River County ranchers, and Governor George Mickelson backed the plan as economic development. Yet a number of local landowners questioned the project's noise and potential radioactivity and formed the group Keep the Hills Attractive, which studied the proposal and sought new zoning laws to stop or modify it.[87]

Two couples managing ranches adjacent to the Honeywell property viewed the project not only as a nuisance to their rural way of life but also as a threat to local property values. Cindy Reed and her husband, Marc Lamphere, owned a 7,000-acre ranch that was faring poorly in the era of low cattle prices. Bruce and Linda Murdock ran a 6,000-acre spread that was doing better economically—a status they feared would disappear as soon as the Honeywell shells began to explode. They coordinated a loose group of ranchers who felt that the Keep the Hills Attractive group moved too slowly in its opposition, and they sought a wider range of allies.

Bruce Murdock had attended the University of Colorado with Charlotte Black Elk, a great-granddaughter of the Oglala Lakota spiritual leader Black Elk and an early leader of Pine Ridge support for the Bradley legislation. After reading news coverage of the controversy, Black Elk called Murdock, and was invited to a meeting, which she remembers was "all white people and me."[88] She told the ranchers that her family had been displaced by the U.S. government in the 1800s, so she could identify with farmers and ranchers facing foreclosures or environmental dislocation. Some friends on the reservation thought it was "absolutely outrageous" that she would meet with white ranchers. But she was joined by other tribal members, including Germaine Tremmel, a great-granddaughter of Sitting Bull, who said: "There are areas in the Black Hills that you get strength from . . . where you can talk to the Great Spirit. This is one of those areas."[89] The great-granddaughters of the Lakota leaders had turned their lines of descent into "lines of dissent."

The ranchers invited other Lakota to visit the proposed testing site in Hell Canyon. An elderly spiritual leader from the Standing Rock Reservation saw numerous ancient pictographs carved on rock in the area. Dozens of Lakota from different reservations, including former AIM activists and the Gray Eagles reservation elders group, converged on the Honeywell property and established two tipi camps. Murdock donated meat to the Native occupants, and Reed told news reporters that the occupation was backed by increasing numbers of local ranchers: "This is not Indian versus white. It's a land-based ethic versus a profit-oriented motive. This is a beautiful place. There's no reason to begin to ruin it."[90] Although the ranchers were not using the BHA as a model for an alliance, many of the Native activists were consciously using the lessons from the earlier uranium mining struggle.

Media reports began to describe the Honeywell opponents as a coalition of "cowboys" and "Indians," and the white ranchers and Lakota found that their unusual relationship drew more attention to the project than their actual complaints about munitions testing. By June, they began describing their loose, unorganized coalition as the Cowboy and Indian Alliance, with "CIA" as its poignant abbreviation. Reed believed that the white ranchers and the

Lakota "have more in common than either side acknowledges." She had grown up in the ranching town of Faith, South Dakota, where Native students befriended her in school. She noted that Honeywell and its Hot Springs backers could understand the Lakota opposition to the project but could never understand the opposition from white ranchers.[91]

Pine Ridge Reservation president Joe American Horse praised the CIA: "It's about time the Black Hills residents join with us on these land issues. It's going to benefit all of us and that's important."[92] Honeywell supporters considered the CIA part of an effort to return the canyon to the Lakota, who they claimed had never visited the site until the controversy. "I've hunted down there since 1947," said Hot Springs resident Art Donnell, "and I've never seen an Indian."[93] Pine Ridge tribal vice president Paul Iron Cloud stated: "The main purpose of not wanting Honeywell in there is the sacredness of the Black Hills to our people. They say there could be bloodshed. It's that serious."[94]

Public hearings were held in June 1987 on the Pine Ridge Reservation and in Hot Springs, to listen to the concerns of both the Lakota and residents from near the site. White ranchers drove a long distance to attend the Pine Ridge hearing, and many Pine Ridge Lakota drove to the Hot Springs hearing, presenting a united front in both communities, and the hearings were broadcast by the reservation radio station KILI.

By August 1987, national TV crews and European magazines were regularly reporting on the CIA's opposition to the Honeywell testing range. Black Elk thought that 60–70 percent of rural white residents opposed the gunnery range. She also told Reed of a dream she had of horses running in the canyon.[95]

Honeywell formally dropped its proposal in October 1987. The company took advantage of a state tax-break program by selling the Hell Canyon property to the quasi-governmental Community Foundation. The foundation then sold the land to the Oregon-based Institute of Range and the American Mustang. The group founded the Black Hills Wild Horse Sanctuary on the land, which has since continued as a mustang refuge, popular tourist destination, and Lakota ceremonial site.[96]

Black Elk expressed relief that the canyon had become "safe for at least a century." According to Reed, the informal alliance was based on strengthening social ties between the Lakota and non-Indian ranchers, rather than on formal institutional structures.[97] In the 1990s and 2000s, these ties between Native and non-Native communities became progressively easier to establish in ensuing South Dakota environmental disputes.

The Black Hills Wild Horse Sanctuary, on the site of the formerly proposed Honeywell munitions testing range near Hot Springs, South Dakota. (Photo by the author)

Defending the Black Hills and CIA II

The experiences of the BHA and the CIA had taught Lakota activists that uniting with white ranchers was instrumental in protecting the Black Hills from harmful development. Yet the true test was on reservations such as Pine Ridge and Rosebud, where tensions persisted between Lakota and the white ranching community over issues such as grazing, water rights, and political representation and realities of racism and economic power.

In 1990, the Amcor company proposed a toxic waste dump on the Pine Ridge Reservation. Joanne Tall, a former Lakota organizer against the Honeywell testing range, took the forefront in educating her community about the toxic threat through the Native Resource Coalition. Tall remembers that the reservation's white ranchers came to the coalition's first meeting and heard about the possible water pollution and increased truck traffic that could result from the dump operation. Tall told them that "these projects don't know a color—they impact anybody."[98] The tribe declared a moratorium, and the company dropped the plan. A similar toxic waste project was then proposed on adjacent Rosebud Reservation, where the Good Road Coalition led a campaign that also included white ranchers and defeated the proposal.[99]

In 1994, a development corporation owned by Kevin Costner (ironically of *Dances with Wolves* fame) and his brother Daniel proposed the 838-acre Dunbar resort complex on Lakota sacred ground near Deadwood, in the northern Black Hills. Local residents concerned about increased taxes joined with Lakota, including former BHA organizer Madonna Thunder Hawk, to form the Black Hills Protection Committee.[100] Thunder Hawk expressed relief that Lakota opposition to the project was no longer the "overwhelming struggle" as in the 1970s and 1980s, because she could count on local white landowners to help protect the hills. Under pressure, Costner modified his plan in 2000.[101]

In 1998, another alliance developed on the Rosebud Reservation against a proposed giant hog farm. Small hog farmers opposed the project, fearing overwhelming competition from a huge operation, and local Lakota expressed concern over the threat to groundwater supplies and burial sites. Together they formed the Concerned Rosebud-Area Citizens, which in 2000 convinced a majority of tribal members to vote against the project and the next year set up a protest camp that pressured the tribal council to drop the plan.[102]

On the neighboring Pine Ridge Reservation, a railroad project similar to Montana's Tongue River Railroad met strong opposition beginning in 1999. The Dakota, Minnesota, and Eastern (DM&E) Railroad planned to ship coal from the Powder River coalfields of Wyoming to the Mississippi River in Minnesota. Opponents formed the Alliance for Responsible Development out of concern that the railroad would cause high dust and noise levels, environmental degradation, and wildfires. A 2000 survey showed that 85 percent of landowners in affected areas opposed the railroad.[103] The Sioux National Council expressed concern over the project's impact on petroglyphs and burial sites and on the Pine Ridge village of Red Shirt, and condemned the DM&E as a violation of the Fort Laramie Treaty.[104]

In late 2000, non-Indian ranchers and Lakota tribal members resurrected their alliance, as CIA II, to fight DM&E expansion, and it included some ranchers from the old BHA, as well as ranchers in Wyoming and the wealthy medical community of Rochester, Minnesota. As Lakota organizer and CIA II cofounder Charmaine White Face recalled, some ranchers understood that the tribes possessed legal pull with the federal government because of the treaty, tribal archeological sites, and Native Americans' environmental justice role in the U.S. Environmental Protection Agency.[105]

Drawing on earlier experiences, the CIA II group drew Lakota tribal citizens and white ranchers to a 2001 rally in Rapid City, where they all took part in a feast and round dance. The U.S. Surface Transportation Board gave its go-ahead to the project in 2002 and faced a joint lawsuit by Lakota tribes, environmental groups, and ranchers' groups.[106] The $6 billion coal shipping plan was dropped in 2009 when the DM&E's new Canadian Pacific owners determined it was a risky investment.[107]

Starting in 2002, the Defenders of the Black Hills, led by Charmaine White Face, Brian Brademeyer, and other Lakota and non-Native community members, campaigned to protect the sacred peak of Bear Butte (near the biker rally town of Sturgis) from a proposed shooting range and biker bar that would disrupt ceremonies and vision quests. The group also highlighted concerns about gold mining, roads, and timber sales in the Black Hills.[108] When uranium mining companies took a renewed interest in exploring the southern Black Hills in 2005, the defenders took the initial lead in educating and organizing in local towns and the Pine Ridge Reservation.

A new "uranium rush" began in 2007, as the price of uranium jumped from $20 to $138 a pound, due to growing markets in China and India. About ten companies sought new uranium exploration leases in Fall River and Custer counties. The Powertech (later Azarga) Uranium Corporation targeted the Dewey-Burdock site near Edgemont, which was rich in archeological sites, attracting opposition from the Defenders of the Black Hills and a handful of small local conservation and wildlife groups. The company proposed in situ leach mining to extract uranium using 13 million gallons a day of a pressured water-based solution and reinjecting massive amounts of radioactive liquid waste back into and onto the ground.[109]

BHA veterans Lilias Jones Jarding and Bruce Ellison formed the Black Hills Clean Water Alliance in 2010 to provide a center for the new anti-uranium campaign. According to Jarding, although the organizing was going well in Lakota communities, the "Rapid City and southern Black Hills non-Indians weren't organized very well."[110] The Black Hills Clean Water Alliance was later bolstered by other Lakota organizers such as Dennis Yellow Thunder, Debra White Plume, and Carla Marshall, as well as by the non-Native organizations Southern Hills Citizens Group and Dakota Rural Action.

At a 2013 state Water Management Board hearing, about 250 people packed the room. According to Jarding, "[The one hundred] people in the back of the room were all Native. For the most part they were standing and very visible. They had [a] public comment period, and first the non-Indian experts got up. . . . Toward the end, the Native people started getting up and talking about treaty issues and the Black Hills being sacred. The last guy that went was an old AIMster, . . . and the last thing he said was, 'The Black Hills are not for sale.' He was saying that loudly. The board was kind of stunned, and everyone clapped in the crowd."[111]

Jarding noted how the non-Indians who came "with very little background in Native issues now have some background, but it's been done in a relatively smooth, friendly, easy fashion." She observed: "There hasn't been a lot of people shutting each other out. . . . It's unusual in my experience for it to go smoothly. We may have bumps in the road, but from the beginning of the process it's gone relatively smoothly." On treaty rights, she said, "There's a difference in tone than there was thirty-five years ago." [112]

The alliance joined with Owe Aku / Bring Back the Way, It's About the Water, and Dakota Rural Action to accuse the federal Nuclear Regulatory Commission of not following its own regulations to protect Native cultural and water resources. In April 2015, the Atomic Safety and Licensing Board ruled that the commission needed to partake in further consultation and cultural site studies before the uranium mine could go forward.[113] At the August 2015 Sturgis Motorcycle Rally, riders made a statement against Black Hills mining, by using six hundred of their bikes to spell out "Honor Vets, Protect Water."[114] This time, even the bikers were joining the cowboys and Indians.

Two Steps Forward, One Step Back

The BHA and the CIA of the 1980s were not anomalies in Native/non-Native relations in South Dakota but instead set a precedent and a standard for later alliances. Yet these new alliances were counterbalanced by examples of continuing tensions between the Lakota and white institutions. Confrontations flared over police shootings and unsolved murders of Lakota tribal members, liquor sales just outside reservation boundaries, the federal transfer of treaty lands along the Missouri River to state control, and many other issues. The U.S. Commission on Civil Rights backed up the Lakota perception that South Dakota maintains a racial "dual system of justice."[115] Lakota groups tended to focus more attention on institutional racism in government agencies than on repeating the 1970s confrontations with local white ranchers and farmers. Indeed, a few ranchers such as Marvin Kammerer spoke out against the murders of Lakota men outside the reservations.

Just as in the case of Montana alliances, the initial success of the BHA and the CIA enabled the later establishment of successor coalitions. A common enemy may improve relations between a tribal community and a neighboring white community, but then the alliance can lay dormant or even face reversals over local issues. Yet previous experience of building bridges makes the formation of new alliances, even around different issues, much easier to accomplish.

The ranchers or farmers may initially only emphasize how Native sovereign powers might benefit their particular environmental cause but later come to learn more about the land ethics of their Native neighbors and, in turn, allow their neighbors to learn more about their land ethics. The "two steps forward, one step back" process that is evident in both Montana and South Dakota has reduced organized anti-Indian sentiment, but not entirely. It has built a greater understanding between the communities, in separate episodes that individually appear not to leave a deep impression, but collectively do. As Kammerer commented: "This is a lifelong struggle. You don't make big waves. If you have any successes, they will be small ones. It's like taking a stone and throwing it in the water."[116]

As BHA co-founder Bruce Ellison observed, each environmental coalition is "a ripple in the pond, it builds greater understanding." After each particular alliance ends, "the circle retracts, but not all the way, and a new alliance expands it farther outward," for "it couldn't retract back to where it was." When discussing the BHA, Ellison asks: "Did the alliance turn [western South Dakota] into utopia? Absolutely not. Did it go a long ways to build understanding? Absolutely. It was a contributing factor to real changes. . . . Prejudice is still substantial, but there is less and it is no longer acceptable."[117]

The South Dakota experience also demonstrates that the initial caution of some white environmental groups in working with tribal members in the late 1970s was unfounded. By strengthening the relationship between Native and white rural communities, the alliances were able to build lasting bonds. The environmental groups that avoided an alliance with Lakota communities faded away, while those that worked with the tribes generally succeeded.

A number of activists also ironically asserted that had the Wounded Knee confrontation not happened in the early 1970s, the formation of the BHA would not have happened in the late 1970s, and the later alliances may not have prevailed. AIM's militancy put it at odds with white ranchers in the short term, but it also helped in the long term to bring critical attention to the treaty and Lakota culture and how they could help defend the Black Hills. As in Montana, it was some of the most outspoken pro-treaty activists—such as Bill Means and Charmaine White Face—who made the first moves to ally with white ranchers. Their "carrot-and-stick" approach, as in Montana, fused particularist confrontation around racism and treaty rights with universalist cooperation around environmental issues. The strategy was crafted to dismantle the racist past, make tribal members more equal partners with non-Indians in the present, and work toward a common future on sacred land.

SHARING SACRED LANDS

On a deeper level, there is something more profound about Native alliances with settlers living on their claimed historic lands. After all, many Native peoples hold a spiritual attachment to the landscape of the Black Hills or the Sweetgrass Hills that non-Indians do not share. In spiritual traditions, sacred places symbolize the primordial creation of the Earth and human beings, creating order out of chaos.[118] It was in fighting for the sacred Black Hills that the Lakota united as a nation in the 1870s and reasserted nationhood in the 1970s. The fight pit Native religious views of the hills as a sacred place against the non-Native quest for gold and tourist dollars. The Black Hills have become an icon for Lakota nationhood and, since the construction of Mount Rushmore, also serve as an icon for American patriotism.

The Black Hills are an example of a place, like Jerusalem, that has assumed greater value through historic conflicts. As the geographer Yi-Fu Tuan has noted: "Conflict over a resource and place has the effect of drawing attention to them: things (walleyes and a beautiful river) that a people might have taken for granted suddenly become a center of attention, assume heightened value, when they are threatened. You learn to truly appreciate a place when another praises it—or when another wants to take it away from you."[119]

Yet as part of their tribal land claim, the Lakota propose sharing that sacred land with the descendants of the original settlers. The sacredness of certain ranges, instead of only dividing Native people from white ranchers, has actually helped bring them together. The strongest environmental alliances in the Northern Plains have been formed to protect the most sacred or culturally significant sites. The white ranchers supporting the alliances no longer seek to exclude Native influence or presence from the hills, and Native Americans do not seek the return of privately held lands. The goal of both groups is instead to exclude outside forces that do not value the ranges as either sacred or significant. In such instances, spiritually sacred sites "assume historical or political importance."[120]

The growth of Earth consciousness in non-Native society (sometimes called "geopiety" or "topophilia") has to some extent blurred the distinction between Native and non-Native views of sacred space.[121] When Native people and white ranchers/farmers agree that the "sacred" Black Hills or Sweetgrass Hills need to be protected, they are agreeing not on religious questions but on the significance of a place to their cultures and lifestyles. These discussions can take an alliance beyond short-term environmental issues, to long-term mutual cultural understanding, and open up ways that sacred spaces can be shared, without degrading either tradition. Within this framework, settler interests can fully "come to terms" with Indigenous religious freedom.[122]

The Lakota scholar Vine Deloria Jr. acknowledges that "a good many non-Indians have some of the same emotional attachment to land that most Indians do" and that "critical to the recognition of this attachment is the family, the community, as functioning parts of the landscape."[123]

Many rural whites value the land because of long-standing family and community history and a transcendent memory of a free way of life. A white teacher in Chester, Montana, for example, wrote of his childhood growing up at the base of the Sweetgrass Hills: "I really enjoyed riding horses with dad on the mountain surrounded by the beauty of the hills. . . . Mom would also take me for hikes in the hills to see what kind of new flowers we could find. . . . When we would find a deep spot in the creek we would stop and lie on our stomachs and feel for the fish under the bank . . . the joy I felt inside was awesome. . . . I love to sit and watch the elk and deer graze while sitting on the side of the mountain in the grass. . . . Growing up in the hills is so peaceful."[124]

The writer incorporated memories of freedom, yet his perspective was not escapist or centered on a non-human "wilderness." His memories instead resemble Native views of a landscape alive with family relationships that bond human beings to a place. Though they have different ties to the rural landscape, both Indigenous people and white farmers/ranchers have in common a sense of place that they view as under siege by globalizing forces. They value place not simply as a recreational landscape but as a connection to their ancestors and a refuge for an endangered way of life.

Native people want some control over territory not simply for political or economic power but for the ability to continue practicing cultural lifeways and spiritual ceremonies. Non-Native agriculturalists want control over territory not simply to continue making money, especially under poor market conditions, but to be able to practice family farming and ranching. The disruption of the agrarian way of life not only threatens individual families with property foreclosure but tears at the fabric of rural community. The identification of the land with continuity of family and community life is perhaps one of the strongest bonds between rural Native and non-Native neighbors.

Indigenous peoples, however, can claim genealogical and cosmological roots in the land stretching back millennia, during which time they have developed an intimate knowledge of the land. Non-Native farmers/ranchers can perhaps claim family roots on the landscape, on the basis of private land ownership, dating back only a century or two. Native spiritual traditions, centered on natural places rather than church buildings or prophetic events, are not accepted in the double standards of Western legal doctrine. A mining company would not extract coal from Mount Sinai, and governments would not ask Christians or Jews to prove the significance of their sacred places. Yet Native peoples who object to projects affecting sacred sites are constantly asked to justify their claims or are accused of using their religion in a scheme to stop development. Because the histories of Indigenous peoples in their ancestral territories go much deeper back in time, they seek the return of land held by non-Native governments.[125]

Although Native and non-Native people may both possess a "sense of place," there is a difference between settler families belonging to a landscape for multiple decades, with their religious and political memberships not fundamentally tied to the place, and Indigenous peoples belonging to a landscape because of spiritual traditions and political sovereignty for multiple centuries. If non-Native people are uprooted, they can settle in a different landscape and more easily develop a new sense of place. When Indigenous people are uprooted, they lose a fundamental connection to their ancestors who are buried in their homeland, origin stories and cultural memories tied to specific places (and place-names), and plants and animals that form the basis of their diets, ceremonial cycles, and clan systems.

Even Indigenous peoples who have migrated—forcibly or otherwise—to new territories generally have transported their sense of indigeneity with them and reconnected their stories to new sites and their "traditional" diets to new plants and animals. Rupturing those relationships through mass removal or contamination can cause an Indigenous nation to diminish or disappear, resulting in cultural genocide. Although rupturing non-Native ties to the land can harm a valuable way of life and reduce the richness of American society, it does not threaten to eliminate American cultural or political existence. There is a difference between a threat to a group of people within a large country and an existential threat to a smaller nation. It can certainly be argued that destroying the Earth and its climate is an existential threat to all of humanity, but even the climate crisis imperils Indigenous existence more quickly and profoundly.

Given these differences, how could Native Americans and European Americans possibly hope to share the same sacred places in the present, much less protect them in the future? Native nations often shared sacred places, even if they had different kinds of ties to the places. The Lakota and Cheyenne, for example, jointly view Bear Butte as one of their most sacred locations, but owing to very different stories, and each group performs tribal-specific ceremonies in their shared sacred space.[126] Religious groups have proposed to share sacred sites in several conflict zones, such as Cyprus, Bosnia, and even Palestine.[127] Some Christians have shared Holy Land sacred sites despite their historical doctrinal schisms.[128] In some cases, such as sacred forest groves in India, moral and spiritual taboos can help preserve the integrity of a local ecosystem, even protecting its biodiversity to a greater extent than in national parks.[129]

Native Americans and white ranchers/farmers have joined to protect sacred "island mountain ranges" as oases of life in the Northern Plains. Although they have differed on the reasons for the ranges' significance, their common bond is their strong cultural attachment to place. Land is not just a material commodity to be contested but carries multiple meanings that can establish both identities and relationships.[130] Native and non-Native neighbors have been questioning the right of faceless corporations or agencies that do not believe in the land's sacredness—however it is defined—to determine its future.

A group's bond to the land is no longer simply being used to "prove" its nationhood—either of Native homelands or of the settler society. A claim can also be made in the name of all human beings who value the land. Control over the place has become less important than what happens in that place, whether land-based cultures can continue to survive and develop a common "sense of place." In defending the land together, using the treaty agreements between their nations, they can also begin to look toward sharing the land into the future. As new threats are emerging in the early twenty-first century to the people and water of the Northern Plains, these treaty partnerships have taken on new life and vigor.

CHAPTER 5

Fossil Fuel Shipping and Blocking

Northern Plains and Pacific Northwest

IN THE TWENTY-FIRST CENTURY, THE CLIMATE JUSTICE MOVEMENT, including Indigenous groups and nations, has identified fossil fuel shipping as the Achilles' heel of the energy industry. The industry needs to ship equipment from ports into its inland oil, gas, and coal fields and to transport the fossil fuels via rail, barge, and pipeline to coastal ports for shipment to global markets.[1] As the climate crisis has unfolded, multiple fronts in the fossil fuel wars have emerged across North America.[2] Earlier Native/non-Native collaborations reemerged as powerful, interconnected campaigns and, for the first time, put themselves on the map in the public consciousness, notably in the Northern Plains and Pacific Northwest.

The three growing fossil fuel sources in North America are in the interior of the continent: the Alberta tar sands, the Powder River coal basin in Montana and Wyoming, and the Bakken oil shale basin centered in North Dakota.[3] Every step of the way, alliances of environmental and climate justice activists, farmers and ranchers, and Native peoples are blocking plans to ship carbon and the technology to extract it, becoming a key part of the global movement that journalist Naomi Klein labels as "Blockadia."[4]

In the 2010s, energy companies proposed to ship Powder River Basin coal by train to Northwest ports, to be loaded onto ships for Asia. Given the widespread success of environmental alliances in rolling back the coal industry in the United States, the industry began to turn toward exports to growing Asian economies (particularly China) as the key to keeping the industry alive. Such plans have reinvigorated Native/non-Native alliances from the Northern Plains to the Pacific Northwest, as the Internet and globalized shipping routes connected communities into larger networks of resistance.

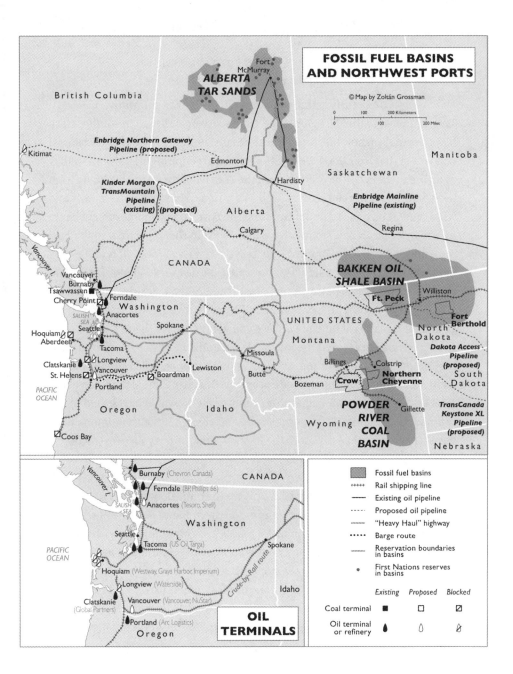

FOSSIL FUEL BASINS AND NORTHWEST PORTS

©Map by Zoltán Grossman

0   100   200 Kilometers
0   100   200 Miles

British Columbia

ALBERTA TAR SANDS

Fort McMurray

Enbridge Northern Gateway Pipeline (proposed)

Kitimat

Edmonton

Hardisty

Manitoba

Saskatchewan

Kinder Morgan TransMountain Pipeline (existing) (proposed)

Enbridge Mainline Pipeline (existing)

Alberta

Calgary

Regina

CANADA

BAKKEN OIL SHALE BASIN

Williston

Vancouver
Burnaby
Tsawwassen
Cherry Point
Ferndale
Anacortes

Ft. Peck

Washington

Spokane

UNITED STATES

North Dakota

Fort Berthold

SALISH SEA

Seattle

Montana

Dakota Access Pipeline (proposed)

Hoquiam
Aberdeen

Tacoma

Missoula

Billings

Colstrip

Clatskanie
St. Helens
Longview
Vancouver

Lewiston

Butte

Crow

Northern Cheyenne

South Dakota

PACIFIC OCEAN

Portland

Boardman

Bozeman

POWDER RIVER COAL BASIN

Gillette

TransCanada Keystone XL Pipeline (proposed)

Oregon

Idaho

Wyoming

Nebraska

Coos Bay

Burnaby (Chevron Canada)
Ferndale (BP, Phillips 66)
Anacortes (Tesoro, Shell)

CANADA

SALISH SEA

Vancouver I.

Seattle
Tacoma (US Oil, Targa)

Washington

Spokane

PACIFIC OCEAN

Hoquiam (Westway, Grays Harbor, Imperium)

Longview (Waterside)

Idaho

Clatskanie (Global Partners)
Vancouver (Vancouver, NuStar)

Portland (Arc Logistics)

Oregon

OIL TERMINALS

Crude-by-Rail route

Fossil fuel basins
+++++ Rail shipping line
―― Existing oil pipeline
----- Proposed oil pipeline
~~~~ "Heavy Haul" highway
••••• Barge route
―― Reservation boundaries in basins
• First Nations reserves in basins

	Existing	Proposed	Blocked
Coal terminal	■	☐	☒
Oil terminal or refinery	⬤	◌	⦸

TWENTY-FIRST-CENTURY NORTHERN
PLAINS FOSSIL FUEL WARS

Tongue River Railroad and Otter Creek Coal Mine

The simmering alliance against the Tongue River Railroad in southeastern Montana took on new life in 2008, as the State Land Board sought to lease coal deposits in the Otter Creek Valley. Northern Cheyenne highly value the valley as an area rich in cultural sites where they settled after returning home from Indian Territory in the 1880s, as well as an area to harvest edible plants and wild game. The tribe's annual run from the Fort Robinson internment camp in Nebraska has helped to involve tribal youth in the opposition to the coal mine and railroad. Otto Braided Hair Jr., a descendant of survivors of the 1864 Sand Creek massacre, said: "I've got spiritual ties to this land. Emotional ties. . . . Is this whole place going to be turned into a black pit, and then it's gone? Are you going to have grandchildren? Are you going to have great-grandchildren? What kind of land are you going to leave them?"[5]

White ranchers feared the inevitable groundwater drawdown, coal dust, herbicides, and coal spills into cattle drinking water and the railroad's use of eminent domain to acquire private property. Rancher Clint McRae, son of the cowboy poet Wallace McRae, whose family property would be bisected by the railroad, commented: "For 40 years, the citizens of southeast Montana have been repeatedly asked to absorb the impacts of natural resource extraction."[6] He said that the mine and railroad project would "wreak havoc with our water, go through our towns."[7]

The Otter Creek mine would supply up to 20 million tons of coal via the Tongue River spur line and Burlington Northern Santa Fe (BNSF) tracks to Pacific Northwest ports and on to Asian markets. Montana opponents of the coal mine and railroad have worked with Northwest alliances against coal export terminals, which they see stopping as key to stopping new coal mines. Clint McRae joined Northern Cheyenne tribal members to testify at 2012 Washington State hearings on coal terminals. At a Seattle hearing, McRae stated that he was "vehemently opposed to a private, for-profit corporation to use eminent domain to condemn [his] private land for a rail line to export coal to China . . . [with] staggering impacts on [his family's] 125 years of ranching."[8] Self-described conservative rancher Nick Golder, seventy-eight years old, said: "This steamrolling over people's property rights is a dangerous thing. Where's the public necessity to ship coal to China?"[9]

The Saint Louis–based company Arch Coal, which co-owned the Tongue

River Railroad Company with BNSF, applied for a permit for a strip mine at Otter Creek in 2012. The U.S. Surface Transportation Board invited public input in its environmental impact statement process.[10] Northern Cheyenne youth organizer Vanessa Braided Hair commented:

> Arch Coal understands money. What Arch Coal doesn't understand is community. They don't understand history. They don't understand the Cheyenne people whose ancestors fought and died for the land they are proposing to destroy. They don't understand the fierceness with which the people, both Indian and non-Indian, in southeastern Montana love the land. This is why not one dragline will rip the coal from the earth. . . . It is why not one burial site will be dug up and why not one elk will be displaced. It is why our water will continue to run clean and plentiful and our wildlife will continue to roam free.[11]

Northern Cheyenne tribal member Adriann Killsnight recalled that Vanessa Braided Hair, Otto Braided Hair Jr., and others "stood up and spoke out during that time." She said: "We were slowly working together. . . . Public meetings [were] held in different towns locally. We've started meetings with hearing others' concerns, and we all realized we share similar concerns."[12] The meetings led to the formation of ecoCheyenne, a grassroots association of tribal members that worked together with the white ranching community.

Alexis Bonogofsky, senior coordinator of the National Wildlife Federation's Tribal Lands Partnerships Project, agreed: "There is a very long history between the homesteading ranchers and the Cheyenne families . . . it's mutual respect and a lot of history between their families. The Cheyenne have been there for a long, long time. The ranchers obviously came during the homesteading, but those relationships have been there for generations. . . . One thing I can tell you for sure is that the people in southeastern Montana, whether they're Northern Cheyenne or they're the ranchers, love that place. . . . There is a specialness about it."[13]

Bonogofsky added: "[The ranchers] do understand the irony of the fact that they're talking about land that was taken from the Indians. . . . When you hear [Wallace] McRae talk, he'll say that this isn't our land. We're stewards of it. We're taking care of it for future generations. All of the cultural and historic sites are the tribes'. We don't own those sites. It's not ours to decide what happens to them. It's a very respectful relationship between them."[14]

Clint McRae spoke of his family's land ethics: "My philosophy . . . is that everything's a balance. The ranch ground we are taking now was taken out of production of buffalo. We have replaced those buffalo with cattle. And it is my responsibility as a rancher to not harm the ground. We try to graze it like the buffalo did. We graze it at certain times of the year, it's rested, and we go back into that area again."[15]

Killsnight remembered that Wallace and Clint McRae attended a tribal council meeting and "took time out . . . to come down and express their concern." She recalled that "Wally" McRae gave tribal members an exclusive tour of their homestead, to show them sacred cultural sites on the property that he promised to protect. Killsnight observed that McRae "didn't want nobody else to know where those places were because he knew . . . lootings and things like that happen."[16]

The Otter Creek coal mine was also opposed by affected tribes outside Montana. In 2013, five Lummi tribal members traveled twelve hundred miles from the Pacific Northwest to Northern Cheyenne, since Lummi sacred ground would be affected by the coal export terminal at the other end of the BNSF rail line. Lummi carver Jewell James led the Kwel Hoy' Totem Pole Journey (the first of three such journeys), taking a twenty-two-foot healing pole he carved from a 300-year-old red cedar back to the coast, to demonstrate the unity of Indigenous peoples and allies along the route. The pole was blessed by Northern Cheyenne spiritual leader Kenneth Medicine Bull because, as he said, "we need to protect our way of life."[17] Lummi has been at odds with the Crow tribal government, which wants to export its own reservation coal through Northwest ports.[18]

Rancher Roger Sprague, whose family has traded with Northern Cheyenne in the Rosebud Valley since 1881, attended the ceremony. He commented: "We're neighbors with these people, and we're proud to work with these people. We don't want this mine in here. We don't want the railroad in here. It's our life. We've fought hard to put it together, and we'd like to keep it that way."[19] Birney rancher Jeanie Alderson told the participants: "I would like to pass on to my children a ranch that is no longer threatened by coal in hopes that they can pass it on to their children. Our fates are tied together despite the distance. . . . We will stand and fight with you."[20]

Also in 2013, the Oglala Lakota passed a resolution against the project, citing their ancestral ties to the area, including as hunting grounds for Tashunka Witko (Crazy Horse).[21] Tribal citizens and their allies had gathered at Deer Medicine Rocks, a sacred site and national historic landmark "to honor and recognize a place where Native Americans have carved their prophecies, their history and their dreams for thousands of years," where "petroglyphs

Northern Cheyenne tribal members and white ranchers thanking Lummi carvers on the 2013 Totem Pole Journey from Washington to Montana. (Courtesy: Alexis Bonogofsky)

cover the walls of the sandstone face of the rocks, including a rock art inscription of the prophecy of a tribal victory at the Battle of the Little Bighorn," which was around the same time that Hunkpapa Lakota spiritual leader Tatanka Yotanka (Sitting Bull) held a Sun Dance in the Rosebud Valley.[22]

Bonogofsky described how the Tongue River Railroad Company attempted to divide the alliance between white landowners and tribal citizens. Part of the railroad's environmental impact statement involved natural and cultural surveys of the proposed rail route. Although white landowners objected to the company's conducting natural surveys on their private lands, they had no objections to the tribe's conducting cultural surveys. However, the railroad company kept saying to the tribes: "These landowners won't let us on. We don't have landowner access. It's a dangerous thing. We don't know if you'd be safe if you went on there." They were "implying that the landowners would shoot someone if the tribes were on their land . . . [and] it's just not true," she said.[23]

Bonogofsky, noting that even though white ranchers are more able than tribal citizens to move away from a contaminated landscape, stated: "They see the ranching culture as permanent as someone might see the reservation. They want a permanent ranching community that is passed down from generation to generation. If anything, this alliance is really strengthening already existing relationships, and it will better help us in the future as we do renewable energy projects. . . . The tribal community can also benefit the ranching community."[24] She cited ranch manager Brad Sauer, who protects cultural sites located on his property outside the reservation and volunteers with the tribal group Red Feather to learn to build straw-bale houses for energy efficiency.

Sauer commented on the Tongue River Valley: "[It's] country you can make a living in, as long as you figure out how to get along with it. . . . Down through time, there were people here that fought hard to keep it. They're our neighbors. I'm starting to understand a little of what they went through . . . during the Indian Wars. Not trying to compare myself to them at all, I'm just starting to gain a little more empathy . . . why they feel the way they feel about this country. . . . With a little care, things can keep on going here for a long, long time."[25]

Bonogofsky acknowledged that the process of building cross-cultural alliances can be difficult: "Even though we're all speaking English to each other, a lot of times we have different ways of communicating. When I say something in English it might mean something different to a person who is a native Cheyenne speaker. It's a very deliberate, slow process that is very long term, and it takes a lot of work. It's not easy to do. . . . I think everyone is so committed to it that everyone is willing to make it work."[26]

Bonogofsky reported that at 2015 Surface Transportation Board hearings, white ranchers "rose to defend the cultural heritage of their Northern Cheyenne neighbors." She said: "They spoke with passion and conviction of their resolve to protect burials and ceremonial sites located on their land. Northern Cheyennes stood in defense of the property rights of the ranchers, land that 150 years ago belonged to their ancestors." Backed by this support, the Northern Cheyenne Tribal Council unanimously opposed the Tongue River Railroad.[27] In November 2015, the Tongue River Railroad Company submitted a request to the Surface Transportation Board to "suspend the permitting process due largely to the ongoing delays."[28] The newly bankrupt Arch Coal withdrew its Otter Creek mine application in March 2016, and the Northern Cheyenne and their allies declared victory.[29]

Oglala Lakota community organizer Krystal Two Bulls, who grew up on the Northern Cheyenne Reservation and participates in the anti-coal campaign, concluded that a true alliance is "like a family": "I think because of these alliances being built, I think it's going to set precedents for other relationships. . . . These farmers and ranchers are going to be leading the way in paving the road for other farmers and ranchers to be able to see we can work together. . . . I think that's the role of a true ally."[30]

Two Bulls contrasted the alliance to many larger urban-based environmental groups: "In looking at, historically, these big green organizations coming into Indigenous communities and parachuting in, and just doing whatever their framework says they should do and then leaving, that's been the precedent for so long. Now you're looking at these alliances where these people are working together on a common ground, so they're actually showing and exhibiting true allyship, where they're coming in and meeting them at the same level, as opposed to coming in and saying this is how we're going to do it, you can be a part of it."[31]

Keystone XL Pipeline and CIA III

The resource wars in the Northern Plains escalated in the 2010s, as part of the continent-wide movement to block the shipping of bitumen oil from the tar sands of northern Alberta.[32] As British Columbia First Nations and their allies mobilized to stop oil pipelines from reaching West Coast ports, Indigenous nations joined environmentalists and white farmers and ranchers to stop other pipelines in the Great Plains and Great Lakes regions. Although the Barack Obama administration had permitted the southern leg of the Keystone XL pipeline to be built in the Southern Plains to the Gulf of Mexico, strong public pressure opposed the approval of the 1,179-mile northern leg from Alberta, through Montana, South Dakota, and Nebraska, first proposed in 2008.

For the Lakota, Nakota, and Dakota (Oceti Sakowin) and other Indigenous nations, the pipeline would imperil treaty lands, brush against reservation boundaries, harm sacred burial and ceremonial sites, bring in "man camps" of outside workers, and endanger the air and sacred waters. For the white ranchers and farmers, the pipeline would condemn private property under eminent domain laws, risk oil spills into creeks and rivers, harm the sensitive Sand Hills of northern Nebraska, and endanger the Ogallala Aquifer, an enormous but vulnerably shallow groundwater reservoir. The Native people and some of the ranchers were also motivated to curb climate change.

The two communities converged over protection of groundwater, but that did not mean they worked together closely, either internally or across the cultural divide. Dakota Rural Action director Paul Seamans, also a rancher and board member of the Western Organization of Resource Councils, recalled: "[Ranchers] had been working separately on Keystone XL, and the tribes were working really separately . . . [The] Pine Ridge tribe was working by themselves against the Keystone. The Rosebud tribe a few miles down the road was working separately, and the Yankton tribe was working separately."[33] Ponca tribal members also opposed the pipeline as desecrating the route of the 1877 Ponca Trail of Tears, on which they were forced to march from Nebraska to Oklahoma.[34]

Through President Obama's first term, the main task was for tribes to begin to work together against Keystone XL and for the farmers and ranchers not to be pitted against each other over routes proposed by the TransCanada pipeline company. In Nebraska, fourth- or fifth-generation landowners such as Randy Thompson led the fight using a property rights argument: "I've never seen any asterisk in the Constitution that says this property is only yours until a big corporation wants it."[35]

The farmers and ranchers coalesced around the group Bold Nebraska, led by Jane Kleeb, whose husband's family had homesteaded in the Sand Hills. As Kleeb recalls: "I knew how tough they were, how much they protected their land, and how much it meant to them in a soulful way. If you don't know ranchers or farmers, you don't immediately get how connected to the land they are—even more so than the environmentalists."[36]

Yet Kleeb also noted that Thompson and other landowners' resistance was not based solely on self-interest: "We did a whole campaign called 'Stand with Randy' when we first started organizing on the pipeline. TransCanada pretty quickly went around him, because they thought that would then shut him up. They've done that to about ten of our very vocal ranchers, but it obviously doesn't shut them up, it just makes them quite stronger."[37]

On the tribal side, Indigenous community organizers were moved by how the tar sands have been affecting First Nations in Alberta and furious that the U.S. and Canadian governments had not consulted with their sovereign tribal nations as mandated. They deemed the Keystone XL pipeline a "black snake," which prophecies had warned their people about.[38] Most Lakota bands strongly opposed the pipeline and launched the Shielding the People project to organize tribal communities along the route, but not all bands participated. Intertribal solidarity began to be realized in September 2011, when Indigenous governments, treaty councils, and Alberta First Nations chiefs joined to sign the Mother Earth Accord to Oppose Keystone XL, "affirming our responsibility to protect and preserve for our descendants, the inherent sovereign rights of our Indigenous nations, the rights of property owners, and all inherent human rights."[39]

Seamans recalled that an old high school friend, Rosebud Lakota renewable energy activist Patrick Spears, invited him and a few other ranchers to participate in the accord meeting in Mission, because Spears was a "let's-get-

along type guy" and "was always working to get people to work together."
For the first time, the tribes were formally welcoming white ranchers to join
with them in the opposition to Keystone XL, even as the Lakota were emphasizing the 1868 treaty. Seamans asserted:

> [The Lakota] feel the government should step up and do what's right by
> them on the 1868 treaty. . . . They're not after the deeded land. They would
> like the government to recognize that they've been screwed and . . . to have
> the federal and state lands back. . . . I don't think there's really any feeling
> of real tension between us at these meetings, because of their talk of that
> treaty. I'd say, maybe five years ago, I would've felt threatened by that, but
> I think after being around them and listening to their point of view, I get to
> thinking, "Hey, if I was Indian, I would be doing the exact same damn thing
> that they're doing."[40]

On the reservations, Native youths joined the Moccasins on the Ground
campaign to train for nonviolent direct action, and some tribal members took
part in blockading construction trucks on the Pine Ridge Reservation in 2012.[41]
The direct action training camps were organized by Debra White Plume, a
veteran of other tribal sustainability alliances, with the Owe Aku / Bring Back
the Way International Justice Project. Greg Grey Cloud, of the Rosebud Sioux
Tribe, said of the spiritual camps: "[They] will band all Lakota to live together
and you can't cross a living area if it's occupied."[42] Ihanktonwan (Yankton)
Nakota/Dakota elder Faith Spotted Eagle observed that the spiritual camps
are "not just publicity stunts": "They're actually talking to Mother Earth. . . .
In Western science you call it metaphysical, and in our world it's actually in-
voking that connection with Mother Earth. I believe that when that happens,
miracles happen. It puts people in touch with Creation. With the Facebooking
and everything else, you lose touch with the outdoors."[43]

The key turning point in the alliance occurred in January 2013, when Indigenous nations and their allies held the "Gathering to Protect the Sacred
from the Tar Sands and Keystone XL" at the Yankton Sioux Reservation in
South Dakota. The gathering was held to commemorate the signing of an 1863
peace treaty between the Pawnee and Ihanktonwan (Yankton) Nakota/Dakota
nations, to stand together against the United States and white settlers. The
gathering was an organized effort of the Yankton Sioux Tribe, through the
Ihanktonwan Oyate Treaty Steering Committee and the grandmothers of
the Brave Heart Women's Society, in collaboration with the Pawnee Nation.

The gathering helped to build bridges between First Nations, tribes, farmers and ranchers, businesspeople, and environmentalists fighting Keystone XL on both sides of the United States–Canada border.

The gathering culminated in the International Treaty to Protect the Sacred, signed first by the sovereign nations—six First Nations and four U.S. tribal governments—and then by agricultural and environmental allies. Ihankton-wan Nakota/Dakota chief Phil Lane Jr. said, "We have achieved this not only with our indigenous relatives who have joined us here, but also with our relatives, the ranchers and farmers who treasure Mother Earth as we do."[44]

In recalling that she invited Jane Kleeb "to come up and bring the ranchers," Spotted Eagle said: "It was really a historical time, because they were very emotional and you could see the impact, and I think that broke through to the Native folks, because there's always been that historical trauma and fear. When it came to the land and water, it just became natural common ground. And it's been a real powerful friendship that developed out of there. I think it's an important crossroads in history."[45] At Spotted Eagle's suggestion, the gathering participants began to use the name Cowboy Indian Alliance to describe the loose affiliation, although only some of the Lakota activists were aware of the earlier incarnations of the "CIA." Kleeb explained: "The name, I think, rocked people a little bit. . . . When we brought everyone together on this, we decided to revive it."[46] She said:

> [In South Dakota] none of us knew what to expect, because we hadn't done any organizing with tribal communities at that point. There were a lot of unknowns to us . . . and at first folks were kind of nervous. Within a couple of hours, we were in the same room together and sharing our stories. It was remarkable. I remember that moment one of the ranchers stood up and said, "I finally understand how you feel having your land taken away," and one of the tribal leaders stood up and said, "Welcome to the tribe." There was honor, and there was this amazing connection. Everyone went, "You know what? We're all in this together in the fight."[47]

Chief Phil Lane Jr. recalled the pivotal moment in more detail:

> Those ranchers came in and spoke to that council, and they shared their heart. . . . So finally we came back after the treaty signing . . . we had about ten or fifteen ranchers there, they all got up to speak . . . and one after another they got up and said they're infuriated. They said . . . "How could this

happen? How can people take our land? . . . How can they do this to us?"
And of course . . . we didn't see a smile, but everybody knew what we was
thinking about from our side. . . . So finally, this last sister got up to speak,
and she just said, "I just am so infuriated, they're coming and taking our
land . . . they just can do it without our consent. . . . This is our land that our
families have lived in since . . . you know, how long they have been there."
And said, "They're treating us just like . . . just like . . . ," and then one of the
relatives said, "Just like the Indians." And all of the sudden there was this
beautiful pause and everybody's like, "Yes!" And one of my relatives walked
over to her and says, "Welcome to the tribe, *welcome* to the tribe."[48]

Nebraska rancher Tom Genung, whose ranch lies two miles from the pipeline route, remembered the treaty signing as the first time he had been invited
to a reservation: "Not to mean any disrespect, but it was sort of a novelty when
I was a kid. . . . But on the cowboy end of things, to be invited, that was exciting." He added: "It was kind of spiritual. . . . The original treaty was with some
tribal folks that were opposed to each other—warring. They realized they had
to get together and stand together to deal with the United States better than
what they were used to. And the reason they were doing that was because they
wanted to protect the land for the next seven generations. . . . That was 150
years ago, so in a way we renewed that treaty for the next seven generations. . . . We're going to do this for the future, and the past."[49]

The alliance deepened through a series of spiritual camps, including the
Ponca Trail of Tears Spiritual Camp held in November 2013 on the northeastern
Nebraska farm of Art and Helen Tanderup, on the route to Oklahoma of both
the Ponca Trail and the Keystone XL pipeline. The participants jointly laid flowers at the gravesite of an eighteen-month-old girl who had died on the Ponca
Trail of Tears in Neligh, where the townspeople had for 136 years honored her
father's request to tend to her grave.[50] Ponca tribal members later planted sacred corn in the path of Keystone XL at Neligh, in their original homeland.[51]
The Ponca and Pawnee had been working with Nebraska gardeners for several
years to plant in their original homeland their rare heirloom native corn, which
could not grow on their post-removal lands in Oklahoma.[52]

Ponca grandfather Mekasi Horinek commented: "Living on the rez', it's
usually us against them. You kind of grow up with that mentality. . . . The
pipeline is dividing the land, but it's bringing people together."[53] Ponca, Lakota, Omaha, and white participants brought their families, gathered around
a sacred fire, shared meals, and told stories that created deeper bonds than

meetings about technical or legal aspects of the pipeline did. Kleeb noted: "The mealtimes were great, because you would sit around the fire and eat the food that was being made all day. It's when everyone would take a deep breath and do business with each other."[54]

The social aspects of the alliance created new friends but also built on earlier social ties between Native and non-Native communities.[55] Spotted Eagle remembered: "I grew up in my father's era and he was friends with some of the farmers, and whenever he'd go to their houses they'd have these barn gatherings. They'd call it Tiger Meat, and they'd have these different types of food. It felt like their whole activity was created around food. And it's the very same thing with our Native people. Food brings the cultures together."[56]

Recalling his high school friendship with Spears, Seamans remembered that in the 1960s and into the 1970s, Lakota families "still lived in the small towns": "I think about every small town had Indian families living in them. . . . I had two Indian families that were classmates, and very good friends. . . . When [the federal government] start[ed] building housing, they start[ed] building it on reservations. A lot of these Indian families moved out of these small towns, onto the reservation [and into the cities]." Without social interaction with Native families, he said, "I think I've kind of become a touch racist myself. . . . Now, since I'm back reconnecting with Indian people, I think I've lost that sense of racism. . . . These alliances have been real good for me, personally. . . . maybe people are just getting more tolerant."[57]

The recurring irony in the alliance, of course, is that the ranchers have been fighting against the corporate theft of their "private property" that their pioneer forebears had themselves stolen from Native people. Nebraska landowner Randy Thompson opposed TransCanada's confiscation of his property because the company "didn't earn" the land: "They didn't carry heavy milk buckets and walk through the snow and the slop like my Mom did."[58] Using the same criteria of hardship and survival on the land, the tribal members should still retain their previous ownership of the same grassy hills that the settlers later homesteaded. By failing to protect private property from confiscation, the settler state broke the "social trust" of the settlers themselves.[59]

Ponca elder Casey Camp-Horinek agreed that the ranchers "are suffering under things like eminent domain" and that "they, too, have had their lifestyles impinged upon by these major corporations." But she said that in the early CIA meeting with the ranchers: "We pulled no punches with them, about how the land that they live on now became land that they could buy and sell. It was our blood." She insisted: "It's part of their history as well as ours. And it has to be brought out and spoken of, or else there isn't an alliance." Camp-Horinek holds out hope: "The people that we are aligning ourselves with, I really believe they're going to help us uphold those treaty rights."[60]

Kleeb asserted:

Even with the property rights, from farmers' and ranchers' perspective, it's because they don't want the government and the corporations overdeveloping that land for corporate gain. What the farmers and ranchers believe is what they [are] doing is feeding people, and they feel a deep responsibility to that land because their ancestors had homesteaded on it. It is a difficult thing to grapple with, as you start to understand on an emotional level the history of that place. The pictures that we have in our living rooms of our homesteaders' families, that did take tribes' land away, it is difficult to grapple with. All of us see that as the reality, but now we have a responsibility to keep passing that land down to future generations.[61]

Kleeb concluded: "The tribes and the farmers and ranchers all share this very spiritual connection to the land we live on. . . . Working together, we've been getting past this horrible thing that happened between the families that were homesteading on the land and the tribes. We've been coming together to protect the land. It's been a chance for healing."[62] Faith Spotted Eagle agreed: "We come from two cultures that clashed over land, and so this is a healing for the generations."[63]

Spotted Eagle remembered: "Back in the day when I was not so open-minded, I was in Kansas one time with a friend at this farmer's place, and they were just plowing up the Earth. You know how it smells when you first plow the grass? And that old man was standing there, and he was looking out in the field, and he said, 'Y'know, when I smell that smell, I know Creator is here.' And I looked at him and thought, 'I never thought of that.' Whenever I saw farmers plowing the ground it would make me angry because they were ruining the ground." She continued: "I think if we cut through the property rights and the government restrictions, the money, at that quiet moment at the end of the day before the sun goes down, we're all the same. . . . I think it's a geographical thing, because we know when the sun rises and when it goes down, and how cold the winters are, and how to talk to the land. You have to come from the same region."[64]

When Spotted Eagle worked on a cultural survey on the North Dakota farm of Jim Hegland, to prevent wind turbines from destroying tribal sacred sites, she told him: "This is your land now, but you have to promise that you'll protect it." And he said, "I promise." As she recounted:

> And then we get a call from Mr. Hegland the next summer. He said, "I just wanted to tell you that I took you up on your words, and I am going to protect the land for the generations. . . . I got a permanent conservation easement in perpetuity," and he said, "Nobody's going to be able to break up this land . . . my children have agreed." And I thought, "Wow, if we had not crossed paths that would never have happened." In essence, they've been taking care of the sacred sites after the land was taken from us, and most of the farmers and ranchers will know where those sites are when we go onto the land.[65]

Spotted Eagle recognized that a gap in understanding existed within the alliance, and although the corporations may be treating white ranchers as Native people were treated, the ranchers have not experienced the genocide and historical trauma that has been inflicted on Indigenous peoples. She remembered developing literature for the CIA: "I was asked to draft something, and just out of my way of thinking I put down 'treaty lands,' and when I got the draft back they had crossed it out, and when I redrafted it I put it back in, and then they sent it back to me and they crossed it off, so then I put it back in. So it's a process, but I'm kind of persistent about it."[66] She acknowledged: "At some point we have to backtrack and unpack our bags, and begin to figure out what happened between us as neighbors. [Native people] sometimes feel like we have a monopoly on this trauma, because we've lost so much land, because we've had a holocaust happen to us. . . . Seeing [white landowners] cry about the loss of their land has softened our hearts. And that made a difference. . . . Ranchers and landowners like Tom [Genung], they *get it* in a way that politicians don't."[67]

The need for the people of the land to explain their situation to the politicians led the Cowboy Indian Alliance to call a five-day gathering in Washington, D.C., in April 2014. The CIA III faced its greatest test and success in holding the "Reject and Protect" gathering, ostensibly to pressure the Obama administration to reject Keystone XL, but in the process showing the country and the world the moral and historic power of Native/non-Native alliances. The nation's capital had never seen anything like it: "cowboys" and "Indians" together erecting a tipi encampment on the National Mall between the Capitol and the White House, riding on horseback in their regalia down Pennsylvania Avenue,

The 2014 "Reject and Protect" march against the Keystone XL oil pipeline, led by the Cowboy Indian Alliance in Washington, D.C. (Courtesy: Bold Nebraska)

and conducting a water ceremony and prayers to protect the land. Ojibwe environmental leader Winona LaDuke later told me that "a protest in the streets of Washington, D.C., with the traffic, photographers, and shouting, is not the optimum place for a horseback ride." But the image of the horseback protest, even more than the anti–big oil message, attracted unprecedented news coverage and commentary. In an image-driven media market, the photos spoke for themselves.

The alliance leaders followed Indigenous protocol to gather before Piscataway chief Billy Red Wing Tayac, whose tribe originally owned the District of Columbia, to formally ask permission to enter tribal territory. Nebraska rancher Bob Allpress, whose land would be transected by the pipeline, presented a blue-jean blanket as an offering to Chief Tayac, who replied, "We welcome you, and we welcome all cowboys in the fight against the pipeline." Allpress came from a ranching family that homesteaded south of the Keya Paha River in 1882, four years before Lakota families were relocated north of the river under a treaty provision. His family maintained good relations with the Lakota, and his great-uncle and grandfather both spoke Lakota. Allpress joked at the protest: "I'm a redneck Republican. . . . Standing there in cowboy boots and a hat next to people in peace necklaces and hemp shirts . . . it's been— an experience. A good experience. We've enjoyed the hell out of it."[68] Jane Kleeb recalled, shortly after the march: "I got an email for the first time from the White House saying, 'OK, you've got our attention.' They literally said that."[69]

"Reject and Protect" was not the typical environmental protest, as high-lighted by freelance journalist Kristin Moe: "The environmental movement has long come under criticism for being led by the so-called Big Greens—largely white, middle class membership groups whose interests don't often represent those actually living in the frontline communities where the pipeline will be built. But the coalition of cowboys and Indians offers a radical depar-ture from this history. Moreover, it is a model of relationship-based organizing, rooted in a kind of spirituality often absent from the progressive world, and—given the role of indigenous leaders—begins to address the violence of colo-nization in a meaningful way."[70]

Ojibwe journalist Mary Annette Pember recognized that the new alliance went beyond the pipeline: "More than a classic Sociology 101 class experiment that draws disparate groups together by introducing a common enemy, the CIA . . . represents a consciousness shift among non-Natives. In the traditional Native worldview, the land, water and wildlife are also members of the com-munity. We care for these relatives as we would care for other members of our families. As they have learned about this continuity of Native culture and environmental responsibility, the non-Native participants are embracing this philosophy, grateful that someone has finally given them permission to ex-press it."[71]

Nebraska rancher Ben Gottschall commented on the Reject and Protect movement's website: "Historically, cowboys and Indians have been at odds, but no more. The CIA shows our cooperation and working together in mutual respect. That shared bond proves that we pipeline fighters are not just a few angry landowners holding out or environmentalists pushing a narrow agenda. We are people from all walks of life and include the people who have been here the longest and know the land best. Sadly, they know what it's like to lose their land, to lose the ground that gives a nation its identity. . . . Together this time, we cannot lose."[72]

Beaver Lake Cree activist Crystal Lameman, from the tar-sands region, noted after a U.S. rancher spoke: "Coming from Alberta . . . to have that rancher step forward and acknowledge the treaty obligations of the beneficiaries of his treaty and remind the farmers and the ranchers that it's their treaty, too, it was beautiful."[73] Citing Idle No More and the Cowboy Indian Alliance, Mani-toba Cree climate justice activist Clayton Thomas-Muller noted that if they continue to integrate environmental and social justice work, "our coalitions that have risen up in response to climate justice will continue to grow in power rather than becoming fractured."[74] He observed that the alliance "represents an important step towards reconciling America's bloody colonial history."[75]

After the Cowboy Indian Alliance returned home, it continued to face challenges. When TransCanada enlisted the support of the Lower Brule Band's government for a pipeline-linked transmission line, in exchange for financial assistance, tribal members started a spiritual camp to oppose the move.[76] As Spotted Eagle had said: "For those of us who have the history, it smacks of repetitive economics, when they put us in forts and they wanted our land. . . . All we're willing to do here is sell our soul, just for the economy. That's the dark side."[77] She explained at a Rapid City gathering: "All this is based on capitalism. The model of capitalism is trying to suffocate us, because with capitalism you need an underclass. Capitalism cannot survive without poor farmers, without poor Indians, without poor people in the cities who are selling their souls. That's what we're combating. . . . We didn't learn it in our communities."[78]

Later in 2014, the alliance held a buffalo roast with the Rosebud Sioux Spirit Camp. Lakota again feasted, spoke from their hearts, and circled up in a round dance.[79] Paul Seamans commented: "An alliance might seem unlikely, but it's not really. We have a lot of the same interests. Historically, it may have been so, but things are changing, especially with the advent of social media, which has made it a lot easier to keep in contact. A lot of us have given more consideration to their Native American treaty rights and see things more from their perspective now." He concluded: "I really think it'll be a lasting relationship, because even if the Keystone XL problem is resolved to our liking or whether it's not, we still have lots of other issues that we have a common interest in. . . . I think these alliances that we've formed now, I expect them to remain."[80]

In November 2015, President Obama rejected the construction of the northern leg of the Keystone XL pipeline, killing the "black snake" for the time being. The successful grassroots pressure on Obama was hailed as a historic victory for the U.S. climate justice movement.[81] Kleeb stated, "Our unlikely alliance showed America that hard work and scientific facts can beat Big Oil's threat to our land and water."[82] Spotted Eagle concluded, "We stood united in this struggle, Democrat, Republican, Native, Cowboy, Rancher, landowners, urban warriors, grandmas and grandpas, children, and through this fight against KXL we have come to see each other in a new better, stronger way."[83] Spotted Eagle received an electoral vote for president in December 2016 (from Robert Satiacum Jr. of the Puyallup Tribe). The electoral victor, Donald Trump, sought to resurrect KXL, and faced renewed resistance.

Dakota Access Pipeline and Standing Rock

The Bakken oil shale formation is located around the western North Dakota boomtown of Williston. The process of "fracking" (or the hydraulic fracturing of bedrock with water and chemicals) made the state number two in U.S. oil production, after Texas.[84] Fracking has been an environmental concern, lowering water tables and contaminating water with chemicals, gases, and oil spills, yet the process is exempt from the Safe Drinking Water Act.[85]

The oil boom has also been a social scourge, with housing shortages, rising crime, prostitution and sexual assaults around "man camps," and endless traffic of chemical and water trucks. Because the companies care only about profitable oil, the natural gas is flared off, causing the entire Bakken Basin to glow so intensely at night that it is visible from Earth orbit.

Although the Fort Berthold tribal government in North Dakota has supported the fracking for economic development, some Mandan, Hidatsa, and Arikara tribal members have been displaced, and others fear an increase in cancer rates, which have already been climbing from previous oil and coal development.[86] Tribal member Kandi Mossett, of the Indigenous Environmental Network, has been outspoken against the expansion of the fossil fuel industry.[87] Mossett testified: "Several community members, including myself, are tired of being sick and are tired of seeing everyone, even babies, dying from unprecedented rates of cancer. We are taking a stand and fighting back, not only for our own lives but for the lives of those who cannot speak for themselves, and we will not stop fighting until we have a reached a true level of environmental and climate justice in our Indigenous lands."[88]

In 2016, Energy Transfer Partners began to construct the Dakota Access Pipeline from the Bakken oil shale basin, to carry 450,000 barrels of crude oil a day through North and South Dakota, Iowa, and Illinois. The route originally was proposed to cross under the Missouri River near the state capital of Bismarck, but the company rejected the northern route because it "could jeopardize the drinking water of the residents in the city of Bismarck."[89] In a classic case of a racialized "shell game" at work, the route was diverted southward to cross the Missouri just north of its confluence with the Cannonball River, the northern boundary of the Standing Rock Sioux Reservation and the main source of reservation drinking water.[90]

The Oceti Sakowin (Seven Council Fires of the Lakota, Dakota, and Nakota nations) objected to the 1,172-mile-long "black snake" and the disproportionate risk it posed to tribes and their sacred sites.[91] The Cannonball River was named after the large, round sacred stones formed at the confluence before dams created the Lake Oahe reservoir, and numerous other cultural sites were located in the 150-foot-wide pipeline right-of-way. Standing Rock organizer LaDonna Bravebull Allard noted: "The place where [the] pipeline will cross on the Cannonball is the place where the Mandan came into the world after the great flood, [and] it is also a place where the Mandan had their Okipa, or Sundance.... This is also where the sacred medicine rock [is located], which tells the future."[92]

In April 2016, Allard and other tribal members set up the Camp of the Sacred Stones in the path of the $3.8 billion pipeline, as a center of prayer and action, asking "everyone who lives on or near the Missouri River and its tributaries, everyone who farms or ranches in the local area, and everyone who cares about clean air and clean drinking water [to] stand with us."[93] The Standing Rock Sioux and other tribes unsuccessfully attempted to have meaningful consultation with the Army Corps of Engineers about their concerns, backed by Dakota Rural Action, Bold Iowa, and other regional groups.[94] A Native youth relay run also delivered 140,000 signatures against the pipeline to the White House.[95] By July, the Army Corps began to issue permits for the pipeline to cross under the Missouri, despite its federal trust responsibility to consult with tribes over federal laws protecting the environment and grave sites, within lands covered by the 1851 and 1868 treaties.

A few landowners began to cooperate with Standing Rock. For example, on September 2, the tribe announced that a non-Native landowner had allowed a tribal cultural survey on Cannonball Ranch in the pipeline corridor north of the reservation, violating his easement agreement with the company. The tribe documented at least twenty-seven burials, sixteen stone rings, nineteen effigies, and other features.[96] A former tribal historic preservation officer described a stone representation of a constellation as "one of the most significant archaeological finds in North Dakota in many years."[97] The following day, the company took its bulldozers to level the same burial site, and its private security contractors unleashed attack dogs and pepper spray on two hundred unarmed Native activists, injuring six (including a pregnant woman and a six-year-old girl).[98] The landowner unexpectedly sold the ranch to the company, perhaps because he faced huge fines for allowing the survey.[99]

In the face of this harsh repression and steadfast resistance, the camp quickly mushroomed in size, support arrived from around the continent and the world, and "water protectors" began to lock themselves to equipment to halt construction.[100] Crowds of ten thousand and more gathered at times in the Standing Rock camp (expanded to include the Oceti Sakowin and Red Warrior camps), and more than three hundred tribal flags lined the entry to

Pacific Northwest canoes arrive at North Dakota's Cannonball River, in a display of solidarity with the Standing Rock Sioux Tribe's fight against the Dakota Access Pipeline, on September 8, 2016. (Photo by the author)

the main camp in an "embassy row." When I visited on September 5–8, a flotilla of Pacific Northwest canoes paddled in solidarity down the Missouri from Bismarck.[101] The camp felt like a liberated zone, a free community of thousands that fed itself, danced and sang together, and celebrated every time a new tribe arrived. It reminded me of the 1980 Black Hills International Survival Gathering and included veterans of earlier alliances.

The Standing Rock standoff generated perhaps the greatest public and media interest in Native resistance since the 1973 Wounded Knee siege and showcased an unprecedented degree of intertribal unity, even including tribes (such as Fort Berthold) with their own fossil fuel development. The camp also became a place of intratribal convergence, with tribal government leaders, traditional chiefs, and Indigenous activists sharing a common goal, even if they did not always agree on strategies and tactics. The tribal organizers were also very open to cooperation with local ranchers and farmers and were supported by Keystone XL opponents from South Dakota and Nebraska. Farmers in Iowa had strongly opposed Dakota Access, resulting in many protests and dozens of arrests, and they had plenty of reasons for their opposition.[102]

Indigenous Environmental Network organizer and Cheyenne River tribal member Joye Braun stated: "When this proposed pipeline breaks, as the vast majority of pipelines do, over half of the drinking water in South Dakota will be affected. How can rubber-stamping this project be good for the people, agriculture, and livestock? It must be stopped . . . with our allies, both native and non-native."[103] Standing Rock descendant Waniya Locke noted: "The Missouri River gives drinking water to 10 million people. We are protecting everyone. We are standing for everyone. . . . They are violating not only my people of Standing Rock, but they are violating ranchers and farmers and everybody else who lives along this river."[104]

According to Braun, Linton-area landowners had visited the camp, and other landowners were "pretty upset about what's going on."[105] One Emmons County landowner said: "The first thing I thought about when I heard about the Bakken pipeline was that beautiful black soil that my grandmother taught me to love. . . . She'd always point it out to me when she'd see that beautiful topsoil . . . the best soil there is. . . . It hurts me to see it trenched and piled up and eroded the way it has been."[106]

But in contrast to the Keystone XL fight, North Dakota farmers and ranchers were only rarely visible in the pipeline fight. Most local landowners gave in to the "eminent domain" confiscation of their property for the pipeline, even if they mistrusted the companies' promises of safety, while others promoted the construction jobs or sowed fear of the Native "protesters" on the roads.

Three factors may explain the relative lack of visible rural white participation in North Dakota to stop the pipeline. First, the oil fracking industry has become so powerful in the state that fatalistic private landowners assume that they would lose any legal battle against eminent domain. Braun explained: "There is support from non-Native landowners, not as overtly as in Nebraska or even South Dakota, because of the political atmosphere here in North Dakota, because oil is such a big deal. . . . There has been contact; it's very difficult for them to come out. Sometimes we'll be at a rally in Bismarck, and some of the local people will come to give out cupcakes, but they don't want their name known or anything. That's a hard sell."[107]

The second, related factor is that the Dakota Access permitting and construction has been "fast-tracked," in contrast to the drawn-out, multiyear process around permitting the Keystone XL. The pipeline company perhaps realized that delays could allow rural Native/non-Native relationships to develop and solidify into a strong alliance. Braun stated that as soon as landowners "start seeing the raping of the land, the bulldozing, and they start seeing how big [the

company's] so-called small tract of land is, then they start to get really worried."[108]
The company appeared almost obsessed with constructing the pipeline seg-
ments as facts on the ground that would be difficult to reverse. A dozen irate
landowning families sued the company for fraudulently pressuring them to
quickly sign away an easement for a low price.[109]

The third factor was that state government and media accounts of the
controversy tended to demonize and even criminalize the water protectors.
After a Lakota spiritual leader was heard urging others to "load your pipes"—
meaning the chanupa wakan (sacred pipe)—Morton County sheriff Kyle Kirchmeier announced at a press conference that the activists had "pipe bombs."
Indigenous Environmental Network organizer Dallas Goldtooth replied,
"These are dangerous statements by Sheriff Kirchmeier and only foster greater
resentment between local native and non-native residents."[110] After Governor
Jack Dalrymple declared a "state of emergency," one rancher told a reporter
that he "had confrontations with protesters."[111]

The New York Times reported that sheriff's officers were escorting the local
school bus and that "ranchers and residents in the conservative, overwhelmingly white countryside view the protests with a mix of frustration and fear,
reflecting the deep cultural divides and racial attitudes in Indian country."[112]
A state patrol roadblock on State Highway 1806 initially prevented access to
the camp and reservation to all but local residents. It was later transformed
into a National Guard "traffic information point," still criticized by water protectors as a "blockade."[113] The concrete, war zone–style checkpoint made it
more difficult for Native supporters to reach the camp but also had the (perhaps calculated) side effect of discouraging white North Dakotans from joining or even seeing the camp, and causing them to blame the camp for long
detours.

Although the Army Corps at first met tribal demands to allow an EIS on
the river crossing, the Trump administration forcibly evicted the camp and
completed the pipeline. Whatever the outcome, the historic stand at Standing
Rock has created ripple effects throughout Indian Country and has deeply
affected Native/non-Native relations in North Dakota.[114]

The oil fracking industry proposed other eastbound pipelines in the Northern Plains, such as Enbridge's Sandpiper pipeline through Minnesota, where
it met strong opposition from tribal and non-tribal landholders in 2013–16.[115]
But the industry's main westbound shipping strategy switched from pipelines
to trains, and the arena of struggle over fossil fuel shipping shifted toward the
Pacific Northwest.[116]

FOSSIL FUEL WARS IN THE PACIFIC NORTHWEST

In the 2010s, the Pacific Northwest has become the leading region of the United States in curbing carbon emissions and in raising public consciousness about climate change. But its efforts to mitigate greenhouse gases or switch to renewable energies will become moot if the fossil fuel industry continues to expand in the Alberta tar sands, the Powder River coal basin, and the Bakken oil shale basin. All three of these sources need outlets via ports in Washington and Oregon, so both states (along with California and British Columbia) are functioning as a chokepoint for the fossil fuel industry, a "thin green line" between North American fossil fuel basins and the growing Asian market.[117]

Tar-Sands Oil Pipelines

The first major source of fossil fuel shipments to the Pacific Northwest is via an oil pipeline from the Alberta tar sands. Bitumen oil is pumped from northern Alberta through the Kinder Morgan Trans Mountain pipeline to Burnaby, near Vancouver, British Columbia, to the Ferndale refinery on former Lummi Reservation land, and to Anacortes refineries on former Swinomish Reservation land—both lands taken by White House executive orders in the 1870s. The pipeline has ruptured at times, affecting First Nations along the route, but in 2012 the company proposed a second, parallel pipeline along the existing route. The proposed second pipeline would vastly increase oil tanker traffic in the narrow interisland straits of the Salish Sea. To guard their prime salmon and crab fishery (and orca whale habitat), several First Nations in British Columbia and Washington tribal governments joined in 2014 to intervene against the second pipeline.[118]

Also in 2014, the Nawtsamaat Alliance brought First Nations and tribes together with environmental groups, interfaith communities, and frontline residents "who love the land and waters of the Salish Sea and call it home" and want to protect it from oil and coal shipments. Together they signed the International Treaty to Protect the Sacredness of the Salish Sea to declare the Kinder Morgan pipeline illegal under Coast Salish laws.[119] The treaty was modeled on the Great Plains cross-border treaty against the Keystone XL pipeline. The Nawtsamaat Alliance is "an empowered coalition . . . to heighten awareness of the increased risks and threats to our beautiful region by a fossil fuel industry that continues to exploit and destroy it." The alliance "mobilizes international, cross-cultural, and co-creative joint action to block fossil fuel projects."[120]

Edmonds climate justice activist Carlo Voli explained: "Nawt-sa-maat means 'one heart, one house, one prayer.' It's an alliance . . . to show unprecedented unified opposition to a lot of these fossil fuel threats."[121] Chief Phil Lane Jr., who lives in British Columbia, commented: "I was here during the fishing wars, so I know how deeply felt this conflict was between all concerned. . . . What we're faced with is a loss of fish for everybody. We're at loss [from] the pollution of not only the waters of which farmers depend and ranchers depend, or fish supplies that fishermen depend on . . . the fact [is] that all of this is being threatened. . . . Fifty percent of nothing is 50 percent of nothing. This is what I believe the challenge is about, we need to have abundance back for our future generations."[122]

Oil companies also engaged in a "heavy haul" of gargantuan mining equipment, called "megaloads," *from* Pacific Northwest ports to the Alberta tar sands. Direct actions by Nez Perce Tribal Council members and other Idaho residents in 2013 forced the cancellation of a proposed heavy haul along winding river roads through Lolo Pass.[123] In 2013 and 2014, members of the Umatilla and Warm Springs tribes confronted the megaload off-loaded from Columbia River barges in eastern Oregon, joined by urban climate justice groups and some local non-Indian residents.[124] Native and non-Native Montanans joined blockades around Missoula.[125] The Port of Seattle was also the target of major May 2015 protests against the basing of Shell Oil's Arctic drilling fleet, with "kayaktivists" and tribal canoes together confronting a huge drilling rig.[126] After spending $7 billion, Shell ended up withdrawing from the Arctic in November 2015.[127] But the main sources of fossil fuel shipping to Pacific Northwest ports are from two lesser-known basins.

Coal Export Terminals

The second major source of fossil fuels is from the Powder River coal basin in Wyoming and Montana, which companies propose to ship by rail to Northwest ports and load onto ships for Asia. Environmentalists, farmers, ranchers, and tribes fear the coal dust from the long trains (up to a ton of dust from each of 150 railcars) would endanger waterways along the routes and the health of local people and livestock.[128] The proposed coal terminals also would pump huge amounts of groundwater to control the dust and vastly increase ship traffic in the Salish Sea, sparking opposition from the tribes and First Nations of the transborder Coast Salish Gathering.[129] The Columbia River Inter-Tribal Fish Commission (CRITFC) tribes raised objections to coal trains and barges along the Columbia River.[130]

Only one West Coast port, in Tsawwassen, British Columbia, currently has a coal-export terminal. In 2012–14, local alliances blocked four new coal terminals proposed in Aberdeen, Washington, and in Saint Helens, Coos Bay, and Boardman, Oregon. CRITFC tribes played a key role in the defeat of the Port of Morrow terminal on the Columbia at Boardman / Turkey Point.[131] The Gateway Pacific Terminal project at Cherry Point, near Bellingham, and the Millennium Bulk Terminal, near Longview on the Columbia River, were the two remaining proposals, both in Washington.[132] Although some labor unions supported the terminals for jobs, some rank-and-file members opposed them as helping to export jobs to China and for contributing to carbon pollution and climate change.

At least seventeen thousand people attended scoping hearings on coal terminal projects in the two states, and dozens of towns and cities passed resolutions against the plans, with local governments questioning the long trains' noise and tie-ups of auto traffic. About forty Northwest local and tribal elected officials together formed the Leadership Alliance Against Coal to oppose coal trains and coal exports.[133] It incorporated oil safety issues and grew into the Safe Energy Leadership Alliance, involving up to seventy elected officials by 2014.[134] The Affiliated Tribes of Northwest Indians strongly opposed both coal and oil transportation and exports through the region as an "infringement and endangerment upon indigenous, inherent, and treaty-protected resources, impacts on human health, economies, sacred places and our traditional way of life."[135]

Cherry Point would be the largest coal terminal on the West Coast and the largest new terminal proposed in the United States, exporting 48 million metric tons a year. But Cherry Point is the site of the 3,500-year-old Lummi village of Xwe'chi'eXen and its sacred burial ground, which the company damaged when it constructed a road and exploratory drill holes. The rail trestle would be built three hundred feet out into a historic reef-net salmon fishing area, where ancient anchors have been found. The area is rich in crab and has historically hosted one of the few herring spawning grounds in the Northwest.[136] As Lummi fisher and tribal council member Jeremiah "Jay" Julius said, "One accident inside the Salish Sea and my way of life is gone."[137] At the 2013 launching of the Safe Energy Leadership Alliance, Julius described Cherry Point as "our Mecca, our Jerusalem, the sacred ground of our people . . . the proposed project must not and will not go forward."[138] In response, the national anti-Indian network Citizens Equal Rights Alliance (CERA) held a meeting in Bellingham to oppose the use of treaties for environmental protection.[139]

Lummi Nation council members protest the proposed coal export terminal at Cherry Point, Washington, by burning a large check stamped "non-negotiable" in 2012. (Courtesy: AP Photo / Philip A. Dwyer, *Bellingham Herald*)

The Lummi viewed the coal plan as a violation of the 1855 Point Elliot Treaty, and elders urged the tribe to "warrior up!" to stop it.[140] In 2012, the Lummi Tribal Council symbolically burned a $1 million check, to make the statement that no amount of company money will convince them to back the project. From 2013 to 2016, Lummi carver Jewell James led several totem pole journeys between the Salish Sea and Montana's Northern Cheyenne Reservation, the Alberta tar sands, and the Dakota Access Pipeline, to heal the land, water, and people along the fossil fuel shipping routes.[141]

Standing at Cherry Point, James recalled how commercial fishermen's backlash to the 1974 Boldt Decision was particularly violent in the waters around Lummi: "From '75 to '78, right here, there were non-Indians up in the woods here, shooting at the tribal fishermen out here. Those were pretty ugly times. Non-Indian boats were ramming Indian boats, and non-Indian fishermen were taking and dropping heavy-chained cement blocks down on our tribal nets and sinking them to the bottom. It continued until people started hearing that the United States was going to start charging them with acts of piracy."[142] At the same time in the late 1970s, James recounted, Lummi helped defeat a plan for a dry-dock facility for oil-drilling platforms, which was also opposed by non-Indian fishermen. The Lummi also defeated a proposed commercial fish farm near Lummi Island in 1996, by convincing the Army Corps of Engineers that Lummi treaty rights would be violated.[143]

Through the co-management era, the Lummi Fisheries Department slowly built coalitions with commercial fishers and farmers, in response to declining water quantity and quality in the watershed. James remembered that in 2001, he had a "big major scream-out over treaty fishing rights" with fisheries director Randy Kinley. As James recalled: "[I yelled], 'It's time to get the non-Indians off the water, there's not enough fish.' And then [Kinley] said, 'Those are our friends.' I said, 'They're your friends, they're not my friends.' Ha, ha."[144] Lummi fisher Dana Wilson commented that after the "shake-up" of the Boldt era, non-Indian fishers began to back the tribe because, as he explained: "If we disappear, they're going to be gone too. We've proven that we can manage [the fishery] on par or even better than the state. They call us before they call the state."[145]

Bellingham resident Sandra Palm is indicative of the local commercial fishers who shifted in their stance toward the tribes in the post-Boldt era. She began commercial reef-net fishing in the early 1970s off Lummi Island, but then "the Boldt Decision came along." She said: "I wasn't able to access fish. . . . And I was one of the people who were pretty upset about that. But keeping an open mind, and wanting to learn more over time. . . . I have been fortunate to be exposed to the frustrations of both sides. And I've actually done a 180 in my perspective and become extremely supportive of treaty rights." Palm attended forums, studied the Cherry Point site, and began to work with Lummi against the coal terminal. She reported, "Now, when I visit my fishing friends, they'll say . . . 'We have to make these partnerships if we want to continue our fishing way.'"[146]

When the time came to close ranks over the coal terminal, the tribal and non-tribal fishers had even begun to overlap in their roles. Eleanor Kinley is a Lummi fisher who has served as vice president of the Whatcom Commercial Fishermen's Association. In 2011, she and association president Milan "Sipa" Slipcevic organized commercial fishers against the moorage fees charged by the Port of Bellingham, then the highest in the state. She recalled: "We formed an alliance between the tribal fishermen and the non-tribal fleet, and that scared the hell out of the Port of Bellingham. One of them said, 'You mean you're actually working with the Indians?' Then President Sipa was like, 'Yes, actually our vice president is a Lummi tribal member.' . . . And that scared them, and they were like, 'Okay, we can meet Seattle's rate.' And we got two dollars off a foot for our boats."[147]

The cooperation over the moorage fees made the alliance to stop the coal terminal that much easier to form. Even though the non-tribal fleet in the Cherry Point area was five times larger than the tribal fleet, the Lummi had to assist non-Indian fishers to have their voices heard. During a 2012 crab harvest opening, Slipcevic and Kinley organized tribal and non-tribal boats in a protest flotilla, in which the twenty fishing and crabbing vessels displayed signs such as "Our Goal: No Coal."[148]

In 2013, polls began to show that a majority of Washington and Oregon voters opposed the coal export terminal plans.[149] Lummi chairman Tim Ballew II invoked treaty rights in a plea to the Army Corps of Engineers to reject the Cherry Point plan.[150] Montana's pro-coal ex-governor admitted, "Unless that local resistance changes, coal is not going to be shipped at Cherry Point."[151] In 2014, Goldman Sachs sold off its share in the Cherry Point project.[152] In 2015, Lummi and Northern Cheyenne joined seven Washington tribes to take a stand against the Cherry Point plan.[153] Lummi youth also joined a Native canoe flotilla in Paris, to call attention to Indigenous demands during the United Nations climate talks.[154]

Beth Brownfield, a member of the Bellingham Universalist Fellowship, asserted: "[The Lummi] are protecting their own culture and their children's children, but they are also protecting everyone else. In our political system, you have no voice, it's write a letter or go to a meeting, you are like a drop of water. But with their treaty and their sovereignty and their history, people are looking at that and saying, that will make a difference."[155]

Finally in May 2016, the Army Corps of Engineers rejected the Cherry Point permit, due solely to the coal terminal's impacts on Lummi treaty rights.[156] The Whatcom County Board later placed a moratorium on new or expanded facilities that would lead to increased shipment of unrefined fossil fuels.[157] (Arch Coal dropped its stake in the Longview coal terminal shortly afterward and the state denied a key permit in January 2017.)[158] Swinomish chair Brian Cladoosby, also president of the National Congress of American Indians, commented on the Army Corps' decision: "Today was a victory not only for tribes but for everyone in the Salish Sea. I hope we are reversing a 100-year trend of a pollution-based economy, one victory at a time."[159] Lummi chairman Ballew, describing the victory as "a celebration of treaty rights," stated, "But it's also a celebration of the power of treaty rights to protect all of us, to preserve our lands and waters for everyone who calls this place home."[160]

Bakken Oil Terminals

The third major fossil fuel basin, the Bakken oil shale formation, is the source of skyrocketing numbers of crude oil trains that traverse the continent, including the Pacific Northwest. Bakken crude is more gaseous and volatile than other oil, so when the oil trains derail they erupt in huge explosions, like the Quebec fireball that killed forty-seven people in 2013. There were more oil train spills that year than in the thirty-seven years prior.[161]

In 2008, Washington and Oregon refineries began to receive rail shipments of fracked crude oil from North Dakota, at first to ship not overseas (due to a 1975–2016 crude oil export ban) but to West Coast refineries.[162] From 2008 to 2013, the number of oil railcars coming to Northwest facilities increased more than 4,000 percent, and the industry proposed more port terminals.[163] According to the Sightline Institute, if all Northwest oil, coal, and gas projects proceeded, they would cumulatively ship the carbon equivalent of five Keystone XL pipelines.[164]

A Tesoro oil terminal planned for Vancouver, Washington (across the Columbia River from Portland), met strong opposition, including from the Longshore Union and the CRITFC tribes along the Columbia River.[165] Yakama and Umatilla asked that the environmental impact review include treaty rights.[166] Their opposition intensified in June 2016, after a derailed oil train burned in the Columbia Gorge.[167] The Nisqually Tribe also objected to oil and coal trains along its Nisqually River and estuary, and tribal members such as Grace Ann Byrd spoke out at public hearings.[168]

Up to fifty oil trains a month, each 1.5 miles long, would supply up to three proposed Grays Harbor oil terminals in Hoquiam, where Bakken oil would be loaded into enormous tankers, next to key migrating bird habitat.[169] The Quinault Indian Nation and Grays Harbor residents became concerned about the effects of an oil tanker spill on local fisheries and shellfish beds.[170] Quinault treaty territory extends into Grays Harbor, and the coastal reservation is famed for its pristine beaches, razor clams, and blueback sockeye salmon.[171]

Collaboration between the Quinault Nation and Grays Harbor environmental groups had extended back to 2008, when Joe Schumacker, marine resources scientist for the Quinault Department of Fisheries, was the tribal liaison on the Grays Harbor Marine Resource Committee. He kept contact with the Friends of Grays Harbor and Grays Harbor Audubon, as well as the Citizens for a Clean Harbor, which defeated a proposed coal terminal in 2012, only to face three proposed oil terminals later the same year.[172] A consolidated appeal by the Quinault Indian Nation, Sierra Club's Earthjustice, and local environmental groups convinced the state Shoreline Hearings Board in 2013 to revoke Washington Department of Ecology permits for two of the oil terminals, pending a state environmental impact statement.[173]

Nearly unanimous public opposition began to emerge in 2014 during a series of Department of Ecology hearings along the proposed oil train route.[174] On the morning he passed away that year, Billy Frank Jr. supported the Quinault stand in his last blog: "It's clear that crude oil can be explosive and the tankers used to transport it by rail are simply unsafe. . . . Everyone knows that oil and water don't mix, and neither do oil and fish. . . . It's not a matter of whether spills will happen, it's a matter of when."[175] Fawn Sharp, president of the Quinault Indian Nation, agreed: "Not all the oil gets cleaned up, no matter how good the effort. That oil affects the habitat, and can make it uninhabitable by fish for decades."[176]

The Grays Harbor community had historically been hostile to outside mainstream environmentalists, whom they blamed for the closure of local timber mills during the Northwest "spotted owl wars." Working only with Earthjustice would reinforce that perception, but Quinault leaders made a point of working also with local environmental groups and fishermen and pushing a "no oil trains" message on local billboards and in newspapers. As Quinault vice president Tyson Johnston commented, "[Some local residents] will lump us in too with a lot of the environmental groups, and we do carry a lot of those values, but we're in this for very different reasons such as sovereignty, our future generations."[177] Quinault leaders also point out that climate change, generated by the burning of fossil fuels, has detrimentally affected salmon and shellfish for both Quinault and non-tribal fishers.[178]

The Quinault Nation had usually been at odds with the Washington Dungeness Crab Fishermen's Association, which has challenged treaty-backed crab harvests. But as association vice president Larry Thevik pointed out about the oil terminal issue: "[It has] united us in the preservation of the resource that we bicker over. It has also kind of created a new channel of communication because those of us at the bottom of the food chain, the actual fishers, have been able to talk somewhat directly to another nation."[179] Schumacker, the Quinault Nation marine resources scientist, agreed: "With no resource, there's no battle . . . we have to maintain what's out there. Those people, those local crabbers out here are almost as place-based as the tribes. I will never say that they are *as* place-based, but they feel so deeply rooted here and it's part of their lives. . . . We find ourselves working together on these matters."[180]

Quinault president Fawn Sharp (also president of the Affiliated Tribes of Northwest Indians) was born in 1970 "at the height of the fishing rights conflict." She commented: "I was a young child, but was very impressionable. At eight years old, I understood what treaty abrogation meant, that there were others trying to wipe out the entire livelihood of not only my family, but my larger Quinault family. That was very real. My perspective is a product of that era." She remembered being called names in neighboring communities and her family's tires being slashed. Even as late as 2000, when she testified for a fisheries enhancement project, "some irate sports fishermen in the audience" kicked her chair.[181]

Sharp reflected: "Part of the relationship that we have today arose out of generations of disputes. Through those disputes, whether they liked us . . . didn't like us . . . they came to know and understand Quinault and our values. . . . For us, a lot of the relationships we have with our neighbors arose out of a relationship of much division, strife, and conflict, but through that . . . they've come to know who we are. That, to me, is a foundational bit of understanding."[182]

Sharp was later impressed, however, in meeting Larry Thevik and other local crabbers when they worked for a renewable energy project and against a coal terminal and agreed to work together with Quinault even as they disagreed about crab harvest allocation. When the oil terminal issue emerged Sharp thought, "We need to develop these partnerships because this oil issue is so much larger than Quinault Nation." Adding a "footnote of hope," she said: "The cooperation that we're seeing now is going to provide another sort of step of maturity and good faith and alliance and looking beyond special interest or individual interest to the greater good. Perhaps today's generation and younger people growing up in this political climate will come to understand that it is so much better to work together with neighbors."[183]

Sharp and Thevik published a March 2016 editorial portraying crude oil as a risk to fishing and tourism and pointing to 57 percent opposition among county residents.[184] By then, two of the three oil terminals had been dropped, and the third was under sustained public pressure.[185] The Quinault Nation sponsored the July 2016 "Shared Waters, Shared Values" rally, including a flotilla of fishing boats, tribal canoes, and kayaks. Notably, the rally's roster highlighted tribal and local speakers, but none from outside environmental groups.[186] Quinault had begun to explore sustainable economic options to crude oil (around industries such as tourism, port exports, forestry, and fisheries), in collaboration with other Grays Harbor County communities.[187] A January 2017 Washington State Supreme Court decision appeared to block the third terminal.

The Quinault Indian Nation hosts the "Shared Waters, Shared Values" rally against a proposed Grays Harbor oil terminal, at Hoquiam City Hall on July 8, 2016. Quinault president Fawn Sharp and vice president Tyson Johnston are joined by representatives of the Quileute, Makah, and Lummi tribes, Washington fishing association representatives, and local environmentalists. (Photo by the author)

The Bakken oil shipping controversy extended far beyond Quinault. Oil trains were rolling into Washington to oil terminals at Anacortes and Ferndale / Cherry Point. As the trains neared two Anacortes refineries (built on former Swinomish Reservation land at March Point), they traversed the existing Swinomish Reservation. The Swinomish tribal government went to U.S. District Court in 2015 to stop the "bomb trains" from crossing tribal lands, partly on the basis of the railroads' lack of authority to build the original tracks in 1889.[188] A large May 2016 climate justice direct action, including an Indigenous Action Day and rail blockade, targeted the refineries on March Point.[189] Shell dropped its oil-by-rail plans to the March Point refinery in October 2016.[190] Other tribal governments expressed support for the positions of Quinault and Swinomish, whether from a concern about exploding trains or a goal of keeping fossil fuels in the ground as a necessary step to limit climate change.[191]

TEMPLATES FOR THE CLIMATE CRISIS

Climate change from carbon pollution has shifted and intensified prospects for Native/non-Native alliances in the Pacific Northwest and Northern Plains. First, climate change expands the scope of conflict to encompass a wide range of rural and urban communities, whose geographic strategies to block fossil fuel industry shipments are becoming more coordinated. Despite the enormous scale and reach of energy corporations, their top-heavy operations are actually quite vulnerable to social movements that creatively use spatial strategies and tactics.[192] Climate justice enables a wider spatial scale of collaboration than local approaches that can succumb to "divide and conquer" tactics, so each local battle over a pipeline or port terminal is ultimately about the global climate.[193]

Second, climate change provides an urgency in overcoming divisions between tribal and local governments, in order to safeguard common livelihoods based on land and water.[194] Tribal and local governments that have been locked in conflict have only each other to depend on when a storm floods their lands or a landslide cuts them off from outside help. Tribes can provide models of resilience to non-Indian communities on how to proactively prepare for climate change, respond to emergencies, and recover from disasters.[195] For example, the Swinomish Tribe collaborated with local governments in its Swinomish Climate Change Initiative in 2009–10, to respond to increased flooding in the Skagit River delta, despite a long history of contention with local lawmakers and citizens over water rights and jurisdiction in the Skagit watershed.[196]

Third, tribal/non-tribal cooperation to restore salmon habitat provides a template for collaboration in climate change adaptation and mitigation.[197] The Nisqually Tribe and the city of Olympia agreed in 2008 to shift their main source of freshwater from the sacred McAllister Springs to wells on higher ground, and by 2017 they had proactively moved their freshwater source out of the reach of future sea-level rise, and returned the springs to the tribe.[198] The Tulalip Tribes defused a long-standing source of conflict between dairy farmers and tribal fishers over cattle waste in the Snohomish watershed's salmon streams by converting the waste into biogas energy.[199] The Tulalip Tribes are also exploring collaborative plans to store glacial and snowpack runoff to lessen spring floods and summer droughts that have been exacerbated by warming temperatures.[200]

As in the Northern Plains, treaty rights have played a pivotal role in resistance to oil and coal infrastructure in the Pacific Northwest and in protecting fisheries from climate change.[201] If the Boldt Decision had gone the other way in 1974, or if the tribes had not fought tooth and tail for the Boldt II process to restore fish habitat, the Northwest would be more industrialized and damaged than it already is. The 2010s resistance to fossil fuel shipping shows the fruit of tribal alliances at both the political and social levels, again demonstrating how both government-to-government relations and people-to-people relations can reinforce the larger nation-to-nation relationship. Working against the common enemy of the energy corporations has helped strengthen a common sense of place and develop a common sense of understanding.

Quinault president Fawn Sharp concluded:

> When we're confronted with issues like this oil terminal, where it's all about corporate greed . . . I think we can help lead and understand with our values system . . . proven through centuries. It's just my hope that future generations, including our own, will go back to that value system that we have of interdependence and interrelationships. There's so much more positive that can come out of coming together than all of that time, energy, headache, heartache that's extended in conflict and disputes. If we could focus on the greater good and very broad vision for what we want for our children, we'll all be so much better off.[202]

As Naomi Klein told an audience in Seattle:

> One of the most exciting parts of the emergence of this fossil fuel resistance . . . is the way in which it is building really powerful ties between non-Native and Native communities. Whenever there's a big resource battle we see these connections, but there's something new happening. We saw this really clearly with the emergence of Idle No More and all these resistance movements—whether it's to the Cherry Point coal export terminal or the Northern Gateway pipeline through B.C. I think what more and more of us are starting to understand is that Indigenous First Nations' treaty rights and aboriginal title are the most powerful legal barrier to the plans to just flay this continent. And those rights become more powerful when there are mass movements defending them, and when they are embraced by whole societies. . . . I think it's actually changing the way we think, as well as the way we fight.[203]

PART IV

AGREEING ON THE WATER

"Sooner or later, people in Northern Wisconsin will realize that the environmental threat is more of a threat to their lifestyle than Indians who go out and spear fish. . . . I think, in fact, that we have more things in common with the anti-Indian people than we have with the state of Wisconsin."

—Walter Bresette (Red Cliff Ojibwe)

THE INLAND WATERS OF THE GREAT LAKES REGION WERE LATER THE setting for a fish war similar to that in the Pacific Northwest, with just as unlikely an outcome. The 1983 Voigt Decision, modeled on the Boldt Decision, triggered a strong anti-treaty movement that protested Ojibwe (Chippewa) exercising their tradition of spearfishing, to the point of mob violence by crowds of white sportsmen. Racist sportfishers viewed the Ojibwe as outsiders in treaty-ceded territory, by violating the social and territorial boundaries of "white man's land," where they were literally and figuratively "out of place."

Even as the racist harassment and violence raged in the late 1980s and early 1990s, Ojibwe treaty rights leaders such as Walt Bresette and Tom Maulson presented their treaty rights and tribal sovereignty as legal obstacles to resources companies' plans for large metallic mines that would pollute the fishing streams and drawdown groundwater supplies. Instead of continuing to argue over the fish, by the mid-1990s, the followers of some sportfishing groups began to cooperate with the Ojibwe, Menominee, Potawatomi, and other tribes to protect the fish.

Although their fishing rights resembled those in Washington State, the northern Wisconsin alliances more closely resembled those of the Northern Plains. With a state government hostile to tribal co-management, the Native/ non-Native relationship had to be built from the bottom up. Tribes, sport-fishers, and farmers often cooperated in opposition to state agencies' pro-industry policies.

Both Native and non-Native fishers held a strong sense of place to the relatively clean waterways of northern Wisconsin, from Lake Superior to the Wolf River. They had clashed over the beautiful lakes in the fishing wars, found that both their resource-based ways of life were endangered, and strengthened their attachment to their mutual "home," as described by Frances Van Zile and Mike Wiggins Jr. Tribal members' and non-Indian sportfishers' loyalty to the Northwoods gave them more in common with each other than with the corporations that they identified as their common enemies or even with mainstream environmental groups.

Though constructing a common identity was more difficult in the tense racial climate, the alliances succeeded in redirecting social anger away from neighbors and toward distant institutions. From the late 1990s to 2010s, their powerful environmental alliances took on the world's largest mining companies in four separate sites near Ojibwe reservations: at Ladysmith near Lac Courte Oreilles, at Lynne near Lac du Flambeau, at Crandon next to Mole Lake, and at the Penokees near Bad River.

In the strangest twist of the story, the areas that had the most intense conflict and polarization over fishing rights are where the anti-mining alliances became the easiest to form and the most effective. In the areas where conflict had been largely avoided during the fishing wars, the cooperation was more difficult and less fruitful. The treaty struggles had educated white neighbors that Native cultures and legal rights were not artifacts of the past and that the same treaty and sovereign rights they had resisted could protect the fish and water for everyone.

As both Native and non-Native residents felt disenfranchised in the rapidly changing economy and environment of northern Wisconsin, they both saw unwanted changes to their "home" region and felt under siege by outside interests. How in that context could they construct a common sense of understanding based on their rural lifestyle and their place-based attachment to their local watersheds? How could they start to redefine and expand the mental boundaries of their home to include their neighbors and to redefine the "outsiders" as "insiders" with ecosystem boundaries? Moreover, how could their cooperation begin to extend beyond environmental protection to economic development and cultural resilience? Where could they find a more stable concept of "home" where they could belong and where they could still exercise some control over their lives?

CHAPTER 6

Fishing and Exclusion

Northern Wisconsin

IN THE LATE 1980S AND EARLY 1990S, NORTHERN WISCONSIN WAS IN the grip of a conflict between whites and the Ojibwe (Chippewa) over the ancient tribal practice of spearfishing. Under two treaties, the Ojibwe had reserved rights to harvest off-reservation natural resources in their ceded territories— such as fish, game, wild rice, and medicine plants.[1] The federal recognition of these rights in 1983—nine years after the Boldt Decision—gave rise to one of the most powerful anti-treaty movements seen in North America.

Thousands of sportsmen and sportswomen, clad in blaze orange clothing, protested against the spearfishing as an environmental "rape" of the inland fishery and as a denial of equal rights for white citizens. As riot-clad police watched and National Guard helicopters hovered overhead, the white protesters harassed Ojibwe spearers with racial epithets and hurled rocks and beer bottles at their boats and vehicles.[2] The protests sparked race-based harassment and hate crimes against Wisconsin Native Americans, whatever their tribes.[3]

The irony of the Ojibwe treaty rights conflict was that both Ojibwe spearfishers and anti-treaty protesters shared certain basic values. Fishing has long been a central cultural icon for both groups, and the "natural, pristine, and clean" Northwoods was a strong source of identity. The difference between the groups involved how and where the fishing would happen. Anglers took a sportsmanship approach to recreational fishing, and the spearers took a harvesting approach for food gathering.[4] The Ojibwe expanded the view of their territory into the treaty-ceded lands where they had been excluded for decades, and white protesters—with backing from state authorities—saw the Ojibwe "in their place" only within the boundaries of the reservation.

Both the Ojibwe and white fishers portrayed their fishing ethic as best suiting the long-term conservation of the fishery. The hundreds of thousands of anglers would practice "catch-and-release" fishing, while the hundreds of spearers would harvest in a limited fashion to catch only as many fish as their community needed to eat. By presenting themselves as the best guardians of the fishery, they prefigured a converging of their seemingly contradictory ethics.

OJIBWE TREATY RIGHTS CONFLICT

For many centuries, Ojibwe spearfishers used torches at night to illuminate the eyes of large fish such as walleye and muskie, in shallow waters close to the shoreline, where male fish moved slowly during spring spawning. The tribal spearers harvested many fish during this two-week spawning period after the ice breaks.[5] French explorers noted the centrality of spearfishing to Ojibwe life around the village of Waswaaganing (Place Where One Spears Fish), which the explorers then named Lac du Flambeau (Lake of the Torch).

The U.S. government and the Lake Superior Ojibwe Nation signed treaties in 1837 and 1842, securing U.S. access to the region's plentiful timber and copper.[6] Under the treaties, the Ojibwe reserved the usufructuary right to hunt, fish, and gather within the ceded lands, which the federal government recognized as necessary for their physical and cultural survival, much as in the Pacific Northwest.[7]

Many local settlers developed a trading relationship with the Ojibwe through the 1800s and strongly protested when the Wisconsin Ojibwe were temporarily removed to Sandy Lake, Minnesota, in the winter of 1850, resulting in many deaths.[8] The perseverance of the Ojibwe and their allies caused the federal government to rescind the removal order and to form four Wisconsin Ojibwe reservations four years later: Lac du Flambeau, Lac Courte Oreilles, Bad River, and Red Cliff. Two tinier reservations, Mole Lake and St. Croix, were formed in 1934. Some Ojibwe were forcibly removed from their settlements into the reservations.[9] They supplemented their meager reservation resources with game, fish, and wild plants from their ceded territory and from labor in the timber and tourism industries.[10]

The rise of fishing and hunting for sport, and the resulting "conservation ethic," brought both Native and non-Native subsistence hunting and fishing under legal attack. In 1908, the Wisconsin Supreme Court outlawed Ojibwe off-reservation hunting, fishing, and gathering rights. Without access to off-reservation resources, the Ojibwe suffered from an inadequate diet, to add to their poor living conditions and health care.[11] Many Ojibwe, however, continued to clandestinely hunt and fish outside their reservations. Some were

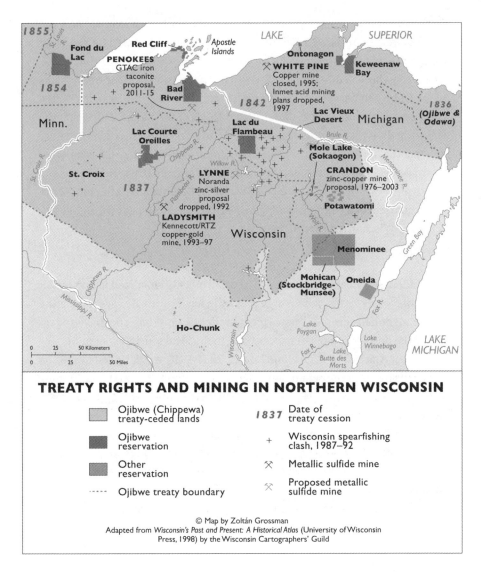

TREATY RIGHTS AND MINING IN NORTHERN WISCONSIN

Ojibwe (Chippewa) treaty-ceded lands

Ojibwe reservation

Other reservation

---- Ojibwe treaty boundary

1837 Date of treaty cession

+ Wisconsin spearfishing clash, 1987–92

✕ Metallic sulfide mine

✕ Proposed metallic sulfide mine

© Map by Zoltán Grossman
Adapted from *Wisconsin's Past and Present: A Historical Atlas* (University of Wisconsin Press, 1998) by the Wisconsin Cartographers' Guild

apprehended by state fish and game wardens and faced fines, equipment and vehicle confiscations, and jail time. Tribal members were defined as "outsiders" in the very lands that their leaders had ceded to the United States, to allow the state of Wisconsin to exist.

In 1974, inspired by the Boldt Decision, Ojibwe brothers Fred and Mike Tribble ice-fished outside the boundary of their Lac Courte Oreilles Reservation. Wisconsin Department of Natural Resources (DNR) wardens cited the

Tribble brothers for fishing off the reservation without a license, and Lac Courte Oreilles initiated a federal lawsuit. The move touched off the Voigt treaty case, named after the Wisconsin DNR administrator at the time.

In 1983, the Seventh Circuit U.S. Court of Appeals affirmed the treaty rights of the Ojibwe to harvest off-reservation natural resources.[12] Drawing on the precedent of the Boldt case, Judge James Doyle subsequently ruled that the Ojibwe had a right to half the harvestable natural resources in ceded territory and that the harvest had to be set in negotiations with the state government.[13] Wisconsin Ojibwe governments formed the Voigt Inter-Tribal Task Force and met to set harvest standards with the Wisconsin DNR. In 1985, after more than three-quarters of a century, the Ojibwe legally began to spear fish again outside their Wisconsin reservations.

Anti-Treaty Movement

Anti-Indian sentiment in northern Wisconsin quickly mobilized in opposition to Ojibwe treaty rights, fed in large part by inaccurate media reports that the government had "granted" new rights to the tribes. White sportfishers predicted the destruction of the fishery, vital to the local tourist economy.

Protect Americans' Rights and Resources (PARR) was founded in 1985 by Park Falls paper mill foreman Larry Peterson. Republican candidate Tommy Thompson visited with PARR during his successful 1986 campaign for governor and agreed with the group that "spearing is wrong, regardless of what treaties, negotiations or federal courts may say."[14] In 1986 and 1987, protesters clad in hunters' blaze orange began gathering at boat landings on spring nights during the two-week tribal spearfishing season. They chanted racist taunts such as "timber niggers," "welfare warriors," and "spearchuckers" and carried signs that read "Save a Spawning Walleye, Spear a Pregnant Squaw" and "Too Bad Custer Ran out of Bullets."[15] The often drunken crowds threw rocks, bottles, and full beer cans.[16] The image-conscious PARR leadership let individual members decide whether or not the group would protest at the lakes. This initial timidity led to the formation of a more militant group, Stop Treaty Abuse (STA), led by Dean Crist, a pizza parlor owner who had moved to the area from Illinois. Crist marketed an alcoholic beverage he dubbed Treaty Beer, in order to raise funds for the cause, and organized mass rallies and civil disobedience at the boat landings.

Both PARR and STA became part of the national anti-treaty coalition Citizens Equal Rights Alliance (CERA), the leading voice of the national anti-treaty movement.[17] During the Ojibwe treaty dispute, Wisconsin-based anti-treaty groups took the helm of this national coalition and emphasized three major themes based on "equal rights," environmental protection, and protecting the local tourism-based economy.[18]

First, the anti-treaty groups advocated "equal rights" for whites. They defined civil rights as individual liberties and therefore viewed the treaties as giving one racial group "special rights" to natural resources.[19] One PARR leader wrote: "The good people of northern Wisconsin will no longer accept being branded as racist because we share Martin Luther King's dream. A dream that how many fish a person can catch will be judged not by the color of his skin but by the strength of his fishing line." He added, "Any person who opposes Apartheid in South Africa but supports American Indian treaty rights is giving new meaning to the word hypocrisy."[20] He was contradicted by none other than South African Anglican archbishop Desmond Tutu, who proclaimed during a 1988 visit to Madison: "I appeal to you . . . to assure that your native Indians in this state can see there are people who want to see justice done for them. Become as committed to racial justice here as you are committed to racial justice in South Africa."[21]

Second, Wisconsin anti-treaty protesters wrapped themselves in the mantle of conservationism, which has historically been more respected by rural Wisconsin sportsmen than by most other U.S. rural groups.[22] On the one hand, PARR and STA activists were skeptical of the continued existence of Native cultural lifeways, viewing Ojibwe "traditionalism" as a mere excuse to steal resources. On the other hand, the anti-treaty activists contrasted the modern aspects of Ojibwe resource harvesting to more "authentic" traditional practices.[23] They particularly singled out Ojibwe use of metal boats, halogen lights, and spears, instead of the more "traditional" use of birch bark canoes, torches, and wooden spears.[24]

Third, anti-treaty protesters effectively appealed to fears of economic decline and social disruption. Protesters often repeated a populist appeal to "working people" who were going through hard times in the economic periphery of the North Country and had to work at fast-food outlets to make a living. Crist called his Treaty Beer the "true brew of the working man." Anti-treaty groups exposed a deeper economic anxiety, termed by one scholar as a reaction to the economic "transformation" of the north under the impetus of globalized corporate development.[25] Another scholar agreed that the conflict's "deeper structural underpinnings" were economic rather than racial and were a "deflection" of working-class whites away from acting in their own interests.[26] But white residents were not so quick to side with Native Americans out of some sense of class loyalty—quite the opposite. By the thousands, they converged on the northern boat landings during cold spring nights, to protest against treaty rights.

Boat Landing Protests

Starting in 1988, STA organized protesters to rally at the boat landings, and the level of violence increased markedly.[27] On the roads leading to and from the lakes, spearers' and other treaty supporters' tires were slashed, vehicles forced into ditches, and elders nearly run down. On the landings, tribal families were assaulted, threatened with death, and harassed with whistles and mock drum chants and pipe bombs were discovered or exploded. On the lakes, spearing boats were rammed, swamped, and blockaded by protest boats, and youths fired metal ball bearings with high-powered "wrist-rocket" slingshots. Snipers often fired rifles from the shoreline, forcing spearers to shut off their boat lights and fishing lights because they made them such visible targets.

At the height of the protests in 1989 and 1990, protests of five hundred to a thousand whites confronted Ojibwe spearers and their families at the boat landings, and their boats shadowed Ojibwe boats on the lakes. National Guard helicopters, DNR patrol boats, and riot-clad police from around the state were deployed at northern lakes. The National Guard, as part of Operation Northern Lights, prepared to enforce a "state of emergency."[28] Walt Bresette, a Red Cliff Ojibwe spearer, said in 1990, "Currently, the only Chippewa who are spearfishing are those willing to risk their lives."[29] Hundreds of anti-treaty protesters were arrested for civil disobedience actions or violent assaults, yet only a few Ojibwe were arrested, because the spearers' leadership had decided early in the conflict not to physically fight back.

The incidents of harassment and violence were concentrated in Vilas and Oneida counties near the Lac du Flambeau Reservation in the north-central part of the state.[30] Protest signs in the white "border towns" of Minocqua and Woodruff proclaimed: "Send Rambo to Flambeau." Tribal members, and Native Americans of other tribes, were often harassed in off-reservation grocery stores, schools, and bars.

The Ojibwe band with the second-largest spearing contingent was from the Mole Lake Sokaogon Chippewa Community, in northeastern Wisconsin. During the 1989 spearing season, PARR protested in the white border town of Crandon and threatened to bring a thousand protesters to disrupt tribal bingo operations. Rock throwing, bomb threats, and gunfire were directed against Mole Lake spearers on nearby lakes. Incidents of violence and harassment also

occurred against spearfishers from the St. Croix, Red Cliff, and Bad River reservations, though not in as highly organized a fashion as the protests around
the PARR/STA home base in north-central Wisconsin.

The one Ojibwe band that held back on exercising off-reservation treaty
rights was from the Lac Courte Oreilles Reservation, in northwestern Wisconsin. The band had initiated and won the federal treaty rights case, yet tribal
chair Gaiashkibos emphasized preventing friction with sportsmen and resort
owners around the border town of Hayward. Lac Courte Oreilles reduced their
fish quota on some lakes and declined to fish entirely on other lakes. Governor
Thompson and the DNR often portrayed Lac Courte Oreilles as a "model" band,
in contrast to the more "aggressive" Lac du Flambeau and Mole Lake bands.

Some protesters not only criticized the practice of spearfishing but also
questioned the very presence of Native people outside reservation boundaries. I often heard protesters' chants that revealed their view that ceded territory was "white man's land" or that ordered "Indians go home!," presumably
back to the reservation. I was in the border town of Minocqua when Lac du
Flambeau tribal members formed a contingent in the 1989 Independence Day
parade, and local white citizens turned their backs.

The hostility extended to off-reservation schools. In a grade school near
Lac du Flambeau, white students drew sketches of fish spearing an Indian and
similar pictures with the words "Shoot the Indian, save the fish."[31] During the
1989 spearing season, parents from Lac du Flambeau and Mole Lake pulled
their children out of the local high school due to intensified racist taunts and
bomb threats.[32]

As anti-treaty protests escalated, they became less focused on environmental or "equal rights" rhetoric and more openly racist. Angry protesters
threw rocks not only at Ojibwe but also at media representatives and even
police they perceived as being "soft on the Indians." One protester yelled, "The
squaws smell worse than the fish."[33] Other protesters shouted at spearers,
"Let's scalp 'em."[34] A threatening poster appeared around shops in northern
Wisconsin announcing the "First Annual Chippewa Shoot," specifying "No
hunting within 500 feet of teepees, liquor stores, food stamp / welfare offices,
or parole offices," and asking hunters to "register kills with the DNR (Dead
No-good Redskin)." This poster would become a prototype of similar posters
in Montana and South Dakota.

Some links to national far-right movements slowly became evident in 1989,
with an armed anti-treaty "death squad" offering money for the assassination
of Lac du Flambeau leaders.[35] The same year, notes were found of a phone call

Anti-treaty protesters at a boat landing during the Ojibwe spearfishing
conflict in northern Wisconsin. (Courtesy: Great Lakes Indian Fish and
Wildlife Commission)

from the "AN Underground" (viewed as a reference to the Aryan Nations) urging snipers to open fire on spearing boats on their way to the lakes. Crist affirmed the following year that former Klan leader David Duke was "saying the
same stuff we have been saying, like he might have been reading it from STA
literature."[36]

Away from the boat landings, some protest leaders attempted to disassociate themselves from the violence and open racism. The United Sportspeople
Alliance (USA), a short-lived alliance of anti-treaty groups, resort business

Ojibwe spearfishers and allies at a boat landing in northern Wisconsin, targeted by anti-treaty protesters. (Courtesy: Great Lakes Indian Fish and Wildlife Commission)

owners, and sports goods store owners, held a 1989 state capitol rally to convince the public that spearing hurt the tourism industry. PARR leader Larry Peterson initially portrayed his group as a respectable non-racist alternative to STA that avoided confrontations, but he lost so much support from militant activists that he returned to advocacy of boat landing protests.

Yet as early as 1989, it was apparent to some observers that not all protesters agreed with the racist rhetoric of the hard-core activists. Though they were silently complicit with the racial harassment, they were either troubled or embarrassed by it. Many young people attended the protests partly because it was the only exciting local event on a weekend night. Some families attended the protests because they believed the environmental message of anti-treaty groups and genuinely feared for the future of the fishery. One reporter observed that the "rear ranks of the demonstration were occupied with silent soldiers—protesters who believed their mere presence . . . was the best way to show their opposition" and that "many debated spearfishing rationally with Indians."[37]

Lac du Flambeau spearing leader Tom Maulson likewise observed, "You can kind of pick them out—the ones who are there just out of curiosity, and they don't know all the issues, and you can talk to them."[38] Although protesters called him "the most hated person in Wisconsin," Maulson said he did not "feel animosity . . . because they need to be educated."[39] Maulson would often wade into hostile crowds and engage in dialogue with individuals, even when he literally had a price on his head, because he felt he could reach them with a message that combined a strong legal justification of treaty rights with a strong commitment to protection of the fishery. Although these "moderate" protesters occupied the periphery of the anti-treaty rallies, they would later take center stage.

Pro-Treaty Movement

In response to the anti-treaty protests, a small pro-treaty movement grew in the late 1980s throughout Wisconsin. Foremost among the pro-treaty groups was the Great Lakes Indian Fish and Wildlife Commission (GLIFWC), modeled on NWIFC and CRITFC in the Northwest.[40] GLIFWC published statistical reports that showed the tribes never harvested more than 3 percent of the walleyes in ceded territory. It also maintained that the tourism industry was being negatively affected not by spearing but rather by anti-treaty protests and that the resorts that were declining had not adjusted to the rise of weekend family tourism.[41]

Another early pro-treaty group was Honor Our Neighbors' Origins and Rights (HONOR), which emerged from church and other human rights groups. HONOR initiated a national campaign targeting STA's Treaty Beer—holding rallies where political leaders condemned the beer as "hate in a can," pressuring liquor stores to stop carrying the product and using boycott threats to pressure breweries to stop canning it.[42]

Another parallel pro-treaty network emerged in the western Great Lakes region, involving grassroots human rights and environmental groups. Their work became visible in 1987 when white friends stood with Ojibwe families as a gesture of moral support at the boat landings, so family members would not take all the hostility. In the anti-treaty hotbed between Lac du Flambeau and Mole Lake, a small group of concerned white residents formed the Citizens for Treaty Rights in 1988 and were quickly targeted with harassment at work and telephoned death threats. Much as in the South in the 1950s and 1960s, "outsider" whites most visibly led the solidarity movement, with only a few brave local whites willing to confront the perception that all non-Indians opposed the treaties.

Red Cliff Ojibwe spearer Walt Bresette proposed a more organized presence at northern lakes, modeled on the Witness program that escorted Indigenous refugees back to their homes in Central American war zones, as a way to express that any assault on Indian people could also injure non-Indians.[43] Witness for Nonviolence trainees, or Witnesses, began to fan out across northern Wisconsin in 1988 and 1989 and to draw participants from around the nation and world.[44]

Ojibwe spearing associations and most tribal governments invited Witnesses to monitor the 1989 protests and noticed that the presence of Witnesses reduced the number of violent incidents at lakes where they were present. Lac du Flambeau spearer Nick Hockings, a leader of the Wa-Swa-Gon Treaty Association, thanked Witnesses at a Madison pro-treaty rally and told them, "The last time I saw this many white . . . hands up, they were throwing rocks." Ho-Chunk activist James Yellowbank likewise thanked Witnesses and Native supporters for giving PARR/STA a "nonviolent ass-kicking" at the boat landings.[45] I was there on Tom Maulson's pontoon boat in July 1989, when pro-treaty groups from around the region founded the Midwest Treaty Network to coordinate the Witness program and carry out educational campaigns on treaty rights.[46]

Ojibwe spearing groups asked the Witnesses not to counterprotest against PARR/STA and to identify themselves only with white armbands. Witnesses aimed to deter a high level of tension and violence with the use of cameras and recorders, to use nonviolent tactics to defuse tense or violent situations, and to document them.[47] By 1992, a total of about two thousand Witnesses had been trained, and the Midwest Treaty Network had published three annual reports documenting hundreds of incidents of harassment, violence, and the lack of adequate police response, centering on Vilas and Oneida counties. Some protesters turned their wrath on the Witnesses, saying, "You white people are all traitors" and "We have red niggers, black niggers, and a few white niggers too."[48]

The Midwest Treaty Network also appealed to human rights groups around the world in 1990 and 1991, leading to pro-treaty rallies at six U.S. embassies and consulates and calling for an economic boycott of Wisconsin if any spearers were injured or killed. Lac du Flambeau treaty rights leader Dorothy Thoms testified at a United Nations hearing in Geneva.[49] In 1990, eleven chambers of commerce from around northern Wisconsin issued a joint declaration calling for an end to the protests.[50] The Wisconsin Equal Rights Council and a federal advisory council found that racial hostility had increased in northern Wisconsin, comparing it to the Deep South.[51] A conservative statewide newspaper editorialized that the protests "proved to be more rooted in racial intolerance than concern for the environment of northern Wisconsin."[52]

The Role of the State

During the height of the treaty conflict, the DNR and other state agencies promoted themselves as neutral parties, caught between the unreasonable demands of the Ojibwe and the destructive militancy of anti-treaty protesters. Yet this claim of neutrality began to be questioned by anglers and spearers alike, who began to view the agency as intensifying rather than preventing conflict. Anglers and spearers usually differed in their views of government, but their perspectives grew closer when it came to the DNR leadership. The DNR was viewed by many spearers as providing inadequate law enforcement and "scapegoating" them for lower angler bag limits. Opposition to the DNR leadership became a common basis of understanding between the opposing sides in the treaty rights dispute. State government was being recast as an "outsider" force that challenged the local control of Native and non-Native communities alike.

In 1990, a three-member panel of University of Wisconsin–Madison professors examined the spearfishing controversy, at the request of Chairman Daniel Inouye of the U.S. Senate Committee on Indian Affairs.[53] They contended that the DNR leadership manipulated fish statistics "so as to shift the blame for inconsistent fisheries management from the DNR to the Chippewa" in a way that seemed "coordinated to inflame anti-Indian emotions." The report offered a 1979 DNR study as evidence that bag limits on the angler fish catch would have been cut regardless of spearfishing.[54] It asserted that the DNR timed bag limit reductions before the spearing season, to create "the impression that it is the Chippewa who are bringing forth the new restrictions."[55]

Federal judge Barbara Crabb, who inherited the Ojibwe treaty case from Judge Doyle, agreed that the DNR's lowering of anglers' bag limits was "purely fortuitous" in its timing. She ruled that the Ojibwe had been scapegoated for sportfishing restrictions that "would have been imposed even if the tribes' treaty rights had not been judicially recognized."[56]

Tribes and their allies also criticized the state government for failing to use models that had reduced tensions over tribal fishing rights in the Northwest. Given the similarities between the Boldt and Voigt decisions, it would seem that state/tribal natural resource co-management would be a possible outcome of the Ojibwe treaty crisis.[57] Bresette and Yellowbank advocated a solution closely resembling the Boldt II habitat framework to turn northern Wisconsin into a "toxic-free zone."[58] They tied unemployment and the closing of "mom-and-pop" small businesses to the search for an Indian "scapegoat" that could be blamed for the north's economic decline. They also began to link the corporate common enemy to environmental threats facing both Indian and white communities.[59] The DNR, unlike its Washington State counterpart, took a negative view of co-management proposals.[60] The DNR secretary even banned the use of the term among his employees.[61]

The state government, instead of working with the treaty rights to strengthen environmental protection, chose instead to seek a buyout of the treaty rights in the name of conservation. The Thompson administration quietly initiated discussions with the tribal governments of Lac du Flambeau and Mole Lake, which would accept a "lease" of treaty rights in exchange for millions in payments and peace at the boat landings.[62] The treaty lease offers immediately stoked divisions between and within communities. The lease deals were strongly opposed by PARR and STA leaders, who viewed them as a financial concession to the tribes, by the other four Ojibwe reservation governments, and by Mole Lake and Lac du Flambeau spearing family members who viewed their tribal leaders' deals as a "sellout" of tribal cultural heritage for financial gain.[63] The most pro-treaty Native activists and most anti-treaty white activists found themselves uncomfortably on the same side of the treaty lease controversy, for completely opposite reasons.

At Mole Lake, where Exxon had proposed a copper-zinc mine in 1976–86, another factor entered into tribal discussions. As an attorney prior to joining the Thompson cabinet, administration secretary James Klauser had served both as a mining advisor to the Wisconsin Manufacturers and Commerce (WMC) business association and as a lobbyist for Exxon Coal and Minerals Company. Some Ojibwe spearers developed suspicions that Klauser's eagerness to "settle" treaty rights was based on his desire to eliminate a possible legal obstacle to a resumption of the mine project. Bresette told Mole Lake tribal members, "Amended treaties would open the door to major mining."[64]

At Lac du Flambeau, the Wa-Swa-Gon Treaty Association portrayed the deal as a betrayal of tribal ancestors and stated, "Our treaty rights are not for sale." Voters at both Mole Lake and Lac du Flambeau overwhelmingly rejected the treaty lease, shocking political and media leaders who had assumed that Native people were more interested in financial gain than in continuing what they viewed as an archaic cultural custom.[65] Some state and federal leaders vowed that the intransigent reservation would not receive any more aid. Vilas County sheriff James Williquette, a vocal treaty opponent, predicted that the vote would lead to "all-out war" in the 1990 spearing season.

Wa-Swa-Gon leader Tom Maulson was elected tribal president three years after the treaty lease referendum. Looking back on the spearfishing clashes,

Maulson saw the conflict as an "education process on everybody's part [on] what Indians were about" and that it would "create understanding." Remembering the pre-spearing days when many Wisconsin citizens did not even know of the existence of reservations, he maintained, "It's only because of treaty rights that our white brothers know they have Indian neighbors." He added, "It needed a conflict to wake them up."[66]

Lac du Flambeau elder Dorothy Thoms and her daughter, Wa-Swa-Gon secretary Anita Koser-Thoms, also remembered the 1989 vote as critical in the treaty struggle. Koser-Thoms stood at boat landings and listened to verbal taunts and abuse during the intense 1990 spearing season. She laughed, "We took a licking but kept on ticking." Thoms asserted that it was worth it for tribal members to go through the trauma, because their perseverance enabled them to eventually fish in peace. Her daughter said that if something she believes in "brings suffering and misery," she accepts the consequences. She explained: "It's like childbirth; it's the worst pain, but not when you see the result."[67] In the view of the Ojibwe spearing families, the treaty battle resulted in a rebirth of tribal traditions on the reservation.[68]

Lac Courte Oreilles carried out a different strategy than either Lac du Flambeau or Mole Lake. On the one hand, Lac Courte Oreilles took the lead in the legal case that led to the reaffirmation of Ojibwe treaty rights and refused to consider a lease of the treaty rights. On the other hand, Gaiashkibos and other Lac Courte Oreilles leaders pursued spearfishing in a much less assertive way than either Lac du Flambeau or Mole Lake, by reducing the band's spearing quotas and refraining from spearing on many lakes. Lac Courte Oreilles historically had a more positive relationship with resort owners than other Ojibwe bands had with local resort interests. In 1989, Lac Courte Oreilles accommodated the requests of resort owners to raise the walleye bag limits and to agree to end the spearing season early. As one resort association leader contended, "I think LCO has been exceedingly responsible in its spearing on all area lakes."[69] Governor Thompson and the DNR upheld Lac Courte Oreilles as a "model of cooperation" that other bands should emulate.

The accommodating strategy worked to reduce tensions in Sawyer County, which includes the Lac Courte Oreilles Reservation and Hayward. Residents held some joint events, and no protesters were arrested in the county.[70] The tribal radio station WOJB provided a forum for dialogue between the communities—a forum that was lacking farther east—even if some of its billboards were defaced.[71]

Yet the Lac Courte Oreilles strategy also had a flip side, which created tensions with other Ojibwe bands. By voluntarily modifying some of the treaty rights, Lac Courte Oreilles leaders were sometimes seen by other bands as undermining stronger assertions of tribal sovereignty. Their accommodation was viewed as bending over backward to avoid DNR bag limit reductions that were not the fault of spearfishing in the first place. Were Lac Courte Oreilles leaders failing to directly educate local white residents about sovereignty and Ojibwe cultural survival? Did their avoidance of short-term conflict result in a long-term public underappreciation of treaties' legal strength? Paraphrasing Frederick Douglass, were Lac Courte Oreilles leaders trying to harvest a crop without plowing the ground?

Gaiashkibos admitted to some impatience with the tendency of state and federal officials to treat Lac Courte Oreilles tribal officials as the "good Indians," when he commented: "Being a model of cooperation doesn't mean we have to bend over every time the state proposes something, or that we have to give every time someone says 'give.' We have to draw the line also. The bottom line of all this is protection of the resource."[72] He conceded that relationships were built with tourism business owners, rather than with individual sportfishers—a difference that would become important later.[73] Lac Courte Oreilles's strategy helped in the short term to head off local conflicts around the spearing issue, but inadvertently it may not have helped in the long term to protect the resources from looming environmental threats.

Decline of the Anti-Treaty Movement

During the 1990 spearing season, Witness for Nonviolence reported 279 incidents of violence, racist acts, or ineffective law enforcement on the lakes and landings.[74] In a poll, 78 percent of Wisconsinites surveyed viewed the "current relationship between Indians and Whites in Wisconsin" as "not so good" or "poor."[75] Another poll showed that 49 percent of state residents surveyed opposed Ojibwe spearfishing, including 66 percent of northern residents.[76]

At Lac du Flambeau, Wa-Swa-Gon went on the legal offensive after the 1990 spearing season, filing suit in federal court against STA harassment and violence. In March 1991, Judge Crabb ordered that STA members halt any physical actions that interfere with the treaty rights of Lac du Flambeau spearers and their families. The judge had drawn partly from a civil rights case brought by Vietnamese immigrant fishermen against Ku Klux Klan violence in Texas.[77] The injunction prevented thousands of "moderate" anti-treaty protesters from going to the boat landings during the 1991 spearing season. The remaining hard-core protesters intensified their protests in Vilas County, driving away even more "moderate" protesters.[78] I remember seeing a crowd of Sand Lake anti-treaty protesters single out a small group of Witnesses (that included African American radio journalist James Mincey) and pummel them with racist epithets.[79] Some resort owners and bait shop owners stopped backing the protest groups because racist violence could keep tourists away. Local anti-treaty newspapers printed letters from out-of-state anglers, including one that stated: "You are destroying the Northwoods and making the Indians scapegoats. I will not bring my family back here. . . . It is clearly because I am disgusted with your obscene racism."[80]

As they gradually lost local support, anti-treaty groups began to bring in supporters from outside the Northwoods. PARR and STA had to import numerous treaty foes from the Milwaukee and Waukesha areas, to replace the local so-called rednecks.[81] Anti-treaty activists had portrayed themselves as white insiders defending their resources from outsiders—reservation Indians, meddling Witnesses, and federal judges—but their message grew increasingly muddled by the presence of their own outside allies.

In addition to the federal injunction, increased awareness of Native culture and fish biology reduced anti-treaty sentiment throughout the state. The state legislature passed a 1990 bill asking that Native histories and cultures be taught in schools.[82] A 1991 federal report confirmed many of GLIFWC's statistics that spearing had not harmed either the fishery or the tourism industry.[83] In a 1991 poll, 59 percent of southern Wisconsinites supported treaty rights, and 42 percent of northerners agreed—a substantial growth in pro-treaty sentiment.[84]

The growth of legalized Indian gaming in Wisconsin also affected the treaty controversy. Many protesters shifted their rhetorical focus to Indian casinos, as an unfair tribal economic advantage over non-Indian tavern and restaurant owners. But the growth in local employment undermined anti-treaty groups' claims that the tribes were hurting the tourism economy.[85]

At a halfhearted Minocqua rally before the 1992 spearing season began, anti-treaty Rhinelander fishing guide Wally Cooper openly called for dialogue with the tribes around environmental issues. STA leader Michael Ahlborn maintained that he "was disgusted . . . to see such a meager attendance by local residents."[86] A 1992 survey showed that 73 percent of state residents (including 56 percent of northerners) favored the policy of "protection of Chippewa treaty rights but close regulation of off-reservation fishing and hunting

by the state." Similar numbers backed "co-management of fish and other resources by the Chippewa bands and the state," similar to the policies imple-
mented in Washington State.[87]

The federal injunction on anti-Indian racial harassment dismantled the
anti-treaty groups' image as defenders of "civil rights." Public education on
the biological effects of spearing dismantled many of the groups' claims to be
defending the fishing-based tourism industry. Tribal casinos also dismantled
the groups' claim to be defending the northern economy from welfare and
unemployment. The influx of urban anti-treaty activists was dismantling their
claim to be defending northern rural life from "outsiders."

Finally, the anti-treaty groups began to lose their most basic claimed identity as defenders of the fishery from environmental threats. This lack of cred-
ibility became more obvious in the early 1990s, when mining companies began
to step up their exploration of northern Wisconsin bedrock for metallic minerals such as copper, zinc, silver, and gold, and to use the Thompson administration's pro-industry policies to open new mines. The area of mineral exploration
closely coincided with the extent of Ojibwe ceded territory.

Even at the outset of the boat landing clashes, Walt Bresette had predicted
that non-Indian northerners would realize that environmental problems such
as mercury, toxic wastes, and state mismanagement of fisheries are "more of
a threat to their lifestyle than Indians who go out and spear fish." He concluded, "I think, in fact, we have more things in common with the anti-Indian
people than we do with the state of Wisconsin."[88]

Treaty rights leaders tied the treaties to environmental issues by pointing
out the possible health risks of subsistence harvesting to Ojibwe, who already
suffered a disproportionate risk of illness from mercury and other toxins.[89]
Bresette told white communities, "[Polluting corporations have] gone with
your health and your money, and the only thing that's left is you and I fighting
over some poison fish."[90]

The Native challenge to PARR's and STA's environmental credentials was
heard by some sportfishers, such as Bob Schmitz of the Wolf River Watershed
Alliance. He wrote soon after the 1989 spearing season: "The real danger to
our lakes and streams in Wisconsin is not the Indians. It is industrial and mu-
nicipal pollution, and acid rain." When Schmitz attended state clean water
rule hearings, he observed: "Not once did I see anyone testify who represented
Protect Americans' Rights and Resources, or Stop Treaty Abuse. The Indians
were always there."[91]

The mining issue brought this challenge to the forefront just as the anti-treaty groups were declining in influence and helped to further tarnish their public image. Lac Courte Oreilles chair Gaiashkibos questioned the groups' environmentalist claims when he asked: "Where the hell are these hell-raisers? Where's PARR and STA that are saying they're concerned about the environment, concerned about the resources? Yet I have heard not one peep out of them about the proposed mines that could devastate the whole North-woods. Not one word from these people."[92]

OUTSIDERS AND INSIDERS

In northern Wisconsin, it seemed that the most derogatory name that anyone could be called was an "outsider." Whites saw Native Americans as outsiders in the treaty-ceded territories, and Native Americans saw whites as outsiders on their reservations, or in general. Anti-treaty protesters viewed non-Indian Witnesses as outsiders, until they were also accused of bringing outsiders from southern Wisconsin cities. Mining companies portrayed environmentalists as outsiders, and environmental groups pointed to the outsider status of mining companies.

The battle over who is and is not an outsider was neatly summarized in the exchange on one northern Wisconsin lake in 1989, when an Ojibwe spearer answered protesters' chant of "Indians go home!" by yelling, "This is our home!"[93] The protesters viewed the Ojibwe as violating the boundaries of "white man's land" by leaving the reservation to fish. The Ojibwe saw the white protesters as descendants of the outside settlers who had violated Ojibwe boundaries and taken Native land. The treaty rights conflict reflected a much deeper battle over who *belonged* in northern Wisconsin.

The "outsider" label was not strictly applied along racial lines. A Milwaukee reporter who revisited his home county to cover the anti-spearing protests, wrote of how his sense of place had been altered:

> For me, the north has changed its face and just isn't as pretty as it used to be. The lakes and the land and the people don't look the same. . . . After the spearers went out on the lake, a protester leaned across the fence, addressed me as an outsider, and demanded to know where I was from. . . . I didn't tell her that I was a hometown boy . . . because I was ashamed of the way she and some protesters had acted. . . . She must love this water and this land, but so do the Chippewa. It's not the love that we all share that bothered me, it was the hate that was so loud.[94]

Yet at the same time, the reporter understood that the protesters' hatred and hostility could in some way be tied to their feelings for the place: "I remember . . . where bluegills took our lines and wrapped them around lily pads; where we could lie on a dock . . . and count perch darting through our afternoons. . . . Those are images so strong that I've kept them since I was a child. Now I add the images of protesters who threw rocks, and those who brought a Doberman pinscher to threaten Chippewa, and those who sounded like children, thumping their boats with paddles, cruelly mimicking Indian drums."[95]

Both fishing and mining conflicts in northern Wisconsin can be tied to competing definitions of geography, or place. On the one hand was a social definition of place, from which "outsider" racial or ethnic groups could be excluded. On the other hand was a territorial definition of place, where all "insider" residents—no matter their culture or race—could feel included. The debate between social or territorial definitions of place goes to the heart of distinguishing between "us" and "them."[96] The powerful make social boundaries seem "normal" by masking them as an everyday geographic rule.[97] Racism, in particular, assigns people of different races to different—and seemingly ordinary—spaces that allow them unequal access to resources.[98] Many forms of racism—from South African apartheid to insurance companies' "redlining" of neighborhoods—enforce racial rules by defining territorial boundaries.[99]

By viewing Ojibwe and their sympathizers as outsiders whose very presence can be challenged in ceded territory, the anti-treaty protesters were practicing "geographies of exclusion," whether through laws or by force.[100] The protesters saw the Ojibwe as "in place" on the reservation but "out of place" outside the reservation.[101] By harnessing the arguments of environmentalism, the anti-treaty protesters were labeling Native people as an "ecological other."[102] By condemning Ojibwe spearfishers for crossing reservation boundaries, they were accusing Native people of transgressing social boundaries between the races.[103] The spearfishing conflict was a classic illustration of how "place becomes race," or how racialized spaces are created and reinforced by laws, and how they expose social hierarchies.[104]

One night while witnessing during the 1992 spearing season, after listening to too many chants of "White man's land," I decided to warm up for a minute in a car. The car radio had on graphic news reports on the civil war then erupting in Bosnia. It struck me that the ultranationalists chanting for a Greater Serbia or Croatia were using the same rhetoric as the anti-treaty protesters on that cold boat landing. Rather than blaming their own leaders for their economic problems, they blamed the ethnic group living next door and cleared them out of "their" new, ethnically defined territory. This so-called ethnic cleansing in Bosnia closely resembled nineteenth-century forced removals of Native Americans.[105]

Using an opposite perspective, environmental alliances against mining projects began to define all northerners as insiders, using "geographies of inclusion." They constructed a common territorial place as a common home that includes all people who depend on it for their livelihood. They accused outsider mining companies of transgressing the boundaries of northern watersheds that belong to both Native and white insiders.

The Romans labeled the social definition of belonging as *jus sanguinis* (law of the blood), defining place on the basis of the identity of those who live there. They termed the territorial definition as *jus soli* (law of the soil), which uses place as the starting point of defining who belongs there. The United States, for example, uses *jus soli* to define anyone born in the United States as a citizen, whereas Germany has used *jus sanguinis* to deny citizenship to many non-Germans born in the country.[106]

Territorial identities may be useful tools in building bridges between tribes and nearby white communities, to offset exclusively racial identities. Native and white neighbors inhabiting the same watershed may perceive each other to be "outsiders"—as in the treaty rights battles—but the arrival of an outside enemy threatening the watershed may cause them to redefine the outsider. In northern Wisconsin, an outside threat from mining companies began to strengthen a territorial place identity over a racial social identity and started to shift the very definitions of insiders and outsiders.

MINING CONFLICTS AND THE TREATIES

In the early 1990s, treaty supporters and opponents alike began to draw together treaty issues and mining issues. Witness coordinator Debra McNutt remembered that in 1991 some of the protesters and tribal members dialoguing at the boat landings began to agree that mining was an overriding problem and started to create some "almost unexpected" common ground "at the height of potential violence."[107] Some northerners began to look for underlying causes of the crisis and to treat it as a symptom of larger economic and environmental ills.

Although the treaties do not cover mineral rights, their guarantee of Ojibwe access to fish, wild game, wild rice, medicinal plants, and other natural resources means that the Ojibwe and their supporters interpret damage to those resources as an "environmental violation" of federally backed treaty rights. University of Wisconsin–La Crosse sociology professor Al Gedicks, who was also the executive secretary of the Wisconsin Resources Protection Council, contended that since state mining regulations had been weakened, "any project that would degrade the environment would degrade the treaty rights."[108]

DNR law enforcement chief George Meyer (later the DNR secretary) agreed: "If, in fact, any of these mines would be shown to adversely affect . . . the fisheries or the wildlife in northern Wisconsin, I believe that the Chippewa would be able to sue the mining companies, or the state of Wisconsin if we had granted such a permit, for hurting their treaty rights because it wouldn't make sense for them to have hunting and fishing rights and then turn around and have those damaged by mines."[109]

As anti-spearing protests were ending in 1992, several tribes were getting involved in fighting proposed metallic sulfide mines, which they feared threatened the fishery with sulfuric acid wastes, groundwater drawdown, and toxic chemicals. To their surprise, the tribes began to receive support from a few sportfishing group leaders. These "moderate" anti-treaty protesters found hard-core anti-treaty leaders unresponsive to their pleas to protect the fishery from mining.

In this way, the views of some anti-treaty and pro-treaty citizens converged on the populist critiques of big business, leaving the anti-treaty groups behind. In an official policy statement, PARR said that it "will not endorse any mining controversy solution reached as a result of long-dead treaties."[110] STA leader Dean Crist ridiculed the connection between treaties and environmental protection, stating that he would accept a contribution from Exxon if one were offered.[111]

Links began to develop between interests opposing the treaties and interests supporting resource extraction—including both mining and timber companies. Gedicks described Secretary Klauser and the WMC, whose members included large mining-equipment manufacturing firms, as providing "the convergence between the anti-Indian movement and the state administration's pro-mining policy."[112] Klauser had told the WMC that northern Wisconsin had the potential for six to ten major metallic mining operations.[113] Klauser helped weaken state mining laws and supported a national conference of county governments and anti-treaty leaders to roll back treaty rights that blocked timber and mineral sales.[114]

Links also began to develop between tribes or treaty rights activists and environmental groups opposing a "minerals resource colony" in northern

Wisconsin.[115] Wa-Swa-Gon leader Nick Hockings maintained: "The real issue wasn't fish. . . . It was always our feeling that there had to be a hidden agenda [in the anti-treaty movement]."[116] Bresette asserted: "As multinational interests are being squeezed out of the Third World, many are coming back home. And home is often rural America: farms, small villages and towns, forests, animals, and Indians."[117] Treaties and environment issues were connected at Protect the Earth gatherings held annually in the Mole Lake and Lac Courte Oreilles areas in 1986–91. By 1992, anti-mining activists began to influence the Wisconsin Conservation Congress, a forum for hunters and fishers that met annually in town hall meetings in every county, to pass anti-mining resolutions.

In 1993–95, a series of meetings gradually brought together an alliance of tribes, environmentalists, and sportfishers against metallic sulfide mining. But this alliance developed unevenly in different areas of the north. They were associated with three distinct watersheds where the spearfishing conflict had affected Native/white relations in different ways and where local people had different attitudes toward environmental integrity. About a dozen major metallic mineral deposits had been identified by mining companies under Ojibwe ceded territory.[118] But only three of the deposits were economically viable enough for the companies to formally propose them as mines, and all three plans met opposition from nearby reservations.[119]

Comparing the opposition to the three projects brings into focus the different strategies that were used by activists in each watershed and reveals that the treaty rights conflict had important effects on the makeup and the success of the later anti-mining alliances. The alliances used different mixtures of treaty politics and environmental politics, and their different approaches brought different results. Some Native and non-Native communities worked through their new relationship with the former rival community to redefine and reconstruct their common place.

The Ladysmith Mine and the Lac Courte Oreilles Ojibwe

The first alliance slowly developed in northwestern Wisconsin. It opposed the Kennecott Copper Corporation's proposed Ladysmith copper-gold mine in Rusk County, on the Flambeau River. The mine site was thirty miles south of the Lac Courte Oreilles Ojibwe Reservation. After the open-pit mine was proposed in 1970, it was supported by many residents who felt the area needed the jobs and contracts and accepted the company's assurances that new technologies would make the mine safe. It was opposed by others who feared that

mining sulfide ore would leak sulfuric acid and heavy metals into the Flambeau River and that the mine would create social disruptions and a boom-and-
bust cycle.

Mine critics in the area, mainly farmers, formed the Rusk County Citizens'
Action Group in 1976 to fight the project. The group was led by an elderly Ladysmith farming couple, Roscoe and Evelyn Churchill, considered the "grandparents" of Wisconsin's anti-mining movement.[120] They raised Appaloosa
horses on their farm and took pride in driving their Model A car in community
parades. Roscoe Churchill was elected as a Rusk County supervisor and used
the position as a platform to criticize the mine. The DNR expressed enough
concern about the Kennecott proposal's environmental impacts that it quickly
denied the company a mine permit.

During the first round of the Ladysmith mine battle, which participants
term "Ladysmith I," the Lac Courte Oreilles Ojibwe did not participate. Since
the water flow was away from the reservation, potential water contamination
did not directly threaten tribal members. Only when uranium companies began to explore around reservation lakes did Lac Courte Oreilles form a mining
impact committee and evict company biologists from the reservation.[121] In
1982, tribally owned public radio station WOJB went on the air, substantially
increasing discussion about mining in the Hayward area.[122]

Despite growing awareness about mining at Lac Courte Oreilles, the tribal
and non-tribal environmental efforts moved forward on separate tracks, with
public hearings being their main point of contact. Just as the anti-mine groups
had predicted, Kennecott returned to Ladysmith in 1987, after Tommy Thompson was elected governor, and resumed its pursuit of a mine permit in "Ladysmith II." The company was purchased by the world's largest mining company,
London-based Rio Tinto.

In 1987, anti-mine activist Sandy Lyon asked tribal chair Gaiashkibos to
attend a Ladysmith hearing on the mine. Gaiashkibos told the hearing that
his band viewed mining as "a camel's head in the tent" that would ultimately
affect the reservation.[123] He also described his memories of joining his father
in canoeing the Flambeau River to gather medicinal plants and watch nest-
ing eagles. Gaiashkibos announced in 1990 that Lac Courte Oreilles would
legally intervene to protect endangered species at the mine site.[124] In London,
he told Rio Tinto shareholders and a throng of media: "I believe that we, Indian
and non-Indian, must stand together to demand the non-degradation of the
environment."[125]

Environmentalists such as Bresette, Lyon, and Gedicks formed Anishinaabe

Niijii (Friends of the Ojibwe) to back Lac Courte Oreilles's opposition to the project and to help finance the lawsuit.[126] Lyon recalled that "when the tribe came on board, it was like the cavalry had arrived."[127] Yet the alliance developed mainly as a coalition between environmental leaders and Gaiashkibos and other Lac Courte Oreilles community leaders such as Eugene Begay, Mary Ellen Baker, Al Baker, Eddie Benton Banai, and Marilyn Benton (veterans of a 1971 occupation of the Winter Dam on the reservation), rather than as a deeper link between their communities. Gedicks remembered that while environmentalists met with a "core group" of tribal leaders, the "grassroots tribal members were not so well informed."[128] Lyon observed that more pressing community concerns such as diabetes understandably took precedence over mining issues thirty miles downstream from the reservation.[129]

Even a limited anti-mine coalition, however, made progress in cultural understanding. Gedicks remembered white farmers visiting the reservation for the first time to attend the annual Protect the Earth gathering, where they participated in smudging ceremonies.[130] Lyon points to two instances of mine opponents Al and Sheryl Barker and Ted Styczynski deeding a total of 120 acres of their farms into Lac Courte Oreilles's tribal trust, to prevent their farms from falling into the hands of mining companies.[131] This kind of close cooperation showed a deep trust in the Ojibwe by anti-mining activists, but such trust rarely was exhibited by the white community as a whole.

Without a large following in either community, the anti-mine coalition was vulnerable in Rusk County to company charges that it represented "outsiders," the label given to urban environmentalists and to Lac Courte Oreilles tribal members from adjacent Sawyer County. Roscoe Churchill replied that "the only outsiders here are the mining companies," but the political damage had been done.[132]

A series of rallies and direct actions in 1991, which activists named "Flambeau Summer," drew environmentalists from around the state, including some Witness for Nonviolence members such as myself. Walt Bresette used a "war club," which he was told was originally carried by Black Hawk, to bludgeon mining equipment within the mine site. Yet in the final civil disobedience action at the mine site, the only Ojibwe activists who participated were Wa-Swa-Gon's Anita Koser-Thoms and Minneapolis elder Bea Swanson.[133] Gedicks recalled that Flambeau Summer "floundered" because it lacked a "broad-enough base," and enough activists to effectively stop the mine.[134]

Despite the protests, the DNR and Klauser's administration department granted a permit for the mine. With its casino success still years in the future,

Lac Courte Oreilles lacked the financial resources to pursue their case beyond a temporary injunction. The Ladysmith mine operated on an accelerated schedule from 1993 to 1997. A federal court found in 2011 that the mine had violated the Clean Water Act by discharging contaminated runoff into the Flambeau River.[135]

The geography of the Flambeau River and Rusk County region offers some explanations for the floundering of the alliance against the Ladysmith mine. Area residents considered the dammed-up Flambeau as neither "wild" nor especially scenic, and the tourism industry was not highly developed in the farming region as elsewhere in the north. Fishing on the river had been ruined for decades by discharges from upstream paper mills. The Flambeau River flowed away from the Lac Courte Oreilles Reservation, and tribal members were primarily concerned about protecting medicinal plants rather than fish. Neither the Native nor the non-Native "sense of place" was strongly centered on the Flambeau River.

The politics of treaty rights in northwestern Wisconsin offers another explanation. Area residents largely experienced the spearfishing dispute in the media, rather than in their backyards. Roscoe Churchill remembered: "What we saw on TV didn't affect us." He observed that while treaty rights brought tribal powers "out into the open" elsewhere in the north, around the Lac Courte Oreilles Reservation the non-Indian public "didn't have anything to spur them on." Churchill felt that "the terrible force of the mining companies" helped bring together the alliance with the tribe but that white members of the alliance had little awareness of Ojibwe culture or legal powers. He recalled that a few local mine opponents even questioned the alliance and warned him, "Boy, your skin is getting darker."[136]

The lack of a direct relationship between Lac Courte Oreilles and sportfishers—even a negative one—may have affected the participation of sportfishers in the Ladysmith mine issue. With the exception of one or two leaders, such as Muskies Inc. local chairman Kermit Benson, sportsmen's groups had virtually no role in the alliance against the Ladysmith mine. Benson, who was married to an Ojibwe woman, testified at a 1990 mine hearing that "mining is [a] long-term threat to the environment and the fishery in Northern Wisconsin" and "has the potential to make the Indian spearfishing controversy look like a piece of candy."[137]

Al Gedicks observed that in the Ladysmith anti-mine alliance, both the tribe and a few sportfishing groups participated at the level of their leadership, rather than involving their members. He remembered that Rusk County resi-

dents in the alliance appreciated Lac Courte Oreilles but had little contact with
the tribe beyond a cautious, distant relationship. He maintains that it "would
have been different" if the treaty rights issue "had been in their face . . . they
would have had to have an opinion, get educated."[138] Midwest Treaty Network
organizer Debra McNutt agreed that there were few connections made between the treaty and environmental issues in the Ladysmith fight, even as the
spearfishing conflict was raging elsewhere.[139]

Sandy Lyon of Anishinaabe Niijii contended that Lac Courte Oreilles was
"not interested in pissing off its neighbors."[140] The Lac Courte Oreilles tribal
government began to directly connect the spearing and mining issues in 1991,
when tribal spearers listed a waterway downstream from the proposed Ladysmith mine site, to legally establish a tribal use of the river system potentially
affected by mine runoff.[141] On the one hand, Lac Courte Oreilles could strongly
assert spearfishing rights, face a violent backlash, and risk alienating potential allies in environmental protection. On the other hand, the tribe could
hold back on off-reservation spearing and face less animosity from its white
neighbors but, in the process, fail to impress on its neighbors the legal powers
of the treaties and the continued vitality of Native lifeways. Lac Courte Oreilles
chose the course of accommodation, whereas Lac du Flambeau and Mole
Lake—after internal struggles of their own around this same quandary—
chose the course of confrontation. As Walt Bresette summed up after the
Ladysmith mine opened: "Where you have Native rights, non-Indians can win.
Where you don't have Indian rights, non-Indians lose."[142]

The Lynne Mine and the Lac du Flambeau Ojibwe

The second major anti-mining alliance developed in 1990 in north-central
Wisconsin. It opposed the Noranda company's proposed metallic sulfide mine
in Oneida County, on the Willow River, about twenty miles south of the Lac
du Flambeau Reservation. The Lakeland area around the site had been the
scene of some of the most intense clashes during the spearfishing conflict.[143]
Nevertheless, an alliance against the mine proposal developed in a remarkably
short order after the Toronto-based company announced the discovery of the
zinc-silver deposit on county lands.

Wa-Swa-Gon Treaty Association member George Amour, Potawatomi elder
Billy Daniels, and Rhinelander environmental leader Karl Fate led tours and
pipe ceremonies at the proposed mine site, inviting tribal members and non-
Indian Witnesses.[144] Amour had lived as a child in the Potawatomi village of
McCord next to the Willow River. The old refugee village held ruins of a tribal

roundhouse and a cemetery with thirty Native graves, and both Ojibwe and Potawatomi continued to gather medicine plants in the area. The Lac du Flambeau tribal government joined with Wa-Swa-Gon to oppose the mine, despite their differences over the treaty lease and the fact that the reservation was not downstream from the mine.[145]

White area residents such as Tomahawk sporting supplies store owners Jim and Pam Wise and Lac du Flambeau grade school teacher Carolyn Parker formed the Environmentally Concerned Citizens of Lakeland Areas (ECC-OLA). The group focused on the environmental impacts of the mine on the Willow Flowage, which it backed as a candidate for state Outstanding Resource Water protected status. ECCOLA invited sportfishers, deer hunters, small loggers, business owners, and—in a controversial move—Wa-Swa-Gon members from Lac du Flambeau to their meetings.[146] As Tom Maulson recalled, "The people that we met made us comfortable," despite the years of animosity over spearing in the Lakeland area.[147]

By 1991, crowds at Lynne mine hearings—including many sportsmen and loggers—began to outnumber the anti-treaty protesters at the boat landings. One reporter saw 120 people cramming into a DNR hearing on the Lynne plan and observed: "On the same night at a boat landing outside of Rhinelander, a damp crowd of about 25 people gathered to half-heartedly protest Chippewa spearfishing. The contrast between the two gatherings was obvious, evidence that while the issue of spearfishing may be on the wane in northern Wisconsin, the issue of mining is taking on more and more importance."[148]

The geography of the Willow Flowage area offered some explanations for the quick development of the alliance. The Willow River was the location of a walleye spawning bed and rich deer and grouse hunting grounds. ECCOLA co-founder Jim Wise described the Willow Flowage as an "undiscovered jewel" valued by Indians and non-Indians alike.[149]

Among the sportsmen attending anti-mine events was Rhinelander fishing guide Wally Cooper, who had participated in anti-spearing rallies but worked with Karl Fate to oppose the Lynne project. Witness coordinator Debra McNutt expressed shock when she saw Cooper at an anti-mine meeting, but then she realized that he "took the risk" because "sportsmen don't want their water dirty" and "they knew one thing they could agree on was keeping water clean."[150]

Cooper, who had been Oneida County chair of the Wisconsin Conservation Congress, grew up in a family that lived near McCord village, and he practiced subsistence fishing (including illegal spearfishing) in his younger days. He opposed the Ojibwe treaties in the 1980s from an "equal rights" perspective, but he came to believe that in a clean environment there would be "plenty of fish to go around." In the early 1990s, Cooper observed that detailed state and federal studies have been made of northern fish resources because of the spearing conflict and thought that the tribes were doing a better job of regulating the fishery than the DNR's "botched" effort.[151]

The divisiveness of treaty politics in the Lac du Flambeau area may have in odd ways contributed to the development of the alliance against the Lynne mine. The intense conflict in the Lakeland area served as a catalyst driving some area residents to find some bit of common ground, if only to prevent someone from getting killed. ECCOLA co-founder Carolyn Parker felt that "after the hot fights at the landings," the anti-mine alliance was an "opportunity to work on something together" and served as a way to make people "more comfortable." Parker asserted that spearing "closed some people's minds but awakened others" and "brought more of an awareness of Indian culture."[152] She was elected as a Vilas County Board member in 1994, despite her obvious support for the treaties, but was defeated in a 1996 bid for a state assembly seat held by a PARR supporter who used the slogan "If you like Tom Maulson, you'll love Carolyn Parker."

McNutt also believed that spearfishing mobilized reservation residents around Wa-Swa-Gon's leadership and resulted in an unprecedented "serious trust" between tribal and non-tribal treaty supporters—both necessary to form an alliance.[153] Maulson agreed that, although most tribal members were not involved in Lynne mine activism, Lac du Flambeau had been so mobilized by the spearing fight that it remained "a war camp, ready to be called out" over the mining threat.[154] McNutt maintained that the spearing conflict also showed white residents and mining companies that Lac du Flambeau was a "powerful community" that could not be ignored or "pushed around."[155]

Karl Fate, a paper mill worker and director of the Rhinelander chapter of the Wisconsin Resources Protection Council, was one of the Citizens for Treaty Rights founders who had been silenced by death threats during the spearing conflict. He viewed the Lynne mine controversy as a "turning point" in public awareness about both mining and the power of the tribes. But he recalled that white co-workers and friends had very conflicting and sometimes contradictory feelings about the relationship between treaties and mining. One co-worker who adamantly opposed the treaties expressed the hope that the tribes would stop the mine; Fate told him that the tribes cannot stop the mine without the treaties.

Another one of Fate's co-workers who strongly opposed the mine expressed

anger at the tribes for being involved in the mining issue, because that prevented him from getting involved. Fate detected a "realization in the back of
people's minds" that the treaties could stop the mine, but he also observed that
this realization was "easy to suppress." The cautious balance, he contended,
made the alliance "tenuous at times." But he also observed that in the course
of the battle, "some bonding . . . occurs that you don't lose easily."[156]

Even early in the Lynne dispute, Noranda had acknowledged the potential
role of the treaties in protecting tribal "rights to hunting and gathering."[157] The
company lobbied heavily against state Outstanding Resource Water status for
the Willow Flowage, which cast a shadow over the project. In September 1992,
Noranda suspended its exploration program in Wisconsin.[158]

Lac du Flambeau developed several legacies from the spearing and mining
conflicts. Maulson, a Wa-Swa-Gon leader, was elected Lac du Flambeau tribal
president in October 1992 and expanded the tribal casino to become an economic engine for the area and the largest employer in Vilas County. Whereas
the reservation economy had long been dependent on the white border towns
of Minocqua and Woodruff, the roles became almost reversed, generating tourist dollars for the local economy. Wa-Swa-Gon secretary Anita Koser-Thoms
laughed when she recalled first seeing former anti-treaty protesters, who had
to keep their racial attitudes hidden, employed at the tribal casino.[159]

The fallout from spearing had an important effect on a controversy about
a burial ground on the Lac du Flambeau Reservation. The tribe opposed a
condominium development on Strawberry Island, a site of an Ojibwe-Dakota
battle, on a parcel of reservation land that had been obtained by a white family
during the Allotment era. As a Vilas County Board member, Lynne mine opponent Carolyn Parker led county support for tribal protection of the burial
ground. The Vilas County Zoning Board sided with the tribe in 1995, by voting
to deny the developer a construction permit. Though its position was later
overturned, the vote lessened the tribal mistrust of officials from what Maulson had called "Violence County."[160] The tribe finally acquired the sacred island
in 2013.[161]

The spearing and mining conflicts spawned several programs to educate non-
Indians about Ojibwe history and culture. Wa-Swa-Gon leader Nick Hockings
built the Waswagoning traditional village for educating tourists about Ojibwe
culture. Hockings asserted: "If it were not for anti-Indian sentiment, I don't
think I would have seen the need [to build the village]." Hockings ironically
credited anti-treaty leaders for mobilizing a greater sense of tribal identity and
greater outside support for their treaties and Native curriculum. Hockings

recalled that the more "anti-Indian rhetoric" that STA leader Dean Crist put out, "the more we had to come back with information."

Hockings explained: "This negative state of affairs actually in the long run helped us. . . . It built a self-esteem that was never there before. It brought out our culture in many different ways . . . gave us a chance to prove we were a nation." He agreed that there is "still a lot of anti-Indian sentiment" in the Lakeland area, but the organized anti-treaty movement had faded and been replaced by a greater emphasis on environmental issues.[162]

McNutt, like Parker, saw the Lynne mine issue as an opportunity for tribal leaders to consciously establish ties with some members of the rival white community during the spearing conflict, but only "if the fight has the component of building bridges in the midst of fighting." While some treaty supporters may have seen the spearfishing war as "burning bridges" with neighboring communities, McNutt noted that the conflict "can also create new things" and "you can change things through your struggle."[163]

In 1990, when Lac du Flambeau was at the center of the storm over treaty rights, no one could have predicted that the band and its allies would defeat the Lynne mine, whereas Lac Courte Oreilles—at the more peaceful periphery of the treaty conflict—would be unable to defeat the Ladysmith mine. Lac du Flambeau chose to combine a strong assertion of spearfishing with a strong environmental bridge to non-Indians in ceded territory and defeated both the anti-treaty groups and a major mining company. This combination of particularist and universalist approaches drew from a common sense of place and combined it with a strong common purpose against the mining companies.

But Lac du Flambeau's mining struggle lasted only a few years in the 1990s. When mining companies returned to apply for exploration permits in 2009, a similar loose, decentralized alliance reassembled and, by 2012, convinced an initially pro-mining Oneida County Board to discontinue talks with the companies. As a reelected tribal president, Maulson told the board: "We have a stake in Wisconsin. We have a stake in America today. And whatever it's going to take . . . we won't let it happen."[164] The previously powerful anti-treaty movement had been replaced by a powerful pro-treaty movement that could run some of the world's largest mining companies out of northern Wisconsin, and it had even larger battles to face.

CHAPTER 7

Mining and Inclusion

Northern Wisconsin

WHEN CHUCK SLEETER FIRST FISHED ON PICKEREL LAKE IN NORTH-eastern Wisconsin in 1983, he fell in love with the stillness of the lake, with the cry of the loons in the distance, and with his success in catching walleyes by hook and line. Sleeter had no inkling that the same natural beauty and abundance that he sought would spark two intense civil conflicts in the area, over spearfishing and mining. Nor did he conceive that he would find himself at the center of both battles in Wisconsin history—from fighting over the fish to uniting for the fish.

During the Ojibwe spearfishing conflict, Sleeter was one of hundreds of riot-clad sheriff's deputies from around the state who were deployed to northern boat landings to prevent further violence. "These were not pleasant duties," he remembered, describing the long dark hours and the snow piling on deputies' shoulders. Like some other police officers, he became concerned by the racial epithets he heard and "noticed that the bigger the news coverage, the bigger the problem."[1]

The sheriff's deputy from Wood County, in central Wisconsin, decided to return to fish in Pickerel Lake every spring and eventually decided to spend the rest of his life there in the Forest County town of Nashville, which includes the Mole Lake Reservation. The area, about one hundred miles northwest of Green Bay, is covered with pine and birch forests, lakes, streams, and wetlands. It is common to spot bald eagles circling overhead and see the bright green stands of *manoomin* (wild rice) in the lakes. Most residents make a living from either logging or tourism.

Nashville had an unusual geography for Wisconsin townships, as it was divided into two separate thirty-six-square-mile blocs. The small area, at the headwaters of the 223-mile-long Wolf River, was called home by three distinct groups of residents. Upper Nashville, or the "north end," was inhabited by Sokaogon Ojibwe tribal members at Mole Lake and by descendants of Kentuckians who had moved to the area to log in the early twentieth century. The Sokaogon Ojibwe gained a tiny 1,700-acre reservation in 1934, including huge wild rice beds. They would harvest the "food that grows on the water" by knocking the ripe kernels into their canoes. The most prominent feature on the flat landscape is Spirit Hill, where many Ojibwe warriors were buried after an 1806 battle with the Dakota over the wild rice beds.

The north-end "Kentuck" family logging firms in the late 1970s sold many of their properties (including Spirit Hill) to the Exxon mining company, which bought up an area larger than the reservation in preparation for opening a zinc and copper sulfide mine.[2] The proposed mine site was divided between the townships of Nashville and Lincoln, and Mole Lake was one mile downstream. Yet the mining company named its Crandon mine proposal after the predominantly white village eight miles to the north. Its plans would create "one of the country's fiercest grass-roots environmental face-offs."[3]

Despite its tiny size, the Mole Lake Sokaogon Ojibwe Community came in second place among Ojibwe bands in the number of speared fish. The tribe opposed the mine because it could contaminate its wild rice beds and fish with sulfuric acid wastes and reduce groundwater levels that feed its community wells. Tribal members were galvanized when an Exxon biologist referred to their treasured wild rice as "lake weeds."[4] Tributaries of the Wolf River (a Class I trout stream) flowed south away from the mine site toward Mole Lake and lower Nashville, not toward Crandon, upper Nashville, and Lincoln.

Lower Nashville, or the "south end," was dominated by lakefront property owners, many of them pension retirees, from around the Midwest. They tended to join Mole Lakers in opposing the mine as a threat to natural beauty and social stability. In 1983, the same year that Sleeter first fished on Pickerel Lake, 41 percent of Nashville voters had voted for a moratorium on the mine, but they were defeated by a 49 percent pro-mine vote, mainly from white north-end voters. Exxon dropped its mine permit application three years later, citing low metal prices. During Exxon's absence in the late 1980s, the treaty rights conflict over spearfishing divided Native from white residents.

In 1992, Sleeter retired on a tract of land next to Pickerel Lake he purchased from longtime friends Ward and Dorothy Tyra. As a former nurse, Dorothy Tyra had come to know tribal members at Mole Lake and the nearby Forest County Potawatomi Community and found a bond with the tribal members through their families, observing that "they have strong family ties" and "it's such a deep feeling."[5] Sleeter fell in love with the Tyras' Illinois friend Joanne Tacopina, who had summered on the lake since she was two years old.

Also in 1992, Exxon returned to reapply for a permit to open the Crandon metallic sulfide mine. When Sleeter asked Exxon representative Don Moe if the company could guarantee that Nashville's water would not be contaminated, Moe replied no, and Sleeter accused the company of "depriving" residents of "the right to live secure."[6]

THE CRANDON MINE AND THE MOLE LAKE OJIBWE

The mine site at Mole Lake was also five miles upwind of the Forest County Potawatomi community and forty miles upstream (via the sacred Wolf River) of the Menominee Nation. Those tribes joined with the Stockbridge-Munsee (Mohican) Community to form the Niiwin Tribes (using the Ojibwe word for "four") in opposing the Crandon mine.[7] At a 1993 anti-mining conference in Ashland, Mole Lake and Menominee officials asked the Midwest Treaty Network to take on political organizing around the Crandon mine, while the tribes would do the legal, technical, and spiritual work necessary to protect the water.[8] The network formed the Wolf Watershed Educational Project as a campaign to organize Native and non-Native communities downstream from the proposed mine site.[9] The new alliance organized a 1994 anti-mine rally at the state capitol in Madison.[10]

Though they began to oppose the mining proposal, only a few local whites actually attended Native events opposed to the mine, including a 1994 national gathering sponsored by the Indigenous Environmental Network and the Midwest Treaty Network, which drew one thousand people to Mole Lake. Menominee elder Hilary "Sparky" Waukau said after a march to the mine site, "If the white man's society would listen to some of the things we are saying, this would be a lot better society for everyone."[11] Because the schisms of the spearfishing war were still too fresh, non-Natives were not listening to the tribes.[12] Native and non-Native mine opponents therefore tended to work separately.

That reticence began to change the following year, partly as a result of public relations blunders on the part of Exxon and its Rio Algom partner. Their Crandon Mining Company subsidiary proposed a thirty-eight-mile pipeline from the mine to the Wisconsin River to dispose of treated liquid mine wastes, in effect admitting that it could not meet the state Outstanding Resource Water standards for the Wolf River. Bob Schmitz asserted that the pipeline plan could

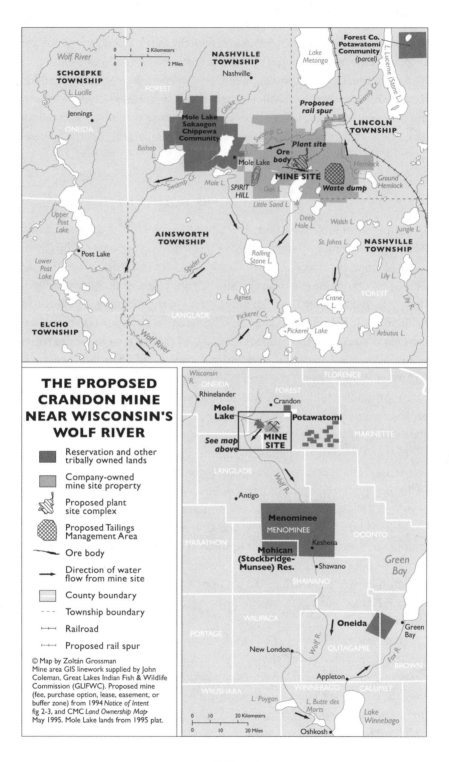

be seen as an attempt "to split us up," by assuring Wolf River sportfishers that their trout stream would be safe, while leaving Mole Lake to face the localized impacts of the solid mine tailings alone.[13] Al Gedicks agreed that the company intended the pipeline to disrupt the "fragile marriage of convenience" between tribes and sportfishers and to "evaporate white opposition" to the mine.[14]

If the pipeline plan was indeed a "shell game" to shift the burdens of waste disposal away from white opponents, the strategy did not work. Wolf River mine opponents kept their central focus on the issues of groundwater drawdown and solid mine wastes and strengthened their relationship with the tribes. Meanwhile, dozens of townships along the Wisconsin River passed resolutions against the pipeline and the mine, for more than two hundred miles along its course.[15]

Crandon Mine and the Menominee

The alliance between the tribes and sportfishers was severely tested in January 1995 when the Menominee Nation filed a lawsuit on treaty rights in its ceded territory of east-central Wisconsin, including sturgeon fishing in the Wolf River and Lake Winnebago, commercial fishing in Lake Michigan, and deer hunting. The delicate, slowly developing alliance between tribes and sportfishing groups was immediately jeopardized by a new division over fishing rights.

The Menominee had successfully resisted removal west of the Mississippi River in 1848, built a sustainable timber industry, and reversed the 1961 federal termination of their tribal status.[16] The boundaries of the reservation can be seen from outer space, because the land around had been cleared by timber barons and farmers, and the biodiverse Menominee forest is still relatively intact.[17] The sturgeon, however, could no longer migrate up the Wolf River to the reservation, because they were blocked by a dam built in 1892.[18]

Restoration of federal status in 1973 did not resolve the tribe's problems. When in 1975, the Menominee Warrior Society carried out an armed occupation of an off-reservation Catholic novitiate, demanding the building be turned into a tribal hospital, white vigilantes attacked and residents of neighboring Shawano and Langlade counties turned against the tribe.

The treaty suit two decades later rekindled strong opposition from fishermen. The case went to the federal court of Judge Barbara Crabb, who had ruled largely in favor of Ojibwe fishing rights. One Lake Michigan charter boat captain predicted an "Indian war" and warned: "It could get rough out there. Some of these people would destroy Indian boats."[19] An angry sportsman told a reporter that she would "see dead Indians floating" down the Wolf River.[20]

Warrior leader Louis Hawpetoss, who had become a respected tribal judge, dismissed charges that the Menominee would harm the fishery, replying, "Just come to our reservation, and see how we have preserved our timber resources." Hawpetoss became a county delegate to the Wisconsin Conservation Congress, the statewide sportsmen's assembly, to work on mining issues and reassure anglers of the tribe's intentions. He found that some anglers were open to dialogue and that "mistrust" of the Wisconsin Department of Natural Resources (DNR) had, he said, "put us together."[21]

In August 1995, the tribal government took the unusual move of combining its work on treaty rights and on mining into one office. Treaty Rights and Mining Impacts Office director Kenneth Fish remembered that some tribal officials objected to the mixing of "a negative and a positive"—the divisive treaty issue with the unifying environmental issue, but he convinced them that the treaties could be used to clean up polluted waters. Fish, a Vietnam veteran, also emphasized the military record of many Menominee, as a way to build bridges to non-Indian veterans.[22]

Sturgeons for Tomorrow representative Tom Soles (from the Lake Winnebago city of Fond du Lac) contacted Fish, and both agreed that there was "going to be no fight over the resources." Soles recalled telling Fish, "We can sit down as friends and still disagree."[23] Soles did not end his opposition to Menominee treaty rights, but joined with the tribe to confront what he saw as a greater threat to the fishery.[24]

Judge Hawpetoss viewed the anti-mine coalition as "not just a tactical alliance" but a long-term relationship developed out of necessity, which could "rub off on other issues." He added that the success of the Keshena casino "completely reversed" the tribe's relationship to the white border town of Shawano. He said: "We were dependent on them . . . and now the roles are reversed. . . . Never in their wildest dreams did they think they'd be forced to work with us."[25] The economic relationship deepened further as the tribe and Shawano County established a joint "heritage area" to attract tourists.[26]

Judge Crabb ruled in 1997 that Menominee treaties had not explicitly guaranteed off-reservation harvesting rights.[27] Despite the tribal loss in the courts, Fish felt that the case may have ironically helped build a "better understanding" with sportfishers, who were forced to "evaluate their own internal feelings." Like the Umatilla dual-track strategy in Oregon, the Menominee mixed treaty confrontation with environmental cooperation. Confrontation alone would have guaranteed a repeat of the Ojibwe spearing clashes, whereas cooperation alone would have risked being ignored by non-Indians unaware of tribal legal and cultural interests far outside reservation boundaries.

The sense of place attached to the Wolf River ultimately provided the bond for the Menominee and sportfishers to see past the treaty dispute. Fish said that white anglers "experience the same thing—touch, vision, hearing . . . quietness" and "they appreciate the river—hear it, smell it, feel it." Fish saved the alliance with his call to sportsmen's groups: "Let's not create evilness for this river."[28] His office opened the Niiwin House next to the proposed Crandon mine site, and it became a key meeting venue for the Wolf Watershed Educational Project.

The Alliance Coalesces

In 1996, the Wolf Watershed Educational Project began a series of speaking tours along the Wolf and Wisconsin Rivers, to organize communities against the Crandon project. At the twenty-two towns visited by the first tour, representatives of tribes, environmental groups, and sportfishing groups spoke, drawing about eleven hundred people. Instead of sending the speakers only to address their own constituencies, organizers decided to show all three parts of the alliance at each of the stops. Some of the sportfishers in the audience heard a tribal member speak for the first time in their lives. At one tour stop at a meeting of the Merrill Sportsmen's Club, a Mole Lake tribal speaker even won the door prize.[29] The speaking tour culminated with a rally at the mining company's local headquarters in Rhinelander, attended by one thousand people.[30]

The series of speaking tours from 1996 to 2000 resulted in small grassroots anti-mine groups being formed along the rivers and around the state, such as Protect Our Wolf River (POWR) in Shawano.[31] Dave Blouin of the Mining Impact Coalition said: "One of our goals is to cement some of those relationships where people were at each other's throats not very long ago. And to help them understand that they have more in common than they realize."[32]

Mole Lake tribal judge Fred Ackley was one of the main tour speakers and often offered guidance at alliance meetings. His lengthy admonitions described the Earth fighting back against exploitation through hurricanes, floods, and other natural disasters. When Ackley had lived in Milwaukee, he had helped to manufacture mining equipment.[33] Frances Van Zile, his companion, was a feisty defender of fishing and hunting traditions, who urged women to join the alliance as the "keepers of the water."[34]

The tour speakers also included a trio of elderly trout fishermen from White

Lake, downstream on the Wolf River in Langlade County, who had befriended tribal environmental leaders, notably Menominee elder Sparky Waukau.[35]

Herbert (Herb) Buettner was the owner of the Wild Wolf Inn resort, treasured by rafters and kayakers who shot the whitewater rapids of the Wolf River. He served as president of the Wolf River chapter of Trout Unlimited (TU) and as chairman of the Langlade County Republican Party. For decades, Buettner had protected the Wolf River from dams and waste dumps, quietly encouraged by his wife, Genie. The successful battles contributed to the 1968 federal declaration of a portion of the upper Wolf as a National Wild and Scenic River. In the 1990s, Buettner was so disgusted by the pro-mine stance of Republican governor Tommy Thompson that he removed his campaign literature from the party table at the county fair and replaced it with anti-Exxon literature.[36]

George Rock was a retired engineer with a biting wit who lived with his wife, Marilyn, in an 1872 log cabin downstream on the Wolf River and served as vice president of the TU chapter and president of the local chapter of the Wisconsin Resources Protection Council. Though he did not live in Nashville, he served as an important bridge between the white residents and local tribal members he had met when his father had been a local schoolteacher.

Bob Schmitz was a white-bearded retired telephone workers' union president from Green Bay, where he had become experienced in the art of rank-and-file organizing, along with his wife, Millie, and had gotten to know Oneida tribal members. As an avid hunter and fisherman, he had a cabin in White Lake and joined fellow World War II veteran Sparky Waukau in a "mutual love of the river."[37] Schmitz's gruff language and colorful humor punctuated alliance meetings. He also brought Roscoe and Evelyn Churchill from Ladysmith's anti-mine movement to collaborate with the new mining fight.

Native and white elders were joined by younger activists concerned about the growth of corporate power. University of Wisconsin students from Stevens Point, including Dana Churness and Deanna Erickson, attended anti-globalization protests around the country but returned home to assist the local "people power" movement in their own backyard. At alliance meetings, they listened as Ackley and Buettner stood to speak about the environment and democracy, drawing from their respective oral traditions.

The Wolf Watershed Educational Project meetings were held monthly at different reservations and border towns and brought together organizers face-to-face in one circle. According to organizer Debra McNutt, the hosting group would provide a potluck lunch, sharing food and giving people the opportunity to get to know one another. Participants often brought birthday cakes and passed around cards for those who were ill. They also sent sympathy cards to the different executive teams that revolved in and out of the mining company, advising them to "rent, don't buy" their homes, because their stay would be temporary. McNutt recalled that Buettner would tell others at the meeting, "[I feel] closer to you people than to people I attend church with on Sundays."[38]

Building the Alliance

The anti-mine movement epitomized Wisconsin's history of progressive populism and of rural conservation ethics (represented by John Muir and Aldo Leopold).[39] It harnessed northern resentment of state agencies in Madison, usually a conservative strategy. It also drew from historic resilience and perseverance of Native nations. In poor logging communities such as Forest County, resource companies had been able to portray mainstream urban-based white environmental activists as yuppies or hippies who do not care about rural jobs. Mining companies attempted to pit white residents against Native people, environmentalists against union members building mining equipment, and rural northerners against urban residents and students. But they failed each time to divide Wisconsinites by race, by class, or by region.

What mining companies faced along the Wolf River was something new—an environmental movement that was rural-based, middle-class and working-class, intergenerational, and multiracial. The Wolf Watershed Educational Project never met during deer hunting season, because nearly all of its members' families hunted. This movement addressed not just a corporation's environmental threats but also its threats to rural cultures, local economies, and democratic institutions, and drew in former followers of the anti-treaty movement.

Rhinelander fishing guide Wally Cooper had spoken at anti-treaty rallies in the late 1980s, but by 1996 he was on stage with Mole Lake tribal members at rallies against the Crandon mine "because Native Americans can stop the mine." Cooper also reported, "We've seen a lot more cultural awareness" as "the tribes grow more prosperous."[40] Frances Van Zile remembered feeling "really surprised" at seeing Cooper at anti-mine meetings. She had discussed her environmental concerns with him at the boat landings and "always wondered if someone was listening, and he was."[41]

In 1997, a diverse range of groups around the state came together to pass the Sulfide Mining Moratorium Bill (originally proposed by Evelyn Churchill), forcing companies to "prove it first" by showing examples of sulfide mines that had operated and been reclaimed without violating environmental laws.[42] Mining interests spent more than $2 million on lobbying and public relations

Mole Lake Sokaogon Chippewa judge Fred Ackley and Shawano mine opponent Joe Skaleski (wearing cheesehead) at a 1998 Wisconsin state capitol
rally against the proposed Crandon mine. (Courtesy: Al Gedicks / Wisconsin
Resources Protection Council)

to defeat the bill.[43] They also tried to appeal to labor unions in a series of TV
ads, but education by anti-mine union members (led by Schmitz, McNutt, and
Milwaukee Steelworkers member Gerry Gunderson) educated labor unions
about the poor health and safety in Exxon and Rio Algom mines. Many union
locals and federations, with members who enjoy Northwoods fishing, passed
anti-mine resolutions.[44]

The successful fight to pass the moratorium bill (signed by normally pro-mining Governor Thompson) did not stop the permit process, but brought the local Crandon fight to a statewide level. Another rural alliance, Save Our Unique Lands (SOUL) tried unsuccessfully to stop a northwestern Wisconsin electric transmission line, which could have provided power to the Crandon project, and held joint rallies with the Wolf Watershed Educational Project.[45]

The Nashville Revolt

In the Town of Nashville, Exxon and Rio Algom worked behind the scenes to secure a local agreement from the pro-mining town board, made up of three north-end members, to waive local zoning authority that could hamper the mine's construction or operation. Townspeople were infuriated when they found out about the board's secret negotiations with the Crandon Mining Company.

On December 7, 1996, about 340 Nashville citizens met in a special town meeting, including retirees, small loggers, lakefront property owners, and Mole Lake tribal members, to prevent their board from signing the agreement. Town chair Richard Pitts adjourned the meeting before it began and called in county police to close the building. Pitts was loudly booed by the crowd, as retired men and women stood on their chairs and shouted: "This is America? This is democracy?" The Nashville revolt had begun.

Tom Ward, an outspoken north-end elderly resident who was county chapter president of the Wisconsin Resources Protection Council, commented of the aborted town meeting: "What we are seeing here is government of Exxon, by Exxon, and for Exxon."[46] The town board signed the local agreement, as Pitts called the mine opponents "newcomers." Mole Lake tribal judge Fred Ackley recalled his amusement that the north-end "old-timers" would accuse the south-end retirees of being "newcomers," when his Native family lived in the area "far longer than either of them."[47]

Ward and others urged Chuck Sleeter to run against Pitts in the next local election and recruited candidates to run for the other two board posts, including Joanne Tacopina and Mole Lake tribal member Robert Van Zile, a serious, thoughtful spiritual leader. Sleeter explained that a Native candidate would help boost tribal voter turnout.[48]

In the April 1997 election, 98.4 percent of Nashville's eligible voters cast ballots—the highest turnout of any election in the history of Wisconsin at that time—and Sleeter won 55 percent of the vote.[49] Some tribal members complained of having their voting credentials challenged by mine backers.[50] For them, Robert Van Zile's unprecedented victory had a special resonance. His sister Frances Van Zile remembered: "I was surprised when my brother was elected... I sat down and I cried. I never thought it could happen, but it did."[51]

The Nashville revolt involved many local white residents whose main concern was not environmental but rather how their local democratic process had been undermined by secret talks with an outside corporation.[52] Wisconsin Resources Protection Council organizer George Rock had told Nashville residents that they were "being treated like a Third World country," in a way that Native Americans had been treated, and that "now white people are being treated the same way because they're in the way."[53]

The new town board rescinded the local agreement, touching off a legal battle with the mining company in state courts and support from around the state and country.[54] De Pere schoolchildren played out the Nashville conflict in class skits, though the teacher faced difficulty in finding students who wanted to play the mining company representative instead of Sleeter.[55] Nashville lost its case in the state courts in 2002, but more importantly had won in the court of public opinion.

Tribal and Local Governments

With media attention focused on Nashville's revolt against the Crandon mine, few observers noticed that the township was going through another transformation: a remarkable improvement in the township's relations with the reservation within its boundaries. Sleeter appointed tribal members to town boards and attended every Mole Lake Tribal Council meeting, where he was put first in the agenda. Tribal members who had previously sat in the back of town board meetings, Sleeter noted, gradually moved to the front and joined discussions. The township passed an intergovernmental cooperation resolution promising to consult with the tribe on issues of mutual concern.[56]

In 1994, Mole Lake had purchased 1,306 acres just to the north of the reservation, to overcome a severe housing shortage, and applied to put the land in federal trust. The old town board opposed trust status as a cut in its tax revenue, but the new board actually asked the feds to approve it and received compensation in the form of tribal services.[57] The township and tribe exchanged snow plowing, garbage pickup, and medical protection and consolidated their fire districts. When the tribe faced delays in paying a contractor for road grading, the township treasury fronted the funds. When the township was mandated to provide elderly emergency shelters, the tribe allowed access to its new elderly services building. The tribe even gave Sleeter the unprecedented status of a

U.S. Bureau of Indian Affairs "screener," enabling the township to join the tribe in receiving free equipment no longer needed by federal agencies.[58]

The tribal-local government cooperation created more social mixing and cultural understanding. Mole Lake children helped Sleeter put up campaign signs and turned to him after a racist incident on a school bus.[59] Tribal spiritual leaders provided prayer invocations at non-Indian events, such as the 2000 wedding of Sleeter and Tacopina. Rock commented that "passing a pipe" had become "part of the understanding" that extended the alliance beyond mere tactical convenience.[60] Ainsworth mine opponent Sonny Wreczycki decided to protect Indian burial mounds on his Rollingstone Lake property and looked at restoring wild rice beds destroyed by settlement.[61] Frances Van Zile remarked that non-Indians began to ask her how to prepare wild rice, because "before, they thought Indians don't still do that stuff."[62]

Sleeter observed that the "heart-lifting" emotional battles over the mine enabled residents to examine the "racial part of the puzzle" and understand why tribal members "don't trust white people."[63] Tom Ward saw the alliance as "breaking down the racial gap" to protect the "mystique" of the "wild and untamed" Wolf River. Ward credited the tribes for taking a "no-compromise position," asserting that many whites had until 1996 seen the mine as "inevitable," with an attitude of "let's see what we can get." Tribal leadership shifted the debate away from a middle-ground "safe mining" stance, by providing a model of people who "have stood up for themselves."[64]

Wisconsin Resources Protection Council organizer Sylvester Poler of Mole Lake praised open-minded white residents who no longer view Indians as the "other people" and tribal members who are no longer "good Indians" who can be safely ignored or patronized. He viewed the fishing war as "an education in itself" as more white residents "come to understand that sovereignty is a reality." "Sportfishermen are coming to realize there is more of a threat from corporations than from us," he said. "Our protections are their protections. They'll circle their wagons with us."[65]

Nashville and other townships along the Wolf River supported the tribe's successful application to the U.S. Environmental Protection Agency (EPA) to set zero-degradation standards for waters flowing into the reservation, under the Clean Water Act.[66] Their support was key in the 1999 EPA approval of Mole Lake's Treatment as State status.[67] A state appeal of the approval was opposed by the Wisconsin Council of TU and a petition of 454 individuals from 121 Wisconsin communities.[68] In 2002, the U.S. Supreme Court refused to hear the state appeal.[69]

The Forest County Potawatomi, who had parcels of land five miles downwind from the mine site, redesignated the air over its reservation as Class I air quality (as at Northern Cheyenne). The move was aimed at heavy metallic dust from the proposed mine site, by then owned by Rio Algom's Nicolet Minerals Company.[70] Business lobbies and local and county governments strongly opposed the redesignation.[71] One Republican legislator described the tribal clean-air plan as "a black cloud over our heads."[72] Yet the Potawatomi also gained support from some citizens who wrote the EPA to support the air redesignation.[73] The tribe ultimately won Class I air redesignation in 2008.[74]

At least one 1997 poll showed that non-Indian state residents would prefer tribal regulations if they safeguarded the environment more than state laws did.[75] The alliance was using parallel tracks in its strategy, concurrently using the powers of local, state, tribal, and federal governments to stop the mine. Even if some of these efforts were set back, the movement was moving forward on at least one of the tracks at all times.

Economic Cooperation

To keep both Native and non-Native youth in the economically depressed area, Nashville and Mole Lake also began to explore economic development initiatives, as alternatives to the boom-and-bust mining economy and to the initially shaky tribal gaming industry. They opened a tourist information center and carried out a survey of community economic needs. Sleeter recalled that, at the first survey meeting, tribal members sat on one side of the town hall room and non-Indian residents sat on the other side. Each side slowly discovered their needs were virtually identical, and subsequent seating arrangements were more mixed.[76]

In 1999, the U.S. Department of Agriculture's Rural Development Office chose Mole Lake and Nashville as part of a federally funded enterprise zone. The Northwoods NiiJii Enterprise Community also included the partner communities of the Menominee Tribe with the city and county of Shawano and the Lac du Flambeau Ojibwe Band with six neighboring non-Indian townships.[77] *NiiJii* is the Ojibwe word for "friend," and each of the sets of partner communities created "Indian and non-Indian working relationships" in what had been the most intense areas of conflict in Wisconsin.[78]

Lac du Flambeau, Mole Lake, and Menominee had previously had contentious relationships with white border towns, which even flared into violent conflict. The list of Northwoods NiiJii communities resembles the communities once mentioned prominently in police incident reports—of clashes between Menominee warriors and white vigilantes in 1975, between Lac du Flambeau spearfishers and white anglers in 1989, and between anti-mine Mole Lake tribal members and pro-mine Nashville leaders in 1996.

Even aside from these open conflicts, the white border towns were places of tension and fear for tribal members, leading tribes to build new schools and grocery stores on the reservations. White border-town residents would rarely venture to the reservations, which they believed were havens of poverty and crime and the source of economic and environmental threats that transgressed reservation boundaries.

By the 2000s, the relationship between reservations and border towns was turned on its head. The very same communities that had been in Wisconsin headlines as the worst flashpoints of Native-white conflict became those most at the forefront of collaboration. The borders of fear between them became borders of cooperation and began to blur their social and political borders within a common watershed. Resource conflicts had ironically educated non-Indians that tribes had retained their Indigenous cultures and their legal powers as sovereign nations.

Reservations and border towns turned their proximity to each other from a problem into an advantage. Tribes with successful casinos funded festivals and musical events in border towns, which had trivialized and commercialized Native cultures for decades. Mole Lake's small casino hosted country bands, drawing many local "Kentuck" residents. Racial prejudice and job discrimination still occurred in white-owned stores and restaurants, but there were fewer and weaker organized anti-Indian groups. Some white businesses continued to resent the casinos and tribal environmental rules, but northerners increasingly began to view them as enhancing the tourism economy.[79]

This process reached an advanced stage in Nashville and Mole Lake, but the participants agreed that there was still a long way to go. Sleeter reported that pro-mine citizens continued to call him an "Indian lover."[80] Poler pointed out an essential difference between the two communities when he warned: "Whites can move away. . . . We are here; we are going to fight. . . . This is our last stand. We don't have any other reservation to go to."[81]

The Death of the Crandon Mine

By 2001, Exxon and Rio Algom had been replaced as Crandon mine project companies by the Australian / South African mining conglomerate BHP Billiton, the world's largest mining company. A poll showed that 57 percent of north-eastern Wisconsinites opposed new metallic sulfide mines in the state, roughly even with the statewide figure of 55 percent statewide.[82]

A bill to ban cyanide in mining passed the Wisconsin State Senate in 2001. It was blocked in the State Assembly, but not before it had "branded" the mine with toxic cyanide.[83] Forest County Potawatomi used $250,000 for a statewide ad campaign that mocked mining company representatives as bumbling, irresponsible outsiders loudly asking, "Where's the best fishing?" Meanwhile, opponents of mining, power lines, and springwater pumping converged in a 2001 "Citizens' Assembly" to "unite opponents of corporate rule in Wisconsin and to build a democratic and sustainable future."[84]

Wisconsin's movement made an impression on the global mining industry. One industry journal identified the state as one of four battlegrounds for the global mining industry. A London-based industry journal stated that "the Wolf Watershed Educational Project (WWEP), a U.S.-based alliance of environmental groups, Native American nations, local residents, unions and students . . . is just one example of what is becoming a very real threat to the global mining industry: global environmental activism."[85] The Vancouver-based Fraser Institute rated Wisconsin at or near the bottom of its annual "mining investment attractiveness score" from 1998 through the 2000s because of the state's "well-publicized aversion to mining."[86] Toronto's *North American Mining* claimed, "The increasingly sophisticated political maneuvering by environmental special interest groups has made permitting a mine in Wisconsin an impossibility."[87] The National Mining Association complained that Wisconsin websites run by "barbarians at the gates of cyberspace" were spreading anti-mining strategies around the world.[88]

On October 28, 2003, the twenty-eight-year fight to stop the proposed Crandon mine came to a sudden and dramatic end, when the Mole Lake and Potawatomi tribes gained ownership and control of the mine site. The Forest County Potawatomi and the Sokaogon Ojibwe paid more than $16.5 million for the 5,939-acre mine site. The grassroots movement had driven away potential corporate partners for the company and had caused the sale price to drop by tens of millions of dollars.[89]

Tribal members and their allies flooded into the Nicolet Minerals Information Center to celebrate. The Nicolet Minerals Company was acquired by Mole Lake and dropped all mining permit applications. As he hung a giant sold sign on the building, Potawatomi tribal member Dennis Shepherd exclaimed: "We rocked the boat. Now we own the boat."[90] The two tribes divided the Crandon

Crandon mine opponents celebrate at the headquarters of the Nicolet Minerals Company, after its 2003 purchase by the Mole Lake Sokaogon Chippewa and Forest County Potawatomi tribes in northern Wisconsin. (Photo by the author)

mine site between themselves, to ensure that the mine could never come back from the dead.

Nicolet Minerals ex-director Gordon Connor Jr. complained that Wisconsin's "anti-corporate culture" defeated the mine. He added: "We have engaged every significant mining interest in the world. The message is clear. They don't want to do business in the state of Wisconsin."[91] Ex-president Dale Alberts said: "[The Crandon mine] is dead and gone forever. I think it is essentially the end of mining in the state. It is a bitter pill."[92] In testimony before Congress, he admitted that Mole Lake's Treatment as State water quality standards "established a very difficult hurdle for the mining project."[93]

Wisconsin media tended to tie the Crandon mine victory to tribal casino profits, rather than to tribal sovereignty itself. A reporter who had covered both the spearing and mining fights critiqued this tendency: "The changes in Wisconsin's Native American community . . . seem too deep and too profound to be credited only to more money. . . . As important was the growth in cultural pride that came in the years after the treaty rights decision. When visiting the reservations 20 years ago, it was rare to come across indigenous language classes or cultural teachings. Now they are the norm. . . . Wisconsin's tribes have not only demonstrated they are an economic and political power in the state, they also showed that the strength and the will and the spirit of their ancestors burns strong in them, too."[94]

The national weekly *Indian Country Today* also commented on the Crandon victory as part of the assertion of tribal powers across Indian Country: "Just a few years ago, the mining companies negotiated with local townships and would totally ignore the tribal representations. Now, tribal representatives are buying out whole mining operations. . . . Native tribal peoples often still think outside the big, square, American box. Creativity flows from this extra perspective. Add a good ethical base . . . and the mix can bring positive results, for tribes and for many others. We've said it before: Indian sovereignty is good for America."[95]

The Wolf Watershed Educational Project celebrated at Mole Lake, where anti-mine farmer Roscoe Churchill cut a victory cake jointly with Mole Lake vice chair Tina Van Zile, who had played a pivotal role in environmental research and the site's purchase. The tribes later held a victory powwow, next to Lambeau Field in Green Bay, drawing hundreds of dancers and eleven drums (representing each Wisconsin tribe). Mole Lake opened a new resort hotel and turned the mine site into a series of hiking and ATV trails. The Spirit Hill sacred burial grounds were returned to tribal control, and native tall grasses grew back in what would have been the mine's parking lot. Frances Van Zile later scoffed that a mining company representative had laughed at her when she formed a prayer circle at that spot, because her "tobacco ties aren't going to stop the mine."[96]

The historic defeat of the Crandon mine was more than a victory of "people power" against corporate power. During the treaty war, Ojibwe and sportfishers fought over the fish, but during the mining fight they united to protect the fish and began to heal some of their divisions. The tribal purchase of the mine site brought the relationship full circle and marked a small rollback in the history of Native land dispossession and was a direct example of "environmental repossession."[97]

On a local level, the relationship between white township residents and tribal members changed how they live on the land. When Chuck Sleeter first dropped his hook in Pickerel Lake two decades earlier, most Natives and non-Natives accepted a meaning of home that was based on political and racial boundaries. They lived side-by-side, but not together in the same place, in the treasured headwaters of the Wolf River.

In Nashville and Mole Lake, the meaning of home began to change. No longer did the Native home and the white majority's home stop at the reservation boundary. It encompassed both tribal and non-tribal lands in a common place defined by the flowing of streams and groundwater, the weaving of canoes through wild rice beds, and even the scraping of shared graders and snowplows over local roads.

THE PENOKEES MINE AND THE BAD RIVER OJIBWE

In 2011, new alliances developed to oppose iron taconite mining plans in the Penokee Hills, upstream from the Bad River Ojibwe Reservation. The proposed mine site in the Penokees (also called the Gogebic Range), straddled Ashland and Iron counties. The iron boom started in the 1880s and supplied iron ore to the Great Lakes steel industry until the 1960s.[98] The mines had left a legacy of asbestos and sulfide contamination in Lake Superior and damage to local waterways and mineworkers' health. In the early twenty-first century, a number of firms took a renewed interest in the iron ore, to feed the industrial growth of China and India.

The headwaters of the Bad River flow toward Lake Superior, the world's largest surface freshwater body. Around the mouth of the Bad River are the 16,000-acre Kakagon Sloughs, one of the world's largest freshwater estuaries, a key fish spawning ground, and the largest wild rice bed in Wisconsin. Mike Wiggins Jr., chairman of the Bad River Band of Lake Superior Chippewa, said that the mine "would drop the water table" and "destroy wild rice crops that grow in wetlands" and that "hunting, fishing, and tourism isn't an option if there is sulfuric acid in the trout streams." He added: "We all have one thing in common; we are all made of water. Water announces our arrival at birth and water is in our bodies and our blood until we die. The water we drink is life itself."[99]

Ashland and Iron counties had seen some anti-treaty harassment and violence during the spearfishing conflict, more than around Lac Courte Oreilles but less than around Lac du Flambeau and Mole Lake. The Ashland school was repeatedly a site of racial friction, and the Ashland city government had strongly opposed treaty rights. Bad River was widely known as a traditionalist, pro-treaty stronghold, and its main town of Odanah has been the headquarters of the Great Lakes Indian Fish and Wildlife Commission (GLIFWC) since its 1984 founding. Bad River educator Joe Rose Sr., professor emeritus of American Indian Studies at Northland College, observed: "As each new generation reaches adulthood, then they take on that responsibility to look seven generations ahead. When my grandfathers signed that Treaty of La Pointe in 1854, that was five generations from me. They were looking at my grandchildren's generation."[100]

Bad River was also the scene of an earlier anti-mining struggle, related to a copper mine in the adjacent Upper Peninsula of Michigan. In July 1996, the Anishinaabe Ogichiidaa (Protectors of the People) halted train shipments of sulfuric acid on tracks crossing the Bad River Reservation. The Wisconsin Central Limited railroad had been shipping the acid to extract remaining ore from the closed White Pine copper mine in Michigan. The only tracks to the mine site crossed the Bad River Reservation, where they traversed old, crumbling trestles over rivers and wetlands.[101]

When the EPA granted a permit for the White Pine project, without first holding a hearing, Red Cliff activist Walter Bresette resigned as Indigenous chair of the National Environmental Justice Advisory Council, which formally advises the EPA, and worked to plan the nonviolent blockade. He commented: "Sovereignty is not something you ask for. Sovereignty is the act thereof. This blockade certainly demonstrates that."[102]

The Ojibwe blockade of the tracks was supported by many non-Native locals, some of whom had shown hostility toward spearing. Blockade participant Joe Dan Rose told a Bad River powwow audience of an Ashland anti-treaty activist who said to the Ogichiidaa, "We're behind you 100 percent." Rose added: "That's very significant. This is a gentleman who at one time stood on the opposite side of the spectrum."[103]

The company planned to bypass the blockade by moving acid on an alternate rail track, but a non-Indian support vigil in the town of Mellen signaled that any new route would also be targeted by protests. The mining company was unable to play its geographical "shell game" because of widespread public support for the Bad River position, and it dropped the permit application in May 1997. Even though the Bad River Ojibwe lived in Wisconsin, they had stopped a mine reopening in Michigan, giving pause to mining executives promoting new mines in the region.

In the 2000s, mining companies began a renewed interest in metallic mining in the Lake Superior region. In the Yellow Dog Plains of the Upper Peninsula, the Keewenaw Bay Indian Community in 2002 joined environmentalists in fighting plans for Rio Tinto / Kennecott's copper mine at sacred Eagle Rock.[104] But the movement was defeated, largely due to Michigan's strong pro-mining corporate culture.[105] Another metallic sulfide mining proposal on the

Michigan side of the Menominee River border, known as the Back Forty Project, persisted into the 2010s, opposed by the Menominee Nation (concerned about burial sites) and environmental groups.[106]

In Wisconsin's Penokee Range upstream from Bad River, RGGS Land and Minerals and LaPointe Iron Company took an interest in iron ore exploration in 2004. Activists who had opposed the Crandon mine (such as Deanna Erickson) started the Penokee Range Alliance to oppose the two companies' mining plans, which never materialized.[107]

The Bad River Tribe also opposed the first phase of the Penokee mining plans but did not get centrally involved, partly because it was pursuing Treatment as State status (under the Clean Water Act), which the EPA granted to the tribe in 2009. The tribe said that its water quality standards help protect waterways outside reservation boundaries: "Water knows no boundaries. It is a living, moving part of life."[108]

The Penokees Mine Battle Erupts

The two companies retained the 22,000-acre property between Mellen and Upson, which they leased in January 2011 to Gogebic Taconite (GTAC), a subsidiary of the Cline Group coal mining conglomerate from Florida. Cline planned to spend $1.5 billion in constructing the largest mine in Wisconsin history.[109] Unlike the shaft mine planned at Crandon, GTAC proposed to use millions of tons of explosives to dig a 4.5 mile-long open pit as the first phase of a mountaintop removal operation that could extend 22 miles long. When scientists revealed the presence of asbestos-type rock and sulfides in the deposit, the opposition took off.

The Crandon and Penokees alliances were similar in many ways, but the political context and atmosphere differed radically.[110] In February 2011, the entire state of Wisconsin was swept by grassroots protests against the agenda of newly elected Republican governor Scott Walker, including his attacks on labor unions, public education, and the environment. In many ways, the Crandon struggle had been a precursor to this anti-corporate rebellion, and many Walker opponents joined the new anti-mining fight as a tactic to oppose the governor's policies.[111]

In June 2011, mine opponents founded the Penokee Hills Education Project, inspired by the Wolf Watershed Educational Project that opposed the Crandon mine. It involved activists who had earlier backed the tracks blockade, such as Frank Koehn, and others who had opposed the Crandon mine, such as Dave Blouin of the Mining Impact Coalition and Dana Churness.[112] Project members

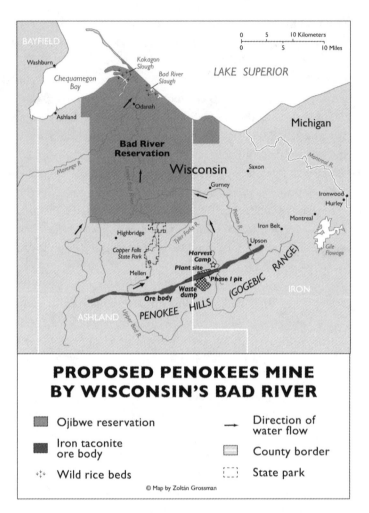

PROPOSED PENOKEES MINE BY WISCONSIN'S BAD RIVER

- ▪ Ojibwe reservation
- ▪ Iron taconite ore body
- ✛ Wild rice beds
- → Direction of water flow
- ▭ County border
- ▢ State park

© Map by Zoltán Grossman

Pete Rasmussen and Bill Heart took visitors on tours of the mine site area around the Tyler Forks River, an idyllic area rich in waterways. A Facebook page helped to keep mine opponents linked throughout the region, and a Penokees Read group brought together writers to extol the beauty of the hills.[113] Koehn told mining opponents: "If you want a seat at this table, this is about the water. . . . You had that common thread, that common passion to protect the water."[114]

Bad River chairman Mike Wiggins Jr. compared the growing public awareness as akin to coming out "of a deep sleep into a lighter sleep, into more of a semi-awoke state where you're wondering what's going on." He continued: "Still trying to ignore it, still trying to engage in the rat race but at the same time, some of the stuff that's hurting people, hurting life, hurting the water is hard to ignore. . . . Then a funny thing happens along the way. Citizens, good citizens, red, black, yellow, white and all the shades between started getting roughed up a little bit . . . they started attending public hearings."[115]

The Penokees mine site was geographically split between different jurisdictions (Ashland and Iron counties) with differing attitudes toward the mine, much as the Crandon site was split between Forest County townships. Many Iron County white residents (particularly around the county seat of Hurley) saw a new mine as reversing the mining bust and devastating job losses of the 1960s, or they were fearful of speaking out. In Ashland County, residents tended to prioritize the tourism industry based on clean water and opposed the mine. The Bad River Watershed Association had formed in Ashland County in 2002 to protect the waterways and sloughs.[116]

Bobbi Rongstad, chair of the association's Mining Impact Committee, lives about ten miles from the proposed mine pit and served on Bad River's energy committee. She reported that she felt, as many other Ashland County mine opponents did, "far closer to my neighbors in Odanah than I do to my neighbors in Hurley." She observed that when Bad River leaders testified to the Iron County Board, they were met with a police presence and were ridiculed for bringing a drum and for speaking Ojibwe. When Red Cliff tribal member Sandra Nevala wore an Ojibwe jingle dress to a hearing, she was evicted for being "noisy" but continued to dance for ninety minutes outside the door.[117]

Potlucks and Fish Fries

Key figures in the initial bridge building between the communities were two Bad River tribal members who had spent much of their lives away from the reservation but returned to live in the area later in life. Tribal attorney Philomena (Phoebe) Kebec and her retired mother, Allie Raven, put their work into building "person-to-person interaction" as "absolutely critical" to building a meaningful alliance. In October 2011, they began to host a series of potlucks in the reservation town of Odanah, welcoming tribal members and non-Native allies into an informal setting they called Organized Chaos for the Penokees.

The monthly potlucks assembled with no funding or written agendas. They always started with a prayer and a smudge of tobacco and cedar, followed by a meal and discussion. The potlucks drew from 6 to 115 people every month, building relationships between the neighbors and creating a "beehive" where people got involved in projects or events around their specific skills and interests. Kebec explained: "We've had to make this struggle our life. We have to have fun, and it can't be stressful and scary."[118]

Raven was a veteran of "Saul Alinsky–style" community organizing in Chicago and Minneapolis. She found that it was easier to draw tribal members to an event on the reservation than to a local border town. But Raven initially felt the potlucks were "never going to work," that they would "never get . . . these white people to go to the rez.'" But as she found: "Feeding them is just a wonderful way of getting them to show up . . . a nice way to unite people and speak in a friendly way. . . . I have seen some really, really deep friendships develop between people who got thrown together in this process and then realized that they have some distinct common interests that go beyond the mining thing."[119]

Jill Hartley, another Bad River tribal member who grew up away from the reservation, got involved in opposing the mine through her cultural work with tribal youth. After attending ceremonies at a log roundhouse and hearing from Bad River elder educator Joe Rose Sr. and Mole Lake spiritual leader Robert Van Zile, she felt she needed to get involved because Ojibwe women are "keepers of the water." Hartley joined the tribal mining committee and saw the alliance as playing out Anishinaabe prophecies of "the lighting of the Eighth Fire" of global peace, based on the "universal value that life comes from water." She noted that white "newcomers" love the area because of the water and that gaming employment has lessened other locals' distance from the tribe.[120]

In Iron County, Hurley resident Maureen Matusewic joined the movement after hearing a "slick" mining company representative speaking "like a used car salesman." Her father was an avid trout fisherman and iron miner who had been crushed in a mine accident. When she heard tribal members testifying against the mine, she "figured most of the white locals would not be moved by testimonies for wild rice." Shortly afterward, while walking her dog by Tyler Forks River, she came across a "miraculously shaped ice spike" that was "in the shape and size of a Native woman wearing a shawl." An academic researcher on ice spikes said it was the most unusual he had ever seen. She contacted the tribe to report on the "ice angel," and Kebec and Hartley welcomed her to the potlucks.[121]

The Penokee Hills Education Project hosted a series of fish fries—a mainstay of Wisconsin culture—in local communities, even drawing some mine supporters. Koehn recalled: "We went from a very adversarial situation to where we got some humor, and people broke down and told the truth. They're just tired of laying people off their businesses. . . . We got to put the human side to economic development. . . . You're never going to get that at a public

Penokees mine opponents gather at the Wisconsin state capitol in Madison, where one of the Bad River drummers was arrested in 2013. (Courtesy: Ros Nelson)

hearing. . . . You find that out by actually face-to-face talking with people."[122] Koehn stated that the Native/non-Native relationship had improved over the three-decade treaty rights conflict. Bad River had worked together with white neighbors to protect the lake, and white kids had learned about treaties in their school curriculum. Koehn asserted: "Those treaties belong to me as much as they do to any tribal member because that's the reason we're here. . . . It's our job to find out why these treaties came about."[123]

Wiggins explained what people began to realize: "If we can acknowledge our differences as human beings but acknowledge the commonality of our home . . . we're on our way to talking about the absolute gorgeous beauty of our home. . . . When people in the particular impacted area stop buying into divide and conquer, stop buying into prejudice and realize that they're all in the same boat . . . we can all turn our attention outward from ourselves, from each other and start to love the big lake. . . . We can start to love those rivers and the thousands of waterfalls that would be destroyed if this thing happened."[124]

Because of the growing alliance, Governor Walker's DNR "fast-tracked" the Penokees mine proposal. Through 2012, Walker and the Republican-dominated state assembly tried to weaken the Mining Moratorium Law and to pass a new mining bill that would drastically weaken environmental regulations.[125] When one such bill was narrowly defeated in the state senate, GTAC temporarily withdrew in December 2012, only to return when a new bill passed and was signed by the governor in March 2013.

Harvest Camp

In the meantime, Bad River and other Ojibwe bands took a strong public stand against the mine plans. Joe Rose Sr. and other tribal members placed seven eagle feather staffs at the springs where the Bad River originates and flows through the watershed to the river mouth on Lake Superior.[126] In February 2013, tribal members converged on the state capitol, the scene of continuing "Solidarity Sing Along" protests against Walker, and media coverage intensified after a tribal drummer was arrested. In April, Lac Courte Oreilles tribal members, led by *News from Indian Country* editor Paul DeMain, established the Harvest Educational Learning Project Camp next to the mine site. Although the Penokees were far from Lac Courte Oreilles, tribal families had acquired plots in the area during the Allotment era.

The Harvest Camp served as a magnet for tribal members, local white residents, and mine opponents from around the region.[127] Up to five thousand people visited the site in 2013 and 2014.[128] The camp effectively included "all human beings since everyone needs water to survive," and the goal was "to instill awareness of the natural resources of the area and how they would be affected by the mine."[129] Mellen fishing and hunting guide Nick Vanderpuy, a longtime ally of tribes in the spearing and Crandon mine fights, played a central role in the Harvest Camp and spoke with other hunters angry at the withdrawal of county forest land for the mine.

The Harvest Camp was supported by some local farmers concerned about the impact of mining on their groundwater and livestock and angered that GTAC never spoke with them. The O'Dovero-Flesia family had been farming and raising beef and dairy cattle on one thousand acres near Mellen at the foot of the hills for five generations, since 1926. The family supplied meat and other necessities for the Harvest Camp, such as equipment, water, and phone and computer connections, and made their dining room table "ground zero" for project opponents.[130] Their strong stance was covered by Al Jazeera America and other international media.[131]

Monica Vitek remembered when two young Native men offering tobacco to the "ice angel" stopped at the farm for directions. She recalled: "They weren't afraid to come in our yard. How sad is that if they're out of the reservation, they have to be afraid of whose house they go to for help or directions."[132] Mark Vitek echoed Bad River tribal members in the family's veneration of the land, which was "passed down from generation to generation": "You take care of the land, and you take care of the animals. My grandpa's philosophy was, you never take more off the land than you can put back. You don't overwork the land. . . . A lot of people think the whole sustainable thing is something new, but the Natives have been doing it forever."[133]

As the mining fight recast Ojibwe and white neighbors as insiders defending common land and water, the Penokees became a battleground for defining who constituted the "outsiders." A June 2013 confrontation between masked anti-capitalist protesters and company employees at the mine site led to the arrest of a Stevens Point activist and media hysteria about so-called eco-terrorists. The Harvest Camp disavowed the action and committed to using nonviolent tactics. Yet the next month, GTAC used the confrontation as a pretext to hire a private security contractor company from Arizona to bring in guards armed with automatic weapons to patrol the mine site.[134]

The presence of camouflage-dressed, heavily armed "mercenaries" back-fired on the company, attracting heavy national and international media attention and inflaming public opinion against the company, particularly in an area where deer hunters feared they could be accidentally targeted.[135] Mark Vitek told the Harvest Camp that his family farm's private property could function as a haven from Iron County law enforcement and company mercenaries. He said: "It doesn't matter if it's cops, anybody. They're bothering you, you come in my yard and you'll be safe here. . . . Nobody is going to come in this yard and touch you."[136]

Public education and the polarization around mine "security" shifted local public opinion. A 2013 survey showed that 61 percent of Iron and Ashland county residents opposed the GTAC mine.[137] Ashland mayor Bill Whalen backed the Bad River stance: "This is not a Native Sovereign issue vs. the State of Wisconsin. This is a water and legislative issue that affects us all."[138] The Ashland County Board, which had initially voted 15–5 to back "responsible mining," ended up voting 18–1 for a zoning ordinance that would severely limit mining. Joe Rose Sr. noted that the entire county board "had done a 180" and that county chair Pete Russo, who once threatened to throw him out of a board meeting, became his "closest ally."[139]

In Ashland County, Chairman Wiggins remembered: "All of a sudden we started to see . . . more and more non-tribal people are waking up to the reality that this isn't just going to harm tribal people. Then, that's when I started seeing mom-and-pops and some of the surrounding towns wake up. It was local leadership that had absolutely no affiliation to corporations. Local elected leadership who represented human beings and their homes . . . started waking up."[140]

Yet the Iron County Board voted to evict the Harvest Camp from county land, forcing it to move to another site nearby.[141] Matusewic faced down the board members for their "pattern of blaming and villainizing the Natives and people who disagree with this mine and making them out to be subhuman."[142] Joe Rose Sr. said that in Iron County, the mining consortium had "a propaganda machine" that was "so strong that they have many people voting against their own interest." He explained: "What they rely on is divide and conquer, and they rely on the prejudices of people and that the solution to that, of course, is education."[143]

Aileen Potter, a resident of the Iron County historic mining town of Montreal, urged the county board to respect the Harvest Camp:

> I was told to duck as a child when we drove through the Bad River Reservation, so I wouldn't get hit by bows and arrows, and I was afraid. I was taken fishing on the Bad River by my father . . . and I was afraid. It took a lot of courage for me to take the first stop at the Harvest Camp, alone, but I did it. I got out of my car, and I started down a path, and I was still afraid, until I was greeted by a single Native man, who said, "Welcome." . . . I've been back there many times since and met old friends there concerned about the mine. . . . I've sat around the fire, swatting mosquitoes and listening to stories. I've seen the river I fished as a child. . . . I found a sense of peace there.[144]

Looking to the Future

Exploratory drilling in the Penokees proceeded in 2013, and the following year Wiggins and other Bad River officials visited Washington, D.C., to convince the EPA to stop the drilling and threatened a lawsuit to stop the drilling operations.[145] Sportfishers and hunters approved a Wisconsin Conservation Congress anti-mine resolution by 67 percent.[146] Joe Rose Sr. was elected to the Ashland County Board, with 57 percent of his district's vote, and Russo named him to the Mining Impact Committee. As the government-to-government relationship failed with the state of Wisconsin, tribal leaders "shape-shifted" their strategy to engage federal and local governments and directly engage Wisconsin citizens.[147]

Rongstad commented: "The thing that many of us have in common is that we love this place. We hunt the land and fish the waters. We hike the trails and paddle the rivers and lakes. We *need* the water." But she also noted that anti-mine people "have probably put too much faith in the tribe's ability to invoke treaty rights."[148] Although non-Native residents now talk positively about treaty rights, Rose agreed: "[They] come up to me and they say . . . 'It's going to be you guys that will win it.' My response is, 'We can't win it by ourselves.' What it's going to take is a strong grassroots movement, and that's going to include all of you. And that's what will beat it."[149]

On February 27, 2015, the company closed its Hurley office and finally admitted that its exploration "revealed wetland issues that make major continued investment unfeasible at this time."[150] It later withdrew its permit requests, and opponents celebrated their victory, while proposing a future Penokee Hills Heritage Park.[151] Some activists soon turned toward opposing plans for a factory hog farm in Bayfield County or questioning an oil pipeline along the Lake Superior shoreline.[152] Bad River refused to renew the lease of an Enbridge pipeline in 2017.[153]

As the alliance's attention shifted in 2015–17, it organized economic alternatives summits on the Red Cliff Reservation.[154] Seeing high levels of poverty both on and off the reservation, Kebec asserted: "[The alliance is] going beyond mining. . . . We are building a new society." She hoped to expand it to "people who have lost hope and don't engage at all because they are so overrun by other stuff." She said that "creating a new vision that embraces everyone, including a large number of underclass people, is our big challenge."[155]

Wiggins is also looking beyond the mine fight to building economic alternatives in the Lake Superior region, which is "unbelievably blessed" with clean water and sustainable farms and orchards and has the potential for renewable energies and wood-based small-homes construction. He concluded: "How we're going to coexist and, ultimately, how we're going to end up with a model that is enviable on a planetary scale is we're going to love our neighbor. . . . We're going to share. We're going to understand that we don't want to be billionaires. . . . The seeds of change are all around us and are already in bloom, and all we got to really do is just go with the flow."[156]

FROM OUTSIDERS TO INSIDERS

The recent history of northern Wisconsin is a story of unintended outcomes. The Ojibwe and Menominee intended to use treaty rights to resurrect their tradition of fishing, only to find that many of the fish had been poisoned by mercury and other toxins. Anti-treaty groups intended to roll back Native rights, but ended up focusing more public attention on Indigenous traditions and sovereignty. Mining companies intended to take advantage of racial divisions to open new mines, but found that Native and non-Natives realized that mine contamination would leave them fewer fish to argue about.

The Wisconsin Ojibwe case studies show how the differing levels of conflict over *resource use* in each watershed may have affected the level of cooperation over *resource extraction*. During the spearfishing conflict, centered on Lac du Flambeau and Mole Lake, it seemed almost utopian that these two bands would be able to successfully work with sportfishing groups against proposed mines. Similarly, it seemed easy to predict that Lac Courte Oreilles, with a carefully cultivated relationship with white neighbors, would be best positioned to work with them to stop a mine.

But counterintuitively, precisely the opposite happened. After rejecting compromises and deciding to strongly assert their treaty rights, Lac du Flambeau and Mole Lake (and later Menominee and Bad River) managed to build the strongest environmental bridges to their non-Indian neighbors. By pushing their identity and ties to the environment, the tribes began to shed their outsider image in treaty-ceded territory and to gain insider status in previously white-defined areas. While the reemergence of tribal powers outside reservation boundaries alienated some non-Indians, it educated and informed others. The tribes' emphasis on their particular identity made it more likely, not less likely, that they would find a convergence with non-Indians around shared universal values.

The areas of Wisconsin where the harshest treaty rights conflict raged in the late 1980s (such as the townships around Lac du Flambeau and Mole Lake) were the same areas that had the most advanced environmental alliances by the 2000s. Forest County resident Dorothy Tyra remembered that before the spearing conflict "people never had taken time to understand the history of Indian tribes." "It's lack of education," she said.[157]

Racism did not disappear from the region, and prejudice is certainly alive and well in the twenty-first century. *Organized expressions* of racism, however, were weakened by the growth of environmental collaborative strategies. The tribal gaming economy added the fortuitous element of economic equalization, although cooperation also deepened around reservations (such as Mole Lake and Bad River) with relatively small casinos.

Unlike Washington tribal governments, which sought to build cooperation with non-Indian governments from the top down, Wisconsin tribes built their relationship from the bottom up. Former Mole Lake environmental officer Bill

Koenen said: "The strength of the movement is among ordinary people. If it was among governments—whether state, local, or tribal governments—it would be inherently ineffective. There is always a back door they can run out. There is also a front door that can be closed on people." Koenen added that a grassroots alliance is "where spirit can evolve" and "there is a spirit that evolves that no government can stop."[158]

Koenen contended that "land is the bond" between Indigenous people and "farmers who have lived on the land all their lives." He realized: "In the country talking with country people, [we] use the same wavelength, talk in terms of partridge and trout. . . . I might end up going fishing with them."[159] Walt Bresette agreed that Indians and small farmers "were in many ways part of the same people—those who reside in rural America." He said of other rural whites who protested treaties, "Though they were trying to kill us, they were our allies." He contended that "those who foment anger" against the treaties "distract from sustainability." The key moment in the alliance was when non-Indians moved "from talking about Indians to talking about fish."[160]

Anti-Indian sentiment reflected even deeper economic and social anxieties that the spearing conflict brought to the surface. Some Native activists came to understand that the protesters' anger and frustration at the loss of their rural lifestyle was misdirected, because it emerged from a depressed economy and disempowerment that was not the tribes' fault. Bresette condemned the anti-treaty protesters not for throwing rocks but for "throwing rocks at the wrong people"—at tribal members rather than at corporate or state policies that were responsible for the economic alienation.[161]

The initial contact between the two communities was almost always made by individuals whose personal history had brought them into contact with the other group, and they were thus best able to confront prejudice. Among the key individuals were the few rural whites who had some prior contact with Native neighbors, whether as schoolteachers, nurses, shop owners, or members of mixed families. The trust building was carried out by these individuals and then expanded to the wider community.

Unlike the alliances in Nevada and southern Wisconsin, environmentally minded northern whites did not "sell out" the tribes even when they had ample opportunity—such as when the Crandon pipeline plan moved liquid wastes away from the Wolf River. Al Gedicks noted that the treaty rights struggle solidified the non-Indian community's "perception that [they were] now dealing with equals rather than with a community perceived as victims."[162] With no incentive to listen to their Native neighbors, rural whites would have had little reason to sit down at the table. Facing an unequal relationship with their neighbors, the Native residents likewise would have little incentive to unite with them.

In certain areas (such as Lac du Flambeau and Mole Lake), the assertion of Native rights began to equalize the two communities and thus build better ties between them. In places where the treaty conflict was prevented or did not occur (such as Lac Courte Oreilles), the later cooperation was not as fully developed, and the alliance may have fallen short as a result. Lac Courte Oreilles started the treaty conflict era in a better position than other Ojibwe bands, with a better relationship with neighboring non-Indians. But the white communities around Lac du Flambeau and Mole Lake gained a quicker understanding of tribal powers—the hard way.

Both spearfishing and the Treatment as State program projected tribal powers outside of reservation boundaries and began to reconstruct all of northern Wisconsin as "Indian Country" for the first time in a century and a half. Treaty rights "became a legal tool used to decentralize power and restructure the organization of political scale in Wisconsin."[163] Native influence was no longer confined within reservation boundaries, but extended outward to both harvest and protect natural resources.

As Philomena Kebec asserted: "What I've been working for is an expansion of the concept of Bad River Nation to extend out through the watershed. The building of networks, and a society, that's about place. It brings the Natives and non-Natives together. . . . Our interests are very much aligned." She concluded: "The United States as an entity . . . and the state of Wisconsin is diminishing in importance. Because, frankly, we're a throw-away community that doesn't get a lot of resources back. This is really the state of rural America. We're forgotten . . . in another sense it's liberating because maybe we get to write our own story . . . we have a chance to create something that's different, outside [the] hegemony of the industrialized capitalist state."[164]

This process of extending tribal power involves not simply transgressing boundaries but shifting or *reconfiguring* the boundaries themselves.[165] The Ojibwe are no longer simply the outsiders who violate the boundaries of white communities by spearfishing on "their" lakes. The outsiders can become the insiders, because new and more threatening outsiders have appeared on the scene. Members of both groups have drawn new, larger defensive mental boundaries that view outside institutions as more of a threat to their lifestyle than their neighbors.

Making Insider Boundaries

For Native Americans and whites in northern Wisconsin, the political boundaries of reservations long served as neat social lines between insider and outsider identities. Some whites remember the time when they rarely saw Native people outside the reservations—except for school and sports matches—and sometimes portray the era as marked by social harmony between the races. Native people view this period as marked by white supremacy so pervasive that it seemed normal and unchangeable. Other whites were not even aware of the continued existence of Native cultures; Indian reservations did not appear on some state maps until the 1970s.

Then the Menominee siege and Ojibwe spearfishing war marked the reemergence of tribal members into ceded territory, ending the invisibility of the tribes and forcing whites to reassess their relationships to Native people. The conflicts blurred the reservations' territorial boundaries and altered the social boundaries between Indian and white worlds.

The poet Robert Frost wrote that "good fences make good neighbors," yet neat boundaries can also prevent social interaction and understanding between neighbors. The geographer Yi-Fu Tuan has noted: "Conflict is actually a way of relating: you get to know your adversaries well in conflict. Good neighbors . . . are neighbors who do not relate to one another, except to throw out a hasty 'good day' in passing. When such neighbors are threatened by an external force, they may find themselves unprepared to respond effectively, for they have not had a prior way of relating." Tuan agreed that "bad fences—that is, boundary lines that are not clear-cut, that allow of overlapping jurisdictions— produce conflictual situations that force farmers and Indians together, making them into adversaries; and yet that very adversarial relationship can be a basis of cooperation in the event of a greater threat to both."[166]

When social or territorial boundaries become blurred or ambiguous, the result is often a struggle along the boundaries to clarify or redefine them.[167] Anti-treaty groups tried to clarify ambiguous legal boundaries by excluding Native people from harvesting resources in ceded territory. Anti-mining alliances responded to the blurring of boundaries by including neighbors as part of a common ecosystem. Rural people share experiences of marginality that can also encourage their solidarity.[168] The commonalities of their resource-based cultures can also help make "them" part of "us."[169]

If the worst thing one can be called in the Northwoods is an "outsider," perhaps the best thing one can be called is an "insider." By territorially defining the Wolf River or Bad River watersheds as homes of insiders, Ojibwe are not turning away from their political sovereignty. Far from it: *the alliances have been made possible not by their assimilation into the dominant society but by their strong stand to remain distinct from it.*

Sidelining treaty rights would have lessened their conflict with the white community but not guaranteed them a seat at the table. Instead of accepting the white community's terms of one-way "inclusion" (meaning official recognition and integration), the tribal nations began to set their own terms of *mutual inclusion*, including a projection of tribal powers in resource management outside the reservations. Boundaries obviously still exist between Mole Lake and Nashville, Menominee and Shawano, Lac du Flambeau and Minocqua, Bad River and Ashland, but they can be supplanted by the boundaries of common watersheds. In such hybrid areas, neither community has absorbed the other, but they can include each other in a common home and develop a common sense of understanding to last beyond the mining wars.

Frances Van Zile asserted that the shift in thinking in Wisconsin emerged from northerners' redefinition of the meaning of home. She said that many white neighbors now "accept Mole Lake as part of home": "It's not just my community. It's everybody's home." She concluded: "This is my home; when it's your home you try to take as good care of it as you can, including all the people in it. . . . We have to take care of this place, including everybody in it. I mean everybody that shares these resources should take care of it. It's not just my responsibility . . . everyone in the community takes care of home."[170]

Conclusion

THE COLLABORATION OF NATIVE AMERICANS AND RURAL WHITES TO defend their common home against outside interests was a rare anomaly in the 1980s. At that time, clashes over treaty rights and tribal sovereignty were considered the norm, whether in the fish wars in Washington and Wisconsin, water wars in Oregon, or treaty rights battles in South Dakota and Montana. But by the 2010s, cooperation between Native and non-Native rural organizers were starting to become almost commonplace.

The assertions of Native rights had created intense conflicts with rural whites in all these states, yet they were followed by some of the strongest environmental alliances seen anywhere in the country. Furthermore, the same Native leaders who had fought tooth and nail for tribal sovereignty were among the first to build bridges to their white neighbors, and the rural whites who least trusted outsiders were often those who built the bridge from the other side. Both sides had discovered that their own bonds to the land were shared more by the "Other" that had contested it than by the jaded and disengaged majority of North Americans.

For the first time in over a century, tribal influence was being projected outside reservation boundaries, both to harvest and to protect natural resources. Since the 1974 Boldt Decision, Washington tribes have redefined the Salish Sea and the Pacific Coast as a common home of Indians and non-Indians, where decisions have to be made together in order for the fish to survive. In Oregon, the Umatilla Tribes used their treaty to successfully assert their water rights and bring back a fishery previously feared extinct. The removal of fish-blocking dams in Klallam and Klamath ceded territories likewise would have been impossible without treaty rights.

When Wisconsin and Montana tribes enhanced their environmental regulations, under the federal Treatment as State program, they could use them to block harmful projects near their reservations. Gaming income also enabled some tribes to resist mines and to reach out to white neighbors with employment and cultural programs. These tribal powers have begun to blur the boundaries between the reservations and border towns and make them a zone of cultural and economic mixture rather than solely confrontation.

Social tensions, and sometimes violence, obviously continue between Native and white neighbors, and the groups still see view the other as "in place" either on the reservation or in the border town. But this process is only beginning, after centuries of white domination. Some barriers will be difficult to break down, and some will need to stay in place to safeguard tribal sovereignty, as Native nations feel more confident in asserting their powers again in their ceded lands.

In general, the places with the strongest assertions of treaty rights are where the later environmental alliances were strongest. In the early 1970s, the Lakota and Northern Cheyenne were engaged in some of the most heated land rights and water rights conflicts anywhere in the country, yet in the late 1970s they built the country's earliest environmental alliances with white ranchers. Lac du Flambeau and Mole Lake assertively pursued spearfishing in the late 1980s, yet these two tribes had the greatest success in joining with white neighbors to stop mining proposals.

In places where an initial conflict was prevented or did not occur, the environmental collaboration with white neighbors was not as fully developed. The Lac Courte Oreilles Band pursued an accommodationist strategy, after its treaty victory in the courts, but its anti-mining alliance did not strongly benefit. In Oregon, Warm Springs cooperated with local ranchers and state agencies in the 1990s, but confronted the Nestlé water bottling company in the 2010s.[1]

In more highly developed cases (such as Umatilla and Menominee), treaty conflicts and environmental-economic cooperation were interwoven into a single tribal strategy. Umatilla leaders creatively mixed a confrontational approach around water allocation with a cooperative approach around enhancing water flows, asserting treaty rights to protect the resources for everyone. A Menominee office worked both on fishing rights and on protecting the fish from mining. The conscious mixing of particularist and universalist strategies gave the tribes a greater chance to set the agenda and to fluidly maneuver into place-based relationships.

And of course in a number of cases, relations remain tense between environmentally minded tribes and anti-environmental whites. Right-wing property-rights movements often view both tribes and environmentalists as their enemies and assert their "sense of place" to exclude them. In other cases (such as Navajo, Crow, Uintah-Ouray, and Fort Berthold), tribal governments have taken a strong stand for fossil fuel development, so the only option for a (complicated) alliance is between tribal dissidents and non-Native environmentalists.

In a few instances, a positive Native/non-Native relationship developed without much of a prior conflict. The Sweetgrass Hills in Montana, where tribes and white farmers stopped a gold mine project, are perhaps too far from reservations to have been the scene of a conflict. The Wallowa Valley in Oregon also was too far from Nez Perce reservations to have been the point of conflict, at least since the forced expulsion of the tribe in the 1870s. Ho-Chunk and Wisconsin farmers similarly were not in intense conflict in the late twentieth century, though resentment surfaced during the Kickapoo Valley and Sauk Prairie land claims. It may indeed have been this lack of contact that caused the alliance against military flight and bombing range expansion to split in the mid-1990s and increased contacts that caused the later alliances against springwater pumping and frac sand mining to grow.

The Native/non-Native alliances demonstrate that particularism and universalism are not necessarily in contradiction. Although a strong assertion of Native identity may in the short run create conflicts with the majority white community, in the long run it can set the stage for greater cooperation, *but only under certain conditions*. While the case studies each have unique profiles, they also share some important patterns.

These patterns may be caused by communication between the different areas, as one group is inspired by the success of another group in defending treaties and forming alliances. The patterns can also help explain why and how the alliances are formed and, in so doing, can provide some more general insights into reconciling cultural identities with cross-cultural goals.

Three conditions seem to be necessary for the successful formation of a Native/non-Native environmental alliance. Each of these conditions can take multiple forms, and each of the possible forms does not have to be completely developed, but at least needs to be recognized and addressed for an alliance to get off the ground. They are a sense of common place, a sense of common purpose, and a sense of common understanding.

COMMON SENSE OF PLACE

The most successful of the alliances were born out of a common "sense of place." The geographic setting of the environmental issue, and the hold that the landscape has on the Native and non-Indian neighbors, literally helps build common ground. A sense of place can be shaped by harvesting and other activities, cultural and familial heritage, personal emotional and cognitive experiences, and social connections.[2] Even after an alliance is no longer needed, it can leave a legacy in increased public understanding of Native land ethics. Improved cultural education is not simply a means of building an alliance, but is largely a *result* of successful alliances.

The geographic setting clearly affected the outcome of all the case studies. Native Americans and rural whites may be more likely to be bonded in defense of a landscape that both groups perceive as "sacred" or "significant"—such as the Black Hills, the Wolf River, or the Salish Sea—rather than a landscape where one or both groups see mostly economic potential. As Lakota activist Bill Means observed in South Dakota, the sacred resource of water became the "source of understanding" between tribes and white neighbors.[3] Yet in other cases, as in the Klamath Basin and the Skagit Valley, tribal water rights remained a source of conflict.

The proximity of a reservation to the environmental threat, and whether it is downstream, influenced the outcome of most case studies. Court-affirmed treaty rights could put the tribe in a position of co-manager of off-reservation natural resources, as at Nisqually. At Northern Cheyenne and Mole Lake, treaty rights were not as effective in protecting the reservation environment as federally backed Treatment as State status was. At Ho-Chunk and Standing Rock, geographic "shell games" burdened Native residents with greater harm.

The landscape can serve as a unifying concept that transcends divisions between communities. In Wisconsin, sportfisher Herb Buettner remembered speaking with Menominee tribal leader Hilary Waukau about the "truths" of the Wolf River, and, conversely, Ojibwe activist Walt Bresette recalled speaking with white farmers. Bresette commented: "They identified with us, showed respect. . . . They showed they loved the Earth as much as the Anishinaabe, by the way they lived."[4]

Alliances around rural environmental issues appear to be stronger if they involve rural neighbors, rather than rural people cooperating with a group located in an urban area. In Minnesota, rural whites—in an area with very few Native people—worked with urban Native groups to stop a power line in the late 1970s.[5] Mdewakanton Dakota tribal members also worked with urban white environmentalists to stop nuclear waste storage next to the Prairie Island Reservation in the early 1990s.[6] Both groundbreaking movements used sophisticated organizing strategies and helped to lessen racial divisions, but

Big Smokey Falls on the Wolf River in the Menominee Reservation, downstream from the proposed Crandon mine in northern Wisconsin. (Photo by the author)

they did not establish a sense of a *local* bicultural place and—perhaps not coincidentally—were both also defeated by the electric utilities.[7] In the Montana movement against gold mining, the alliance between Fort Belknap and urban environmental groups did not fare as well as the Sweetgrass Hills alliance that united tribes and local white farmers and ranchers. A locally based rural alliance is able to claim a defense of the place against outside interests more effectively than a purely urban-rural alliance, and frontline voices are more compelling in public relations strategies than staff members of urban-based environmental groups.

Cultural education is a possible by-product of the alliances, and a lasting cultural impression can alter relationships. Wolf River sportfisher George Rock said: "Things we've gained from knowing who people are will not go away. . . . When you work with people, you don't just work on the issue." Rock stated that his family "didn't appreciate Mother Earth, or the concept of the Seventh Generation," which he learned from Native people.[8] Menominee judge Louis Hawpetoss expressed amazement at meeting sportfishers such as Rock and noted: "'Seventh Generation' just rolls off their tongues. I've never heard non-Native people talk like that."[9]

The alliance building went beyond environmental goals into shifting cultural attitudes. In Wisconsin, Wolf River–area residents began a program to reintroduce wild rice to their off-reservation lake, and in South Dakota and Nebraska, ranchers participated in round dances and learned how to protect sacred burial sites on their property. At Umatilla and Lac du Flambeau, non-Indians were educated through new museums and cultural programs founded in the midst of crisis. South Dakota white ranchers joined Lakota in demanding that white youths be prosecuted for murdering a Lakota man in Sturgis.[10]

An alliance that begins to alter white views of Native cultures, and to improve the image of local whites in the eyes of Native residents, has greater potential than an alliance that limits dialogue to the environmental threat. Each alliance takes the relationship forward through mutual education. Even if the relationship recedes after the alliance, it generally does not return to the previous status quo. This pattern of "two steps forward, one step back," highlighted in the South Dakota case study, can be seen in many of the alliances as they succeeded each other over the decades.

COMMON SENSE OF PURPOSE

Second, the alliances are often born out of a common "sense of purpose," or the idea that Native Americans and rural whites are in it together to meet their legal, political, or economic goals. Tribes that have enhanced their legal powers through treaty or sovereignty struggles are looked upon by many neighbors as possessing powers to protect the land. Corporations and uncooperative state and federal agencies provide ready-made common enemies for both communities. Tribal gaming can help strengthen relationships, by giving Native nations the financial resources to carry on the fight and to build influence in previously impenetrable circles, but it is not necessary.

Tribal legal powers are perhaps the mostly commonly cited reason by rural whites for building ties with a Native nation. The tribe's treaty and sovereign rights provide legal "clout" or "aces to play" that ordinary U.S. citizens do not possess. The first phase of the Crandon mine struggle, in 1976–86, saw the tribes and rural whites both opposing the mine on parallel tracks without close cooperation. After the treaty rights struggle, the second phase of the Crandon fight began in 1992 with the tribes in a stronger position on treaty rights.

In Wisconsin, Sonny Wreczycki praised the role of "sovereign governments protecting our waters . . . doing better than the federal government."[11] Town of Nashville resident Tom Ward similarly credited Mole Lake's "no-compromise stance" as providing a stronger barrier against unwanted mining than the compromise-oriented stance of many white environmentalists.[12] Al Gedicks saw treaty victories as showing that the Ojibwe "are not about to back down, not going to be intimidated."[13]

One negative aspect of this attitude was pointed out by Wisconsin treaty activist Debra McNutt. White people are once again "using" something owned by Native Americans, in this case treaty or sovereign rights, for their own ends—to stop a project that may threaten their livelihoods.[14] Author Naomi Klein agrees that "it has to be more than an extractive relationship to those rights: 'those rights are useful to us, because they help us protect our water, so we want to use those rights'—that's exactly the wrong way of thinking about this."[15]

Perhaps cynical non-Indian exploitation of tribal powers is inevitable, yet in some places this exploitation has also been made into a reciprocal deal. Non-Indians continue to "use" treaties to further their environmental goals, as long as Native people and their supporters can also "use" environmental issues to deepen public understanding of Indigenous self-determination and cultures. But in most alliances, the rural whites who at first exploited tribal powers later came to realize the value of those powers on their own merits. As Klein concludes: "These are rights that come out of a vision of how to live well, that were hard-won and hard-protected, and they point us toward a non-extractive regeneration-based way of living on this planet. That is the most hopeful and exciting part of this new wave of activism."[16]

Common political adversaries are a necessary basis for an alliance. The most obvious "common enemy" is the corporation or agency that is planning a harmful project, but similar historical experiences also resonate. Ho-Chunk tribal representatives in Wisconsin, for example, often compared the dispossession of white farmers for military or dam projects with their own expulsion from the same land a century before. A stance against racist anti-Indian organizations can also mobilize non-Indian support for tribal environmental regulations. Even a common wariness of urban-based environmental groups can be a point of agreement between Native and white rural neighbors.

The role of ostensibly "neutral" government agencies often invites mistrust from Native and rural white groups, even if for different reasons. Hawpetoss, a Menominee environmentalist, recalled that "mistrust" of the Wisconsin Department of Natural Resources "brought us together" with angling groups, much as tribes and fishing groups in the Columbia and Klamath Basins often expressed a common mistrust of state and federal agencies.[17] If tribal and local

Native and non-Native members of the Wolf Watershed Educational Project celebrate their 2003 victory over the Crandon mine project, at the Mole Lake Sokaogon Chippewa tribal headquarters in northern Wisconsin. (Photo by the author)

governments begin to see eye-to-eye, or even if a few local white officials shift racist patterns, cooperation can begin to flourish.

A consistent message from both Native and white organizers is that an alliance is best built at the grassroots, rather than only between government officials. The experience of being in the opposition serves as a bond between community organizers. Whether the movements oppose a mine or a pipeline, they can help redirect white anger away from their Native neighbors and toward distant institutions.

Economic equalization can even the playing field between rural Native and white residents. In Wisconsin and Washington, new casinos were beginning to generate new income just at the time that environmental alliances were founded. As recently as the 1980s, reservations were economically dependent on white border towns, yet the former anti-Indian protesters were employed at some casinos by the 2000s. Gaming income gave tribes access to technical expertise, public relations and lobbying resources and respect in the local business community. Wreczycki observed that local whites got to know the Mole Lake community "better when the casinos opened."[18]

Yet even within successful tribal gaming states such as Wisconsin and

Washington, only a handful of tribes were located close to population and tourism centers. Overstating the role of gaming revenue in the alliances overlooks the tribal cultural renaissance.[19] In Montana, South Dakota, and especially Nevada, non-Indian gaming was far more pervasive than small and isolated tribal enterprises.

COMMON SENSE OF UNDERSTANDING

Third, the alliances emerge out of a common "sense of understanding." They sometimes are created in the process of mediating a conflict between reservation and off-reservation communities, as a conscious method of making connections. In this scenario, a certain type of cooperation can be seen as an outgrowth of conflict, to put tribes on a more equal footing with the white community.

Conflict management may prove to be a result of building an alliance, but it may also be an initial reason for building the alliance in the first place. A few of the alliances, such as in Washington State, the Klamath Basin, and around Menominee, were directly born out of discussions to settle Native/non-Native resource conflicts. The conflict forced key players to sit down at the table, where they discovered their common concerns for the natural resources. Had tribes not strongly asserted their rights, the rural whites may not have sat at the table to begin with. An alliance, however difficult to form, can also be viewed as a welcome diversion from racial strife.

As Bill Means observed in South Dakota: "A lot of education takes place in areas of conflict . . . both sides back up their claims with documentation. . . . It increases understanding."[20] "We can find lots of reasons not to cooperate," said Wisconsin angler Herb Buettner, "but we have to overcome those differences."[21] After years of frustration at the epicenter of the Ojibwe spearfishing conflict, Wisconsin schoolteacher Carolyn Parker welcomed anti-mining sentiment as an "opportunity to build an alliance *over anything*."[22]

Building a bridge is perhaps the primary visible aspect of building an alliance. The initial bridge between two communities is almost always built by key individuals whose social positionality brings them into contact with both groups, and in the process they get stepped on a lot. The "middle person" has a personal or family history in contact with the other group and is in a position to confront the prejudice that surfaces.

In general, Native Americans tend to have more experience and knowledge of white communities than whites have of Native communities. The key individuals, then, tend to be those few whites who have had some prior contact with the tribal community. In Wisconsin, Carolyn Parker taught at the Lac du Flambeau school, Bob Schmitz caddied with Oneidas at a golf course, and Dorothy Tyra was a nurse who served tribal members. In Montana, Mert Freyholtz owned a pawn shop near three reservations, and in Nevada, Native ranchers and ranch hands worked with white ranchers.

The cross-cultural inviting and trust building was carried out by these individuals and then expanded to the wider communities. A significant minority is all that is really needed to break a preexisting anti-Indian consensus, though it is difficult to form a pro-tribal consensus without majority support, as sometimes appears now in Washington State.

Political equalization can be strengthened through conflict. Violent treaty conflicts in Washington and Wisconsin, or even armed standoffs in South Dakota, did not prevent environmental cooperation with the white community. Some of the most assertively pro-treaty Native activists, such as Billy Frank Jr. and Joe DeLaCruz in Washington, Gail Small and Jim Main in Montana, Bill Means and Faith Spotted Eagle in South Dakota, and Walt Bresette and Louis Hawpetoss in Wisconsin, initiated much of the cooperation with their rural white neighbors. Their "carrot-and-stick" approach sought to address past injustices and make real changes in the present, to move toward a more positive future.

The strong assertion of Native rights opened up possibilities that would not have existed had the relationship remained stable and unequal. With no incentive to listen to their Native neighbors, whites would have had little reason to find common ground. With an unequal relationship with their white neighbors, the Native residents would have little incentive to collaborate with them. Mere "unity" is not enough, since a unity between unequal partners is generally short-lived. True "unity" has the prerequisite of a process of political, economic, and cultural equalization, to set the stage for an alliance based on a relatively more level playing field. It is not a matter of waiting for full Native self-determination, or the end of capitalism, but for the process of decolonization to be moving forward and not stagnating or regressing.

A politically passive Native community that does not assert its rights faces the risk of being patronized as "good Indians" by non-Indian governments and of being perceived as politically weak partners by non-Indian communities. Cooperation would have certainly been possible without prior conflict, and conflicts do not inevitably lead to collaborative projects. But certain conflicts— in a particular form and met with a particular response—serve as an embryo from which cooperation can be born. The conflict should have the component of building bridges in the midst of fighting—a *conscious* effort by Native and non-Native leaders to find common goals.

APPLYING THE CONDITIONS

It appears that all three of these senses—of a common place, purpose, and understanding—are to some extent necessary preconditions for a successful alliance. These ingredients do not have to be equal in intensity, but they should be deciphered on their own merits.

A common sense of place without a common purpose may lead, at best, to joint cultural festivals or ecotourism programs, but not to political unity or action. Many regions have programs to educate non-Indians about Native cultures. Some of these efforts (such as in the Wallowa Valley) try to combine Indian and non-Indian versions of local history. Yet in other cases, these programs have not been politicized and so have not defused white anger or refocused it on an outside enemy. At worst, a strongly held common sense of place without a common sense of purpose or understanding could fuel conflict.

A sense of a common purpose without a sense of a common place may create temporary political alliances against a common enemy. But these alliances may not always build a lasting convergence between insiders defending their positive vision of the place. The Black Hills Alliance, and the Cowboy Indian Alliances, had dramatic success in blocking resource corporations. Yet because a strong "insider" sense of place has not been shared by Lakotas and white ranchers, the success has not translated into widespread white support for the Black Hills treaty claim.

A sense of a common place or purpose without a sense of a common understanding may provide the objective conditions for an alliance, but not the conscious leadership necessary to set it in motion. Native and non-Native neighbors may share a strong appreciation of the place and seek to defend it from unwelcome intruders, but that does not mean that they will defend the place together. In the first phases of the Crandon and Penokees mine battles, Wisconsin tribes and white neighbors defended the watershed from mining companies, but on parallel tracks with little cooperation. In southern Wisconsin, the Ho-Chunk and white farmers never had such a recent conflict and so were never forced into dialogue.

A common sense of understanding without a common sense of place or purpose, or both, can also emerge out of a conflict. The Native and non-Native communities may consciously realize that they need to build bridges between them, but lack the materials to build such a bridge. Without a common sense of place, they cannot begin to define the local landscape as a common home. That may be one reason that alliances are more difficult to construct in urban areas with more mobile demographics. Without a common sense of purpose, they cannot construct an insider identity to confront an outside threat.

State-sponsored negotiations between Native and non-Native communities (such as in South Dakota and Montana) sometimes appear to promote reconciliation for its own sake. Such efforts try to weaken ethnic or racial identities, rather than try to promote a real shift in power relations. The "reconciliation" strategy is in keeping with state views of Native sovereignty as a threatening form of "nationalism" that has to be reduced from an anti-colonial struggle to a mere demand for racial "minority rights." Anti-Indian leader Elaine Willman reinforces this view by describing Native sovereignty as a dangerous parallel to "Middle Eastern tribalism."[23] Pentagon counterinsurgency doctrine targeting "tribal regions" around the world similarly include Indigenous movements in a "global war on tribes."[24]

A MORE UNIVERSALIST NATIONALISM?

Even some progressive scholars and activists minimize or dismiss local cultural resistance as an example of an intolerant, exclusive nationalism, which overlooks working-class unity or ignores global economic structures that shape local realities.[25] Indigenous peoples are sometimes told that if they only look out for their own liberation, they will miss the "bigger picture" that can make fundamental change.

There is a certain amount of truth that by jettisoning universalism in favor of particularism, "narrow nationalist" movements are not interested in a broader liberation of humankind from capitalist structures. Yet universalist movements that downplay cultural resistance are also limiting their options. As Black Consciousness Movement leader Steve Biko pointed out in the 1970s, South African blacks needed to build their own political confidence, cultural self-esteem, and economic institutions, before blacks and whites could truly unite as equals.[26]

As the poet Aimé Césaire wrote in 1956: "I'm not going to confine myself to some narrow particularism. But I don't intend either to become lost in a disembodied universalism. . . . I have a different idea of universal. It is a universal rich with all that is particular, rich with all the particulars there are, the deepening of each particular, the coexistence of them all."[27] Black Studies scholar George Lipsitz agrees that in an interconnected world, "there is no 'universal' that is not actually the project of some dominant particular, and there is no 'particular' that exists outside of the totality of social relations."[28]

Indigenous movements rarely face a stark either-or choice between particularist "identity politics" and universalist "common ground." In many countries, such as the Philippines, Indigenous and leftist rebels have united to oust dictators and halt corporate megaprojects.[29] Other creative Native movements interweave their own liberation with appeals to the larger working class, particularly in Indigenous regions of "Latin" America.[30] These alliances include people joining together or finding common ground: Ecuadoran Indigenous peoples with workers and farmers, Guatemala Indigenous with poor Ladinos, Bolivian Indigenous peoples with other farmers and miners, Brazilian Amazon Indigenous people with rubber tappers, Indigenous activists and striking teachers in Oaxaca, and the Zapatista movement in Chiapas with the mestizo poor.[31]

Huge crowds cheered a 2001 Zapatista caravan in Mexico City, showing that the insurgents' message resonated beyond their Mayan heartland. Zapatista subcommander Marcos proclaimed: "The march for indigenous dignity must be a march of indigenous and non-indigenous. Only thus can we build a house called the world in which all of us fit, where all are equal and each one different."[32]

In these instances, the particularist demands of Indigenous peoples did not contradict larger universalist demands for a socio-economic shift away from capitalism but instead complemented or even enhanced them. Because of their histories, the most oppressed groups are in a favorable position to lead national movements for change.[33] They have the least emotional investment in the colonial culture, are less naive that the elite had the best interests of the people at heart, and are generally less willing to compromise with state institutions. In short, they have less to lose and more to gain than their allies do.

Native/non-Native alliances are small-scale versions of these collaborations, in which Indigenous nations take a leading role in fighting not only for their own powers but for larger changes that strengthen the whole society. Native movements in North America are on the cutting edge in environmental and economic change, as dramatized by Idle No More and Standing Rock. They generally insist not on reclaiming the private property of white landowners— even if such a claim would be justified—but on ensuring that the land-based cultures of both Native and non-Native peoples can survive and prosper into the future. Tribes' legal and political rights are serving as tools to reframe economic and cultural relations. Even if they had the power to exclude non-Indians, many Native activists claim, they would prefer to work together with them to protect land-based lifeways. They pose Indigenous sovereignty as carving out space for the application of universalist values.

The roots and histories of Native sovereignty movements differ from those of the "exclusivist" right-wing nationalism and sectarianism that has torn apart regions of Europe and Asia.[34] Native national self-determination emerged not out of a feudal past or modernity but out of the colonial encounter and "interaction" with white-supremacist settler colonial states.[35] Indigenous pre-colonial societies also had generally more egalitarian economic structures than the hierarchical European societies they confronted. Karl Marx and Friedrich Engels even read U.S. anthropologist Lewis Henry Morgan's studies of Haudenosaunee (Iroquois) society for clues into what a relatively classless society may look like.[36] Glen Coulthard asserts that contemporary Indigenous demands are "based on an articulation of reciprocity which rendered not only colonial domination but also capitalist domination over the natural world as profoundly harmful and wrong. When that's the cultural base that you're making a claim to defend, it's profoundly anticapitalist and anticolonial."[37]

In addition, Indigenous movements treat the land and water as the source of all life, rather than life only for the human beings of their own nation. The modern Native interest in defending their political boundaries is a reaction to the sovereign state system—to build a hard "outer shell" to protect Native lifeways from state control. It remains to be seen what role non-Indians would have on reservations and reclaimed Native lands in the future. They could be seen as a continuing threat or allowed under the condition that they not usurp Indigenous governance or cultures (much like ethnic Russians in the Baltic states). The Institute for the Advancement of Hawaiian Affairs, for example, has issued the "Settler's Code of Conduct," requiring a commitment to awareness, fairness, and action.[38]

Native movements have also developed a strong universalist commitment to an ecologically sustainable future, such as responding to the threat of climate change to all species, including human beings. Indigenous movements can point out possible paths that differ from paths taken by nationalists around the world. Oppressed nations can free themselves, while at the same time appealing to some citizens of the oppressor nation that they may have some common interests. The unlikely environmental alliances are only one example of how a movement for national self-determination can make this appeal.

LESSONS OF THE ALLIANCES

These unlikely alliances may seem to some outside observers like a "man-bites-dog" story—an exotic exception to the normal realities of Native-white conflict. They not only can more effectively defeat environmental threats than racially divided movements can. Some alliances also can claim success by extending cooperation beyond the environmental issue and having that convergence last after the immediate threat recedes.

The stories of Native/non-Native alliances are replete with seemingly contradictory lessons. Native and non-Native neighbors have constructed relationships most effectively at a local grassroots scale, but only after tribes have used the national (federal) scale to shift local power relationships. They have constructed a territorial place as common ground, but only after tribes have strongly asserted their social claim to belong on that ground. They have built geographies of inclusion, but only after tribes have convinced local whites to exclude other outsider whites. Finally, they have emphasized universalist environmental values, but only after tribes have begun to uphold their particularist cultural identity. Again paraphrasing Frederick Douglass: the ground of conflict had to be plowed up before the crops of cooperation could be harvested.[39]

The experience of the Cowboy Indian Alliance revealed another important contradiction. In order to build an effective alliance against corporate dispossession of their land, white ranching families had to begin to understand and deal with their own history of dispossessing Indigenous land and *renegotiate* the meaning of home with their Native neighbors. As Scott L. Morgensen asks: "What does it mean for non-Natives . . . knowing one feels at home only to the degree that others remain dispossessed [and] being accountable to histories of Native displacement by questioning one's sense of place?"[40]

Although the phenomenon of Native/non-Native alliances is relatively recent in U.S. history, and this study examined only a few dozen examples, some general trends cut across the case studies. These criteria can be used to judge the success of an alliance, though they should be taken as general observations rather than a set of hard rules.

First, alliances seem to be more successful if they emphasize building grassroots rather than only institutional relationships. The "bottom-up" alliances are able to involve members of the community, rather than simply their leaders or government officials. Although "top-down" relationships can help to set a positive political tone and example to the society, they cannot substitute for social and cultural interaction between community members and can even generate resentment at the base of society. To achieve lasting success, state/tribal resource co-management structures need to be matched by cooperation among the Native and non-Native resource users, as seen in emerging watershed councils. Grassroots oppositional alliances also need to make some changes at the top of society, in government circles, or their best intentions will probably be frustrated by bureaucracies and ambitious politicians (as happened in the Klamath Basin). A parallel track of governmental relations and grassroots community relations is the most effective strategy.

Second, alliances seem to be more successful if they emphasize local place identity, rather than only state citizenship. The point of Native sovereignty is for Indigenous nations to be able to govern themselves outside the confines of non-Indian governments. Instead of waiting for official "recognition" from a state apparatus, *Indigenous nations can themselves recognize and designate their own potential partners.* The United States and each of its component states are too geographically large and socially impersonal as places to build positive relationships. They also carry the baggage of centuries of white supremacy and of the exclusion of Native voices and powers. It may be easier to reframe a local or subregional place—at the human scale of the Umatilla Basin, Black Hills, Tongue River Valley, or Salish Sea—as an inclusive place of convergence. Instead of appealing to a common U.S. citizenship, with all of its boundaries and limitations, alliances can begin to define a place membership, appealing to people's attachment to their local geography.

Third, alliances seem to be more successful if they define this local place in territorial and inclusive terms, rather than in social and exclusive terms. Using a territorial definition, "Indian Country" extends far beyond the reservation boundary, and rural whites can view the reservation as part of a common and valued home, based around a natural region. Outsiders who do not share the value of home can be excluded, but those who do value the place can be recast as insiders. The geographies of inclusion define a local, cross-cultural territorial area as the home of all who live there, despite political boundaries that cut across the landscape.

Fourth, alliances seem to be more successful if they recognize and respect particularist identity differences among their members, rather than if they only promote an overarching universalist message. Unity around common goals cannot succeed in the long run unless different groups in the alliance gain roughly equal resources and powers. The assertion of difference does not

Otter Creek near the Northern Cheyenne Reservation, in an area of southeastern Montana targeted for a coal mine. (Courtesy: Steve Paulson / Northern Plains Resource Council)

have to stand in the way of unity and can actually make a convergence more attainable. In the regions where Native nations most strongly asserted their rights, they were able to offer rural whites new ways of valuing the local place and new tools to defend it. An alliance can be divided and conquered if its white members succumb to outsider appeals to their self-interest, or it can be strengthened if the rural whites remain loyal to their Native partners.

Though it may seem difficult, or even impossible, to reconcile cultural differences with intercultural similarities, these alliances have just such a combination as the centerpiece of their relationships. As a Lummi totem pole was being erected in Billings, Montana, on the Lummi Nation's Treaty Day, January 22, 2016, Montana rancher Jeanie Alderson declared: "Solidarity is awkward and hard, but there is dignity and strength in our differences. Our unity makes us stronger."[41] When Lummi blocked the Cherry Point coal terminal that year, Chairman Tim Ballew II credited the "power of treaty rights to protect all of us, to preserve our lands and waters for everyone who calls this place home."[42]

This interweaving of particularism and universalism is not simply a matter of initiating dialogue or conversations between different communities. It is also a matter of constructing grassroots relationships around a place, remaking that place into an inclusive home, and correcting the historic wrongs that had made the place less than a secure home. It is a matter of creating empathy and solidarity to replace the oppression and entitlement of settler colonialism, and moving toward decolonization on the ground.

I'll always remember hearing Santee Dakota activist and poet John Trudell deliver his message to the Black Hills International Survival Gathering, held on Marv Kammerer's ranch in the summer of 1980. In the opening session, Trudell identified key differences between Native and non-Native communities, but at the same time recognized the power inherent in all human beings to connect with the Earth and shape reality.

He observed: "When I go around in America and I see the bulk of the white people, they do not feel oppressed; they feel powerless. When I go amongst my people, we do not feel powerless; we feel oppressed. We do not want to make the trade." He went on: "We must be willing in our lifetime to deal with reality. It's not revolution; it's liberation. We want to be free of a value system that's being imposed upon us. . . . We don't want change in the value system. We want to remove it from our lives forever. . . . We have to assume our responsibilities as power, as individuals, as spirit, as people."

To the white community, Trudell warned: "They don't need you any more, because they've got an entire potential world market with millions and millions of consumers. So, all the lies they've dangled in front of your faces, well, they're going to start pulling back on these lies a bit, and they're going to start slapping you all with a bit of reality." To the Native community, he predicted: "We Indians are going to have to act as runners and messengers. We are going to have to run and act as teachers. We are going to have to talk to all the people who will listen to us about what we believe, what it is that we know to be right."

Trudell concluded: "They have been attacking Indigenous people, and they have been misusing white people, and they want to push us all into a position where all we think about is ourselves. They want us to forget the Earth. . . . We must build a resistance in our hearts that says we will not accept it, we will *never* accept it."[43]

NOTES

NOTES TO FOREWORD

John Trudell, speech in New York (1979), in documentary *Trudell*, directed by Heather Rae (2005).

NOTES TO PREFACE

1   Zoltán Grossman, "The Kindness of Strangers: Today's Refugees in Hungary and My Family during WWII," Common Dreams, September 21, 2015, www.commondreams .org/views/2015/09/21/kindness-strangers-todays-refugees-hungary-and-my-family -during-wwii.

NOTES TO INTRODUCTION

1   Indigenous Peoples Specialty Group of the Association of American Geographers, "Declaration of Key Questions about Research Ethics with Indigenous Communities" (2010), www.indigenousgeography.net/IPSG/pdf/IPSGResearchEthicsFinal.pdf.

2   Zoltán Grossman, "Some Guidelines for Working with Native Communities" (2012), http://academic.evergreen.edu/g/grossmaz/NativeCulturalRespectGuidelines.pdf.

3   Sissel A. Waage, "(Re)claiming Space and Place through Collaborative Planning in Rural Oregon," *Political Geography* 20, no. 7 (2001): 839–858.

4   Joy Porter, *Native American Environmentalism* (Lincoln: University of Nebraska Press, 2014); Jonathan Clapperton, "Stewards of the Earth? Aboriginal Peoples, Environmentalists, and Historical Representation" (master's thesis, College of Graduate Studies and Research, University of Saskatchewan, 2012); Mik Moore, "Coalition Building between Native American and Environmental Organizations in Opposition to Development," *Organization and Environment* 11, no. 3 (1998): 287–313; D. Prybyla and S. Barth, *Building Bridges between American Indians and Conservation Organizations*, WWF Topics in Conservation Report (Washington, D.C.: World Wildlife Fund, 1996).

5   Carolyn J. Stirling, "Decolonize This—Settler Decolonization and Unsettling Colonialism: Insights from Critical Ethnographies with Indigenous and Allied Educator-Activists in Aotearoa / New Zealand, the U.S., and Canada" (Ph.D. diss., Department of Educational Leadership and Policy, State University of New York at Buffalo, 2015).

6   Sherry L. Smith, *Hippies, Indians, and the Fight for Red Power* (Oxford: Oxford University Press, 2014).

7   Lynne Davis, ed., *Alliances: Re/envisioning Indigenous–Non-Indigenous Relationships* (Toronto: University of Toronto Press, 2010); Indigenous Action Media, "Accomplices Not Allies: Abolishing the Ally Industrial Complex," May 2, 2014, www.indigenousaction .org/wp-content/uploads/Accomplices-Not-Allies-print.pdf.

8   Jill M. Bystydzienski and Steven P. Schacht, eds., *Forging Radical Alliances across*

Difference: Coalition Politics for the New Millennium (Lanham, Md.: Rowman and Little-field, 2001).

9   Waage, "(Re)claiming Space and Place."

10   David Sibley, *Geographies of Exclusion: Society and Difference in the West* (New York: Routledge, 1995); Tim Cresswell, *In Place / Out of Place: Geography, Ideology, and Transgression* (Minneapolis: University of Minnesota Press, 1996).

11   Joe Bryan and Denis Wood, *Weaponizing Maps: Indigenous Peoples and Counterinsurgency in the Americas* (New York: Guilford Press, 2015); Zoltán Grossman, ed., "Geographic Controversy over the Bowman Expeditions / México Indígena" (2010), http://academic.evergreen.edu/g/grossmaz/bowman.html.

12   Kristi Giselsson, *Grounds for Respect: Particularism, Universalism, and Communal Accountability* (New York: Lexington Books, 2012); Charles Hampden-Turner and Fons Trompenaars, *Building Cross-Cultural Competence* (New Haven, Conn.: Yale University Press, 2000); Ernesto Laclau, "Universalism, Particularism, and the Question of Identity," in *The Politics of Difference*, ed. Edwin N. Wilmsen and Patrick A. McAllister (Chicago: University of Chicago Press, 1996).

13   Glen Coulthard, *Red Skin, White Masks: Rejecting the Colonial Politics of Recognition* (Minneapolis: University of Minnesota Press, 2014), 12.

14   David Harvey, *Spaces of Hope* (Edinburgh: Edinburgh University Press, 2000), 242.

15   Rodney King, "Can We All Get Along?," video, May 1, 1992, http://abcnews.go.com/US/video/rodney-king-16589937.

16   Barack Obama, "Caucus Speech," *New York Times*, January 3, 2008.

17   Barack Obama, "Remarks by the President during the Opening of the Tribal Nations Conference," White House, November 5, 2009.

18   Maya Rhodan, "Obama Defends Black Lives Matter," *Time*, October 22, 2015.

19   Jamelle Bouie, "Black Lives Matter Protests Matter," *Slate*, August 17, 2015, www.slate.com/.

20   Jacqueline Keeler, "'Are You Going to Honor the Treaties?' Clyde Bellecourt Asks Bernie Sanders," Indian Country Today Media Network, February 15, 2016, http://indiancountrytodaymedianetwork.com/; Zach Cartwright, "Bernie Sanders Replaces Stump Speech with Epic Call for Native American Justice in Arizona," U.S. Uncut, March 18, 2016, http://usuncut.com/.

21   Ta-Nehisi Coates, "The Enduring Solidarity of Whiteness," *Atlantic*, February 8, 2016.

22   Ian Haney-López and Heather McGhee, "How Populists like Bernie Sanders Should Talk about Racism," *Nation*, January 28, 2016.

23   Ghassan Hage, *White Nation: Fantasies of White Supremacy in a Multicultural Society* (Annandale, Australia: Pluto Press, 1998).

24   Lani Guinier and Gerald Torres, *The Miner's Canary: Enlisting Race, Resisting Power, Transforming Democracy* (Cambridge, Mass.: Harvard University Press, 2002).

25   Florence Gardner and Simon Greer, "Crossing the River: How Local Struggles Build a Broader Movement," *Antipode* 28, no. 2 (1996): 175–192.

26   Harvey, *Spaces of Hope*, 88.

27   Ibid., 240.

28   Guinier and Torres, *Miner's Canary*.

29   Kino-nda-niimi Collective, ed., *The Winter We Danced: Voices from the Past, the Future, and the Idle No More Movement* (Winnipeg, Man.: ARP Books, 2014).

30   Sylvia McAdam, Idle No More co-founder, talk at South Puget Sound Community College, Olympia, Wash., March 14, 2013.

31 Gyasi Ross, "Still Don't Know What #IdleNoMore Is About? Here's a Cheat-Sheet," *Huffington Post*, January 15, 2013, www.huffingtonpost.ca/.

32 Naomi Klein, "Dancing the World into Being: A Conversation with Idle No More's Leanne Simpson," *Yes!*, March 5, 2013.

33 Tom Holm, J. Diane Pearson, and Ben Chavis, "Peoplehood: A Model for the Extension of Sovereignty in American Indian Studies," *Wicazo Sa Review* 18, no. 1 (2003): 7–24.

34 Aileen Moreton-Robinson, *The White Possessive: Property, Power, and Indigenous Sovereignty* (Minneapolis: University of Minnesota Press, 2015).

35 Susan Sleeper-Smith, Juliana Barr, Jean M. O'Brien, Nancy Shoemaker, and Scott Manning Stevens, eds., *Why You Can't Teach United States History without American Indians* (Chapel Hill: University of North Carolina Press, 2015).

36 Carolyn Merchant, *The Death of Nature: Women, Ecology, and the Scientific Revolution* (New York: Harper and Row, 1980).

37 Silvia Federici, *Caliban and the Witch: Women, the Body, and Primitive Accumulation* (New York: Autonomedia, 2004), http://libcom.org/files/Caliban%20and%20the%20Witch.pdf.

38 Peter Linebaugh, *Stop, Thief! The Commons, Enclosures, and Resistance* (Oakland, Calif.: PM Press, 2013); E. P. Thompson, *The Making of the English Working Class* (London: Vintage, 1966), 472–575.

39 Roxanne Dunbar-Ortiz, *An Indigenous Peoples' History of the United States* (Boston: Beacon Press, 2015), 132–139.

40 William Cronon, *Changes in the Land: Indians, Colonists, and the Ecology of New England* (New York: Hill and Wang, 1983), 147.

41 Nancy Isenberg, *White Trash: The 400-Year Untold History of Class in America* (New York: Viking, 2016), 105.

42 Mason Hersey, "Lewis Henry Morgan and the Anthropological Critique of Civilization," *Dialectical Anthropology* 18, no. 1 (1993): 53–70; Bruce E. Johansen, *Forgotten Founders: How the American Indian Helped Shape Democracy* (Boston: Harvard Common Press, 1982).

43 The Oklahoma story is discussed in Dunbar-Ortiz, *Indigenous Peoples' History*, 166–167. The Nisqually, Ho-Chunk, and Ojibwe examples are referred to elsewhere in this book.

44 C. Joseph Genetin-Pilawa, *Crooked Paths to Allotment* (Chapel Hill: University of North Carolina Press, 2012).

45 Roxanne Dunbar-Ortiz in interview with Laura Flanders, "From Indigenous Socialism to Colonial Capitalism," Truthout, October 14, 2014, www.truth-out.org/.

46 Glenda Riley, *Women and Indians on the Frontier, 1825–1915* (Albuquerque: University of New Mexico Press, 1984).

47 Dunbar-Ortiz, *Indigenous Peoples' History*, 59.

48 Janet Mawhinney, "'Giving Up the Ghost': Disrupting the (Re)production of White Privilege in Anti-Racist Pedagogy and Organizational Change" (master's thesis, Department of Sociology and Equity Studies in Education, University of Toronto, 1998).

49 Eve Tuck and K. Wayne Yang, "Decolonization Is Not a Metaphor," *Decolonization: Indigeneity, Education, and Society* 1, no. 1 (2012): 1-40.

50 Allen Buchanan, *Secession: The Morality of Political Divorce from Fort Sumter to Lithuania and Quebec* (Boulder, Colo.: Westview Press, 1991), 39.

51 Rodolfo Stavenhagen, "Indigenous Peoples: Emerging International Actors," in *Ethnic Diversity and Public Policy: A Comparative Inquiry*, ed. Crawford Young (Basingstoke, U.K.: Palgrave in association with UNRISD, 1998), 138.

52   Steven E. Silvern, "Scales of Justice: American Indian Treaty Rights and the Political
     Construction of Scale," *Political Geography* 18, no. 6 (1999): 645.

53   Donald L. Fixico, "Federal and State Policies and American Indians," in *A Companion
     to American Indian History*, ed. Philip J. Deloria and Neal Salisbury (Malden, Mass.:
     Blackwell, 2004), 379–396.

54   Francis Paul Prucha, *American Indian Treaties: The History of a Political Anomaly* (Berke-
     ley: University of California Press, 1997).

55   Patricia Albers and Jeanne Kay, "Sharing the Land: A Study in American Indian Terri-
     toriality," in *American Indians: A Cultural Geography*, 2nd ed., ed. Thomas E. Ross,
     Tyrel G. Moore, and Laura R. King (Southern Pines, N.C.: Karo Hollow Press, 1995).

56   John P. Bowes, *Land Too Good for Indians: Northern Indian Removal* (Norman: University
     of Oklahoma Press, 2016).

57   Vine Deloria Jr., *Behind the Trail of Broken Treaties* (Austin: University of Texas Press,
     1985).

58   Vine Deloria Jr. and David E. Wilkins, *Tribes, Treaties, and Constitutional Tribulations*
     (Austin: University of Texas Press, 2000).

59   Kristin T. Ruppel, *Unearthing Indian Land: Living with the Legacies of Allotment* (Tucson:
     University of Arizona Press, 2008); Janet A. McDonnell, *The Dispossession of the Ameri-
     can Indian, 1887–1934* (Bloomington: Indiana University Press, 1991).

60   David Wallace Adams, *Education for Extinction: American Indians and the Boarding
     School Experience, 1875–1928* (Lawrence: University Press of Kansas, 1995); K. Tsianina
     Lomawaima and Brenda J. Child, *Away from Home: American Indian Boarding School
     Experiences, 1879–2000* (Phoenix: Heard Museum, 2000); Brenda J. Child, *Boarding
     School Seasons: American Indian Families, 1900–1940* (Lincoln: University of Nebraska
     Press, 2000).

61   Kevin Bruyneel, "Challenging American Boundaries: Indigenous People and the 'Gift'
     of U.S. Citizenship," *Studies in American Political Development* 18, no. 1 (2004): 30–43.

62   Frederick E. Hoxie, *Parading through History: The Making of the Crow Nation in America,
     1805–1935* (Cambridge: Cambridge University Press, 1995).

63   Thomas Biolsi, *Organizing the Lakota: The Political Economy of the New Deal on the Pine
     Ridge and Rosebud Reservations* (Tucson: University of Arizona Press, 1992); Richard O.
     Clemmer, *Hopis, Western Shoshones, and Southern Utes: Three Different Responses to the
     Indian Reorganization Act of 1934* (Louisville, Ky.: Applied Anthropology Documentation
     Project, 1986).

64   David E. Wilkins, *Hollow Justice: A History of Indigenous Claims in the United States* (New
     Haven, Conn.: Yale University Press, 2013).

65   Charles Wilkinson, *Blood Struggle: The Rise of Modern Indian Nations* (New York: W. W.
     Norton, 2005), 57–86.

66   Roberta Ulrich, *American Indian Nations from Termination to Restoration, 1953–2006*
     (Lincoln: University of Nebraska Press, 2010).

67   Donald L. Fixico, *Termination and Relocation: Federal Indian Policy, 1945–1960* (Albu-
     querque: University of New Mexico Press, 1986); Daniel M. Cobb, *Native Activism in Cold
     War America* (Lawrence: University Press of Kansas, 2008).

68   Alvin M. Josephy Jr., Troy R. Johnson, and Joane Nagel, eds., *Red Power: The American
     Indians' Fight for Freedom*, 2nd ed. (Lincoln: University of Nebraska Press, 1999); Bradley
     G. Shreve, *Red Power Rising: The National Indian Youth Council and the Origins of Native
     Activism* (Norman: University of Oklahoma Press, 2014).

69 Kevin Bruyneel, *The Third Space of Sovereignty* (Minneapolis: University of Minnesota Press, 2007), 195–216.

70 Jessica Cattelino, *High Stakes: Florida Seminole Gaming and Sovereignty* (Durham, N.C.: Duke University Press, 2008).

71 David E. Wilkins and K. Tsianina Lomawaima, *Uneven Ground: American Indian Sovereignty and Federal Law* (Norman: University of Oklahoma Press, 2002).

72 Alexandra Harmon, *Rich Indians: Native People and the Problem of Wealth in American History* (Chapel Hill: University of North Carolina Press, 2010); Jeff Corntassel and Richard C. Witmer, *Forced Federalism: Contemporary Challenges to Indigenous Nationhood* (Norman: University of Oklahoma Press, 2008), 27–81.

73 The "rich Indian" stereotype uncomfortably resembles historic stereotypes of European Jews (also disallowed from owning land) as moneylenders and financial power brokers. Zoltán Grossman, "Rich Tribes, Rich Jews: Comparing the New Anti-Indianism to Historic Anti-Semitism" (presentation to the Association of American Geographers, Denver, April 9, 2005), http://academic.evergreen.edu/g/grossmaz/jewsindians.ppt.

74 Elizabeth Cook-Lynn, *Anti-Indianism in Modern America* (Urbana: University of Illinois Press, 2007), 4.

75 The 1948 United Nations Convention on the Prevention and Punishment of the Crime of Genocide defines *genocide* as the deliberate destruction of members of a national, ethnic, racial, or religious group, through killing, causing serious bodily or mental harm, inflicting deadly conditions of life, preventing births, or forcibly removing children. "Ethnocide" intends to destroy cultures, even if the group is not physically eliminated, through restricting language, religion, kinship, customs, arts, histories, education, and other social institutions or separating a group from its cultural resources and land base.

76 Patrick Wolfe, "Settler Colonialism and the Elimination of the Native," *Journal of Genocide Research* 8, no. 4 (2006): 387–409.

77 Deloria and Wilkins, *Tribes, Treaties, and Constitutional Tribulations.*

78 Rudolph C. Rÿser, *Indigenous Nations and Modern States* (New York: Routledge, 2012).

79 Oren Lyons, Haudenosaunee Six Nations Confederacy, talk to Indigenous Environmental Network gathering, South Fork Reservation, Nev., July 19, 2008.

80 Coulthard, *Red Skin, White Masks.*

81 Taiaiake Alfred, *Wasáse: Indigenous Pathways of Action and Freedom* (Peterborough, Ont.: Broadview Press, 2005), 152.

82 Ibid., 153.

83 Simone Poliandri, ed., *Native American Nationalism and Nation Re-building: Past and Present Cases* (Albany: State University of New York Press, 2016).

84 Benedict Anderson, *Imagined Communities: Reflections on the Origin and Spread of Nationalism* (London: Verso, 1991).

85 Eugèn Weber, *Peasants into Frenchmen: The Modernization of Rural France, 1870–1914* (London: Chatto and Windus, 1977).

86 Harvey, *Spaces of Hope*, 85.

87 Stephen Cornell, *The Return of the Native: American Indian Political Resurgence* (New York: Oxford University Press, 1988).

88 Gerald R. Alfred, *Heeding the Voices of Our Ancestors: Kahnawake Mohawk Politics and the Rise of Native Nationalism* (Toronto: Oxford University Press, 1995).

89 The Hegelian concept of the "negation of the negation" was not intended to explain

Indigenous decolonization, but it might be the closest explanation that Western philosophy is equipped to provide. Georg W. F. Hegel, *Elements of the Philosophy of Right*,
ed. Allen W. Wood and trans. H. B. Nisbet (Cambridge: Cambridge University Press,
1991), 121–123.

90 Suzan Shown Harjo, ed., *Nation to Nation: Treaties between the United States and American Indian Nations* (Washington, D.C.: National Museum of the American Indian in
association with Smithsonian Books, 2014).

91 Paul Nadasdy, "Transcending the Debate over the Ecologically Noble Indian: Indigenous
Peoples and Environmentalism," *Ethnohistory* 52, no. 2 (2005): 291–331.

92 David Waller, "Friendly Fire: When Environmentalists Dehumanize American Indi-
ans," *American Indian Culture and Research Journal* 20, no. 2 (1996): 107–126; Shepard
Krech III, *The Ecological Indian: Myth and History* (New York: W. W. Norton, 2000);
Michael E. Harkin and David Rich Lewis, eds., *Native Americans and the Environment:
Perspectives on the Ecological Indian* (Lincoln: University of Nebraska Press, 2007).

93 Stephanie J. Fitzgerald, *Native Women and the Land: Narratives of Dispossession and
Resurgence* (Albuquerque: University of New Mexico Press, 2015).

94 Imre Sutton, "Preface to Indian Country: Geography and Law," *American Indian Culture
and Research Journal* 15, no. 2 (1991): 3–35.

95 Theodore W. Allen, *The Invention of the White Race*, vol. 2, *The Origin of Racial Oppression in Anglo-America* (New York: Verso, 1997).

96 David R. Roediger, *The Wages of Whiteness: Race and the Making of the American Working
Class* (New York: Verso, 1991).

97 Joanne Barker, ed., *Sovereignty Matters: Locations of Contestation and Possibility in Indigenous Struggles for Self-Determination* (Lincoln: University of Nebraska Press, 2005),
23–24.

98 Philip Deere, talk to International Indian Treaty Conference, White Earth, Minn., June 5,
1981.

99 Alfred, *Wasáse*, 235.

100 David Rich Lewis, "Skull Valley Goshutes and the Politics of Nuclear Waste," in Harkin
and Lewis, *Native Americans and the Environment*, 304–342; Winona LaDuke, *All Our
Relations: Native Struggles for Land and Life* (Boston: *South End Press*, 1999), 97–114.

101 Angela Parker, "Sovereignty by the Barrel: Indigenous Oil Policies in the Bakken" (presentation to the Native American and Indigenous Studies Association [NAISA], Austin,
Tex., May 30, 2014); Andrew Curley, "Coal and Resource Nationalism: Indigenous Sovereignty in the Navajo Nation" (presentation to NAISA, Austin, Tex., May 31, 2014).

102 On Quebec, see MiningWatch Canada, "Urgent Action: Support the Mohawks of Kane-
satake—Stop Niocan," February 28, 2002. On British Columbia, see Paul Bowles and
Henry Veltmeyer, *The Answer Is Still No: Voices of Pipeline Resistance* (Black Point, N.S.:
Fernwood Publishing, 2014); Sacred Headwaters—Tl'abāne (a.k.a.: Klappan/Klabona),
"Local and Supporting Organizations," November 12, 2013, http://sacredheadwaters.
ca/; Soren C. Larsen, "Place Identity in a Resource-Dependent Area of Northern British
Columbia," *Annals of the Association of American Geographers* 94, no. 4 (2004): 944–960;
Okanagan Nation Alliance (2017), www.syilx.org/. On Ontario, see Rick Wallace, *Merging
Fires: Grassroots Peacebuilding between Indigenous and Non-Indigenous Peoples* (Halifax,
N.S.: Fernwood Publishing, 2013); Anna Willow, "Re(con)figuring Alliances: Place Mem-
bership, Environmental Justice, and the Remaking of Indigenous-Environmentalist
Relationships in Canada's Boreal Forest," *Human Organization* 71, no. 4 (2012): 371–382.
On the Maritime Provinces, see Sam Koplinka-Loehr, "Protectors vs. Destroyers—

Canadians Unite to Stop Fracking in New Brunswick," Waging Nonviolence, October 14, 2013, http://wagingnonviolence.org/.

103 *Two Row Wampum* Renewal Campaign, Partnership between the Onondaga Nation and Neighbors of the Onondaga Nation (2013), www.honorthetworow.org/; Kyra Long Visnick, "SHARE and the SHARE Farm: Strengthening Relationships to Food and Place," *Storying the Foodshed* (blog), October 31, 2013, https://blogs.cornell.edu/foodstories/; Jamie Lewey and Gail Dana-Sacco, "Saltwater Fishery Conflict: Passamaquoddy and the State of Maine" (presentation to NAISA, Washington, D.C., June 5, 2015).

104 Manuel Piño, Laguna-Acoma, Indigenous Environmental Network (Acoma, N.M.), interview, June 13, 1999.

105 Zoltán Grossman, "Maori Opposition to Fossil Fuel Development in Aotearoa New Zealand" (presentation to NAISA, Washington, D.C., June 6, 2015), http://academic.evergreen.edu/g/grossmaz/MaoriOilOppositionArticle.pdf.

106 Bruyneel, *Third Space of Sovereignty*, 218–219.

107 Bunty Anquoe, "Trump Slams Tribal Sovereignty," *Indian Country Today*, October 20, 1993; Fred Francis, "Donald Trump Fights Indian Casinos," *Today*, NBC, August 14, 1994.

108 Felix S. Cohen, "The Erosion of Indian Rights, 1950–1953," *Yale Law Journal* 62 (1953): 348.

109 Audra Simpson, *Mohawk Interruptus: Political Life across the Borders of Settler States* (Durham, N.C.: Duke University Press, 2014).

110 Harsha Walia, "Decolonizing Together," *Briarpatch*, January 1, 2012.

111 Stephanie Irlbacker-Fox, "#IdleNoMore: Settler Responsibility for Relationship," in Kino-nda-niimi Collective, *The Winter We Danced*, 223.

112 Emma Battell Lowman and Adam Barker, *Settler Identity and Colonialism in Twenty-First Century Canada* (Black Point, N.S.: Fernwood Publishing, 2015); Adam Barker, "From Adversaries to Allies: Forging Respectful Alliances between Indigenous and Settler People," in Davis, *Alliances*.

113 Khury Petersen-Smith and Brian Bean, "Nothing Short of Liberation: Ally-ship Isn't Enough," *Jacobin*, June 4, 2015.

114 Quoted in Northland Poster, "Attributing Words," November 3, 2008, *Unnecessary Evils* (blog), http://unnecessaryevils.blogspot.com/2008/11/attributing-words.html.

115 Malcolm X, *The Autobiography of Malcolm X: As Told to Alex Haley*, reissued ed. (New York: Ballantine Books, 1992), 384.

116 Protect the Earth, *In His Own Voice: Speaking for the Generations*, Superior Broadcast Network, 1999, www.protecttheearth.org/Walter/aboutwalt.htm. Excerpt at www.youtube.com/watch?v=q4Vtzj5LwUU.

117 Leanne Simpson, "Oshkiimaadizig, the New People," in *Lighting the Eighth Fire: The Liberation, Resurgence, and Protection of Indigenous Nations*, ed. Leanne Simpson (Winnipeg, Man.: Arbeiter Ring Publishing, 2008), 14.

118 Ibid., 211.

NOTES TO CHAPTER I

1 The transboundary Salish Sea consists of Puget Sound and Hood Canal in the United States, along with the Strait of Juan de Fuca and Strait of Georgia between Vancouver Island and the mainland.

2 Ronald Trosper, *Resilience, Reciprocity, and Ecological Economics: Northwest Coast Sustainability* (New York: Routledge, 2011).

3   Fay G. Cohen, *Treaties on Trial: The Continuing Controversy over Northwest Indian Fishing Rights*, report prepared for the American Friends Service Committee (Seattle: University of Washington Press, 1986).

4   Northwest fish conflicts center on six species of anadromous (oceangoing) salmon and steelhead. They are born in the gravel beds of inland freshwater rivers, streams, and lakes and, after growing to a certain size, migrate to the ocean. After living most of their lives in saltwater, their instinct directs them to return to their freshwater birthplace. The salmon (the name comes from the Latin for "leaper") migrate upstream to their home gravel beds, where they spawn and die. Northwest salmon are divided into five species: chinook (king), pink (humpback), coho (silver), chum (dog), and sockeye (red). They differ according to their size, their preferred spawning waters, their timing of migration, and the desirability for eating. Steelhead are anadromous trout, which are preferred by sportfishers as fighting fish.

5   "Treaty with the Nisqualli, Puyallup, etc. 1854," December 24, 1854, 10 Stat. 1132, in *Indian Affairs: Laws and Treaties*, ed. Charles J. Kappler (Washington, D.C.: Government Printing Office, 1904), 2:661–664.

6   Cohen, *Treaties on Trial*.

7   Charles Wilkinson, *Messages from Frank's Landing: A Story of Salmon, Treaties, and the Indian Way* (Seattle: University of Washington Press, 2000), 55.

8   Alexandra Harmon, *Indians in the Making: Ethnic Relations and Indian Identities around Puget Sound* (Berkeley: University of California Press 1998), 88.

9   Richard Kluger, *The Bitter Waters of Medicine Creek* (New York: Alfred A. Knopf, 2011), 165–166. In 2010, the Nisqually Tribe and the state of Washington agreed to develop the Nisqually State Park, including the massacre site as a tribal ceremonial ground.

10   Ibid., 167–184.

11   Leschi was exonerated in a 2004 historic court hearing involving representatives of the army and state supreme court. Lisa Blee, *Framing Chief Leschi: Narratives and the Politics of Historical Justice* (Chapel Hill: University of North Carolina Press, 2014).

12   Cohen, *Treaties on Trial*.

13   Hank Adams, "A New Analysis of Indian Treaty Fishing Rights and the Division of Salmon Resources in the Pacific Northwest and a Different Interpretation of the Law and Meaning of 'In Common,'" monograph, The Evergreen State College, Olympia, Wash. (April 1979), 6, http://academic.evergreen.edu/g/grossmaz/1979SalmonMono graphHankAdams.pdf.

14   Daniel Boxberger, *To Fish in Common: The Ethnohistory of Lummi Indian Salmon Fishing* (Seattle: University of Washington Press, 2000).

15   American Friends Service Committee, *Uncommon Controversy: Fishing Rights of the Muckleshoot, Puyallup, and Nisqually Indians* (Seattle: University of Washington Press, 1970).

16   Native American Solidarity Committee (NASC), *To Fish in Common: Fishing Rights in the Northwest*, 2nd ed. (Seattle: NASC, 1979), 22–23.

17   The Puyallup Trilogy, a series of three U.S. Supreme Court decisions, later clarified Puyallup rights to net for steelhead, ruling that the state could not discriminate against the tribe by shutting down its commercial fishing but that the tribe must also accommodate non-Indian fishing and "reasonable" state conservation rules.

18   Cohen, *Treaties on Trial*.

19   Carol Burns, *As Long as the Rivers Run*, documentary (1971).

20   Trova Heffernan, *Where the Salmon Run: The Life and Legacy of Billy Frank Jr.*, Washington

State Heritage Center Legacy Project (Seattle: University of Washington Press, 2012); David Wilkins, ed., *The Hank Adams Reader* (Golden, Colo.: Fulcrum Publishing, 2011).

21   Billy Frank Jr., talk to Anti-Indianism class from The Evergreen State College, Wa-He-Lut School, Frank's Landing, Wash., April 14, 2006.

22   "Boldt Decision Upheld Treaty Fishing Rights," *Sin-Wit-Ki* (Toppenish, Wash.), 5, no. 3 (1999).

23   Wilkinson, *Frank's Landing*, 49–65.

24   U.S. District Court of Western District Washington, *United States v. Washington*, 384 F. Supp. 312 (W.D. Wash. 1974).

25   Adams, "Indian Treaty Fishing Rights."

26   "Boldt Decision," *Sin-Wit-Ki*.

27   U.S. Court of Appeals, Ninth District, *State of Washington v. Washington State Commercial Passenger Fishing Vessels Association*, 443 U.S. at n.36 696 (1978).

28   Cohen, *Treaties on Trial*.

29   Rudolph C. Rÿser, *Anti-Indian Movement on the Tribal Frontier*, Occasional Paper 16, rev. ed. (Kenmore, Wash.: Center for World Indigenous Studies, 1992), 11.

30   Jeffrey R. Dudas, "In the Name of Equal Rights: 'Special' Rights and the Politics of Resentment in Post–Civil Rights America," *Law and Society Review* 39, no. 4 (2005): 723–757.

31   Heffernan, *Where the Salmon Run*, 142–155.

32   Boxberger, *To Fish in Common*.

33   NASC, *To Fish in Common*.

34   Adams, "Indian Treaty Fishing Rights," 54–55.

35   According to Rÿser (*Anti-Indian Movement*), Metcalf's father, John Metcalf, was a follower of pro-Nazi Silver Shirts in the 1930s and later a follower of the extreme-right Christian Identity movement. Senator Metcalf was praised by the far-right *Spotlight* newspaper when he spoke to meetings of the Populist Party—led by ex-Klansman David Duke—in the 1980s.

36   Gorton registered in 1987 as a lobbyist for the Non-Indian Negotiating Group to provide technical and legal research to reservation whites on land claims matters.

37   U.S. Supreme Court, *State of Washington v. Washington State Commercial Passenger Fishing Vessels Association*, 443 U.S. 658 (1979).

38   Joseph Cone, *A Common Fate: Endangered Salmon and the People of the Pacific Northwest* (New York: Henry Holt, 1994).

39   Joseph E. Taylor, *Making Salmon: An Environmental History of the Northwest Fisheries Crisis* (Seattle: University of Washington Press, 2001), 4.

40   Quoted in Alex Tizon, "Twenty-Five Years after the Boldt Decision," *Seattle Times*, February 7, 1999.

41   Cone, *Common Fate*.

42   Bruce E. Johansen and Roberto Maestas, *Wasi'chu: The Continuing Indian Wars* (New York: Monthly Review Press, 1979), 175, 189.

43   U.S. District Court of Western District Washington, *United States v. State of Washington*, 506 F. Supp. 187 (1980).

44   Cohen, *Treaties on Trial*, 140.

45   Quoted in Debbie Preston, "Joe DeLaCruz: Boldt Decision Gave Tribes Unified Voice," *NWIFC News*, Summer 1999.

46   Quoted in Tony Meyer, "Boldt 25: A Look Back," *NWIFC News*, Spring 1999.

47   Cohen, *Treaties on Trial*, 143–146.

48 Jim Waldo, "Redefining Winning: The TFW Process," *Forest Planning Canada* 4, no. 3 (1988): 14–19.

49 Bill Lowman, *220 Million Custers* (Anacortes, Wash.: Anacortes Printing and Publishing, 1978), 71.

50 C. Herb Williams and Walt Neubrech, *Indian Treaties—American Nightmare* (Seattle: Outdoor Empire Publishing, 1976), 135.

51 Rÿser, *Anti-Indian Movement*, 24–27.

52 Bruce E. Johansen, "The New Terminators: A Guide to the Anti-Treaty Movement," in *Enduring Legacies*, ed. Bruce E. Johansen (Santa Barbara, Calif.: Praeger, 2004), 305–332.

53 Bill Robinson, Trout Unlimited Washington Council chair and executive director of Washington State Northwest Salmon and Steelhead Council (West Seattle, Wash.), interview, August 11, 1999.

54 Ibid.

55 Ibid.

56 Frank, talk to Anti-Indianism class.

57 Joseph DeLaCruz, Quinault former chairman and NWIFC co-founder (Hoquiam, Wash.), interview, August 14, 1999.

58 Betsy Reynolds, *Building Bridges: A Resource Guide for Tribal/County Intergovernmental Cooperation* (Seattle: Northwest Renewable Resources Center, 1997).

59 B. Robinson, interview.

60 Ibid.

61 Frank Urabeck, Northwest Marine Trade Association (Federal Way, Wash.), interview, August 11, 1999.

62 Bill Robinson estimated that after 1983 half of TU members accepted Boldt as a reality, about one-third left the group in anger over the tribal policy, and the balance of members remained in the middle.

63 Urabeck, interview.

64 Joseph Pavel, NWIFC staff and former Skokomish chair (Olympia, Wash.), interview, August 13, 1999.

65 Tim Stearns, Save Our Wild Salmon director (Seattle), interview, August 10, 1999.

66 Quoted in Debbie Preston, "Chinook Returns Please Tribe, Anglers," *NWIFC News*, Fall 1998.

67 Steve Robinson, NWIFC (Olympia, Wash.), interview, August 11, 1999.

68 DeLaCruz, interview.

69 B. Robinson, interview.

70 Alexandra Harmon, ed., *The Power of Promises: Rethinking Indian Treaties in the Pacific Northwest* (Seattle: University of Washington Press, 2009).

71 In the 1985 Pacific Salmon Treaty with Canada, NWIFC tribes were a formal part of the U.S. delegation and worked in the Pacific Salmon Commission.

72 Governor's Office of Indian Affairs, "Centennial Accord between the Federally Recognized Indian Tribes in Washington State and the State of Washington," August 4, 1989, www.goia.wa.gov/government-to-government/data/centennialaccord.htm.

73 Office of Native Education, Office of Superintendent of Public Instruction, *Since Time Immemorial: Tribal Sovereignty in Washington State*, curriculum resources (2017), www .indian-ed.org/.

74 Cedar Media, *Canoe Way: The Sacred Journey*, documentary (2008), www.youtube.com

/watch?v=QJOC92S98C4; Tribal Journeys Information Site (2017), https://tribal journeys.wordpress.com/.

75 Governor's Office of Indian Affairs, "Institutionalizing the Government-to-Government Relationship in Preparation for the New Millennium," November 3, 1999, www.goia .wa.gov/government-to-government/data/agreement.htm.

76 David E. Wilkins, *Hollow Justice: A History of Indigenous Claims in the United States* (New Haven, Conn.: Yale University Press, 2013), 130–141.

77 Sara Singleton, *Constructing Cooperation: The Evolution of Institutions of Comanagement* (Ann Arbor: University of Michigan Press, 1998), 73–98.

78 S. Robinson, interview.

79 Sara Singleton, "Collaborative Environmental Planning in the American West: The Good, the Bad, and the Ugly," *Environmental Politics* 11, no. 3 (2002): 54–75.

80 Amanda E. Cronin and David M. Ostergren, "Democracy, Participation, and Native American Tribes in Collaborative Watershed Management," *Society and Natural Resources* 20, no. 6 (2007): 527–542.

81 U.S. District Court, Western District of Washington, *United States v. Washington* (Martinez Decision), No. CV 9213RSM, 2007 WL 2437166, at *10 (W.D. Wash.).

82 Northwest Indian Fisheries Commission, "Federal Court Upholds Treaty Rights in Culverts Case," *NWIFC News*, April 1, 2013. The Ninth Circuit Court of Appeals upheld the Martinez Decision in June 2016.

83 Craig Welch, "Tribes Take Salmon Battle into State's Road Culverts," *Seattle Times*, October 20, 2009.

84 Michael C. Blumm and Jane G. Steadman, "Indian Treaty Fishing Rights and Habitat Protection: The Martinez Decision Supplies a Resounding Judicial Reaffirmation," *Natural Resources Journal* 49, nos. 3–4 (2009): 705.

85 Northwest Indian Fisheries Commission, "Treaty Rights at Risk," July 14, 2011, http:// treatyrightsatrisk.org/; Lynda V. Mapes, "Fishing-Rights Victory Empty without Fish," *Seattle Times*, January 6, 2013.

86 Evelyn Pinkerton, *Co-operative Management of Local Fisheries* (Vancouver: University of British Columbia Press, 2003).

87 Chris Carrell, "Snow Job? Is a Proposal to Ban All Fishing Nets from Puget Sound Supposed to Save Salmon or Sports Fisherfolk?," *Seattle Weekly*, April 1, 1999.

88 L. Harris, "Lorraine Loomis: Habitat Key to Salmon Recovery," *NWIFC News*, Fall 1999.

89 The Puget Sound Gillnetters Association was active in anti-treaty lawsuits in the Boldt era, but it is not to be confused with the Puget Sound Anglers, which Carpenter described as continuing a "hate campaign" against tribal and commercial fishing into the twenty-first century.

90 Puget Sound Gillnetters Association, "Gillnet Selectivity in Northern Puget Sound," prepared by Lanny Carpenter (January 1999).

91 Lanny Carpenter, Puget Sound Gillnetters Association (Olympia, Wash.), interview, August 13, 1999.

92 Puget Sound Gillnetters Association, "Gillnet Selectivity."

93 Carpenter, interview.

94 Pamela K. Madson and William Koss, *Washington Salmon: Understanding Allocation*, Washington State House of Representatives Office of Program Research (August 1988).

95 Carpenter, interview.

96   Vicki Monks, "When a Fish Is More than a Fish," *Spokane Spokesman-Review*, January 26, 2000.

97   Marsha Shaiman, "Death of a River . . . and Resurrection," *On Indian Land*, June 1996.

98   David Melmer, "Tribe Sues City, Federal Government over Tacoma, Wash., Dam," *Indian Country Today*, December 1, 1999.

99   Ibid.

100 Shaiman, "Death of a River."

101 American Friends Service Committee, "Bill Matchett's Brainstorm: Indian Shellfish Contract," news update, April 1997, www.afsc.org/; L. Harris, "Cooperation Key to Tribal Shellfish Harvest," *NWIFC News*, Summer 2000.

102 Victor Martino, Skokomish tribal attorney (Bainbridge Island, Wash.), interview, August 10, 1999.

103 Pavel, interview.

104 Lewis Kamb, "TPU: Thirty-Six-Year Pursuit of New License for Cushman Dams Finally Over," *Tacoma News Tribune*, July 19, 2010.

105 Skokomish Watershed Action Team, "Coming Back: Restoring the Skokomish Watershed," 2014, www.youtube.com/watch?v=KeOcE9ENHmo.

106 Trout Unlimited, "Trout Unlimited Celebrates Major Step toward Removal of Washington's Elwha River Dams," press release, February 11, 2000.

107 Lynda V. Mapes and Steve Ringman, *Elwha: A River Reborn* (Seattle: Mountaineers Books, 2013).

108 Lynda V. Mapes, "Back to Nature: Last Chunk of Elwha Dams out in September," *Seattle Times*, August 17, 2014.

109 Lynda V. Mapes, "Roaring Resurgence," *Seattle Times*, February 14, 2016.

110 Quoted in D. Williams, "Tribal Fisheries Still Face Harassment," *NWIFC News*, Winter 1997.

111 Joshua L. Reid, *The Sea Is My Country: The Maritime World of the Makahs* (New Haven, Conn.: Yale University Press, 2015).

112 Charlotte Coté, *Spirits of Our Whaling Ancestors: Revitalizing Makah and Nuu-chah-nulth Traditions* (Seattle: University of Washington Press, 2010).

113 Jeremy Firestone and Jonathan Lilley, "An Endangered Species: Aboriginal Whaling and the Right to Self-Determination and Cultural Heritage in a National and International Context," *Environmental Law Reporter* 34, no. 9 (2004): 10763–10787.

114 Jeff Smith, American Friends Service Committee, Makah (Seattle), interview, August 9, 1999.

115 Robert J. Miller, "Exercising Cultural Self-Determination: The Makah Indian Tribe Goes Whaling," *American Indian Law Review* 25, no. 2 (2000–2001): 165–273.

116 DeLaCruz, interview.

117 From 2008 to 2015, Willman worked for the township of Hobart, Wisconsin, to oppose Oneida Nation attempts to consolidate its reservation land base, and then moved to the Flathead Reservation in Ronan, Montana, to oppose a tribal-state water compact. Charles Tanner Jr., "The Revolutionary War for Citizens of Montana," Institute for Research and Education on Human Rights, September 10, 2015, www.irehr.org/2015/09/10/the-revolutionary-war-for-citizens-of-montana.

118 Mike Barenti, "GOP Politicians Break with Platform on Tribes," *Yakima Herald-Republic*, July 9, 2000.

119 Quoted in Julie Titone, "Resolution Would End Tribal Sovereignty," *Spokane News*, July 3, 2000.

120 David Ammons, "GOP Apologizes for Move to End Indian Self-Rule," Associated Press, July 18, 2000.

121 "GOP's Anti-Indian Stand Weakens State Ticket," *Seattle Times*, editorial, July 14, 2000.

122 Nicholas Christos Zaferatos, *Planning the American Indian Reservation: From Theory to Empowerment* (Syracuse, N.Y.: Syracuse University Press, 2015), 209–236; Zaferatos, "Tribal Nations, Local Governments, and Regional Pluralism in Washington State," *Journal of the American Planning Association* 70, no. 1: (2004): 81–96.

123 Borderlands Research and Education, *Anti-Indianism in the Skagit County, Washington GOP*, Borderlands Background Report (Silverdale, Wash.: Borderlands Research and Education, 2012), https://turtletalk.files.wordpress.com/2012/04/anti-indianism-in-skagit-county-4-15-20121.pdf.

124 Lewis Kamb, "Rift between La Conner, Swinomish Tribe 'Comes down to Taxes,'" *Seattle Times*, April 18, 2015.

125 Mark Yuasa, "Sport Fishermen Protesting in La Conner on Wednesday as Tribal Gill-Net Salmon Fishery Gets Underway," *Seattle Times*, May 3, 2016; Kimberly Cauvel, "Fisheries Frustrations," *Skagit Valley Herald*, July 31, 2016; Charles Tanner Jr., "Bigotry, Calls for Violence Follow Protest of Tribal Treaty Fishing," Institute for Research and Education on Human Rights, May 13, 2016, www.irehr.org/2016/05/13/bigotry-calls-violence-follow-protest-tribal-treaty-fishing.

126 Brian Cladoosby, "The Swinomish Indian Tribal Community's Approach to Governance and Intergovernmental Relations," interview, March 24, 2010, Leading Native Nations interview series, Native Nations Institute for Leadership, Management, and Policy, University of Arizona, Tucson, https://nnidatabase.org/video/brian-cladoosby-swinomish-indian-tribal-communitys-approach-governance-and-intergovernmental-r.

127 Brian J. Cantwell, "Swinomish Leader Brian Cladoosby Fights for Salmon and Sovereignty," *Seattle Times*, June 21, 2015.

128 Brian J. Cantwell, "Northwest's First Citizens Develop Tribal Tourism," *Seattle Times*, June 21, 2015.

129 Charles Tanner Jr., "No Justice on the Plate: Transnational Companies and the Right Oppose Fish Consumption Justice and Tribal Treaty Rights," Borderlands Research and Education special report, September 19, 2014, http://irehr.org/news/special-reports/580-no-justice-on-the-plate.

130 Daniel Sarna-Wojcicki, "Democratizing Scale in Klamath Collaborative Watershed Governance (presentation to the Association of American Geographers, San Francisco, March 29, 2016).

131 Wilkinson, *Frank's Landing*, 66–87.

132 Zoltán Grossman, "From Nisqually to Iraq: Placemaking and Reclaiming Space at Fort Lewis" (presentation to the Association of American Geographers, Las Vegas, Nev., March 23, 2009), http://academic.evergreen.edu/g/grossmaz/fortlewisnisqually.ppt.

133 Nisqually River Task Force, *Nisqually River Management Plan*, Washington State Legislature (June 1987).

134 David Troutt, "Director's Corner," *Yil-Me-Hu: Nisqually Watershed Salmon Recovery Newsletter*, Winter 2009.

135 Nisqually River Council (2017), http://nisquallyriver.org/.

136 Conceptualizing Native Place program, Nisqually Watershed Podcasts, The Evergreen State College, Olympia, Wash., Winter 2009, http://blogs.evergreen.edu/native place/.

137 Katie Big-Canoe and Chantelle Richmond, "Anishinabe Youth Perceptions about Com-

munity Health: Toward Environmental Repossession," *Health and Place* 26 (2014): 127–136.

138 Beth Rose Middleton, *Trust in the Land: New Directions in Tribal Conservation* (Tucson: University of Arizona Press, 2011), 185–194; Nisqually Watershed Podcasts.

139 Nisqually Delta Association (2011), http://oly-wa.us/nda/History.php.

140 Billy Frank Jr., "A Tribute to Kenny Braget," In *Tell the Truth: The Collected Columns of Billy Frank Jr.* (Olympia, Wash.: Northwest Indian Fisheries Commission, 2015), 109–10.

141 Lisa Pemberton, "Refuge That Served as Billy Frank Jr.'s Medicine Now Named for Him," *Olympian*, July 19, 2016.

142 Quoted in Lisa Pemberton, "Nisqually Tribe's Garden Program Cultivates Tradition, Community," *Olympian*, July 16, 2014.

143 Pavel, interview.

144 Arend Lijphart, *Democracy in Plural Societies* (New Haven, Conn.: Yale University Press, 1977).

145 James D. Fearon and David D. Laitin, "Explaining Interethnic Cooperation," *American Political Science Review* 90, no. 4 (1996): 715–735.

146 Yet an economic rebellion that flared in 2014 involved protesters from all three Bosnian ethnic groups, against their own elite ethnic leaders. Tim Judah, "Bosnian Protests: A Balkan Spring?," BBC News, February 7, 2014, www.bbc.com/.

147 Raimo Väyrynen, ed., *New Directions in Conflict Theory*, International Social Science Council (London: Sage Publications, 1991), 5.

148 John Paul Lederach, *Building Peace: Sustainable Reconciliation in Divided Societies* (Washington, D.C.: United States Institute of Peace, 1998), 24.

149 John Burton, *Conflict Resolution and Prevention* (New York: St. Martin's Press, 1990).

150 Tom Holm, J. Diane Pearson, and Ben Chavis, "Peoplehood: A Model for the Extension of Sovereignty in American Indian Studies," *Wicazo Sa Review* 18, no. 1 (2003): 7–24.

NOTES TO CHAPTER 2

1   Andrew H. Fisher, *Shadow Tribe: The Making of Columbia River Indian Identity* (Seattle: University of Washington Press, 2010).

2   Katrine Barber and Andrew H. Fisher, "Remembering Celilo Falls," *Oregon Historical Quarterly*, Winter 2007.

3   Blaine Harden, *A River Lost: The Life and Death of the Columbia* (New York: W. W. Norton, 2012).

4   Benedict Colombi, "The Nez Perce vs. Elite-Directed Development in the Lower Snake River Basin" (Ph.D. diss., Department of Anthropology, Washington State University, 2006).

5   Donald Worster, *Rivers of Empire: Water, Aridity, and the Growth of the American West* (Oxford: Oxford University Press, 1992), 269–272.

6   Paul R. Needham, "Dam Construction in Relation to Fishery Protection Problems in the Pacific Northwest," University of California, Berkeley (1949).

7   Richard White, *The Organic Machine: The Remaking of the Columbia River* (New York: Hill and Wang, 1996).

8   Katrine Barber, *Death of Celilo Falls* (Seattle: University of Washington Press, 2005).

9   Roberta Ulrich, *Empty Nets: Indians, Dams, and the Columbia River*, 2nd ed. (Corvallis: Oregon State University Press, 2007); Michelle Nijhuis, "Fishers of the Yakama Nation," *New Yorker*, December 3, 2015.

10   J. C. Gartland, "*Sohappy v. Smith*: Eight Years of Litigation over Indian Fishing Rights,"
      Oregon Law Review 56 (1977): 680–791.

11   U.S. District Court for the District of Oregon, *United States v. Oregon*, 302 F. Supp. 899;
      1969 U.S. Dist. LEXIS 9899.

12   Keith Petersen, *River of Life, Channel of Death: Fish and Dams on the Lower Snake* (Cor-
      vallis: Oregon State University Press, 2001).

13   Columbia River Inter-Tribal Fish Commission (CRITFC) (2017), www.critfc.org/.

14   Roy Hemmingway, "The Northwest Power Planning Council: Its Origins and Future
      Role," *Environmental Law* 13 (1983): 673–697.

15   CRITFC (1998), www.critfc.org/.

16   Columbia River Fish Management Plan (October 1988), entered into pursuant to *So-
      happy v. Smith*, 302 F. Supp. 899 (D. Or. 1969), *aff'd* 913 F.2d 576 (9th Cir. 1990), http://
      docs.streamnetlibrary.org/ColRivFishMgmtPlan-1988.pdf.

17   Michael C. Blumm, *Sacrificing the Salmon: A Legal Policy History of the Decline of Colum-
      bia Basin Salmon* (Lake Mary, Fla.: Vandeplas Publishing, 2013).

18   Paul Lumley, CRITFC (Portland, Ore.), interview, July 7, 2000.

19   American Fisheries Society, *Salmon at the Crossroads* (1992).

20   Susana Santos, Tygh fisher, former Greenpeace staffer (Warm Springs, Ore.), interview,
      June 29, 2000.

21   U.S. District Court, District of Oregon, *Idaho Department of Fish and Game v. National
      Marine Fisheries Service*, 850 F. Supp. 886 (D. Or. 1994); Michael C. Blumm, Michael A.
      Schoessler, and R. Christopher Beckwith, "Beyond the Parity Promise: Struggling to
      Save Columbia Basin Salmon in the Mid-1990s," *Environmental Law Reporter* 27 (1997).

22   Steven Hawley, *Recovering a Lost River: Removing Dams, Rewilding Salmon, Revitalizing
      Communities* (Boston: Beacon Press, 2011).

23   Lumley, interview.

24   Vicki Monks, "When a Fish Is More than a Fish," *Spokane Spokesman-Review*, January
      26, 2000.

25   Robinson Shaw, "Salmon vs. Dam: The Snake Debate Rushes On," *ENN News*, March 12,
      2000.

26   *Idaho Statesman*, special report on dam breaching (July 20–22, 1997).

27   Reuters News Service, "Clinton Opposes Removing Four Dams on Snake River," July 19,
      2000.

28   *White Salmon Restored: A Timelapse Project—Documenting the Removal of Condit Dam*
      (2014), https://whitesalmontimelapse.wordpress.com/.

29   Salmon for All, "Columbia River Commercial Fishermen: Fishing for the General Pub-
      lic," 2016, www.salmonforall.org/history.

30   Johnny Jackson, Columbia River Chiefs' Council, Cascade/Klickitat (Underwood,
      Wash.), interview, July 6, 2000.

31   Jim Lichatowich, *Salmon without Rivers: A History of the Pacific Salmon Crisis* (Wash-
      ington, D.C., Island Press, 1999).

32   Pacific Coast Federation of Fishermen's Associations (2017), www.pcffa.org/.

33   Glen Spain, Pacific Coast Federation of Commercial Fishermen (Eugene, Ore.), inter-
      view, June 19, 2000.

34   Ibid.

35   Steve Fick, Salmon for All (Astoria, Ore.), interview, August 16, 2000.

36   Donald Sampson, CRITFC chairman, former Umatilla chair (Portland, Ore.), interview,
      July 7, 2000.

37 Les Clark, Northwest Gillnetters Association former president (Chinook, Wash.), interview, August 16, 2000.

38 Ibid.

39 Sampson, interview.

40 Dennis White, Columbia Gorge Audubon (White Salmon, Wash.), interview, July 6, 2000.

41 Jackson, interview.

42 Ibid.

43 Ibid.

44 Santos, interview.

45 Ibid.

46 Native Artist Apolonia Susana Santos, "Her Activism," 2006, www.apoloniasusana santos.com/apolonia/artist/activism.html.

47 Santos, interview.

48 Liz Hamilton, Northwest Sportfishing Industry Association (Portland, Ore.), interview, August 16, 2000.

49 Ibid.

50 Ibid.

51 Bill Bakke, Native Fish Society director (Portland, Ore.), interview, June 22, 2000.

52 Dan Landeen and Allen Pinkham, *Salmon and His People: Fish and Fishing in Nez Perce Culture* (Lewiston, Idaho: Confluence Press, 1999).

53 Jonathan Brinckman, "Clubbing of Salmon Unleashes Outrage," *Oregonian*, March 4, 2000; Mike Federman, "Tribes Object to Salmon Clubbing," *East Oregonian*, June 17, 2000; Associated Press, "Agency Decides It Will Spare Winthrop Hatchery Salmon," *Seattle Times*, June 22, 2000.

54 Sampson, interview.

55 Ted Strong, former CRITFC director, former Yakama chair (Toppenish, Wash.), interview, July 5, 2000.

56 Ibid.

57 Monks, "More than a Fish."

58 Quoted in ibid.

59 CRITFC, *Wy-Kan-Ush-Mi Wa-Kish-Wit* (*Spirit of the Salmon*), 1995, http://plan.critfc. org/; CRITFC, *Wy-Kan-Ush-Mi Wa-Kish-Wit*, update, 2014, http://plan.critfc.org/assets /wy-kan-update.pdf.

60 "Polls Support Tribal Salmon Positions," *Confederated Umatilla Journal*, June 1, 2000.

61 Clackamas County Pomona Grange, "Native Americans' Hatchery Management" (April 22, 2000).

62 Snake River Irrigators Association and Eastern Oregon Irrigators Association, policy memorandum, May 24, 2000.

63 Joseph Cone, *A Common Fate: Endangered Salmon and the People of the Pacific Northwest* (New York: Henry Holt, 1995).

64 Margaret Hollenbach and Jill Ory, *Protecting and Restoring Watersheds: A Tribal Approach to Salmon Recovery* (Portland, Ore.: CRITFC, 1999), 14–16, 24–28.

65 Ben Goldfarb, "The Great Salmon Compromise," *High Country News*, December 8, 2014.

66 Steve Parker, Yakama Fisheries staff (Toppenish, Wash.), interview, July 5, 2000.

67 Salmon Corps (2017), www.salmoncorps.org.

68 Courtenay Thompson, "Preserving Culture and Spirit: Native Americans Thrive in Salmon Corps," *Oregonian*, June 13, 2000.

69 Chris Shelley, Salmon Corps director of education/training (Portland, Ore.), interview, July 7, 2000.

70 George W. S. Aguilar Sr., *When the River Ran Wild! Indian Traditions on the Mid-Columbia and the Warm Springs Reservation* (Seattle: University of Washington Press, 2005).

71 Susan K. Driver, "Confederated Tribes of the Warm Springs Reservation Reach Historic Water Settlement Agreement," *Big River News*, newsletter of the Northwest Water Law and Policy Project, Lewis and Clark College, Winter 1998.

72 Terry Courtney Jr., Wasco/Tingit CRITFC commissioner (Warm Springs, Ore.), interview, June 29, 2000.

73 Claude Smith Sr., Wasco elder/fisher (Warm Springs, Ore.), interview, June 29, 2000.

74 In its 1995 constitution, the nation expressed an official preference for the original spelling of "Yakama."

75 "Hatfield Rates a High Mark," *Oregonian*, editorial, August 13, 1998.

76 Parker, interview.

77 Andrew Garber, "Longtime Foes Unite over Water Plan for Eastern Washington," *Seattle Times*, September 28, 2013.

78 Quoted in ibid.

79 Jennifer Karson, ed., *Wiyaxayxt / Wiyaakaa'awn / As Days Go By: Our History, Our Land, Our People—the Cayuse, Umatilla, and Walla Walla* (Seattle: University of Washington Press, 2006).

80 Michael Bales and Ann Terry Hill, *Pendleton Round-Up at One Hundred* (Portland, Ore.: Graphic Arts Center Publishing, 2009).

81 R. L. Alcorn and G. D. Alcorn, "Jackson Sundown, Nez Perce Horseman," *Montana: Magazine of Western History* 33, no. 4 (1983).

82 Hadley Akins, Umatilla Basin Project former co-chair (Pendleton, Ore.), interview, June 30, 2000.

83 Wil Phinney, "Salmon Returning to Umatilla," *East Oregonian*, April 30, 1988.

84 Akins, interview.

85 Chris Shelley, "The Resurrection of a River: Re-watering the Umatilla Basin" (paper presented at the American Society for Environmental History Conference, March 2000), http://ccrh.org/comm/river/docs/ubasin.htm.

86 Cone, *Common Fate*, 239.

87 Umatilla Basin Project Steering Committee, Umatilla Basin Project Summary Papers (1990).

88 John Shurts, *Indian Reserved Water Rights: The Winters Doctrine in Its Social and Legal Context, 1880s–1930s* (Norman: University of Oklahoma Press, 2000).

89 Quoted in Becky Hiers, "Water Conflict Resolved Cooperatively," Umatilla Tribes Policy Analysis (1996).

90 Quoted in Beverly Kelley, "Umatilla Project Addresses Needs of Irrigators, Fish," *Capital Press*, May 10, 1991.

91 Cone, *Common Fate*, 238.

92 Akins, interview.

93 Ibid.

94 Quoted in Steve Meyers, "Basin Project Backed," *East Oregonian*, February 9, 1988.

95 Steve Meyers, "Basin Project Start Near," *East Oregonian*, June 25, 1990.

96 Shelley M. Espelund, "Umatilla River: Resource Stakeholders Reconcile Conflicting Water Management Goals to Rebuild Salmon Runs" (1998).

97 Dick Cockle, "Testimony Favors Umatilla Basin Plan," *Oregonian*, February 9, 1988.

98   Courtenay Thompson, "Umatilla Revives Spring Salmon Run," *Oregonian*, April 25, 1997.

99   Akins, interview.

100 Steve Meyers, "WaterWatch Challenging Traditional Farm Irrigation," *East Oregonian*, December 9, 1991.

101 Shelley, interview.

102 Cone, *Common Fate*, 233–242.

103 Ibid., 234.

104 Wil Phinney, "Historic Celebration: Sides Join to Sign Pact Ending Water Dispute," *East Oregonian*, February 28, 1992.

105 Michael Farrow, Umatilla Department of Natural Resources director (Umatilla, Ore.), interview, June 30, 2000.

106 Melvin Schmidtgall, S&M Farming Company (Athena, Ore.), interview, July 1, 2000.

107 Quoted in Wil Phinney, "Lawmakers' OK Expected for Fish Run Project," *East Oregonian*, September 14, 1998.

108 Schmidtgall, interview.

109 Quoted in Karson, *Wiyaxayxt*, 231.

110 Antone Minthorn, Umatilla Tribes chairman (Umatilla, Ore.), interview, June 30, 2000.

111 "Saving the Salmon," *Newsweek*, September 30, 1991.

112 "Basin Project Paves Path for Fish Recovery," *East Oregonian*, editorial, May 3, 1991.

113 Jennifer L. Phillips, Jill Ory, and André Talbot, "Anadromous Salmonid Recovery in the Umatilla River Basin, Oregon" (Portland, Ore.: CRITFC, 2000).

114 Karson, *Wiyaxayxt*, 234.

115 Quoted in "Fishers Sing Praises of Umatilla Spring Chinook," *Confederated Umatilla Journal*, June 1, 2000.

116 Quoted in Associated Press, "Umatilla's Restoration Celebrated," *Spokane Spokesman-Review*, May 17, 1998.

117 Akins, interview.

118 Jerome A. Greene, *Nez Perce Summer, 1877: The U.S. Army and the Nee-Me-Poo Crisis* (Helena: Montana Historical Society Press, 2000).

119 Merrill Beal, *"I Will Fight No More Forever": Chief Joseph and the Nez Perce War* (Seattle: University of Washington Press, 2000); Kent Nerburn, *Chief Joseph and the Flight of the Nez Perce* (New York: HarperCollins, 2006).

120 Alex Tizon, "Nez Perce Invited Back to Land of Winding Rivers," *Seattle Times*, May 25, 1997.

121 Nicole Tonkovich, *The Allotment Plot: Alice C. Fletcher, E. Jane Gay, and Nez Perce Survivance* (Lincoln: University of Nebraska Press, 2012).

122 Monks, "More than a Fish."

123 Hawley, *Recovering a Lost River*, 202.

124 Sissel A. Waage, "(Re)claiming Space and Place through Collaborative Planning in Rural Oregon," *Political Geography* 20, no. 7 (2001): 840.

125 Don Bryson, Nez Perce Fisheries biologist (Lostine, Ore.), interview, August 4, 2000.

126 Ibid.

127 Quoted in Kim Murphy, "A Healing Closure to Nez Perce's Sad Voyage," *Los Angeles Times*, June 14, 1997.

128 Ibid.

129 Quoted in ibid.

130 Diane Snyder, Wallowa Resources director (Enterprise, Ore.), interview, July 3, 2000.

131 Ibid.

132 Allen Pinkham, Nez Perce former chairman, CRITFC commissioner (Lapwai, Idaho), interview, July 1, 2000.

133 Ibid.

134 Tizon, "Nez Perce Invited Back."

135 Quoted in Lyris Wallwork Winik, "We're Doing It Because We Think It's Right," *Parade*, June 15, 1997.

136 Quoted in Tizon, "Nez Perce Invited Back."

137 Rich Wandschneider, Nez Perce Homeland Project (Enterprise, Ore.), interview, July 3, 2000.

138 Tizon, "Nez Perce Invited Back."

139 The project had to deal with the inevitable Native perception of the non-Indian supporters as New Age "wannabes." Wandschneider reported that when the Nez Perce at one meeting requested the construction of a basketball court, a white "aging hippie" (who had evidently never visited a reservation) questioned the sport's relevance to "spiritual" Indian culture. In response, a Nez Perce elder stood up to exclaim: "No basketball—no Indians!" The other non-Indians understood the significance of basketball in Native life and helped to start a basketball tournament on the Tamkaliks grounds.

140 Robert T. Anderson, "Treaty Substitutes in the Modern Era," in *The Power of Promises: Rethinking Indian Treaties in the Pacific Northwest*, ed. Alexandra Harmon (Seattle: University of Washington Press, 2008), 328.

141 Donald L. Fixico, *The Invasion of Indian Country in the Twentieth Century: American Capitalism and Tribal Natural Resources*, 2nd ed. (Boulder, Colo.: University Press of Colorado, 2011), 79–102.

142 Holly Doremus and A. Dan Tarlock, *Water War in the Klamath Basin: Macho Law, Combat Biology, and Dirty Politics* (Washington, D.C.: Island Press, 2008).

143 Hannah Gosnell and Erin Clover Kelly, "Peace on the River? Social-Ecological Restoration and Large Dam Removal in the Klamath Basin, USA," *Water Alternatives* 3, no. 2 (2010): 361–383.

144 Stephen Most, *River of Renewal: Myth and History in the Klamath Basin* (Portland: Oregon Historical Society Press in association with University of Washington Press, 2006), back cover.

145 Doremus and Tarlock, *Water War*, 60–76.

146 Gosnell and Kelly, "Peace on the River?," 367–368.

147 Dan Keppen, *The Klamath Project at One Hundred* (Klamath Falls, Ore.: Klamath Water Users Association, 2004).

148 Doremus and Tarlock, *Water War*, 87–111.

149 Gosnell and Kelly, "Peace on the River?," 377; U.S. Court of Appeals, Ninth Circuit, *Klamath Water Users Protective Association v. Patterson*, No. 98-35708 (U.S. Ct. App., 9th Cir. 1999).

150 Gosnell and Kelly, "Peace on the River?," 369.

151 Klamath Bucket Brigade, "A History," 2015, http://klamathbucketbrigade.org/a_history_of_KBB.htm.

152 Theresa May, with Suzanne Burcell, Kathleen McCovey, and Jean O'Hara, *Salmon Is Everything: Community-Based Theatre in the Klamath Watershed* (Corvallis: Oregon State University Press, 2014).

153 Gosnell and Kelly, "Peace on the River?," 370; U.S. Court of Appeals, Ninth Circuit, *Pacific Coast Federation of Fishermen's Associations et al. v. United States Bureau of Reclamation et al.*, 426 F.3d 1082 (9th Cir. 2005).

154 "Klamath Tribes Could Get Land Back," *San Francisco Chronicle*, March 3, 2002.

155 Doremus and Tarlock, *Water War*, 166.

156 Gosnell and Kelly, "Peace on the River?," 371–372.

157 Julia Schreiber, "FERC Relicensing of the Klamath Hydropower Project," University of California, Davis (2009).

158 Glen Spain, "Dams, Water Reforms, and Endangered Species in the Klamath Basin," *Journal of Environmental Law and Litigation* 22, no. 1 (2007): 49–129.

159 Troy Fletcher, "At the Crossroads: In Search of Sustainable Solutions in the Klamath Basin" (presentation at the *Journal of Environmental Law and Litigation* [*JELL*] Symposium, University of Oregon Law School, January 26, 2007).

160 Gosnell and Kelly, "Peace on the River?," 378.

161 Craig Tucker, Klamath coordinator, Karuk Tribe (Orleans, Calif.), interview, July 28, 2015.

162 Klamath Restoration Agreements (2014), www.klamathrestoration.org/.

163 Klamath Hydroelectric Settlement Agreement (2010), http://edsheets.com/Klamath docs.html.

164 Quoted in Indigenous Peoples Issues and Resources, "Klamath Dam Agreement Represents Giant Leap Forward for Largest River Restoration Effort in History," press release, 2009.

165 Sarah Tory, "A New Film Tells the Story of the Klamath River Agreements," *High Country News*, February 4, 2015; Jason Atkinson, *A River Between Us*, documentary (2015), www .ariverbetweenus.com/.

166 Scott Learn, "Victory: Klamath Tribes' Water Rights Upheld by Federal Government," *Oregonian*, June 10, 2013.

167 Konrad Fisher, "Revised Klamath Agreement Signed: New Agreement Bypasses Congress for Dam Removal by 2020," *EcoNews*, June–July 2016; Bettina Boxall, "Pact Reached to Remove Four Klamath River Dams That Block Salmon Migration," *Los Angeles Times*, April 6, 2016.

168 Geoffrey Riley, "FERC Denies Permits for Jordan Cove, LNG Pipeline," Jefferson Public Radio, March 11, 2016.

169 Tucker, interview.

170 Gosnell and Kelly, "Peace on the River?," 365.

171 Aaron Orlando, "Salmon Reintroduction to Canadian Columbia River Recommended by U.S. Entity," *Revelstoke Times Review*, December 27, 2013.

172 Tim Stearns, Save Our Wild Salmon director (Seattle), interview, August 10, 1999.

173 Voyages of Rediscovery, *Treaty Talks: A Journey Up the Columbia River for People and Salmon*, documentary (2015), http://voyagesofrediscovery.blogspot.com/.

174 Steven E. Silvern, "Scales of Justice: American Indian Treaty Rights and the Political Construction of Scale," *Political Geography* 18, no. 6 (1999): 640.

175 Yi-Fu Tuan, *Topophilia: A Study of Environmental Perception, Attitudes, and Values* (Englewood Cliffs, N.J.: Prentice-Hall, 1974), 101.

176 Ibid.

177 For example, for a resident of a multiethnic Kosovo city to expand his or her scale of identity has meant expanding to a larger but monoethnic Greater Serbia or Greater Albania. Members of a local Iraqi tribe that includes both Shi'as and Sunnis may expand their scale of identity to a larger but sectarian religious identity.

178 In Macedonia, warring Slavs and Albanians lived together in peace around the natural springs town of Vevcani, which disassociated itself from the majority Slav republic.

Associated Press, "Macedonia Tolerates a 'Republic' in Its Midst," *New York Times*, January 6, 2000.

179 The conflict management group Search for Common Ground promoted joint environmental projects and tree plantings involving Macedonian Slav and Albanian youth. Search for Common Ground, "Macedonia," October 1998, www.sfcg.org/macedonia/.

180 Kyle Whyte, "Renewing Relatives: Nmé (Sturgeon) Stewardship in a Shared Watershed," *Humanities for the Environment*, December 1, 2014.

181 To use another international analogy: leaders of Israel and the Palestinian Authority have signed several peace accords since the mid-1990s. But the closed-door talks did not "trickle down" to affect local relations. Conversely, if dialogue is opened between Israelis and Palestinians, it has tended to founder because signals from the top have favored a continuation of occupation and war.

NOTES TO CHAPTER 3

1 Robert Gottlieb, *Forcing the Spring: The Transformation of the American Environmental Movement*, rev. ed. (New York: Island Press, 2005).

2 Robert D. Bullard, Glenn S. Johnson, and Angel O. Torres, *Environmental Health and Racial Equity* (Washington, D.C.: American Public Health Association, 2011); Robert D. Bullard, ed., *The Quest for Environmental Justice* (Berkeley, Calif.: Counterpoint, 2005); David E. Camacho, ed., *Environmental Injustices, Political Struggles: Race, Class, and the Environment* (Durham, N.C.: Duke University Press, 1998).

3 Vicki Been, "Locally Undesirable Land Uses in Minority Neighborhoods: Disparate Siting or Market Dynamics?," *Yale Law Journal* 103, no. 6 (1994): 1383–1422.

4 Ronald D. Sandler and Phaedra C. Pezzullo, *Environmental Justice and Environmentalism: The Social Justice Challenge to the Environmental Movement* (Cambridge, Mass.: MIT Press, 2007).

5 Mark David Spence, *Dispossessing the Wilderness: Indian Removal and the Making of the National Parks* (Oxford: Oxford University Press, 2000).

6 Ibid., 136; Robert H. Keller Jr. and Michael F. Turek, *American Indians and National Parks* (Tucson: University of Arizona Press, 1998).

7 Danny Westneat, "Save-the-Whales Movement Failed to Rally Opposition to Makah Hunt," *Seattle Times*, October 24, 1997.

8 Rob Nixon, *Slow Violence and the Environmentalism of the Poor* (Cambridge, Mass.: Harvard University Press, 2013).

9 Donald S. Moore, Jake Kosek, and Anand Pandian, eds., *Race, Nature, and the Politics of Difference* (Durham, N.C.: Duke University Press, 2003), back cover.

10 Melissa K. Nelson, ed., *Original Instructions: Indigenous Teachings for a Sustainable Future* (Rochester, Vt.: Bear and Company, 2008); Winona LaDuke, *All Our Relations: Native Struggles for Land and Life* (Boston: South End Press, 1999); Donald A. Grinde and Bruce E. Johansen, *Ecocide of Native America* (Santa Fe, N.M.: Clear Light Publishers, 1995).

11 Gregory Cajete, *Native Science: Natural Laws of Interdependence* (Santa Fe, N.M.: Clear Light Publishers, 2000).

12 Regina Austin and Michael Schill, "Black, Brown, Poor, and Poisoned: Minority Grassroots Environmentalism and the Quest for Eco-Justice," *Kansas Journal of Law and Public Policy* 1 (1991): 69–82.

13 Michael Heiman, "From 'Not in My Backyard' to 'Not in Anybody's Backyard': Grassroots

Challenge to Hazardous Waste Facility Siting," *Journal of the American Planning Association* 65, no. 2 (1990): 359–362.

14 Stella M. Capek, "The 'Environmental Justice' Frame: A Conceptual Discussion and an Application," *Social Problems* 40, no. 1 (1993): 5–24.

15 Heiman, "Not in My Backyard."

16 Laura Pulido, "A Critical Review of the Methodology of Environmental Racism Research," *Antipode* 28, no. 2 (1996): 142–159.

17 Andrew Hurley, *Environmental Inequalities: Class, Race, and Industrial Pollution in Gary, Indiana, 1945–1980* (Chapel Hill: University of North Carolina Press, 1995), 123.

18 Thomas D. Beamish and Amy J. Luebbers, "Alliance Building across Social Movements," *Social Problems* 56, no. 4 (2009): 647–676; Laura Pulido and Devon Peña, "Environmentalism and Positionality: The Early Campaign of the United Farmworkers' Organizing Committee, 1965–71," *Race, Gender and Class* 6, no. 1 (1998): 33–50.

19 Pulido, "Environmental Racism Research."

20 Jake Kosek, *Understories: The Political Life of Forests in Northern New Mexico* (Durham, N.C.: Duke University Press, 2006).

21 Tom Goldtooth, Indigenous Environmental Network executive director (Bemidji, Minn.), interview, August 6, 1997.

22 Luke W. Cole and Sheila R. Foster, *From the Ground Up: Environmental Racism and the Rise of the Environmental Justice Movement* (New York: New York University Press, 2001), 134–150.

23 Ned Blackhawk, *Violence over the Land: Indians and Empires in the Early American West* (Cambridge, Mass.: Harvard University Press, 2008).

24 United States Treaty with the Western Shoshone, Oct. 1, 1863, 18 Stat. 689.

25 Scott Robert Ladd, "Stealing Nevada," 1996, www.dickshovel.com/def.html.

26 Rob Bhatt, "State of Conflict," *Las Vegas Weekly*, December 2, 1999.

27 Raymond Yowell, "Outline of Western Shoshone National Government's Finding of Facts against the United States" (January 1998).

28 James Rainey, "Cash vs. an Allegiance to Heritage," *Los Angeles Times*, February 9, 2000.

29 Beth Gage and George Gage, *American Outrage*, documentary (2008).

30 Yowell, "Finding of Facts."

31 U.S. Supreme Court, *United States v. Dann*, 470 U.S. 39 (1985).

32 Rebecca Solnit, *Savage Dreams: A Journey into the Hidden Wars of the American West*, 2nd ed. (Berkeley: University of California Press, 2014), 159–190.

33 Associated Press, "Nevada Cowboys, Indians Allies in Fed Face-off over Seized Cows," June 1, 2002.

34 Mark Miller, "The Timbisha Shoshone and the National Park Idea: Building toward Accommodation and Acknowledgment at Death Valley National Park, 1933–2000," *Journal of the Southwest* 50, no. 4 (2008): 415–445.

35 Richard L. Miller, *Under the Cloud: The Decades of Nuclear Testing* (The Woodlands, Tex.: Two-Sixty Press, 1999).

36 Solnit, *Savage Dreams*, 58–60.

37 Matthew Glass, "Air Force, Western Shoshone, and Mormon Rhetoric of Place and the MX Conflict," in *The Atomic West*, ed. Bruce Hevly and John Findlay (Seattle: University of Washington Press, 1998).

38 Jerry Mander, "This Is Not Air Force Land," *Village Voice*, December 17, 1979.

39 Raymond Yowell, Western Shoshone National Council chief (South Fork, Nev.), interview, November 30, 2000.

40 Raymond Yowell, "Land Yes, M-X No," Western Shoshone Sacred Lands Association (April 1980).

41 Dagmar Thorpe, "The MX Missile and the Western Shoshone," Western Shoshone Sacred Lands Association (Spring 1981).

42 Quoted in ibid.

43 Great Basin MX Alliance, "Resolution of the Great Basin MX Alliance," Western Shoshone Sacred Lands Association (April 1980).

44 Yowell, interview.

45 Glass, "MX Conflict."

46 Quoted in Ladd, "Stealing Nevada."

47 Yowell, interview.

48 Bret Lortie, "How Low Can You Go?," *Bulletin of the Atomic Scientists* 56, no. 3 (2000): 6.

49 Jane Braxton Little, "Military Watchdog," *Audubon*, December 2000.

50 Grace Potorti, Rural Alliance for Military Accountability (Reno, Nev.), interview, September 25, 1997.

51 Ibid.

52 Jennifer Allen, "US Navy Crashed and Burns in Austin, NV," Western Shoshone Defense Project (Spring 1997).

53 Ibid.

54 Salisbury, quoted in David C. Henley, "Navy Expansion Plans Opposed by New Central Nevada Committee," *Lahontan Valley News / Fallon Eagle Standard*, September 9, 1997.

55 Potorti, interview.

56 Virginia Sanchez, Citizen Alert Native American Program, Western Shoshone (Reno, Nev.), interview, August 6, 1997.

57 Ken Butigan, *Pilgrimage through a Burning World: Spiritual Practice and Nonviolent Protest at the Nevada Test Site* (Albany: State University of New York Press, 2003).

58 Yowell, interview.

59 Potorti, interview.

60 After Mary Dann passed in 2005, her sister Carrie kept up the fight to protect their ranch and cattle.

61 Peace Brigades International, "Western Shoshone Situation," report from PBI North America Project, January 16, 1995.

62 Jennifer Allen and Chris Sewall, Western Shoshone Defense Project (Crescent Valley, Nev.), interview, August 6, 1997.

63 Corbin Harney, *The Nature Way* (Reno: University of Nevada Press, 2009).

64 Corbin Harney, Western Shoshone National Council (Sparks, Nev.), interview, June 13, 1998.

65 Quoted in Ladd, "Stealing Nevada."

66 Quoted in Bhatt, "State of Conflict."

67 Harney, interview.

68 Yowell, interview.

69 Quoted in Solnit, *Savage Dreams*, 172.

70 Florence Williams, "The Shovel Rebellion," *Mother Jones*, January–February 2001.

71 Jaime Fuller, "Everything You Need to Know about the Long Fight between Cliven Bundy and the Federal Government," *Washington Post*, April 15, 2014. The Moapa Band of Paiutes has also sought federal protection for lands within the Bundy ranch. Henry Brean, "Moapa Band of Paiute Members March to Protect Gold Butte," *Las Vegas Review-Journal*, April 23, 2016.

72   Steve Russell, "Confronting the Feds: Armed Ranchers and Peaceful Native Water Pro-
      tectors," *Indian Country Today*, August 25, 2016.
73   Evelyn Nieves, "Never Mind Cliven Bundy: Here's the Real David vs. Goliath Story be-
      tween Ranchers and Feds," *AlterNet*, April 19, 2014, www.alternet.org/.
74   David Edwards, "'Pissed as Hell' Rancher Blows Up at Bundy Militants: 'I'm Not Going Let
      Some Other People Be My Face,'" The Raw Story, January 7, 2016, www.rawstory.com/.
75   William James Smith Jr., Zhongwei Liu, Ahmad Saleh Safi, and Karletta Chief, "Climate
      Change Perception, Observation, and Policy Support in Rural Nevada: A Comparative
      Analysis of Native Americans, Non-Native Ranchers and Farmers, and Mainstream
      America," *Environmental Science and Policy* 42 (2014): 101–122.
76   Carol Miller, "Speak Your Piece: Take Back the Skies," *Daily Yonder*, January 5, 2012.
77   Tribal members view the effigies of thunderbirds, bears, panthers, and other animals
      as representing their clans. Rock art on various cave ledges symbolizes legends that
      tribal members still tell to their children. Robert A. Birmingham and Leslie E. Eisenberg,
      Indian Mounds of Wisconsin (Madison: University of Wisconsin Press, 2000).
78   Ho-Chunk Nation Department of Historic Preservation, *The Ho-Chunk Nation* (1997).
79   Patty Loew, *Indian Nations of Wisconsin: Histories of Endurance and Renewal*, 2nd ed.
      (Madison: Wisconsin Historical Society Press, 2013), 44–58.
80   *Reedsburg Remembers 150 Years* (Reedsburg, Wis.: Sesquicentennial History Committee,
      1998), 32–33.
81   Kendall Marie Tallmadge, "Tourism, Place, and Identity: Economic History and Political
      Sovereignty in the Ho-Chunk Nation" (master's thesis, University of Colorado–Boulder,
      2013); Ho-Chunk Nation Department of Historic Preservation, "The Cranberry People,"
      brochure (1996).
82   Wisconsin Cartographers' Guild, *Wisconsin's Past and Present: A Historical Atlas* (Madi-
      son: University of Wisconsin Press, 1998), 8–9.
83   Tribal members were instrumental in starting the Highground Veterans' Memorial near
      Neillsville, where Ho-Chunk artist Harry Whitehorse also sculpted the National Native
      American Vietnam Veterans Memorial.
84   Tom Jones, Michael Schmudlach, Matthew Daniel Mason, Amy Lonetree, and George A.
      Greendeer, *People of the Big Voice: Photographs of Ho-Chunk Families by Charles Van
      Schaick, 1879–1942* (Madison: Wisconsin Historical Society Press, 2011), 93.
85   Marilyn Leys, *Denting Goliaths: Citizens Unite against Regional Low-Level Flights*
      (Bloomington, Ind.: AuthorHouse, 2015).
86   Air National Guard Readiness Center (ANGRC) Environmental Planning Branch, *Ex-
      pansion of Hardwood Air-to-Ground Gunnery Range, Wisconsin* (April 1992), 1–3.
87   "Why Now, and Why Here?," *Wisconsin Trails*, editorial, July–August 1995.
88   Susan Lampert Smith, "Opposition to Military Flyovers Taking Off," *Wisconsin State
      Journal*, October 8, 1995.
89   Wisconsin Department of Natural Resources, *Environmental Assessment on the Planned
      Expansion of the Hardwood Bombing and Gunnery Range, Wood County* (1996), 11.
90   Ho-Chunk Nation Geographic Information Systems (GIS), "Ho-Chunk Nation Popula-
      tion Distribution in Wisconsin" (October 18, 1995).
91   Ona Garvin, Citizens Opposed to Range Expansion (CORE), former Ho-Chunk tribal
      legislator (Pittsville, Wis.), interview, August 22, 1997.
92   CORE, "Don't Bomb Our Forests!" (October 1996).
93   Ibid.

94 Susan Lampert Smith, "More Oppose Plan to Add Practice Bombing Runs," *Wisconsin State Journal*, May 24, 1995.

95 Wood County Board of Supervisors (Wisconsin), Resolution 95-2-9, February 21, 1995.

96 Kurt Rentmeester, "Public Air Travel in Jeopardy from Bombing Range Expansion: Gaier," *Marshfield News-Herald*, August 18, 1995.

97 Patricia Conway, "Prayer Rally Opposes Bombing Range Expansion and Low-Level Flights," press release, September 1995.

98 A 1996 environmental assessment claimed that the expansion "will have no effect on Native American archeological resources." Wisconsin Department of Natural Resources, *Environmental Assessment on the Planned Expansion of the Hardwood Bombing and Gunnery Range, Wood County* (1996), 15.

99 Patricia Conway, Citizens United Against Low-Level Flights (Ontario, Wis.), interview, August 26, 1999.

100 S. Smith, "Opposition to Military Flyovers."

101 Patrick Slattery, "Noisy Skies Draw Protest, Prayers from Amish, Others," *Times Review*, October 5, 1995.

102 Peter Muller, "Amish Oppose Flight Zone," *Milwaukee Journal Sentinel*, April 11, 1995.

103 Garvin, interview.

104 S. Smith, "More Oppose Plan."

105 Garvin, interview.

106 Susan Lampert Smith, "Air Guard Plan Is under Fire," *Wisconsin State Journal*, March 7, 1995; Gray quoted in ibid.

107 Garvin, interview.

108 Slattery, "Noisy Skies."

109 "National Guard Drops Flight Plan," *Tomah Monitor Herald*, April 15, 1996.

110 "High-Level Democracy," *Hillsboro Sentry-Enterprise*, editorial, April 18, 1996.

111 "Activist Groups Hit Plans to Expand U.S. Bomb Range," *Hillsboro Sentry-Enterprise*, April 18, 1996.

112 Conway, interview.

113 CORE, "Candlelight Vigil to Oppose Expansion of Bombing Range" (September 1997).

114 Air National Guard, *Final Environmental Impact Statement Addressing the Hardwood Range Expansion and Associated Airspace Actions* (Washington, D.C.: National Guard Bureau, 2000).

115 The Air National Guard delayed its planned expansion of the Hardwood Range into the 2010s, as studies were conducted to "minimize encroachment" around the facility. Wisconsin Air National Guard, *Hardwood Range Compatible Use Analysis* (August 2010); North Central Wisconsin Regional Planning Commission, *Volk Field Hardwood Range Joint Land Use Study* (December 2011).

116 Zoltán Grossman, "Removal Reversed: Native/Non-Native Joint Management of Reclaimed Lands" (presentation to the annual meeting of the Association of American Geographers, New Orleans, March 2003), http://academic.evergreen.edu/g/grossmaz/RemovalReversed.ppt.

117 Lynne Heasley, *A Thousand Pieces of Paradise: Landscape and Property in the Kickapoo Valley* (Madison: University of Wisconsin Press, 2012), 129–153.

118 Ibid., 173–194.

119 Susan Lampert Smith, "Ho-Chunk Add to Trust Holdings," *Wisconsin State Journal*, October 29, 1997.

120 Ho-Chunk Nation GIS, "Population Distribution."

121 Jim Parr, Vernon County supervisor (La Farge, Wis.), personal communication, August 9, 1999.

122 S. Smith, "Trust Holdings."

123 Wisconsin Cartographers' Guild, *Past and Present*, 86.

124 Jason Van Driesche and Marcus Lane, "Conservation through Conversation: Collaborative Planning for Reuse of a Former Military Property in Sauk County, Wisconsin, USA," *Planning Theory and Practice* 3, no. 2 (2002): 133–153.

125 Sharon Lynn Hausam, "Native American and Non-Native Involvement in Collaborative Planning Processes: A Case Study of a Planning Process for the Reuse of the Badger Army Ammunition Plant" (Ph.D. diss., Department of Urban and Regional Planning, University of Wisconsin–Madison, 2006).

126 Amanda Fuller, "So What's Happening with Badger?," Community Conservation Coalition for the Sauk Prairie, fact sheet, May 22, 2001.

127 Ho-Chunk Nation GIS, "Population Distribution."

128 Citizens for Safe Water Around Badger, "Klug Opposes Commercial Uses at Badger," *CSWAB Newsletter* (Merrimac, Wis.), Winter 2000.

129 *Shopper Stopper*, "Survey on Future of Badger," June 1998–November 1999.

130 Community Conservation Coalition for the Sauk Prairie, "A Proposal for the Future Use of Land at the Badger Army Ammunition Plant," October 1999, www.saukprairievision.org/.

131 Badger Re-use Committee, "Badger Army Ammunition Plant Reuse Plan" (December 2001).

132 Ron Seely, "Badger Ammo Future on Tap," *Wisconsin State Journal*, January 6, 2002.

133 Sauk Prairie Conservation Alliance, "Landowners at Badger," 2012, http://saukprairievision.org/resources_future_landowners.

134 Laura Olah, "An Opportunity for Solidarity," *CSWAB Newsletter*, Spring 1999.

135 Anita Weir, "Ho-Chunk to Get Less Land," *Capital Times*, October 25, 2003.

136 Tim Damos, "Ho-Chunk Gives Up on Badger Ammo," *Baraboo News Republic*, October 11, 2011.

137 Dee J. Hall, "Ho-Chunk to Finally Get Fifteen Hundred Acres at Closed Badger Army Ammunition Plant," *Wisconsin State Journal*, December 5, 2014.

138 Kim Lamoreaux, "Ho-Chunk Return to Ancestral Land That Was Part of Badger Army Ammunition Plant," *Wisconsin State Journal*, June 24, 2015; Wisconsin Public Television, "What the Future Holds for Former Propellant Facility," July 1, 2016, http://wpt.org/Here_and_Now/what-future-holds-former-propellant-facility.

139 Robert Jerome Glennon, *Water Follies: Groundwater Pumping and the Fate of America's Fresh Waters* (New York: Island Press, 2004), 3–10.

140 Midwest Treaty Network, "Ho-Chunk Nation Opposes Perrier Pumping Plans," October 2000, http://treaty.indigenousnative.org/perrier.html; Erik Ness, "Perrier Didn't Reckon on an Angry Citizenry When It Looked to Expand into the Midwest," Grist, May 21, 2011, http://grist.org/.

141 Arlene Kanno and Hiroshi Kanno, "When the Grassroots Said No (Way)," Angling Matters, 2003, www.anglingmatters.com/ww_when.htm.

142 Steve Lopez, "And Nary a Drop for You, Wisconsin," *Time*, September 25, 2000.

143 Michigan Citizens for Water Conservation (March 2002), www.savemiwater.org/; Robert Downes, "The Bad Taste of Perrier," *Northern Express*, March 14, 2002.

144 Thomas W. Pearson, "Frac Sand Mining in Wisconsin: Understanding Emerging Con-

flicts and Community Organizing," *Culture, Agriculture, Food, and Environment (CAFÉ)* 35 (2013): 30–40.

145 Ho-Chunk Nation Legislature, "Ho-Chunk Nation Opposition to Frac Sand Mining Operations," Resolution 12-4-12K, December 4, 2012.

146 Cassandra Colson, "Ho-Chunk Lobbying against Mining," *Tomah Journal*, February 7, 2013.

147 Zahra Hirji, "Frac Sand Mining Boom: Health Hazard Feared, but Lawmakers Aim to Ease Regulation," *InsideClimate News*, November 5, 2013.

148 Rebecca Kemble, "Jon Greendeer: Frac Sand Mining Is an Insidious Industry," SB349 public hearing, October 24, 2013, www.youtube.com/watch?v=Hlh5B3WmYd4.

149 Cassandra Colson, "Residents Unite for Anti–Frac Sand Mining Conference," *Tomah Journal*, June 6, 2013.

150 Lissa Blake, "Bus Trip to Land of Frac-Sand Mining Provides Insight to 'New' Industry," *Decorah Newspapers*, August 14, 2013.

151 Quoted in Rich Kremer, "Ho-Chunk Members Call for Coalition against Frac Sand Mining," Wisconsin Public Radio, November 21, 2013.

152 Juliee de la Terre, "Ho-Chunk Nation Adds 'Rights of Nature' to Their Constitution," Global Alliance for the Rights of Nature, September 19, 2015.

153 Save the Hills Alliance, "Information about the Buses to the Madison Rally," *Frac Sand Sentinel*, January 9, 2016.

154 Theodore W. Allen, *The Invention of the White Race*, vol. 2, *The Origin of Racial Oppression in Anglo-America* (New York: Verso, 1997).

155 Peter Kolchin, *American Slavery, 1619–1877* (New York: Hill and Wang, 2003).

156 David R. Roediger, *The Wages of Whiteness: Race and the Making of the American Working Class* (New York: Verso, 1991); Herbert Hill, *Race and Ethnicity in Organized Labor* (Madison: University of Wisconsin–Madison, Industrial Relations Research Institute, 1984).

157 Noel Ignatin, "Black Worker, White Worker," in *White Supremacy: A Collection* (Chicago: Sojourner Truth Organization, 1970).

158 Michelle Alexander, *The New Jim Crow: Mass Incarceration in the Age of Colorblindness* (New York: The New Press, 2012), 22.

159 Amory Ballantine, "'Whiteness as Property': Colonialism, Contamination, and Detention in Tacoma's Puyallup Estuary" (master's thesis, Master of Environmental Studies program, The Evergreen State College, 2016); George Lipsitz, *How Racism Takes Place* (Philadelphia: Temple University Press, 2011); Audrey Kobayashi and Linda Peake, "Racism out of Place: Thoughts on Whiteness and an Antiracist Geography in the New Millennium," *Annals of the Association of American Geographers* 90, no. 2 (2000): 392–403.

160 David R. Roediger, *Working toward Whiteness: How America's Immigrants Became White* (New York: Basic Books, 2006); Matthew Frye Jacobson, *Whiteness of a Different Color: European Immigrants and the Alchemy of Race* (Cambridge, Mass.: Harvard University Press, 1999); Noel Ignatiev, *How the Irish Became White* (New York: Routledge, 1995).

161 Birgit Brander Rasmussen, Eric Klinenberg, Irene J. Nexica, and Matt Wray, eds., *The Making and Unmaking of Whiteness* (Durham, N.C.: Duke University Press, 2001); Redneck Revolt (2017), www.redneckrevolt.org.

162 Theodore W. Allen, *Class Struggle and the Origin of Racial Slavery: The Invention of the White Race* (Somerville, Mass.: New England Free Press, 1976).

163 Katherine T McCaffrey, *Military Power and Popular Protest: The U.S. Navy in Vieques, Puerto Rico* (New Brunswick, N.J.: Rutgers University Press, 2002); Jonathan

Kamakawiwoʻole Osorio, "Hawaiian Souls: The Movement to Stop the U.S. Military Bombing of Kahoʻolawe," in *A Nation Rising: Hawaiian Movements for Life, Land, and Sovereignty*, ed. Noelani Goodyear-Kaʻopua, Ikaika Hussey, and Erin Kahunawaikaʻala Wright (Durham, N.C.: Duke University Press, 2014), 137–160; Mansel G. Blackford, "Environmental Justice, Native Rights, Tourism, and Opposition to Military Control: The Case of Kahoʻolawe," *Journal of American History* 91, no. 2 (2004): 544–571.

164 LaDuke, *All Our Relations*, 49–74.

165 As the geographer David Harvey notes: "All propositions for social action (or conceptions of social justice) must be critically evaluated in terms of the situatedness or positionality of the argument and the arguer. But it is equally important to recognize that the individuals developing such situated knowledge are not themselves homogeneous entities but bundles of heterogeneous impulses, many of which derive from an internalization of 'the other' within the self." David Harvey, *Place and the Politics of Identity*, ed. Michael Keith and Steve Pile (London: Routledge, 1993), 63.

NOTES TO CHAPTER 4

1   Joseph G. Jorgensen et al., *Native Americans and Energy Development* (Boston: Anthropology Resource Center, 1978).

2   Peter Iverson, *When Indians Became Cowboys: Native Peoples and Cattle Ranching in the American West* (Norman: University of Oklahoma Press, 1997), 219. See also Miriam Horn, *Rancher, Farmer, Fisherman: Conservation Heroes of the American Heartland* (New York: W.W. Norton & Co., 2016).

3   National Academy of Sciences, *Rehabilitation Potential of Western Coal Lands*, document drafted with the National Academy of Engineering (Washington, D.C.: Ford Foundation, 1973), 135.

4   Roger Richardson, "Rising Coal Exports Have Montana Rail Communities Braced for Worst," The Daily Climate, May 3, 2012, www.dailyclimate.org/.

5   James N. Leiker and Ramona Powers, *The Northern Cheyenne Exodus in History and Memory* (Norman: University of Oklahoma Press, 2011).

6   Winona LaDuke, *All Our Relations: Native Struggles for Land and Life* (Boston: South End Press, 1999), 78–90.

7   Ibid., 83.

8   James Robert Allison III, *Sovereignty for Survival: American Energy Development and Indian Self-Determination* (New Haven, Conn.: Yale University Press, 2015), 75–88.

9   Marjane Ambler, *Breaking the Iron Bonds: Indian Control of Energy Development* (Lawrence: University of Kansas Press, 1990), 67–69.

10 Northern Plains Resource Council (2017), http://northernplains.org/.

11 Michael Parfit, *Last Stand at Rosebud Creek: Coal, Power, and People* (Hialeah, Fla.: Dutton Press, 1980).

12 Northern Plains Resource Council, *Annual Report 1996* (Billings, Mont.).

13 Joseph G. Jorgensen, "Land Is Cultural, So Is a Commodity: The Locus of Differences among Indians, Cowboys, Sod-Busters, and Environmentalists," *Journal of Ethnic Studies* 12, no. 3 (1984): 1–22.

14 Teresa Erickson, Northern Plains Resource Council (Billings, Mont.), interview, August 5, 1997.

15 Alaina Buffalo Spirit, Northern Plains Resource Council (Lame Deer, Mont.), interview, May 15, 2015.

16 Gail Small, "The Search for Environmental Justice in Indian Country," *News from Indian Country*, March 1994.

17 Wallace McRae, *Stick Horses and Other Stories of Ranch Life* (Layton, Utah: Gibbs Smith, 2009).

18 Wallace McRae, "Things of Intrinsic Worth," in *New Cowboy Poetry*, ed. Hal Cannon (Layton, Utah: Gibbs Smith, 1990), 54.

19 Carly Calhoun and Sam Despeaux, directors, *Things of Intrinsic Worth*, The Montana Experience: Stories from Big Sky Country (2013).

20 Marjane Ambler, *We, the Northern Cheyenne* (Lame Deer, Mont.: Chief Dull Knife College, 2008), 140.

21 Northern Plains Resource Council, "History," 2016, www.northernplains.org/history.

22 Quoted in Thomas Kotynski, "Ranchers, Indians Oppose Tongue River Railroad Plans," *Great Falls Tribune*, September 29, 1980.

23 Northern Plains Resource Council, "Tongue River Railroad," 2016, www.northernplains.org/issues/tongue-river-railroad.

24 Scott McMillon, "Clinton to Announce Plan to Prevent Mine Construction," *Bozeman Daily Chronicle*, August 8, 1996.

25 Gail Small, "The Coal Wars: Northern Cheyenne Reservation," Southwest Research and Information Center (2005).

26 Yellow Bird, "Environmental Protection," 2016, http://yellowbirdprograms.org/enviromental-protection.

27 James Main Jr., Red Thunder / Indigenous Environmental Network, Gros Ventre (Fort Belknap, Mont.), interview, August 5, 1997.

28 John Smart, "Gold and Ethnocide," *Plains Truth*, Fall 1993.

29 Robert Moran, *Cyanide Uncertainties* (Washington, D.C.: Mineral Policy Center, 1998), www.earthworksaction.org/files/publications/cyanideuncertainties.pdf.

30 Ted Lange, "Big Problems at Montana's Biggest Mine," *Plains Truth*, Fall 1993.

31 Main, interview.

32 Fort Belknap Community Council, "The Struggle to Save the Little Rocky Mountains," pamphlet (1997).

33 Heather Abel, "Montana on the Edge: A Fight over Gold Forces the Treasure State to Confront Its Future," *High Country News*, December 22, 1997.

34 Ted Lange, "BLM Considering Mining Ban for Sweetgrass Hills," *Plains Truth*, Fall 1993.

35 Richard Thieltges, Sweet Grass Hills Protective Association (Helena, Mont.), interview, August 6, 1997.

36 Quoted in Lange, "Sweetgrass Hills."

37 Mert Freyholtz, Environmental Rangers (Gildford, Mont.), interview, August 5, 1997.

38 Main, interview.

39 Quoted in Native Action, "Montana's Sweet Grass Hills: The Gold Rush Is On!," pamphlet (1995).

40 Heather Abel, "On the Trail of Mining's Corporate Nomads," *High Country News*, June 23, 1997.

41 Emily Cousins, "Marching to Stop a Montana Mine," *High Country News*, August 5, 1996.

42 Two decades later, they remobilized and pressured the Department of the Interior to renew the withdrawal in 2017.

43 Thieltges, interview.

44 Ken Toole and Christine Kaufmann, *Drumming Up Resistance: The Anti-Indian Movement in Montana* (Helena: Montana Human Rights Network, 2000), 12–17, 26–29.

45 Rudolph C. Rÿser, *Anti-Indian Movement on the Tribal Frontier*, Occasional Paper 16, rev. ed. (Kenmore, Wash.: Center for World Indigenous Studies, 1992), 34–36.

46 Toole and Kaufmann, *Drumming Up Resistance*, 43.

47 Ericka Schenck Smith, "Indian-State Meeting Plan Debated," *Billings Gazette*, January 10, 2002.

48 Donald L. Fixico, *The Invasion of Indian Country in the Twentieth Century: American Capitalism and Tribal Natural Resources*, 2nd ed. (Boulder, Colo.: University Press of Colorado, 2011), 123–142.

49 Roxanne Dunbar-Ortiz, *The Great Sioux Nation* (Berkeley, Calif.: American Indian Treaty Council Information and Moon Books, 1977), 94.

50 Jeffrey Ostler, *The Plains Sioux and U.S. Colonialism from Lewis and Clark to Wounded Knee* (Cambridge: Cambridge University Press, 2004).

51 Jeffrey Ostler, *The Lakotas and the Black Hills: The Struggle for Sacred Ground* (New York: Penguin Books, 2010).

52 Quoted in Dunbar-Ortiz, *Great Sioux Nation*, 47.

53 Paul Chaat Smith and Robert Allen Warrior, *Like a Hurricane: The Indian Movement from Alcatraz to Wounded Knee* (New York: New Press, 1996), 112–126, 171–193.

54 Donald L. Fixico, *Indian Resilience and Rebuilding: Indigenous Nations in the Modern American West* (Tucson: University of Arizona Press, 2013), 121–150.

55 *Voices from Wounded Knee, 1973* (Rooseveltown, N.Y.: Akwesasne Notes, 1974); Chaat and Warrior, *Like a Hurricane*, 194–268.

56 Edward Lazarus, *Black Hills, White Justice: The Sioux Nation versus the United States, 1775 to the Present* (New York: HarperCollins, 1991), 310.

57 Ibid., 401.

58 Bruce E. Johansen and Roberto Maestas, *Wasi'chu: The Continuing Indian Wars* (New York: Monthly Review Press, 1979), 83–84.

59 Peter Matthiessen, *In the Spirit of Crazy Horse: The Story of Leonard Peltier and the FBI's War on the American Indian Movement* (New York: Viking, 1983).

60 International Leonard Peltier Defense Committee (2017), www.whoisleonardpeltier .info.

61 Black Hills Alliance, *Keystone to Survival: The Multinational Corporations and the Struggle for Control of Land* (Minneapolis: Haymarket Press, 1981), 46–47.

62 Ronald Goodman, *Lakota Star Knowledge: Studies in Lakota Stellar Theology* (Rosebud, S.D.: Sinte Gleska University, 1992).

63 Ostler, *Lakotas and the Black Hills*, 12–25.

64 Donald Worster, *Under Western Skies: Nature and History in the American West* (Oxford: Oxford University Press, 1994), 106–153; Watson Parker, *Gold in the Black Hills* (Lincoln: University of Nebraska Press, 1982).

65 Linea Sundstrom, "The Sacred Black Hills: An Ethnohistorical Review," *Great Plains Quarterly* 17, nos. 3–4 (1997): 208; Sundstrom, *Indian Rock Art in the Black Hills Country* (Norman: University of Oklahoma Press, 2004).

66 Worster, *Under Western Skies*, 110.

67 Bruce Ellison, Black Hills Alliance co-founder, attorney (Rapid City, S.D.), interview, June 24, 1999.

68 Bill Means, International Indian Treaty Council director; Oglala Lakota (Minneapolis), interview, March 21, 1997.

69 The BHA published the *Black Hills–Paha Sapa Report* in 1979–81, archived by Lilias

Jarding on her Oglala Lakota College web page, accessible from http://academic.ever green.edu/g/grossmaz/bha.html.

70 Mark Tilsen, Black Hills Alliance former director (Stillwater, Minn.), interview, August 10, 1997.

71 Paula L. Wagoner, *"They Treated Us Just like Indians": The Worlds of Bennett County, South Dakota* (Lincoln: University of Nebraska Press, 2002), 117–123.

72 Tilsen, interview.

73 Ellison, interview.

74 Madonna Thunder Hawk, Black Hills Alliance, Oglala Lakota (Pine Ridge, S.D.), interview, June 26, 1999.

75 Marvin Kammerer, Black Hills Alliance, rancher (Box Elder, S.D.), interview, July 26, 1997.

76 Quoted in Peter Matthiessen, "High Noon in the Black Hills," *New York Times Magazine*, July 13, 1979.

77 Charles Ray, "Bucking the Trends: Black Hills Crusader Marvin Kammerer," *High Country News*, September 27, 2004.

78 Quoted in C. Michael Ray, "Cowboys and Indians," *OnEarth*, December 1, 2008, http:// archive.onearth.org/article/cowboys-and-indians.

79 Black Hills Alliance, *Keystone to Survival*.

80 Ellison, interview.

81 Means, interview.

82 Lazarus, *Black Hills, White Justice*, 401.

83 Worster, *Under Western Skies*, 108.

84 Christopher McLeod and Malinda Maynor, *In the Light of Reverence*, Sacred Land Film Project documentary (2001); *Run of the Sacred Hoop*, documentary (2006).

85 Ray, "Bucking the Trends."

86 Lazarus, *Black Hills, White Justice*, 419–425; Worster, *Under Western Skies*, 114–116.

87 Cindy Reed, Cowboy and Indian Alliance (Hot Springs, S.D.), interview, June 24, 1999.

88 Charlotte Black Elk, Cowboy and Indian Alliance, Oglala Lakota (Pine Ridge, S.D.), interview, June 25, 1999.

89 Quoted in James Grass, "Battle Flares over Weapons Test Site," *Sioux Falls Argus Leader*, August 17, 1987.

90 Bob Secter, "Indians, Ranchers Oppose Black Hills Weapons Tests," *Los Angeles Times*, August 30, 1987.

91 Reed, interview.

92 Quoted in John Wooliscroft and Joan Morrison, "Ranchers, Indians Join to Oppose Honeywell Plans," *Rapid City Journal*, June 25, 1987.

93 Quoted in Kurt Chandler, "Clash over a Canyon: The Meaning of Sacred," *Minneapolis Star-Tribune*, August 9, 1987.

94 Quoted in Grass, "Battle Flares."

95 Black Elk, interview.

96 Black Hills Wild Horse Sanctuary (2017), www.wildmustangs.com/.

97 Secter, "Black Hills Weapons Tests."

98 Joanne Tall, Good Road Coalition, Oglala Lakota (Pine Ridge, S.D.), interview, June 25, 1999.

99 Ibid.

100 Thunder Hawk and her daughter Marcy Gilbert are the subjects of the documentary *Warrior Women* (2017), http://itvs.org/films/warrior-women.

101 Els Herten, "Kevin Costner Has a Change of Heart," KOLO News (Belgium), April 12, 2000, http://arvollookinghorse.homestead.com/articles_on_chief_arvol_apr2002.html.

102 Joe Kafka, "Rosebud Hog Operation under Fire by Members," Associated Press, June 22, 2000.

103 Jim Kent, "85% Resist Railroad Expansion," *News from Indian Country*, Late Spring 2000.

104 Charmaine White Face, "The DM&E Railroad's Impact on the Great Sioux Nation," *Lakota National Journal*, October 23, 2000.

105 Charmaine White Face, Cowboy and Indian Alliance II, Oglala Lakota (Manderson, S.D.), interview, June 8, 2001.

106 Dan Daly, "Tribes Join Opposition to Railroad," *Rapid City Journal*, April 9, 2002.

107 Doug Dreyer, "Lincoln DM&E Railroad Suspends Effort to Carry Powder River Basin Coal," *Lincoln Journal Star*, August 27, 2009.

108 Defenders of the Black Hills, "Campaigns," 2016, www.defendblackhills.org/.

109 Black Hills Clean Water Alliance (2017), www.sdcleanwateralliance.org/; Prairie Dust Films, *Crying Earth Rise Up*, documentary (2015), www.cryingearthriseup.com/.

110 Lilias Jones Jarding, Clean Water Alliance (Rapid City, S.D.), interview, June 30, 2014.

111 Ibid.

112 Ibid.

113 Clean Water Alliance, Owe Aku / Bring Back the Way, It's about the Water, and Dakota Rural Action, "NRC Ruling Gives Victory to Mine Opponents," press release, April 30, 2015.

114 Alyssa Terry, "World's Largest Motorcycle Sculpture Honors Veterans, Calls for Water Protection," NewsCenter1, August 8, 2015.

115 U.S. Commission on Civil Rights, *Native Americans in South Dakota: An Erosion of Confidence in the Justice System* (March 2000).

116 Quoted in Ray, "Bucking the Trends."

117 Ellison, interview.

118 Mircea Eliade, *The Sacred and the Profane: The Nature of Religion* (New York: Harcourt Brace Jovanovich, 1959), 22.

119 Yi-Fu Tuan, personal correspondence to the author, March 18, 2000.

120 David L. Carmichael, Jane Hubert, Brian Reeves, and Audhild Schanche, eds., *Sacred Sites, Sacred Places* (London: Routledge, 1997), 3.

121 Yi-Fu Tuan, *Topophilia: A Study of Environmental Perception, Attitudes, and Values*, 2nd ed. (New York: Columbia University Press, 1990).

122 Kristen A. Carpenter, "Old Ground and New Directions at Sacred Sites on the Western Landscape," *Denver University Law Review* 83 (2006): 981–1002.

123 Vine Deloria Jr., "Reflection and Revelation: Knowing Land, Places, and Ourselves," in *The Power of Place: Sacred Ground in Natural and Human Environments*, ed. James A. Swan (Bath, U.K.: Gateway Books, 1993), 29–34.

124 Joe Wolery, "The Sweetgrass Hills: Essay of Place" (St. Ignatius: Montana Heritage Project, 1999), www.montanaheritageproject.org/edheritage/HE_99sum/su99jw.htm.

125 Fixico, *Indian Resilience and Rebuilding*, 192–216.

126 Deloria, "Reflection and Revelation," 39–40.

127 Elazar Barkan and Karen Barkey, *Choreographies of Shared Sacred Sites: Religion, Politics, and Conflict* (New York: Columbia University Press, 2015).

128 Chad F. Emmett, "Sharing Sacred Space in the Holy Land," in *Cultural Encounters with*

the Environment, ed. Alexander Murphy and Douglas Johnson (Boulder, Colo.: Rowman and Littlefield, 2000).

129 Fikret Berkes, *Sacred Ecology* (New York: Routledge, 2012).

130 Glen Coulthard, "Place against Empire: Understanding Indigenous Anti-Colonialism," *Affinities: A Journal of Radical Theory, Culture, and Action* 4, no. 2 (2010): 79–83.

NOTES TO CHAPTER 5

1   Zoltán Grossman, "The Achilles Heel of the Fossil Fuels Monster," *Works in Progress*, December 10, 2012, http://olywip.org/the-achilles-heel-of-the-fossil-fuels-monster.

2   Winona LaDuke, *The Winona LaDuke Chronicles: Stories from the Front Lines in the Battle for Environmental Justice* (Ponsford, Minn.: Spotted Horse Press, 2016).

3   Resource Rebels: Environmental Justice Movements Building Hope, Fossil Fuel Connections, The Evergreen State College, Winter 2016, www.fossilfuelconnections.org/.

4   Naomi Klein, *This Changes Everything: Capitalism vs. the Climate* (New York: Simon and Schuster, 2014), 293–336.

5   Quoted in Marc Gunther, "Warren Buffett's Coal Problem," *Sierra*, May 2013.

6   Quoted in Northern Plains Resource Council, "Farmers, Ranchers Have Fought Coal Development for Forty Years," 2012, www.northernplains.org/issues/coal/.

7   Clint McRae quoted in Kim Murphy, "In Montana, Ranchers Line Up against Coal," *Los Angeles Times*, April 26, 2013.

8   Clint McRae, "Testimony to Seattle Scoping Hearing on Cherry Point Coal Export Terminal," December 13, 2012.

9   Quoted in Gunther, "Coal Problem."

10 Alexis Bonogofsky, "The Tongue River Railroad Tries Again: The Little Engine That Couldn't," *Wildlife Promise* (blog), National Wildlife Federation, November 8, 2012, http://blog.nwf.org/2012/11/the-tongue-river-railroad-tries-again-the-little-engine -that-couldnt-part-1.

11 Vanessa Braided Hair, "Why the Otter Creek Coal Mine Will Never Be Built," *Wildlife Promise* (blog), National Wildlife Federation, April 10, 2013, http://blog.nwf.org/2013/04 /why-the-otter-creek-coal-mine-will-never-be-built.

12 Adriann Killsnight, Northern Cheyenne, Ecoregional Ethnographic Assessment Project (Lame Deer, Mont.), interview, November 6, 2015.

13 Alexis Bonogofsky, National Wildlife Federation Tribal Lands Partnerships Project, interview, March 26, 2014.

14 Ibid.

15 Clint McRae, "Big Coal's Slavery of the Land and the Liver of Mother Earth," interview at Seattle coal export hearing, December 18, 2012, www.youtube.com/watch?v= g0v6_b2DLk4.

16 Killsnight, interview.

17 Quoted in John S. Adams, "Mont., Wash. Tribes Join Ranchers to Fight Coal Mine," *USA Today*, September 23, 2013.

18 William Yardley, "In Dispute over Coal Mine Project, Two Ways of Life Hang in the Balance," *Los Angeles Times*, July 21, 2015.

19 Quoted in Adams, "Tribes Join Ranchers."

20 Jeanie Alderson, "Birney, Montana, Rancher," Power Past Coal, 2012, www.powerpast coal.org/voices-of-concern/ranchers-and-farmers.

21 Joyce Whiting, "Oglala Lakota Tribe Calls on Tribes to Oppose Otter Creek Coal Mine,"

Wildlife Promise (blog), National Wildlife Federation, August 8, 2013, http://blog.nwf
.org/2013/08/oglala-lakota-tribe-calls-on-tribes-to-oppose-otter-creek-coal-mine.

22 Alexis Bonogofsky, "Protecting the Cultural and Historic Values of the Powder River
Basin," *Wildlife Promise* (blog), National Wildlife Federation, June 12, 2012, http://blog.
nwf.org/2012/06/protecting-the-cultural-and-historic-values-of-the-powder
-river-basin.

23 Bonogofsky, interview.

24 Ibid.

25 Quoted in John Adams, "Lummi Totem Pole Blessing at Otter Creek," GFTrib.com, September 23, 2013, www.youtube.com/watch?v=_2sXOxQQNeg.

26 Bonogofsky, interview.

27 Alexis Bonogofsky, "Fighting to Keep Coal in the Ground, Montana Activists Score a Global
Victory against Climate Change," Truthout, November 1, 2015, www.truth-out.org/.

28 Matt Volz, "Coal Railroad Plans on Hold Due to Mine Permitting Delays," Associated
Press, November 25, 2015.

29 Matthew Brown, "Arch Coal Suspends Plans for Major New Mine in Montana," Associated Press, March 10, 2016.

30 Krystal Two Bulls, Oglala Lakota, anti-coal organizer on the Northern Cheyenne Reservation (Missoula, Mont.), interview, November 6, 2015.

31 Ibid.

32 Toban Black, Stephen D'Arcy, Tony Weis, and Joshua Kahn Russell, eds., *A Line in the
Tar Sands: Struggles for Environmental Justice* (Oakland, Calif.: PM Press, 2014).

33 Paul Seamans, Dakota Rural Action (Draper, S.D.), interview, April 3, 2014.

34 Kristin Moe, "'Cowboys and Indians' Camp Together to Build Alliance against Keystone
XL," *Yes!*, November 22, 2013.

35 Quoted in Luiza Ch. Savage, "The Untold Story of Keystone: How One Nebraska Farmer
Tried to Kill the Pipeline," *Maclean's*, January 27, 2014.

36 Quoted in ibid.

37 Jane Kleeb, Bold Nebraska executive director (Hastings, Neb.), interview, March 20,
2014, http://boldnebraska.org.

38 Jorge Barrera, "Keystone XL 'Black Snake' Pipeline to Face 'Epic' Opposition from Native
American Alliance," *APTN National News*, January 31, 2014.

39 Mother Earth Accord to Oppose Keystone XL (September 2011), http://ienearth.org
/docs/mother-earth-accord.pdf.

40 Seamans, interview.

41 Sarah Lazare, "Indigenous Groups: 'No Keystone XL Pipeline Will Cross Our Lands,"
Common Dreams, February 5, 2014, www.commondreams.org/.

42 Quoted in Barrera, "Keystone XL."

43 Faith Spotted Eagle, Ihanktonwan Nakota/Dakota (Yankton, S.D.), interview, March 20,
2014.

44 Forward on Climate, "Emerging Cowboy and Indian Alliance Sees Adoption of International Treaty to Block the Keystone XL TransCanada Pipeline" (January 2013).

45 Spotted Eagle, interview.

46 Quoted in Dianna Wray, "Cowboys and Indians Protesting the Keystone Pipeline Together," *Houston Press*, March 26, 2014.

47 Kleeb, interview.

48 Chief Phil Lane Jr., talk at Stommish Sacred Summit, Lummi Nation, July 16, 2014.

49 Quoted in Heather Smith, "The Cowboys and Indians Pipeline Protest was a Throwback—in More Ways than One," Grist, April 2014, http://grist.org/.

50 Sabin Russell, "When a Pipeline Crosses a Trail of Tears," *York News-Times*, November 21, 2013.

51 Elizabeth M. Hoover, "Planting Ponca Corn in the Path of Keystone XL, Neligh NE," *From Garden Warriors to Good Seeds: Indigenizing the Local Food Movement* (blog), June 5, 2014, https://gardenwarriorsgoodseeds.com/.

52 Mike Konz, "Poncas, Nebraskans Hope to Rescue Rare Native Corn," *Kearney Hub*, April 11, 2012.

53 Moe, "'Cowboys and Indians' Camp Together."

54 Kleeb, interview.

55 Ken Winston, "Local View: Respect for 'Reject and Protect,'" *Lincoln Journal Star*, April 26, 2014.

56 Spotted Eagle, interview.

57 Seamans, interview.

58 Quoted in Savage, "Untold Story of Keystone."

59 Sam Markwell, "Keystone XL and the Affective Infrastructures of the Cowboy and Indian Alliance" (presentation to the Association of American Geographers, San Francisco, March 29, 2016).

60 Quoted in Kristin Moe, "When Cowboys and Indians Unite—Inside the Unlikely Alliance That Is Remaking the Climate Movement," Waging Nonviolence, May 2, 2014, http://wagingnonviolence.org/.

61 Kleeb, interview.

62 Quoted in Wray, "Cowboys and Indians."

63 Spotted Eagle, interview.

64 Ibid.

65 Ibid.

66 Ibid.

67 Quoted in Kristin Moe, "Brought Together by Keystone Pipeline Fight, 'Cowboys and Indians' Heal Old Wounds," *Yes!*, April 24, 2014.

68 Quoted in Moe, "When Cowboys and Indians Unite."

69 Quoted in Ben Adler, "The Inside Story of How the Keystone Fight Was Won," Grist, November 6, 2015, http://grist.org/.

70 Moe, "When Cowboys and Indians Unite."

71 Mary Annette Pember, "Cowboys and Indians Unite against Keystone XL," CNN, April 27, 2014, www.cnn.com/2014/04/27/opinion/pember-keystone-cowboys-indians.

72 Cowboy Indian Alliance, "Interview with Ben Gottschall," March 2014, http://rejectand protect.org/.

73 Quoted in Erin Flegg, "First Nations' Anti-Keystone XL Alliance Years in Making," *Vancouver Observer*, April 30, 2014.

74 Quoted in ibid.

75 Quoted in Moe, "When Cowboys and Indians Unite."

76 Natalie Hand, "Power for People or Pipeline?," *Lakota Country Times*, May 1, 2014.

77 Quoted in Rob Hotakainen, "Native Americans Vow a Last Stand to Block Keystone XL Pipeline," *McClatchy DC*, February 17, 2014.

78 Faith Spotted Eagle, talk at "Help Save Mother Earth from the Keystone XL Pipeline" gathering, Rapid City, S.D., February 14, 2014.

79 Mark Hefflinger, "Cowboy Indian Alliance Hosts Buffalo Roast to Mark Expiration of Keystone XL Permit in South Dakota," *Bold Nebraska*, June 24, 2014.

80 Seamans, interview.

81 Adler, "Inside Story."

82 Quoted in "Obama Rejects Keystone XL: 'Does Not Serve National Interest,'" *Indian Country Today*, November 6, 2015.

83 Indigenous Environmental Network, "Tribal, Grassroots, and Treaty Leaders Respond to President Obama Rejecting Keystone XL Pipeline," press release, November 6, 2015.

84 Edwin Dobb, "The New Oil Landscape," *National Geographic*, March 2013.

85 *Bakken Watch* (blog) (2013), http://bakkenwatch.blogspot.com/.

86 Pratap Chatterjee, "North Dakota Oil Boom Displaces Tribal Residents," CorpWatch, April 25, 2012, www.corpwatch.org/article.php?id=15713; Curt Brown, "While North Dakota Embraces the Oil Boom, Tribal Members Ask Environmental Questions," *Minneapolis Star Tribune*, November 29, 2013.

87 Antonia Juhasz, "From North Dakota to Paris with Love," *Newsweek*, November 25, 2015.

88 Indigenous Environmental Network, "Obama's Visit to Canada Must Address Dirty Oil from the Tar Sands in Northern Alberta," press release, February 19, 2009.

89 Valerie Taliman, "Dakota Access Pipeline Standoff: Mni Wiconi—Water Is Life," *Indian Country Today*, August 15, 2016.

90 Jenni Monet, "Climate Justice Meets Racism: This Moment at Standing Rock Was Decades in the Making," *Yes!*, September 16, 2016.

91 Standing Rock Sioux Tribe (2017), www.standwithstandingrock.net.

92 Quoted in Camp of the Sacred Stones, "Stop the Dakota Access Pipeline" (2016), http://sacredstonecamp.org/.

93 Quoted in Camp of the Sacred Stones, "Tribal Citizens Rise Up against Bakken Oil Pipeline," March 29, 2016, http://sacredstonecamp.org/.

94 Camp of the Sacred Stones, "Coalition Support of Tribal Lawsuits against US Army Corps Permits for the Dakota Access Pipeline," August 5, 2016, http://sacredstonecamp.org/.

95 Saul Elbein, "The Youth Group That Launched a Movement at Standing Rock," *New York Times*, January 31, 2017.

96 Amy Dalrymple, "Tribe Submits Evidence of Cultural Sites in Dakota Access Path," Oil Patch Dispatch, September 2, 2016, http://oilpatchdispatch.areavoices.com/.

97 Valerie Taliman, "Judge Temporarily Halts DAPL Construction on Select Land but Not on Desecrated Area," *Indian Country Today*, September 6, 2016.

98 Camp of the Sacred Stones, "Protection of Sacred Sites Leads to Clash with Dakota Access Private Security," September 4, 2016, http://sacredstonecamp.org/.

99 Lauren Donovan, "Camp Organizers Look at Winter Parameters," *Bismarck Tribune*, October 1, 2016; Wasté Win Young, "Cannonball Ranch Sale Resulted from DAPL Bullying," *Censored News* (blog), September 26, 2016.

100 Camp of the Sacred Stones, "Judge Issues Inadequate Emergency Injunction, but Direct Action Stops Construction," September 6, 2016, http://sacredstonecamp.org/.

101 Zoltán Grossman, "Report from Standing Rock," photo albums, September 2016, http://academic.evergreen.edu/g/grossmaz/standingrock.html. Lynda V. Mapes, "United in Fossil-Fuel Fight, NW Tribes Inspire N.D. Pipeline Foes," *Seattle Times*, October 18, 2016.

102 Ron Meador, "Why the Dakota Access Pipeline Fight May Be a Turning Point in U.S. Environmental Politics," MinnPost, September 16, 2016, www.minnpost.com/.

103 Quoted in Camp of the Sacred Stones, "Stop the Dakota Access Pipeline."

104 Quoted in Jason Coppola, "Lakota Lead Native Americans, Ranchers, and Farmers in Fight against Dakota Access Pipeline," Truthout, August 13, 2016, www.truth-out .org/.

105 Joye Braun, Camp of the Sacred Stones, Indigenous Environmental Network, Cheyenne River tribal member, interview, near Cannon Ball, N.D., September 6, 2016.

106 Sacred Stone, "North Dakota Landowner Sees Pipeline Destroy Topsoil," September 8, 2016, www.youtube.com/watch?v=bXDZNnXHyEU.

107 Braun, interview.

108 Ibid.

109 Levi Lass, "Dakota Access Lied to Them, Irate Landowners Say," *Courthouse News*, January 11, 2017.

110 Quoted in Camp of the Sacred Stones, "Tribal Gathering against Dakota Access Faces Aggressive State Repression and Media Manipulation," August 23, 2016, http://sacred stonecamp.org/.

111 Sara Berlinger, "Dakota Access Pipeline Protests Affecting Morton County Landowners," *KFYR TV News*, September 7, 2017.

112 Jack Healy, "Neighbors Say North Dakota Pipeline Protests Disrupt Lives and Livelihoods," *New York Times*, September 13, 2016.

113 Brenda Norrell, "National Guard at Highway Checkpoint on Highway 1806," *Censored News* (blog), September 8, 2016, http://bsnorrell.blogspot.com/; Winona LaDuke, Colonel Ann Wright (U.S. Army Ret.), and Zoltán Grossman, "Public Servants or Corporate Security?: An Open Letter to Law Enforcement and National Guard in North Dakota," Common Dreams, November 2, 2016.

114 Relations had begun to improve in 2012 after state voters rejected (by 2–1) the University of North Dakota's racist "Fighting Sioux" team name and mascot, after a long and divisive conflict. Nick Smith, "North Dakotans Vote to Let UND Retire Fighting Sioux Nickname," *Bismarck Tribune*, June 12, 2012. Stand with Standing Rock, "Standing Rock Denounces Army Easement Announcement, Vows Court Challenge," February 7, 2017, standwithstandingrock.net; Earthjustice, "The Standing Rock Sioux Tribe's Litigation on the Dakota Access Pipeline," February 8, 2017, earthjustice.org; Oliver Milman, "Standing Rock Sioux Tribe Says Trump Is Breaking Law with Dakota Access Order," *The Guardian*, January 26, 2017.

115 Winona LaDuke, "A Pipeline Runs through It," Honor the Earth, June 2, 2014, www .honorearth.org/; LaDuke, "What Happened Enbridge?," *News from Indian Country*, August 2016.

116 Greg Muttitt and Lorne Stockman, *Tracking Emissions: The Climate Impact of the Proposed Crude-by-Rail Terminals in the Pacific Northwest* (Seattle: Sightline Institute and Oil Change International, 2015).

117 Eric de Place, "The Thin Green Line: The Northwest Faces off against Titanic Coal and Oil Export Schemes," *Sightline Daily*, March 20, 2014.

118 Earthjustice, "Kinder Morgan Pipeline Threatens Ecology and Economy of Salish Tribes," February 13, 2014, http://earthjustice.org/.

119 David Ball, "Cross-Border Indigenous Treaty Takes on Kinder Morgan Pipeline, *Tyee*, September 23, 2014; Jeremy Shepherd, "Coastal First Nations Sign Treaty to Stop Kinder Morgan Pipeline," *Business Vancouver*, September 24, 2014.

120 Nawtsamaat Alliance (2017), www.protectthesacred.org/.

121 Carlo Voli, 350.org, and Rising Tide, speech to "Protect the Sacredness of the Salish Sea" rally, Seattle, August 11, 2014.

122 Phil Lane Jr., Nawtsamaat Alliance co-founder, Ihanktonwan Nakota/Dakota chief (White Rock, B.C.), interview, September 7, 2014.

123 LaDuke, *Chronicles*, 76–81; The Rural People of Highway 12—Fighting Goliath (2013), http://fightinggoliath.org/.

124 Klein, *This Changes Everything*, 319; All Against the Haul (2014), www.facebook.com /AllAgainstTheHaul.

125 Nick Engelfried, "Indian People's Action Takes Center Stage in Protests against Tar Sands Partner," Waging Nonviolence, February 15, 2014, http://wagingnonviolence .org/.

126 Sydney Brownstone, "Why Descendants of Chief Leschi Led the Protest against Shell on Saturday," *Stranger*, May 18, 2015; Frank Hopper, "Lummi Youth Learn the Bigger Picture: Canoes Join Kayactivists Protesting Arctic Drilling," *Indian Country Today*, May 22, 2015.

127 Bruce Bulls, "Shellacked: After Almost a Decade and $7 Billion, Shell Withdraws from the Arctic," *WorkBoat*, November 2015.

128 Western Organizations of Resource Councils, *Heavy Traffic Ahead: Rail Impacts of Powder River Basin Coal to Asia by Way of Pacific Northwest Terminals* (July 2012).

129 Association of Washington Tribes and Coast Salish Gathering, *Protecting Treaty Rights, Sacred Places, and Life Ways* (February 2013).

130 Northwest Tribal Coal Summit, "Northwest Tribes Say No Shortcuts for Coal Export Proposals," CRITFC, September 27, 2012, www.critfc.org/blog/press/northwest-tribes -say-no-short-cuts-for-coal-export-proposals.

131 Mara Kardas-Nelson, "Anti-Coal Campaigners Continue to Win in the Northwest," Waging Nonviolence, September 16, 2014, http://wagingnonviolence.org/.

132 Power Past Coal (2017), www.powerpastcoal.org/.

133 Mayor's Media Availability, "Coalition to Oppose Coal Trains," Seattle Channel, April 22, 2013, www.seattlechannel.org/videos/video.asp?ID=1061340&file=1.

134 Safe Energy Leadership Alliance (SELA), King County Executive (2016), www.king county.gov/elected/executive/constantine/initiatives/safe-energy.aspx; Andy Hobbs, "Inslee Says State Will Act on Oil Trains," *Olympian*, November 21, 2014.

135 Affiliated Tribes of Northwest Indians, "Opposing the Proposals for the Transportation and Export of Fossil Fuels in the Pacific Northwest," Resolution 13-47, May 16, 2013.

136 Floyd McKay, "Coal Port Faces Huge Obstacle in Lummi Opposition," Crosscut, August 19, 2013, http://crosscut.com/.

137 Voices of Coal, "Jay Julius: Member of Lummi Nation Tribal Council and Fisherman," EarthFix, 2013, http://vimeo.com/60530689.

138 Quoted in Zachariah Bryan, "Mayor Announces Regional Coalition, Leadership Alliance against Coal," *Ballard News Tribune*, April 22, 2013.

139 Charles Tanner Jr., "'Take These Tribes Down': The Anti-Indian Movement Comes to Washington State," Institute for Research and Education on Human Rights, April 28, 2013, www.irehr.org/2013/04/26/take-these-tribes-down.

140 Lummi Nation Sovereignty and Treaty Protection Office (2014), www.lummi-nsn.org /website/Site/images/Reso%202014-154.pdf.

141 Jewell James, *Protecting Treaty Rights, Sacred Places, and Lifeways: Coal vs. Communities, Totem Pole Journey*, booklet (August 2014), www.totempolejourney.com/.

142 Jewell James, Lummi Nation Sovereignty and Treaty Protection Office (Lummi Nation, Wash.), interview, June 17, 2014.

143 Amber Cortes, "Treaty Rights and Totem Poles: How One Tribe Is Carving out Resistance to Coal," Grist, August 15, 2014, http://grist.org/.

144 James, interview.

145 Dana Wilson, Lummi tribal fisherman (Lummi Nation, Wash.), interview, June 17, 2014.

146 Sandra Palm, commercial fisher (Bellingham, Wash.), interview, June 17, 2014.

147 Eleanor Kinley, Whatcom Commercial Fishermen's Association (Lummi Nation, Wash.), interview, June 17, 2014.

148 Kirk Johnson, "Tribes Add Potent Voice against Plan for Northwest Coal Terminals," *New York Times*, October 12, 2012; Brandi N. Montreuil, "Protest Held at Xwe'chi'eXen (Cherry Point)," *Tulalip News*, October 15, 2012.

149 John Stark, "New Poll Shows Majority Oppose Coal Shipments," *Bellingham Herald*, September 16, 2013.

150 Eric Wilkinson, "Tribe Plays Trump Card That Could Kill Coal Terminal," *King 5 News*, August 1, 2013.

151 Quoted in John Stark, "Coal Booster Says Cherry Point Terminal Is 'Dead,' But Foes Aren't Celebrating," *Bellingham Herald*, February 17, 2013.

152 Amanda Carlucci, "Activists Defeating Coal Export Terminals in the Pacific Northwest," *Examiner*, January 10, 2014.

153 Associated Press, "Tribes Stand against Coal Export Terminal," *Seattle Times*, May 15, 2015.

154 Brenda Norrell, "Indigenous Canoe Flotilla in Paris," *Censored News* (blog), December 7, 2015, http://bsnorrell.blogspot.com/.

155 Quoted in Lynda V. Mapes, "Northwest Tribes Unite against Giant Coal, Oil Projects," *Seattle Times*, January 16, 2016.

156 Samantha Wohlfeil, "Army Corps Rejects Permit for Coal Terminal at Cherry Point," *Bellingham Herald*, May 8, 2016.

157 Samantha Wohlfeil, "Whatcom County Puts New Unrefined Fossil Fuel Exports on Hold," *Bellingham Herald*, August 10, 2016.

158 Clark Williams-Derry, "Arch Coal Backs out of Longview Coal Terminal," Sightline Institute, May 27, 2016, http://sightline.org/; Marissa Luck and Andre Stepankowsky, "Study: Coal Terminal Won't Damage Tribal Fishing," *Daily News* (Longview, Wash.), October 2, 2016; Gene Johnson, "Washington State Denies Sublease for Coal Export Terminal," *News Tribune*, January 3, 2017.

159 Quoted in Lynda V. Mapes, "Tribes Prevail, Kill Proposed Coal Terminal at Cherry Point," *Seattle Times*, May 9, 2016.

160 Tim Ballew II, "Cherry Point Victory Shows Treaty Rights Protect Us All," *Bellingham Herald*, May 14, 2016.

161 Curtis Tate, "More Oil Spilled from Trains in 2013 than in Previous Four Decades, Federal Data Show," *McClatchy DC*, January 20, 2014.

162 Matt Egan, "After Forty-Year Ban, U.S. Starts Exporting Crude Oil," CNN Money, January 29, 2016, http://money.cnn.com/.

163 Matt Krogh, *Off the Rails: The Fossil Fuel Takeover of the Pacific Northwest* (Bellingham, Wash.: ForestEthics, 2014).

164 Eric de Place, *The Northwest's Pipeline on Rails* (Seattle: Sightline Institute, 2013); De Place, *Northwest Fossil Fuel Export* (Seattle: Sightline Institute, 2014).

165 Dameon Pesanti, "Diverse Groups Join Forces against Oil Terminal," *Columbian*, May 29,

2016; Columbia Riverkeeper, "Oil-by-Rail," 2016, http://columbiariverkeeper.org/our -work/oil-by-rail.

166 Ralph Schwartz, "Northwest Tribes Band Together to Stop Oil-by-Rail," *Yes!*, July 12, 2016.

167 Patrick Mulvihill, "Tribes Unite in Opposition to Oil Trains," *Dalles Chronicle*, June 10, 2016; Terri Hansen, "Columbia River Tribes Speak out as Flaming Bakken Train Leaks Oil," *Indian Country Today*, June 6, 2016.

168 George Walter, "Oil Trains Pose Real Risk for Our Communities," op-ed, *Olympian*, July 13, 2015.

169 Citizens for a Clean Harbor (2017), http://cleanharbor.org/; *Railing Against Crude* (blog), (2017), http://cleanharbor.blogspot.com/.

170 Junior Goodell, "Grays Harbor Oil Terminal Would Threaten Quinault Indian Identity," *Seattle Times*, June 1, 2015.

171 Pauline K. Capoeman, ed., *Land of the Quinault*, 2nd ed. (Taholah, Wash.: Quinault Indian Nation, 1991).

172 Arthur (R. D.) Grunbaum, personal communication, February 27, 2015.

173 David Haviland, "Quinault and Earthjustice Hope to Shine Light on Crude by Rail," *KBKW Local News*, April 23, 2013; Haviland, "Quinault Indian Nation Urges Opposition to Oil Transport and Shipment through Grays Harbor," *KBKW Local News*, April 23, 2014.

174 Brad Shannon, "State Oil Trains Run into Heavy Opposition," *Olympian*, May 4, 2014.

175 Billy Frank Jr., "Keep Big Oil out of Grays Harbor," *Being Frank* (blog), Northwest Indian Fisheries Commission, May 5, 2014, http://nwtreatytribes.org/keep-big-oil-grays-harbor.

176 Quoted in Sarah Tory, "Northwest Tribes Are a Growing Obstacle to Energy Development," *High Country News*, May 27, 2015.

177 Tyson Johnston, vice president of Quinault Indian Nation (Taholah, Wash.), interview, October 8, 2015.

178 Ashley Ahearn, "Washington Tribe Confronts Climate Change, Sea Level Rise," KUOW, November 9, 2015, www.opb.org/news/article/a-washington-tribe-confronts-climate -change-sea-level-rise.

179 Larry Thevik, vice president of Washington Dungeness Crab Fishermen's Association (Ocean Shores, Wash.), interview, October 8, 2015.

180 Joe Schumacker, Marine Resources scientist, Quinault Indian Nation (Taholah, Wash.), interview, October 8, 2015.

181 Fawn Sharp, president of Quinault Indian Nation and Affiliated Tribe of Northwest Indians (Taholah, Wash.), interview, October 29, 2015.

182 Ibid.

183 Ibid.

184 Fawn Sharp and Larry Thevik, "Risks Far Outweigh Any Benefit from Proposed Oil Terminals in Grays Harbor," *Daily World*, March 19, 2016.

185 Quinault Indian Nation, "Let's Keep Grays Harbor Safe from Crude Oil," May 2016, www .quinaultindiannation.com/crudeoil.htm.

186 Quinault Indian Nation, "QIN Environmental Defense," July 2016, www.facebook.com /QINDefense.

187 Resource Rebels: Environmental Justice Movements Building Hope, *Economic Options in Grays Harbor* (Olympia, Wash.: The Evergreen State College, 2016), http://academic .evergreen.edu/g/grossmaz/GraysHarborReport.pdf.

188 Sydney Brownstone, "How One Tribe Could Slow the Rate of 'Bomb Trains' through Seattle," *Stranger*, April 15, 2015; Hal Bernton, "Swinomish Tribe Sues to Block Bakken Oil Trains," *Seattle Times*, April 7, 2015.

189 Break Free Pacific Northwest (2016), http://breakfreepnw.org/.

190 *Seattle Times* staff, "Shell Halts Proposed Oil-by-Rail Project near Anacortes," *Seattle Times*, October 6, 2016.

191 Also in 2015–16, the Puyallup Tribe joined the opposition to a proposed liquefied natural gas plant in Tacoma. Adam Lynn. "Puyallup Tribe Asks Court to Halt Permits for Tacoma Gas Plant," *Tacoma News Tribune*, December 20, 2015. Puyallup has also opposed a new methanol-conversion plant and pipeline proposed for the Tacoma tidal flats. Steve Dunkelberger, "Tribe, Federal Way Oppose Methanol Plans," *Tacoma Weekly*, February 18, 2016.

192 Bill McKibben, "Fossil Fuel Resistance," *Rolling Stone*, April 11, 2013.

193 Kyle Powys Whyte, "Why the Native American Pipeline Resistance in North Dakota Is about Climate Justice," The Conversation, September 16, 2016, http://theconversation.com/why-the-native-american-pipeline-resistance-in-north-dakota-is-about-climate-justice-64714.

194 Debra McNutt, "Tribal and Local Government Collaboration for Secure Water Sources in the Salish Sea Basin" (capstone project, Master of Public Administration—Tribal Governance program, The Evergreen State College, 2012).

195 Zoltán Grossman, "No Longer the Miner's Canary: Indigenous Nations' Responses to Climate Change," *Terrain*, October 2, 2012, http://terrain.org/2012/nonfiction/no-longer-the-miners-canary.

196 Swinomish Climate Change Initiative, *Impact Assessment Technical Report* (2009); Swinomish Climate Change Initiative, *Climate Adaptation Action Plan* (2010), www.swinomish-nsn.gov/climate_change/project/reports.html.

197 Zoltán Grossman and Alan Parker, eds., *Asserting Native Resilience: Pacific Rim Indigenous Nations Face the Climate Crisis* (Corvallis: Oregon State University Press, 2012), http://osupress.oregonstate.edu/book/asserting-native-resilience.

198 Matt Batcheldor, "Olympia Will Get Water from Wells, Not Springs," *Olympian*, September 16, 2012; Andy Hobbs, "McAllister Wellfield Water Marks New Chapter for Olympia and Nisqually Tribe," *Olympian*, September 5, 2014; Andy Hobbs, "Olympia's McAllister Springs Site to Return to Nisqually Tribe," *Olympian*, January 11, 2017.

199 Lewis Kamb, "A Methane to their Madness: Tribes and Farmers Come Together—over Cow Manure," *Seattle Post-Intelligencer*, April 22, 2003.

200 Nahal Ghoghaie, "Native/Non-Native Watershed Management in an Era of Climate Change: Freshwater Storage in the Snohomish Basin" (master's thesis, Master of Environmental Studies program, The Evergreen State College, 2011).

201 Climate Change and Pacific Rim Indigenous Nations Project, "Indigenous Climate Justice Symposium," The Evergreen State College, Olympia, Wash., November 5–6, 2015, http://academic.evergreen.edu/g/grossmaz/climate.html.

202 Sharp, interview.

203 Naomi Klein, talk on *This Changes Everything: Capitalism vs. The Climate*, Town Hall, Seattle, September 28, 2014, uploaded by *Talking Stick TV*, www.youtube.com/watch?v=4b2B-ys3N10.

NOTES TO CHAPTER 6

1 Donald L. Fixico, *The Invasion of Indian Country in the Twentieth Century: American Capitalism and Tribal Natural Resources*, 2nd ed. (Boulder, Colo.: University Press of Colorado, 2011), 103–122.

2 Rick Whaley and Walter Bresette, *Walleye Warriors: The Chippewa Treaty Rights Story*,

3rd ed. (Ossipee, N.H.: Beech River Books, 2015); Larry Nesper and Michael Johnson, *The Walleye War: The Struggle for Ojibwe Spearfishing and Treaty Rights* (Lincoln: University of Nebraska Press, 2002).

3 Barbara Perry, *Silent Victims: Hate Crimes against Native Americans* (Tucson: University of Arizona Press, 2008).

4 Steven E. Silvern, "Nature, Territory, and Identity in the Wisconsin Treaty Rights Controversy," *Ecumene* 2, no. 3 (1995): 269–273.

5 Sue Erickson, ed., *Ojibwe Treaty Rights: Understanding and Impact* (Odanah, Wis.: Great Lakes Indian Fish and Wildlife Commission, 2004).

6 David R. Wrone, "Economic Impact of the 1837 and 1842 Chippewa Treaties," *American Indian Quarterly* 17, no. 3 (1993): 332.

7 Ronald N. Satz, "Chippewa Treaty Rights: The Reserved Rights of Wisconsin's Chippewa Indians in Historical Perspective," *Transactions of the Wisconsin Academy of Sciences, Arts and Letters* 79, no. 1 (1991): 125.

8 James A. Clifton, "Wisconsin Death March: Explaining the Extremes in Old Northwest Indian Removal," *Transactions of the Wisconsin Academy of Sciences, Arts and Letters* 75 (1987): 1–39.

9 Erik M. Redix, *The Murder of Joe White: Ojibwe Leadership and Colonialism in Wisconsin* (East Lansing: Michigan State University Press, 2014).

10 Chantal Norrgard, *Seasons of Change: Labor, Treaty Rights, and Ojibwe Nationhood* (Chapel Hill: University of North Carolina Press, 2014).

11 Satz, "Chippewa Treaty Rights," 85–86.

12 U.S. Court of Appeals, *Lac Courte Oreilles Band of Lake Superior Chippewa Indians v. Voigt*, 700 F.2d 341, 345 (7th Cir. 1983).

13 Satz, "Chippewa Treaty Rights," 94–101.

14 Jeff Mayers, "Early Spearing End Urged," *Wisconsin State Journal*, April 3, 1989.

15 Zoltán Grossman, "Wisconsin Treaty Conflict: No End in Sight," *Z Magazine*, July–August 1990, http://academic.evergreen.edu/g/grossmaz/WisTreatyConflict.pdf.

16 Whaley and Bresette, *Walleye Warriors*, 46–47.

17 Bruce E. Johansen, "The New Terminators: A Guide to the Anti-Treaty Movement," in *Enduring Legacies*, ed. Bruce E. Johansen (Santa Barbara, Calif.: Praeger, 2004), 305–332.

18 Zoltán Grossman, "Anti-Indian Movement," in *Encyclopedia of Race and Racism*, ed. John Hartwell Moore (New York: Macmillan Reference USA, 2008), 1:102–105; Grossman, "Indian Treaty Rights," in *When Hate Groups Come to Town: A Handbook of Effective Community Responses* (Atlanta: Center for Democratic Renewal, 1992), http://treaty.indigenousnative.org/anti-indian.html.

19 Stop Treaty Abuse, "Wisconsin's Treaty Problems: What Are the Issues?," pamphlet (1989), 5–6.

20 Kevin Hermening, "We Are Not Racists," *PARR Issue*, June 1987.

21 Quoted in William R. Wineke, "Tutu Points to Indians' Plight," *Wisconsin State Journal*, May 5, 1988.

22 The Wisconsin ecologist Aldo Leopold had inspired a "red shirts" movement of sportsmen to back conservation policies protecting fish and game. Thomas R. Huffman, *Protectors of the Land and Water: Environmentalism in Wisconsin, 1961–1968* (Chapel Hill: University of North Carolina Press, 1994).

23 Paige Raibmon, *Authentic Indians: Episodes of Encounter from the Late-Nineteenth-Century Northwest Coast* (Durham, N.C.: Duke University Press, 2005).

24 Stop Treaty Abuse, "Wisconsin's Treaty Problems," 2.

25 Wrone, "Economic Impact," 335–336.

26 Joseph Damrell, "Some Observations and Interpretations of the Ojibwa Treaty Rights Struggle," *Humanity and Society* 13, no. 4 (1989): 388–389.

27 Ron Seely, "Indians Besieged by Hatred, Incivility," *Wisconsin State Journal*, May 4, 1989.

28 Quincey Dadisman, "Indians to Get DNR Guards on Lakes," *Milwaukee Sentinel*, April 21, 1989.

29 Quoted in Perry, *Silent Victims*, 207.

30 Whaley and Bresette, *Walleye Warriors*, 102–128.

31 James B. Nelson, "Pro-Treaty Group Keeps Watch for Peace," *Milwaukee Sentinel*, April 29, 1988.

32 Ron Seely, "Indian Rallies Lament Racism," *Wisconsin State Journal*, May 7, 1989.

33 Monica Lauer, "Treaty Rights Activist Recounts Racist Violence," *Feminist Voices*, June 1989.

34 Maryann Mrowca, "Racist Jeers Greet Chippewa," *Capital Times*, April 26, 1989.

35 Terry Koper and James B. Nelson, "Calls to Police Threaten Two Indian Leaders' Lives," *Milwaukee Sentinel*, April 29, 1989.

36 George Hesselberg, "Crist Grabs Slice of Treaty Limelight," *Wisconsin State Journal*, January 14, 1990.

37 Matthew Dietrich, "Spearfish Protesters Come in Two Varieties," *Capital Times*, May 8, 1989.

38 Quoted in Maurice Wozniak, "Calm Presence around Storm," *Milwaukee Journal*, April 30, 1989.

39 Quoted in Barbara Isaacs, "Conference Seeks Ways to Stem Racism," *Milwaukee Journal*, June 2, 1988.

40 Larry Nesper and James H. Schlender, "The Politics of Cultural Revitalization and Intertribal Resource Management," in *Native Americans and the Environment: Perspectives on the Ecological Indian*, ed. Michael E. Harkin and David Rich Lewis (Lincoln: University of Nebraska Press, 2007), 277–303.

41 Ron Seely, "Resorts on Ice Up North," *Wisconsin State Journal*, April 23, 1989.

42 Michelle Aguilar-Wells and Barbara Leigh Smith, "Confronting Racism: Treaty Beer Comes to Washington State," Enduring Legacies: Native Case Studies, The Evergreen State College, July 13, 2011, http://nativecases.evergreen.edu/.

43 Patty Loew, *Seventh Generation Earth Ethics: Native Voices of Wisconsin* (Madison: Wisconsin Historical Society Press, 2014), 1–16.

44 David M. Freedman, "The New People: Chippewa Ethos Inspires Non-Indian Supporters," *Isthmus*, July 21, 1989.

45 Quoted in Zoltán Grossman, "Treaty Support Grows in the Face of Right-Wing Violence," *Guardian* (New York), May 31, 1989, http://academic.evergreen.edu/g/grossmaz/Wis TreatyConflict.pdf.

46 Midwest Treaty Network, "Archives" (2006), http://treaty.indigenousnative.org/content .html.

47 Midwest Treaty Network, *1990 Witness Report*.

48 Unidentified racist behind me, Sand Lake (Phelps, Wis.), anonymous comment, April 20, 1991.

49 Zoltán Grossman, "World Is Watching: International Support Growing for Wisconsin Chippewa," *News from Indian Country*, September 1990, http://academic.evergreen .edu/g/grossmaz/WisTreatyConflict.pdf.

50 Will Fantle, "We'll Be There," *Isthmus*, March 30, 1990.
51 U.S. Commission on Civil Rights, *Discrimination against Chippewa Indians in Northern Wisconsin*, summary report of Wisconsin Advisory Committee (December 1989).
52 "Spearing Dispute More than Just Fish," *Milwaukee Sentinel*, editorial, May 8, 1989.
53 Rennard Strickland, Stephen J. Herzberg, and Steven R. Owens, "Keeping Our Word: Indian Treaty Rights and Public Responsibilities," Senate Committee on Indian Affairs (1990).
54 Wisconsin Department of Natural Resources, *Fish and Wildlife Comprehensive Plan*, pt. 1, *Management Strategies, 1979–1985* (1979).
55 Strickland, Herzberg, and Owens, "Keeping Our Word," 18–25.
56 U.S. District Court of Western District Wisconsin, *Lac Courte Oreilles Band of Lake Superior Chippewa Indian et al. v. State of Wisconsin*, 707 F. Supp. 1034 (1989).
57 Satz, "Chippewa Treaty Rights," 125–126; Scott Kerr, "Three-Ring Battle," *Shepherd Express*, November 16, 1989.
58 Walter Bresette and James Yellowbank, "Regional Resources Co-management: Saving the Land for the Next Seven Generations," *Indian Treaty Rights Newsletter*, Winter 1991; Scott Kerr, "The New Indian Wars: The Trail of Broken Treaties Grows Longer," *Progressive*, April 1990.
59 Whaley and Bresette, *Walleye Warriors*, 210–213.
60 Jeff Mayers and Doug Mell, "What Next on Treaty Rights?," *Wisconsin State Journal*, October 27, 1989.
61 Carroll Besadny, "Cooperation in Natural Resource Management with Wisconsin Indian Tribes vs. Co-management of the Natural Resources by the Tribes," memorandum to Wisconsin legislators, November 6, 1989.
62 Satz, "Chippewa Treaty Rights," 119–120.
63 Nesper and Johnson, *Walleye War*, 111, 185–197.
64 Scott Kerr, "Thompson Is Criticized for Treaty Statements," *Milwaukee Journal*, December 20, 1989.
65 Associated Press, "Tribe Rejects Sale of Fishing Rights," *New York Times*, October 27, 1989.
66 Tom Maulson, Lac du Flambeau Ojibwe chair (Lac du Flambeau, Wis.), interview, July 12, 1997.
67 Anita Koser-Thoms and Dorothy Thoms, Wa-Swa-Gon Treaty Association (Lac du Flambeau, Wis.), interview, July 12, 1997.
68 Matthew Dietrich, "Treaty Rights Conflict Stirs Renewed Interest in Indian Traditions," *Capital Times*, May 8, 1989; Sandra Sunrising Osawa, *Lighting the Seventh Fire*, documentary (Upstream Video Productions, 1995).
69 Bill Gardner, "Cooperation Keeps Spearfishing Peaceful," *Wisconsin State Journal*, May 6, 1989.
70 Fantle, "We'll Be There."
71 Maryann Mrowca, "Rights Controversy Has Hurt Chippewa Station," *Milwaukee Sentinel*, November 25, 1988.
72 Gaiashkibos, "Northwoods Leader Speaks out for Land," interview with Zoltán Grossman, *Insurgent*, September–October 1991.
73 Gaiashkibos, Lac Courte Oreilles Ojibwe chair (Hayward, Wis.), interview, July 28, 1998.
74 Midwest Treaty Network, *1990 Witness Report*.
75 St. Norbert College Survey Center, "Wisconsin Survey," report (Spring 1990).
76 "What the Treaty Gives to the Indians," graphic, *Milwaukee Journal*, April 8, 1990.

77 U.S. District Court of Western District Wisconsin, *Lac du Flambeau Band and Wa-Swa-Gon Treaty Association v. Stop Treaty Abuse Wisconsin et al.* (March 15, 1991).

78 Midwest Treaty Network, *1991 Witness Report: Chippewa Spearfishing Season* (1991), 7–11.

79 The Gulf War had also played a role in heating the 1991 boat landing confrontations. National Guard lights that had been used to illuminate boat landings had been withdrawn to Saudi Arabia for base security. Dean Crist regularly compared Tom Maulson to Saddam Hussein, for blocking American access to "our" natural resources.

80 Bill Braden, "Tried to Protest Treaty Rights, but Couldn't," *Lakeland Times*, May 7, 1991.

81 Joel Dresang, "Treaty Foes Claim Influx from Milwaukee Area," *Milwaukee Journal*, September 21, 1989.

82 Whaley and Bresette, *Walleye Warriors*, 242–243.

83 U.S. Department of the Interior, *Casting Light upon the Waters: A Joint Fishery Assessment of the Wisconsin Ceded Territory* (Minneapolis: Bureau of Indian Affairs, 1991).

84 Ron Seely, "Anti-Spearing Fires Burning Out," *Wisconsin State Journal*, May 5, 1991.

85 Robert Imrie, "Spearfishing Requests Show Decline," *Wisconsin State Journal*, May 18, 1992.

86 Michael Ahlborn, "Disgusted with Locals Who Didn't Show Up," letter, *Lakeland Times*, May 1, 1992.

87 Lawrence D. Bobo and Mia Tuan, *Prejudice in Politics: Group Position, Public Opinion, and the Wisconsin Treaty Rights Dispute* (Cambridge, Mass.: Harvard University Press, 2006), 198.

88 Quoted in Marv Balousek, "Indians, Environmentalists Forge Alliance," *Wisconsin State Journal*, August 28, 1988.

89 Ron Seely, "Toxic Fish Taint Spearers," *Wisconsin State Journal*, May 17, 1992.

90 Quoted in Joe Beck, "Indian Blames Firms, Politicians," *Wisconsin State Journal*, November 7, 1989.

91 Robert Schmitz, "Indians Helped Protect the Wolf River," *Milwaukee Sentinel*, editorial, June 21, 1989.

92 Gaiashkibos, interview (1991).

93 Maryann Mrowca, "Racist Jeers Greet Chippewa," *Capital Times*, April 26, 1989.

94 William Janz, "Image of Hate Soils Memories," *Milwaukee Sentinel*, May 9, 1989.

95 Ibid.

96 Fredrik Barth, *Ethnic Groups and Boundaries: The Social Organization of Culture Difference* (Boston: Little, Brown, 1969).

97 These "in/out-of-place rules" regulate our daily lives in ways we barely notice, until the boundaries are violated, such as by homeless people. Robert David Sack, *Homo Geographicus* (Baltimore: Johns Hopkins University Press, 1987), 90–91.

98 George Lipsitz, *How Racism Takes Place* (Philadelphia: Temple University Press, 2011).

99 Peter Jackson, ed., *Race and Racism: Essays in Social Geography* (London: Allen and Unwin, 1987), 14.

100 David Sibley, *Geographies of Exclusion: Society and Difference in the West* (London: Routledge, 1995); David Storey, *Territories: The Claiming of Space* (London: Routledge, 2012), 8, 193–196, 210–211.

101 Tim Cresswell, *In Place / Out of Place: Geography, Ideology, and Transgression* (Minneapolis: University of Minnesota Press, 1996), 153.

102 Sarah Jaquette Ray, *The Ecological Other: Environmental Exclusion in American Culture* (Tucson: University of Arizona Press, 2013).

103 Peter Stallybrass and Allon White, *The Politics and Poetics of Transgression* (Ithaca, N.Y.: Cornell University Press, 1986).

104 Sherene Razack, *Race, Space, and the Law: Unmapping a White Settler Society* (Toronto: Between the Lines, 2002).

105 Zoltán Grossman, "Of Kosovars, Apaches, and 'Ethnic Cleansing,'" *Synthesis/Regeneration* 40 (1999), www.greens.org/s-r/20/20-14.html; Gary Clayton Anderson, *Ethnic Cleansing and the Indian: The Crime That Should Haunt America* (Norman: University of Oklahoma Press, 2014).

106 "Jus Sanguinis Revisited," *Economist*, March 2, 2013.

107 Debra McNutt, Midwest Treaty Network (Madison, Wis.), interview, August 8, 1997.

108 Dave Stewart, "Professor Digs Up New Treaty Theory," *Milwaukee Journal*, April 15, 1990.

109 Marla Donato, *Spearfishing Treaty Rights and Mining*, video (High Park, Ill.: Earth Network, 1991).

110 Protect Americans' Rights and Resources, "PARR Statements of Policy," February 23, 1991.

111 Donato, *Spearfishing Treaty Rights and Mining*.

112 Al Gedicks, "Racism and Resource Colonialism," *Race and Class* 33, no. 4 (1992): 75–81.

113 Ron Seely, "Mining Has Strong Potential in Wisconsin," *Wisconsin State Journal*, January 31, 1982.

114 Lucia Mouat, "Counties Aim to Limit Treaty Rights," *Christian Science Monitor*, July 9, 1990; Wisconsin Counties Association, *Salt Lake City: Trying to Make Sense out of Federal Indian Policy Confusion* (1990).

115 Bonnie Stowers, "Mining Foes Join Forces with Treaty Supporters," *Milwaukee Journal*, November 17, 1989.

116 Nick Hockings, Wa-Swa-Gon Treaty Association (Lac du Flambeau, Wis.), interview, August 24, 1997.

117 Whaley and Bresette, *Walleye Warriors*, 3.

118 Al Gedicks, *The New Resource Wars: Native and Environmental Struggle against Multinational Corporations* (Boston: South End Press, 1993).

119 Ibid., 161–71.

120 Roscoe Churchill and Laura Furtman, *The Buzzards Have Landed: The Real Story of the Flambeau Mine* (Duluth, Minn.: Deer Tail Press, 2007). Full text at https://flambeaumineexposed.files.wordpress.com/2014/04/buzzards_e-book_final_hyperlinked-edition_apr-2014_certified.pdf.

121 Whaley and Bresette, *Walleye Warriors*, 198.

122 Robert Johnson, "Indians Send Signals That Rile Neighbors of Station WOJB," *Wall Street Journal*, July 8, 1988.

123 In 1991–95, Gaiashkibos served as president of the National Congress of American Indians.

124 Kathy Olson, "Tribe Requests Delay in Copper Mine Case," *St. Paul Pioneer Press*, April 25, 1990; Associated Press, "Lac Courte Oreilles to Oppose Mining Plan," *Milwaukee Sentinel*, May 8, 1990; Mary Jo Kewley, "Band Opposes Mine on Spiritual Grounds," *Wausau Daily Herald*, July 16, 1990.

125 Quoted in Barry Denny, "RTZ Shareholders Hear Indian Tribal Land Pleas," *London Morning Star*, May 10, 1990.

126 Gedicks, *New Resource Wars*, 83–162.

127 Sandy Lyon, Anishinaabe Niijii (Springbrook, Wis.), interview, July 16, 1998.

128 Al Gedicks, Wisconsin Resources Protection Council (La Crosse, Wis.), interview, June 20, 1997.

129 Lyon, interview.

130 Gedicks, interview.

131 Lyon, interview.

132 Quoted in Zoltán Grossman, "Indians, Farmers Fight Copper Giant's Global Reach," *Guardian* (New York), July 31, 1990.

133 Ron Seely, "Protest Taken to Mine Site," *Wisconsin State Journal*, July 7, 1991.

134 Gedicks, interview.

135 Laura Gauger, "2010–2014: Clean Water Act Lawsuit," Flambeau Mine Exposed, 2014, http://flambeaumineexposed.wordpress.com/legal-actions/clean-water-act-case-2012-3.

136 Roscoe Churchill, Rusk County Citizens Action Group (Ladysmith, Wis.), interview, May 22, 1997.

137 Quoted in Gedicks, *New Resource Wars*, 116.

138 Gedicks, interview.

139 McNutt, interview.

140 Lyon, interview.

141 "Mine Issue Turns Spearfishers' Eyes South," *Eau Claire Leader Telegram*, March 7, 1991.

142 Walter Bresette, Midwest Treaty Network; Anishinaabe Niijii, Red Cliff Ojibwe (Red Cliff, Wis.), interview, August 17, 1997.

143 Satz, "Chippewa Treaty Rights," 101–124.

144 John Sherer, "Mining Waste Is Cited as Top Concern," *Milwaukee Sentinel*, February 11, 1991.

145 "Tribal Leader Opposes Mining Plan," *Milwaukee Sentinel*, June 23, 1990.

146 Jim Wise, ECCOLA / Northwoods Alliance (Tomahawk, Wis.), interview, July 12, 1997.

147 Maulson, interview.

148 Ron Seely, "Mining Debate Takes Front Seat," *Wisconsin State Journal*, May 12, 1991.

149 David Wahlberg, "Environmentalists Protest Oneida County Mine," *Wausau Daily Herald*, April 9, 1992.

150 McNutt, interview.

151 Wally Cooper, Oneida County fishing guide (Rhinelander, Wis.), interview, August 18, 1997.

152 Carolyn Parker, ECCOLA / Vilas County Board member (Woodruff, Wis.), interview, July 11, 1997.

153 McNutt, interview.

154 Maulson, interview.

155 McNutt, interview.

156 Karl Fate, Wisconsin Resources Protection Council (Rhinelander, Wis.), interview, August 18, 1997.

157 Terry Anderson, "Reclamation Important Part of Mining, Executives Say," *Green Bay Press Gazette*, August 4, 1991.

158 "Noranda Pulls out of Eastern U.S.," *Northern Miner*, October 5, 1992.

159 Koser-Thoms, interview.

160 County zoning administrator John Anderson also found in the Strawberry Island conflict an opportunity to voice moral sympathy for Ojibwe treaty rights and tribal jurisdiction that he felt he could not during the spearing crisis. John Anderson (Boulder Junction, Wis.), interview, July 1, 1997.

161 Meg Jones, "Lac du Flambeau Tribe Buys Island on Wisconsin Reservation," *Milwaukee Journal Sentinel*, December 30, 2013.

162 Hockings, interview.

163 McNutt, interview.

164 Marcus Nesemann, "Oneida County Board Supervisors End Mining Talks," *Lakeland Times*, August 24, 2012.

NOTES TO CHAPTER 7

1   Chuck Sleeter and Joanne Sleeter, Town of Nashville employees (Pickerel, Wis.), interview, January 30, 2000.

2   Al Gedicks, *The New Resource Wars: Native and Environmental Struggle against Multinational Corporations* (Boston: South End Press, 1993), 57–82.

3   Keith Schneider, "A Wisconsin Indian Tribe Tries to Turn Back a Giant," *New York Times*, December 26, 1994.

4   Robert P. W. Gough, "A Cultural-Historical Assessment of the Wild Rice Resources of the Sokaogon Chippewa," in *An Analysis of the Environmental and Socio-Economic Impacts of Mining and Mineral Resource Development on the Sokaogon Chippewa Community* (Madison, Wisc.: COACT Research, Inc., 1980).

5   Dorothy Tyra, Pickerel Lake Association (Pickerel, Wis.), interview, June 15, 1997.

6   Rob Zaleski, "Mine Foes Coo over Coup," *Capital Times*, May 10, 1997.

7   The Niiwin Tribes were often joined by the Oneida Nation of Wisconsin, next to Green Bay.

8   Debra McNutt, Midwest Treaty Network (Madison, Wis.), interview, August 8, 1997.

9   Midwest Treaty Network, "Archives" (2006), http://treaty.indigenousnative.org/content.html.

10 Al Gedicks, *Keepers of the Water*, documentary (1996).

11 Quoted in Will Fantle, "Indians Oppose Exxon Mine," *Isthmus*, June 24, 1994.

12 McNutt, interview.

13 Bob Schmitz, Wolf River Watershed Alliance (White Lake, Wis.), interview, June 13, 1997.

14 Al Gedicks, Wisconsin Resources Protection Council (La Crosse, Wis.), interview, June 20, 1997.

15 Menominee Treaty Rights and Mining Impacts Office, "Resolutions Opposing the Crandon Mine or Pipeline," March 12, 1997, https://flambeaumineexposed.files.wordpress.com/2012/12/cd-120-20.pdf.

16 Patty Loew, *Indian Nations of Wisconsin: Histories of Endurance and Renewal* (Madison: Wisconsin Historical Society Press, 2001), 24–39

17 Menominee Tribal Enterprises, *The Forest Keepers: The Menominee Forest-Based Sustainable Development Tradition* (1997), 25.

18 Menominee Historic Preservation Department, "Menominee Sturgeon Feast and Celebration," program (April 2001).

19 Quoted in Don Behm and Steve Schultz, "Tribe's Lawsuit May Ignite Backlash," *Milwaukee Journal*, January 15, 1995.

20 Quoted in Susan L. Smith, "Wary Anglers Know Crabb, Fear Her Role in Treaty Suit," *Wisconsin State Journal*, January 17, 1995.

21 Louis Hawpetoss, Menominee tribal judge (Keshena, Wis.), interview, August 20, 1997.

22 Kenneth Fish, director, Menominee Treaty Rights and Mining Impacts Office (Keshena, Wis.), interview, June 14, 1997.

23 Tom Soles, Walleyes for Tomorrow (Fond du Lac, Wis.), interview, August 22, 1997.

24 Walleyes for Tomorrow, "Resolution on the Crandon Mine," September 14, 1996.

25 Hawpetoss, interview.

26 Shawano Country Chamber of Commerce, "From the Pineries to the Present: Heritage Area Shawano and Menominee Counties," pamphlet (2000).

27 U.S. District Court, Western District of Wisconsin, *Menominee Indian Tribe of Wisconsin v. Tommy G. Thompson et al.*, No. 95-C-0030 (W.D. Wis. 1997).

28 Fish, interview.

29 Bill Koenen, former Sokaogon Chippewa environmental officer (Mole Lake, Wis.), interview, August 19, 1997.

30 Wolf Watershed Educational Project, "Anti-Exxon Gathering Draws One Thousand to Rhinelander, Wisconsin," Midwest Treaty Network, 1996, http://treaty.indigenousnative .org/content.html/exxon.html.

31 Michael O'Brien, *Exxon and the Crandon Mine Controversy* (Middleton, Wis.: Badger Books LLC, 2008).

32 Quoted in Rob Zaleski, "Here's How to Stick It to Exxon, Tommy," *Capital Times*, March 18, 1996.

33 Fred Ackley, Sokaogon Chippewa tribal judge (Mole Lake, Wis.), interview, August 18, 1999.

34 Patty Loew, *Seventh Generation Earth Ethics: Native Voices of Wisconsin* (Madison: Wisconsin Historical Society Press, 2014), 33–47.

35 Ibid., 17–32.

36 Herbert Buettner, Wild Wolf Inn owner, Trout Unlimited Wolf River chapter (White Lake, Wis.), interview, June 13, 1997.

37 Schmitz, interview.

38 McNutt, interview.

39 Thomas R. Huffman, *Protectors of the Land and Water: Environmentalism in Wisconsin, 1961–1968* (Chapel Hill: University of North Carolina Press, 1994).

40 Wally Cooper, Oneida County fishing guide (Rhinelander, Wis.), interview, August 18, 1997.

41 Frances Van Zile, Mole Lake Sokaogon Chippewa Community (Mole Lake, Wis.), interview, August 18, 1999.

42 Wolf Watershed Educational Project, "Wisconsin Governor Will Sign Sulfide Mining Moratorium Bill," Midwest Treaty Network, 1997, http://treaty.indigenousnative.org /minelaw.html.

43 Ron Seely, "Here's How to Lobby If Other Side Has $1 Million," *Wisconsin State Journal*, March 31, 1998.

44 Committee of Labor Against Sulfide Pollution (CLASP) (1998), http://treaty.indigenous native.org/clasp.html.

45 Save Our Unique Lands (SOUL) of Wisconsin (2005), www.soulwisconsin.org/.

46 Tom Ward, Wisconsin Resources Protection Council (Crandon, Wis.), interview, August 19, 1997.

47 Ackley, interview.

48 Sleeter, interview.

49 "Ousted Officials Refuse to Leave Office," April 18, 1997, *Milwaukee Journal Sentinel*.

50 Sleeter, interview.

51 Van Zile, interview.

52 Will Fantle, "Open Meetings Law Violations May Doom Crandon Mining Pact," *Isthmus*, December 1999.

53 George Rock, Wolf River Watershed Alliance, Wisconsin Resources Protection Council (White Lake, Wis.), interview, June 14, 1997.

54 A 2000 state court hearing on the Nashville case was attended by Green Party vice presidential candidate Winona LaDuke and the musical group Indigo Girls.

55 Sleeter beat back recall challenges and repeatedly won reelection by progressively larger margins, until he left office in 2014.

56 Sleeter, interview.

57 Ibid.

58 Ibid.

59 Ibid.

60 Rock, interview.

61 Sonny Wreczycki, Rollingstone Lake Association (Ainsworth, Wis.), interview, June 15, 1997.

62 Van Zile, interview.

63 Sleeter, interview.

64 Ward, interview.

65 Sylvester Poler, Wisconsin Resources Protection Council, Mole Lake Ojibwe (Mole Lake, Wis.), interview, June 20, 1998.

66 Al Gedicks, *Resource Rebels: Native Challenges to Mining and Oil Companies* (Boston: South End Press, 2001), 127–158; Associated Press, "Tribal Water Plan Supported," November 11, 1996.

67 Lee Bergquist, "Decision Puts Water Quality in Tribe's Hands," *Milwaukee Journal Sentinel*, June 4, 2002.

68 Midwest Treaty Network, "Citizens' Petition to Attorney General James Doyle on Mole Lake's Clean Water Status," April 1999, http://treaty.indigenousnative.org/water.html; Trout Unlimited Wisconsin Council, "A Resolution to Assure That the Mole Lake Sokaogon Chippewa Tribe's Treatment-as-State Rights are Granted to Protect Their Vital Clean Water," September 9, 2000.

69 Bergquist, "Water Quality in Tribe's Hands."

70 Forest County Potawatomi Tribe, "Class I Air Quality Request," June 1995.

71 "Air Redesignation Hearing Takes Public Comments," *Forest Republican*, October 6, 1994.

72 Jeff Mayers, "Businesses Concerned about Tribe's Air Request," *Wisconsin State Journal*, July 25, 1995.

73 Wallace Sundstrom, "Letter from Dickinson Citizens for Clean Air to the Forest County Potawatomi Community," January 5, 1995; Associated Press, "Tribal Water Plan Supported."

74 Forest County Potawatomi Tribe, "Class I Redesignation," 2008, www.fcpotawatomi. com/natural-resources/air-resource-program/class-i-redesignation.

75 Wisconsin's Environmental Decade, "Poll Shows Strong Support for Local, Tribal Environmental Protections," December 8, 1997.

76 Sleeter, interview.

77 Northwoods NiiJii Enterprise Community (2017), www.niijii.org/.

78 Northwoods NiiJii Enterprise Community, "Letter to U.S. Rep. Mark Green," September 20, 2000.

79 Andy Hall, "Survey: Public Supports Tribes' Right to Casinos," *Wisconsin State Journal*, February 24, 2000.

80 Sleeter, interview.

81 Poler, interview.

82 Chamberlain Research Consultants, "Opinion Survey Commissioned by Forest County Potawatomi Community" (July 2001).

83 Midwest Treaty Network, "Wisconsin Campaign to Ban Cyanide in Mining," 2002, http://treaty.indigenousnative.org/content.html/cyanide.html.

84 Midwest Treaty Network, "Citizens' Assembly," March 2001, http://treaty.indigenousnative.org/assembly.html.

85 Tracey Khanna, "Editorial Comment: Minerva," *Mining Environmental Management*, May 2000.

86 Fraser Institute, *Annual Survey of Mining Companies* (Vancouver, B.C., 2001).

87 "Troubled Time; Brighter Future," *North American Mining*, editorial, August–September 1998.

88 Bob Webster, "Barbarians at the Gates of Cyberspace: Inside the Internet Battle over the Proposed Crandon Mine in Wisconsin," *Mining Voice*, January–February 1998.

89 Mole Lake acquired $8 million in debt and later reached a write-off deal with the company. Robert Imrie, "Mining Firm Gives $8M Back to Tribe; Gift Ends Crandon Mine Saga," *Capital Times*, May 31, 2006.

90 Dennis Shepherd, Forest County Potawatomi tribal member, talk at Nicolet Minerals Company headquarters, Crandon, Wis., October 28, 2003.

91 Quoted in "The Best Bet for the Mine Site," *Milwaukee Journal Sentinel*, editorial, October 30, 2003.

92 Quoted in "Developer: Sale Kills Crandon Mine Future," *Green Bay Press Gazette*, October 30, 2003.

93 Dale Alberts, "Testimony before the Energy and Minerals Subcommittee," U.S. House Committee on Natural Resources, March 3, 2004.

94 Ron Seely, "State Tribes' Influence Had Broadened over Years," *Wisconsin State Journal*, November 2, 2003.

95 "'Under New Management' in Wisconsin," *Indian Country Today*, editorial, November 21, 2003.

96 Frances Van Zile, Mole Lake Sokaogon Chippewa Community, personal conversation, August 17, 2015.

97 Katie Big-Canoe and Chantelle Richmond, "Anishinabe Youth Perceptions about Community Health: Toward Environmental Repossession," *Health and Place* 26 (2014): 127–136.

98 Carl Sack, "Potential Environmental Impacts of a Penokee Mine," Midwest Treaty Network, 2006, http://treaty.indigenousnative.org/penokee.html.

99 Midwest Environmental Advocates, "Citizen Voices Matter: In the Penokee Hills," 2014.

100 Joe Rose Sr., professor emeritus of American Indian Studies at Northland College, Bad River tribal member, Ashland County Board member (Odanah, Wis.), interview, October 14, 2014.

101 John Myers, "Greens Protest Train, Method," *Duluth News-Tribune*, July 23, 1996.

102 Quoted in Zoltán Grossman, "Chippewa Train Blockade Upsets Mining Plans," *Progressive*, October 1996, http://treaty.indigenousnative.org/mtn-br x1.html.

103 Ibid.

104 Yellow Dog Watershed Preserve (2017), www.yellowdogwatershed.org/blog/tag/kbic/; Save the Wild U.P. (2017), http://savethewildup.org/tag/yellow-dog-plains/.

105 "Eagle Mine Gets Court Nod as Keweenaw Bay Indian Appeal Overturned," Indian Country Today Media Network, August 14, 2014, http://indiancountrytodaymedianet work.com/.

106 Brian Bienkowski, "Mining Leaves a Wisconsin Tribe's Hallowed Sites at Risk," Environmental Health News, September 19, 2016, www.environmentalhealthnews.org/; Lisa M. Reed. "Anti-Mining Group Voices Concerns," *Eagle Herald*, May 10, 2016; Lee Bergquist, "Plans for U.P. Mine Studied," *Milwaukee Journal Sentinel*, January 11, 2016; Menominee Indian Tribe of Wisconsin, "Resolution No. 15-93: Opposition to Mining Activity That Threatens Menominee Cultural Resources at Tribe's Place of Origin," December 17, 2015.

107 Penokee Range Alliance, "Ceremony to Celebrate Spring Urges Us to Protect Penokee Hills," March 20, 2006, http://treaty.indigenousnative.org/penokee.html.

108 Bad River Band of the Lake Superior Tribe of Chippewa Indians, "Water Quality Standards Resolution," July 6, 2011.

109 Al Gedicks, "Resisting Resource Colonialism in the Lake Superior Region," *Z Magazine*, September 2011.

110 Al Gedicks and Dave Blouin, "Crandon Victory Has Lessons for Today," *Milwaukee Journal Sentinel*, October 9, 2013.

111 Thanks to *Progressive* correspondent Rebecca Kemble for her invaluable assistance (December 30, 2013) in directing me to local sources for interviews.

112 Penokee Hills Education Project (2017), www.miningimpactcoalition.org/; The Water's Edge (2017), www.savethewatersedge.com/.

113 Ros Nelson, Penokees mine opponent (Washburn, Wis.), interview, September 9, 2014.

114 Frank Koehn, The Water's Edge / Penokee Hills Education Project (Herbster, Wis.), interview, June 29, 2015.

115 Mike Wiggins Jr., chairman of Bad River Band of Lake Superior Chippewa (Odanah, Wis.), interview, October 14, 2014.

116 Bad River Watershed Association (2017), www.badriverwatershed.org/.

117 Bobbi Rongstad, Bad River Watershed Association (Gurney, Wis.), interview, July 29, 2014.

118 Philomena Kebec, Bad River Band of Lake Superior Chippewa Tribe staff attorney (Odanah, Wis.), interview, July 25, 2014.

119 Allie Raven, Bad River tribal member (Delta, Wis.), interview, August 13, 2014.

120 Jill Hartlev, Bad River Ojibwe mining committee (Odanah, Wis.), interview, September 15, 2014.

121 Maureen Matusewic, Penokees mine opponent (Hurley, Wis.), interview, September 20, 2014.

122 Koehn, interview.

123 Ibid.

124 Wiggins, interview.

125 Rebecca Kemble and Barbara With, "The Anishinaabe Speak: There Will Be No Mines in the Penokees," Wisconsin Citizens Media Cooperative, January 17, 2012, http://wc mcoop.com/.

126 Rose, interview.

127 Ron Seely, "In Penokees Camp, Tribes Flex Treaty Muscles to Stop Mine," *Sawyer County Record*, July 29, 2013.

128 Rose, interview.

129 Mary Annette Pember, "Fighting Mines in Wisconsin: A Radical New Way to Be Radical," *Indian Country Today*, July 7, 2013.

130 Monica Vitek, Mark Vitek, Donald Vitek Sr., Don Vitek Jr., Wendy Koosmann, and Faye Koosmann, O'Dovero-Flesia Farm (Mellen, Wis.), interview, October 14, 2014.

131 Lucy Kennedy and Josh Rushing, "Wisconsin's Mining Standoff," *Fault Lines*, June 14, 2014, Al Jazeera America, http://america.aljazeera.com/.

132 Vitek et al., interview.

133 Ibid.

134 Rebecca Kemble, "Walker's Mine Imperils Wisconsin," *Progressive*, February 10, 2014.

135 Al Gedicks, "Militarized Mining in Wisconsin," *Z Magazine*, October 2013, http://wcmcoop.com/2013/09/27/militarized-mining-in-wisconsin.

136 Vitek et al., interview.

137 Rick Olivo, "UW–Superior Public Opinion Survey Shows Most Respondents Oppose GTAC Mine," *Ashland Daily Press*, September 19, 2013.

138 Quoted in Gedicks, "Militarized Mining."

139 Rose, interview.

140 Wiggins, interview.

141 Rebecca Kemble, "Walker's DNR Pushes Tribe out for Strip Mine," *Progressive*, July 24, 2013.

142 Penokee Mineinfo, "Maureen Matusewic Calls out Iron County for Racist Policy," July 30, 2013, www.youtube.com/watch?v=ok9w-nTUKQY.

143 Rose, interview.

144 Penokee Mineinfo, "Aileen Potter Urges Iron County to Respect the LCO Harvest Camp," July 30, 2013, www.youtube.com/watch?v=mzs6jxD69lY.

145 Mary Annette Pember, "Dear DC, Stop All Mining in the Penokee Range, Sincerely Bad River," *Indian Country Today*, February 22, 2014.

146 Al Gedicks, "Defeating the Iron Mines of Wisconsin," *News from Indian Country*, June 2015.

147 Paula Mohan, "Intergovernmental Shape-Shifting: Tribal Strategies of Resistance against the State of Wisconsin" (presentation to the Native American and Indigenous Studies Association, Washington, D.C., June 5, 2015).

148 Rongstad, interview.

149 Rose, interview.

150 Steven Verburg, "Gogebic Taconite Says Wisconsin Mine Isn't Feasible," *Wisconsin State Journal*, February 28, 2015.

151 Citizens Preserving the Penokee Hills Heritage Park (2017), www.facebook.com/groups/penokeemine.

152 Citizens Concerned about Lake Superior CAFOs (2017), www.facebook.com/groups/412421685578382; United in Defense of the Water (2017). https://unitedindefenseofthewater.wordpress.com/.

153 John Myers, "Anti-Mine Group Turns Attention to Enbridge Pipelines," *Duluth News Tribune*, January 11, 2017; Phil McKenna, "Wisconsin Tribe Votes to Evict Oil Pipeline from Its Reservation," *Inside Climate News*, January 16, 2017.

154 Chippewa Federation, "Mining Alternatives Summit," Red Cliff, Wis., January 7–9, 2015.

155 Kebec, interview.

156 Wiggins, interview.

157 Tyra, interview.

158 Koenen, interview.

159 Ibid.
160 Walter Bresette, Midwest Treaty Network, Anishinaabe Niijii, Red Cliff Ojibwe (Red Cliff, Wis.), interview, August 17, 1997.
161 Ibid.
162 Gedicks, interview.
163 Steven E. Silvern, "Scales of Justice: American Indian Treaty Rights and the Political Construction of Scale," *Political Geography* 18, no. 6 (1999): 663.
164 Kebec, interview.
165 Henry Giroux and Peter McLaren, *Between Borders: Pedagogy and the Politics of Cultural Studies* (New York: Routledge, 1994).
166 Yi-Fu Tuan, personal correspondence to the author, March 18, 2000.
167 Bradford J. Hall, "Understanding Intercultural Conflict through an Analysis of Kernel Images and Rhetorical Visions," *International Journal of Conflict Management* 5, no. 1 (1994): 62–86.
168 Barbara Ching and Gerald W. Creed suggest that although rural whites "are often identified with . . . racist, ethnocentric or nationalist ideologies, . . . they are made conservative by others." They write that "the marginality of rustic people renders them vulnerable to conservative maneuvering, but efforts at more self-conscious rustic resistance could challenge such manipulation." Barbara Ching and Gerald W. Creed, eds., *Knowing Your Place: Rural Identity and Cultural Hierarchy* (London: Routledge, 1997), 29–30.
169 Janet Fitchen, *Endangered Spaces, Enduring Places: Change, Identity, and Survival in Rural America* (Boulder, Colo.: Westview Press, 1991).
170 Van Zile, interview.

NOTES TO CONCLUSION

1   By 2016, Warm Springs led the fight to stop a Nestlé water bottling plant at Cascade Locks in the Columbia Gorge, and two-thirds of Hood River County voters opposed the plan. David Steves and Chris Lehman. "Nestle Water Bottling Plan Draws Protest—Even after It's Voted Down," Oregon Public Broadcasting / EarthFix, September 21, 2016.
2   Jamie Donatuto and Melissa R. Poe, *Evaluating Sense of Place as a Domain of Human Well-Being for Puget Sound Restoration* (Seattle: Puget Sound Institute, April 2015).
3   Bill Means, International Indian Treaty Council director, Oglala Lakota (Minneapolis), interview, March 21, 1997.
4   Walter Bresette, Midwest Treaty Network, Anishinaabe Niijii, Red Cliff Ojibwe (Red Cliff, Wis.), interview, August 17, 1997.
5   George Crocker, General Assembly to Stop the Powerline (GASP), and Lea Foushee, GASP, North American Water Office (Lake Elmo, Minn.), interview, March 22, 1997; Paul Wellstone and Barry M. Caspar, *Powerline: The First Battle of America's Energy War* (1981; Minneapolis: University of Minnesota Press, 2003).
6   Shean Bjoralt, *Confronting Nuclear Racism: A Prairie Island Coalition Report* (Lake Elmo, Minn.: Prairie Island Coalition, 1996).
7   Faye Brown, Prairie Island Coalition (Minneapolis), interview, August 10, 1997.
8   George Rock, Wolf River Watershed Alliance and Wisconsin Resources Protection Council (White Lake, Wis.), interview, June 14, 1997.
9   Louis Hawpetoss, Menominee tribal judge (Keshena, Wis.), interview, August 20, 1997.
10 Marvin Kammerer, Black Hills Alliance, rancher (Box Elder, S.D.), interview, July 26, 1997.

11 Sonny Wreczycki, Rollingstone Lake Association (Ainsworth, Wis.), interview, June 15, 1997.

12 Tom Ward, Wisconsin Resources Protection Council (Crandon, Wis.), interview, August 19, 1997.

13 Al Gedicks, Wisconsin Resources Protection Council (La Crosse, Wis.), interview, June 20, 1997.

14 Debra McNutt, Midwest Treaty Network (Madison, Wis.), interview, August 8, 1997.

15 Naomi Klein, talk on *This Changes Everything: Capitalism vs. The Climate*, Town Hall, Seattle, September 28, 2014, uploaded by *Talking Stick TV*, www.youtube.com/watch ?v=4b2B-ys3Ni0.

16 Ibid.

17 Hawpetoss, interview.

18 Wreczycki, interview.

19 Ron Seely, "State Tribes' Influence Had Broadened over Years," *Wisconsin State Journal*, November 2, 2003.

20 Means, interview.

21 Herbert Buettner, Wild Wolf Inn owner and member of Trout Unlimited Wolf River chapter (White Lake, Wis.), interview, June 13, 1997.

22 Carolyn Parker, ECCOLA / Vilas County Board member (Woodruff, Wis.), interview, July 11, 1997.

23 Charles Tanner Jr., "Bigoted Nationalism Opens CERA's New Year," Institute for Research and Education on Human Rights, February 3, 2016, www.irehr.org/2016/02/03/bigoted-nationalism-opens-ceras-new-year.

24 Zoltán Grossman, "The Global War on Tribes," *Z Magazine*, June 2, 2010, https://zcomm .org/zmagazine/the-global-war-on-tribes-by-zoltan-grossman.

25 David Harvey, *Spaces of Hope* (Edinburgh: Edinburgh University Press, 2000), 74.

26 Steve Biko, *I Write What I Like* (New York: Harper and Row, 1978).

27 Quoted in Robin D. G. Kelley, "A Poetics of Anticolonialism," introduction to Aimé Césaire, *Discourse on Colonialism* (New York: Monthly Review Press, 2000), 5–6.

28 George Lipsitz, "Unexpected Affiliations: Environmental Justice and the New Social Movements," *Works and Days* 24, nos. 1–2 (2006): 41.

29 Zoltán Grossman, "Inside the Philippine Resistance," *Race and Class* 28, no. 2 (1986): 1–29, http://academic.evergreen.edu/g/grossmaz/raceandclass.pdf.

30 Raúl Zibechi, *Territories in Resistance: A Cartography of Latin American Social Movements* (Oakland, Calif.: AK Press, 2012).

31 On Ecuador, see Marc Becker, *Indians and Leftists in the Making of Ecuador's Modern Indigenous Movements* (Durham, N.C.: Duke University Press, 2008); and Roberta Rice, *The New Politics of Protest: Indigenous Mobilization in Latin America's Neoliberal Era* (Tucson: University of Arizona Press, 2012). On Guatemala, see Charles R. Hale, *Más que un Indio (More than an Indian): Racial Ambivalence and the Paradox of Neoliberal Multiculturalism in Guatemala* (Santa Fe, N.M.: School for Advanced Research Press, 2006). On Bolivia, see Nicole Fabricant, *Mobilizing Bolivia's Displaced: Indigenous Politics and the Struggle over Land* (Chapel Hill: University of North Carolina Press, 2012); Raquel Gutiérrez Aguilar, *Rhythms of the Pachakuti: Indigenous Uprising and State Power in Bolivia* (Durham, N.C.: Duke University Press, 2014); Nancy Postero, *Now We Are Citizens: Indigenous Politics in Postmulticultural Bolivia* (Stanford, Calif.: Stanford University Press, 2006); and Raúl Zibechi, *Dispersing Power: Social Movements as Anti-State Forces* (Oakland, Calif.: AK Press, 2010). On Brazil, see Gomercindo Rodrigues,

Walking the Forest with Chico Mendes: Struggle for Justice in the Amazon (Austin: University of Texas Press, 2007. On Oaxaca, see Lynn Stephen, *We Are the Face of Oaxaca: Testimony and Social Movements* (Durham, N.C.: Duke University Press, 2013); and Diana Denham, *Teaching Rebellion: Stories from the Grassroots Mobilization in Oaxaca* (Oakland, Calif.: PM Press, 2008). On Chiapas, see John Ross, *Zapatistas: Making Another World Possible* (New York, Nation Books, 2006); and Jeff Conant, *A Poetics of Resistance: The Revolutionary Public Relations of the Zapatista Insurgency* (Oakland, Calif.: AK Press, 2010).

32 Quoted in Lorraine Orlandi, "Mexico's Marcos Calls for Support from Non-Indians," Reuters, February 28, 2001.

33 Lani Guinier and Gerald Torres, *The Miner's Canary: Enlisting Race, Resisting Power, Transforming Democracy* (Cambridge, Mass.: Harvard University Press, 2002).

34 James Clifford, *Returns: Becoming Indigenous in the Twenty-First Century* (Cambridge, Mass.: Harvard University Press, 2012), 14.

35 Shantha Hennayake, "Interactive Ethnonationalism: An Alternative Explanation of Minority Ethnonationalism," *Political Geography* 11, no. 6 (1992): 526–549.

36 Lawrence Krader, ed., *The Ethnological Notebooks of Karl Marx* (Assen, Neth.: Van Gorcum and Company, 1974), www.marxists.org/archive/marx/works/1881/ethnographical -notebooks/notebooks.pdf; Friedrich Engels, *The Origin of the Family, Private Property, and the State*, reissued ed. (London: Penguin Classics, 2010).

37 Quoted in Andrew Bard Epstein, "The Colonialism of the Present," *Jacobin*, January 13, 2015, www.jacobinmag.com/2015/01/indigenous-left-glen-coulthard-interview.

38 Poka Laenui, "Settler's Code of Conduct," Hawaiian Perspectives, October 17, 2011, www.hawaiianperspectives.org/?page_id=36.

39 "If there is no struggle there is no progress. Those who profess to favor freedom and yet deprecate agitation are men who want crops without plowing up the ground." Frederick Douglass, "West India Emancipation Speech" (1857).

40 Scott L. Morgensen, "Settler Homonationalism: Theorizing Settler Colonialism within Queer Modernities," *GLQ: A Journal of Lesbian and Gay Studies* 16, nos. 1–2: 122.

41 Quoted in Jaci Webb, "West Coast Totem Pole Symbolizes Power, Solidarity to Montana Tribal Members," *Billings Gazette*, January 22, 2016.

42 Tim Ballew II, "Cherry Point Victory Shows Treaty Rights Protect Us All," *Bellingham Herald*, May 14, 2016.

43 John Trudell, "We Are Power" (speech to the Black Hills International Survival Gathering, July 18, 1980), www.historyisaweapon.com/defcon1/trudellwearepower.html.

INDEX

Please note that page numbers in *italics* refer to figures or maps; those followed by "n" indicate endnotes.

Ackley, Fred, 245, 246, *248*, 249
Adams, Hank, 39, 40, 44
Affiliated Tribes of Northwest Indians, 195
African Americans, 17, 24, 104, 132
Ahlborn, Michael, 224
Akins, Hadley, 80, 81, 83
Alaska, 9, 27, 46, 72
Alberta First Nations, 178
Alberta tar sands, *171*, 177, 193–94
Alberts, Dale, 255
Alderson, Jeanie, 174, 289
Alfred, Taiaiake, 22, 26
Allard, LaDonna Bravebull, 189
All Citizens Equal, 149
Allen, Jennifer, 113
Allen, Theodore W., 24
Alliance for Responsible Development, 162
alliances. *See* Native/non-Native alliances; *specific alliances and case studies*
Allotment era, 16, 19, 43, 83, 237, 264
Allpress, Bob, 185
"allyship," 30
Alves, Maynard, 113
Amcor, 161–62
American Fisheries Society, 74
American Friends Service Committee, 44
American Horse, Joe, 160
American Indian Movement (AIM), 152, 153, 165
Amish farmers, 120
Amour, George, 234–35
Anderson, John, 337n160
Andrus, Cecil, 109
Anishinaabe. *See* Ojibwe
Anishinaabe Niijii (Friends of the Ojibwe), 231–32
Anishinaabe Ogichiidaa (Protectors of the People), 258

anti-treaty movement. *See specific case studies*
Arapaho, 150
Arch Coal, 172–73, 176, 198
Arctic drilling fleet, Shell, 194
Arikara, 188
Arizona, 265
Army Corps of Engineers, U.S., 68, 69, 123, 189, 192, 197, 198
Aryan Nations, 216
assimilation, 15, 18–20, 28, 132, 272
Assiniboine, 138, 146–47
Atkinson, Jason, 92–93
Australia, 27, 253
Azarga Uranium Corporation, 163

Babbitt, Bruce, 55, 77, 148
Back Forty Project, 259
Badger Army Ammunition Plant, Sauk Prairie, *118*, 124–27, *127*, 130, 133
Badger Reuse Committee, 126
Bad River, 210, *211*, 215, 257, 258, *260*, 264, 272
Bad River Band of Lake Superior Chippewa (Ojibwe), 257. *See also* Penokee Hills mine and Bad River Ojibwe
Bad River Watershed Association, 261
Baker, Al, 232
Baker, Mary Ellen, 232
Bakken oil shale basin, *171*, 188, 199–202
Ballew, Tim II, 198, 289
Baltic States, 286
"Ban All Nets" initiative (1999), 54
Barker, Adam, 30
Barker, Al, 232
Barker, Joanne, 25
Barker, Sheryl, 232
basketball, 309n139
Bear Butte, 163, 169

Begay, Eugene, 232
Bellingham, 195–97
Belloni, Robert, 67
Benson, Kermit, 233
Benton, Marilyn, 232
Benton Banai, Eddie, 232
BHP Billiton, 253–54
Big Smokey Falls, Wolf River, 277
Biko, Steve, 284
bioregions, defined, 95
Bismarck, 188
Black Elk, Charlotte, 159, 160
Blackfeet, 138, 147
Black Hills Alliance (BHA), 138, 153–58, 283
Black Hills and Lakota, South Dakota:
    background, 150–53; Bear Butte and
    Defenders of the Black Hills, 163;
    Black Hills Alliance (BHA), 153–58;
    DM&E Railroad and CIA II, 162–63;
    Honeywell gunnery range (Hell Can-
    yon) and Cowboy and Indian Alliance
    (CIA I), 158–60; map, 151; sacred
    lands, sharing, 166–69; toxic waste
    dump proposals for Pine Ridge and
    Rosebud reservations, 161–62; "two
    steps forward, one step back" process,
    164–66; uranium mining and Black
    Hills Clean Water Alliance, 163–64
Black Hills Clean Water Alliance, 163–64
Black Hills Energy Coalition, 154
Black Hills International Survival
    Gathering, 157, 157–58, 290
Black Hills National Gathering of the
    People, 155
Black Hills Protection Committee, 162
Black Hills Wild Horse Sanctuary, 160, 161
blood quantum, 21
Blouin, Dave, 245, 259
boarding schools, 19
boat landing protests against Ojibwe, 214–
    18, 239, 335n79
Bold Iowa, 189
Bold Nebraska, 178
Boldt, George, 42, 45
Boldt I decision, 41–45, 196–97, 204, 273
Boldt II process, 45–47, 204
Bolivia, 12, 285
Bonneville Power Administration (BPA),
    75, 76, 85

Bonogofsky, Alexis, 173, 175–76
border communities. See specific alliances
    and case studies
Bosnia, 62, 117, 169, 227, 228, 304n146
boundaries, blurring or reconfiguring of,
    270–72
Brademeyer, Brian, 163
Bradley, Bill, 158
Braget, Ken, 60
Braget Farm, 60
Braided Hair, Otto, Jr., 172, 173
Braided Hair, Vanessa, 173
Brando, Marlon, 40
Braun, Joye, 191–92
Brave Heart Women's Society, 179
Bresette, Walter (Walt), 30–31, 206, 214,
    218–21, 225, 230–34, 258, 269, 276,
    282
bridge-building and common understand-
    ing, 281–82
British Columbia First Nations, 27, 177, 193
Brownfield, Beth, 198
Bryson, Don, 84–85
Buettner, Herbert (Herb), 246, 276, 281
Buffalo Spirit, Alaina, 142
Bundy, Ammon, 115
Bundy, Cliven, 115
Bundy, Ryan, 115
Bureau of Indian Affairs, U.S. (BIA), 126,
    141, 152
Bureau of Land Management, U.S. (BLM),
    107, 113–15
Bureau of Reclamation, U.S., 77, 79
burial grounds: Back Forty Project and,
    259; Columbia Hills, 71; Concerned
    Rosebud-Area Citizens and, 162; Da-
    kota Access Pipeline and, 189; DM&E
    Railroad and, 162; Ho-Chunk burial
    mounds, 120, 127, 129; Keystone XL
    oil pipeline and, 177; Little Rockies,
    146; Lyle Point, 71; Rollingstone Lake,
    251; Spirit Hill, 240, 256; Strawberry
    Island, 237; Xwe'chi'eXen village/
    Cherry Point, 195
Burlington Northern Santa Fe (BNSF),
    172–73
Burns Paiute, 115
Bush, George W., 90
Byrd, Grace Ann, 60, 199

California, 70, 81, 88–90, 105, 107, 193
Camp-Horinek, Casey, 182–83
Camp of the Sacred Stones, 189
Canada, 9, 13, 21, 27, 180
Cannonball Ranch, 189
Cannonball River, 188–90, *190*
Cantwell, Maria, 56
Carpenter, Lanny, 53, 54
"carrot-and-stick" strategy, 150, 165–66, 282
Carter, Jimmy, 109
Cascade, 70, 71
Cascades, 35, 89
casinos and gaming, tribal: Crandon mine
    victory (Ojibwe) and, 255; economic
    cooperation and, 253; equalization
    and, 268, 280–81; Ho-Chunk, 117, 120,
    125; Lac du Flambeau, 237; land return
    proposals and, 131; Menominee, 244;
    Ojibwe spearfishing conflict and, 224,
    225; rise of, 20–21; Wildhorse Casino
    Resort (Umatilla), 82
Cayuse, 78
Celilo Falls, 66–67, *67*, 70, 80
Centennial Accord (1989), 50
Césaire, Aimé, 284–85
Chaney, Ed, 80–81
Charlton, Marc, 78
checkerboarded land, 43
Chehalis, 51
Cherry Point terminal project, 195–98,
    196
Cheyenne. *See* Northern Cheyenne
Cheyenne River Reservation, 151
Chiapas, 285
Chicanos, 104–5
Chief Joseph Days, 84, 86
Ching, Barbara, 344n168
Chippewa (Ojibwe). *See* Crandon mine,
    Nashville, and Mole Lake Ojibwe;
    mining conflicts, northern Wisconsin;
    Penokee Hills mine and Bad River
    Ojibwe; spearfishing and Ojibwe treaty
    rights conflicts, northern Wisconsin
Chippewa Cree, 138, 147
Churchill, Evelyn, 231, 246, 247
Churchill, Roscoe, 231, 232, 233, 246, 256
Churness, Dana, 246
Citizens Equal Rights Alliance (CERA), 47,
    195, 212

Citizens for Safe Water Around Badger
    (CSWAB), 126
Citizens for Treaty Rights, 218, 236
citizenship, state, 15, 36, 39, 97, 288
Citizenship Act (1924), 19
Citizens Opposed to Range Expansion
    (CORE), 121
Citizens United Against Low-Level Flights,
    120
Citizens United Against Range Expansion,
    122
Cladoosby, Brian, 57, 198
Clark, Les, 70–71, 74, 95
Class I air designation, 143, 252
Clean Air Act, 143
Clean Water Act, 233, 251, 259
climate crisis, templates for, 203–4
Clinton, Bill, 68, 144–45, 149
Cloud, Ani, 128–29
coal export terminals, 194–98
"coal for gold" deal, 144–45, 149
Coalition for Peaceful Skies, 121
coal mining in Montana, 139–46, *145*
coal transport and terminals. *See* fossil
    fuel shipping and blocking
Coast Salish Gathering, 194
Coates, Ta-Nehisi, 12
Cohen, Felix S., 28
Collins, Anita, 111
colonization, historical process of, 15–18
Colorado, 27, 115
Columbia Basin. *See* water wars, North-
    west Plateau
Columbia River Chiefs' Council, 71
Columbia River Fishermen's Protective
    Union, 69
Columbia River Fish Management Plan, 68
Columbia River Inter-Tribal Fish Commis-
    sion (CRITFC), 65, 68, 70, 72–75, 194–
    95, 199
Columbia River Treaty, United States–
    Canada (1964), 94
Colville Reservation, 65, 83–84
co-management, 50–52, 114, 225
"commons," 11, 53
Community Conservation Coalition for the
    Sauk Prairie, 126
Concerned Citizens of Newport, 127
Concerned Rosebud-Area Citizens, 162

conflict management as reason for alliance-building, 281
Connor, Earl "Taz," 86–88
Connor, Gordon, Jr., 255
conservationism as mantle, 213
Conway, Brock, 148
Conway, Patricia, 120, 122
Cook-Lynn, Elizabeth, 21
Cooper, Wally, 224, 235–36, 247
corporate theft, 19th-century land dispossession compared to, 26, 130–31
Cossalter, Tom, 82
Costner, Daniel, 162
Costner, Kevin, 162
Coulthard, Glen, 11, 286
Courtney, Terry, Jr., 77
Cowboy and Indian Alliance (CIA I and CIA II), 159–60, 162–63
Cowboy Indian Alliance (CIA III), 180–81, 184–87, 287
"cowboys and Indians" stereotype, 9–10, 137
Crabb, Barbara, 220, 223, 243, 244
Crandon mine, Nashville, and Mole Lake Ojibwe: death of the mine, 253–57; levels of conflict and levels of cooperation, 268–70; maps, 211, 242; Menominee treaty dispute and, 243–45; Nashville town council revolt, 249–50; Nashville Township and Mole Lake Reservation, 239–41; nature of alliance, 247; Northwood Niijii Enterprise Community and economic development, 252–53; outsiders, insiders, and blurring or reconfiguring of boundaries, 270–72; pipeline proposal, 241–43; speaking tours and coalescing of alliance, 245–47; Sulfide Mining Moratorium Bill, 247–49; tribal and local government cooperation, 250–52; Wolf Watershed Education Project, formation of, 241
Crazy Horse (Tashunka Witko), 174
Creed, Gerald W., 344n168
Crenshaw, Terry, 86–87
Crist, Dean, 212, 213, 216, 229, 238, 335n79
Cronon, William, 16
Crow, 138, 140, 141, 174, 275
cultural education as by-product of alliance, 277–78

Cunningham, Jack, 44
Cushman Hydropower Project and Reservoir, 54–55
Custer, George Armstrong, 150
cyanide ban, 147–49, 254
Cyprus, 169

Dakota, 137–38, 150, 179–80, 276
Dakota, Minnesota, and Eastern (DM&E) Railroad, 162–63
Dakota Access Pipeline, 29, 188–92
Dakota Rural Action, 164, 189
The Dalles Dam, 66
Dalrymple, Jack, 192
dams and dam removal, 54–55, 66–69, 79, 89
Daniels, Billy, 234
Dann, Carrie, 102, 107, 110, 113, 114, 115
Dann, Mary, 102, 107, 113, 115
Death Valley National Park, 107
decolonization: landscape healing and, 60; Native, 9, 23, 29, 282, 290; "reconciliation" and, 17; settler, 30, 31
Deere, Philip, 26
Deer Medicine Rocks, 174–75
Defender of the Black Hills, 163
DeLaCruz, Joe, 35, 40, 42, 46, 48–50, 56, 282
Deloria, Vine, Jr., 167
DeMain, Paul, 264
Department of Agriculture, U.S., 125
Department of the Interior, U.S., 90
"diversity," 11, 12
Dixie Valley, 111
Donnell, Art, 160
Douglass, Frederick, 223, 287
Doyle, James, 212, 220
Duck Valley Reservation, 108, 113
Duckwater, 106, 108
Duke, David, 216, 299n35
Dunbar-Ortiz, Roxanne, 17
Dunbar resort complex, Black Hills, 162
Dunn, Bruce, 84
Duwamish, 51

Eagle Rock, 258
Eberhardt, Urban, 78
ecoCheyenne, 173
"ecological Indian" image, 23–24
economic equalization, 268, 280–81
Ecuador, 285

Eighth Fire prophecy (Ojibwe), 31
Ellison, Bruce, 156, 157, 163, 165
Ellsworth Air Force Base, 156
Elofson, Mel, 56
Elwha River, 55
Enbridge, 192, 267
Endangered Species Act (ESA): Klamath
    River and, 89, 91; salmon and, 51, 68,
    70; Snake River and, 88
Energy Transfer Partners, 188
Engels, Friedrich, 286
environmental justice, 103–5
Environmentally Concerned Citizens of
    Lakeland Areas (ECCOLA), 235–36
environmental movement: Big Greens,
    186; environmental racism and, 103;
    Idle No More movement and, 13; new
    forms of, 247; Ojibwe viewed as eco-
    logical other and, 227; Wisconsin min-
    ing and, 229–30
Environmental Protection Agency, U.S.,
    143, 162, 251–52, 259. See also Treat-
    ment as State program
environmental racism, 103–4
equalization, 13, 132, 268, 280–81, 282–83
Erickson, Deanna, 246
Erickson, Teresa, 144
ethnic cleansing, 228
ethnocide, 21
Evans, Dan, 77
Exxon, 221, 240, 249, 253. See also Crandon
    mine, Nashville, and Mole Lake
    Ojibwe

Fallon Naval Air Station, 108, 111
Farrow, Michael, 81
Fate, Karl, 234, 235, 236–37
Federal Energy Regulatory Commission
    (FERC), 91
federal Indian policy, 18–22, 90. See also
    specific departments and agencies
Federation of Western Outdoor Clubs,
    45–46
Federici, Silvia, 16
Fick, Steve, 70
Fish, Kenneth, 244–45
fishing conflicts, northern Wisconsin
    (Menominee), 243–44
fishing conflicts, northern Wisconsin

(Ojibwe). See spearfishing and Ojibwe
    treaty rights conflicts, northern
    Wisconsin
fish kills, 90, 91
fish wars, western Washington: Boldt I
    decision on harvest and allocation,
    41–45; Boldt II process on habitat, 45–
    47; co-management agreements, 50–
    52; commercial fishers and, 53–54;
    conflict resolution from above and
    below, 61–63; continuing anti-tribal
    sentiment, 55–58; culverts case, 52;
    "fish-ins" (1960s), 40–41; hydropower
    dams and, 54–55; map, 38; Puyallup
    Trilogy decisions, 298n17; salmon
    species and migration, 298n4; sport-
    fishers and Trout Unlimited, 47–50;
    threats to salmon, types of, 36; trea-
    ties, tribes, and reservations, 37–39;
    watershed councils, 58–61. See also
    water wars, Northwest Plateau
Flambeau River, 233
Flambeau Summer, 232
Fleming, John, 57
Fletcher, Troy, 91–92
Forest County Potawatomi, 241, 252, 254.
    See also Crandon mine, Nashville, and
    Mole Lake Ojibwe
Fort Belknap Reservation, 146–47
Fort Berthold Reservation, 188, 190, 275
Fort Laramie Treaties (1851 and 1868), 150,
    151, 152, 156, 162, 179
fossil fuel shipping and blocking, North-
    ern Plains: background, 170; Dakota
    Access Pipeline and Standing Rock,
    29, 188–92; Keystone XL Pipeline and
    CIA III, 14, 177–87; map, 171; Otter
    Creek Mine and Tongue River Rail-
    road, 172–77; sulfuric acid train ship-
    ments at Bad River Reservation, 258;
    templates for the climate crisis, 203–4
fossil fuel shipping and blocking, Pacific
    Northwest: background, 170, 193;
    Bakken oil terminals, 199–202; coal
    export terminals, 194–98; map, 171; tar-
    sands oil pipelines and Nawtsamaat
    Alliance, 193–94; templates for the
    climate crisis, 203–4
fracking. See hydraulic fracturing

Frank, Billy, Jr., 34, 35, 40, *41*, 42, 46, 48, 50, 58–60, 200, 282
Frank's Landing (WA), 58–59
Freyholtz, Mert, 282
Frost, Robert, 271
Funmaker, Bert, 119

Gaffney, Frank, 48
Gaiashkibos, 215, 222, 223, 226, 231–32
gaming, tribal. *See* casinos and gaming, tribal
Garvin, Ona, 100, 119, 120–22
Gateway Pacific Terminal project. *See* Cherry Point terminal project
Gathering to Protect the Sacred from the Tar Sands and Keystone XL, 179–81
Gedicks, Al, 229, 231–32, 243, 269, 279
genocide, 21, 295n75
Genung, Tom, 181, 184
geographic setting, impact of, 276
geographies of exclusion vs. inclusion, 10, 227–28
geopiety, 166
Getches, David, 44
Glines Canyon Dam, 55
Gogebic Taconite (GTAC), 259, 263–64, 265
Golder, Nick, 172
gold mining, 144–45, 146–50
Goldtooth, Dallas, 192
Good Road Coalition, 162
Gorton, Slade, 35, 42–43, 44, 50, 56, 299n36
Gottschall, Ben, 186
Granges, 73, 74
Gray, Dale, 121
Gray Eagles, 159
Grays Harbor, WA, 199–201
Grays Harbor Marine Resource Committee, 199
Great Lakes Indian Fish and Wildlife Commission (GLIFWC), 218, 224, 257
Great Sioux Reservation, 150–51
Green Corn Rebellion, 17
Greendeer, Bill, 128
Greendeer, Jon, 128
Greenpeace, 56, 72, 103
Gregory, Dick, 40
Grey Cloud, Greg, 179
Gros Ventre, 138, 146–47

Guatemala, 285
Gunderson, Gerry, 248

Hamilton, Liz, 72–73
Haney-López, Ian, 12
Hanford Nuclear Reservation, *65*, 66
Hansell, Bill, 80
Hansell, Stafford, 81
Hardwood Bombing Range, 117, *118*, 119–22, 315n115
Harney, Corbin, 110, 113–14
Hartlev, Jill, 262
Harvest Educational Learning Project Camp, 264–66
Harvey, David, 318n165
Hatfield, Mark, 77, 79–80, 81
Haudenosaunee (Six Nations Iroquois Confederacy), 50, 286
Havasupai Reservation, 103
Hawai'i, 27, 133
Hawpetoss, Louis, 244, 277, 279, 282
Heart, Bill, 260
Hegel, Georg W. F., 295n89
Hegland, Jim, 183–84
Hell Canyon, 158–60
Hidatsa, 188
Highground Veterans' Memorial, 314n83
Ho-Chunk. *See* military projects and Ho-Chunk, Wisconsin
Ho-Chunk Nation Department of Historic Preservation, 127
Hockings, Nick, 219, 230, 237–38
hog farm, proposed (Rosebud), 162
Honeywell Corp., 158–60
Honor Our Neighbors' Origins and Rights (HONOR), 218
Hood Canal Coordinating Council, 55
Hoopa, *65*, 89
Horinek, Mekasi, 181
House, Samantha, 127
hydraulic fracturing (fracking), 128–29, 188, 191, 192. *See also* fossil fuel shipping and blocking
hydroelectric dams, 54–55, 66–69, 89

Idaho, 6, 35, 66, 83, 86, 194
identities, complexities of, 22–25
"identity politics," 10, 12, 28, 285
Idle No More movement, 13, 186, 204

Ihanktonwan (Yankton) Nakota/Dakota, 179–80
Ihanktonwan Oyate Treaty Steering Committee, 179
Illinois, 188, 212
India, 27
Indian Claims Commission (ICC), 20, 106, 152–53, 158
Indian removal policy, 18–19, 116, 123, 130, 140, 181, 210, 228, 243
Indian Reorganization Act of 1934 (IRA), 19–20, 106
Indigenous Environmental Network, 105, 188, 191–92, 241
Indigenous Nationhood Movement, 13
Inouye, Daniel, 220
"insider" label and status, 226–28, 270–72
Institute for the Advancement of Hawaiian Affairs, 286
Institute of Range and the American Mustang, 160
International Indian Treaty Council, 153
International Treaty to Protect the Sacred, 180
International Treaty to Protect the Sacredness of the Salish Sea, 193
Interstate Congress for Equal Rights and Responsibilities (ICERR), 43, 44, 47
Iowa, 188–90
Iraq, 96, 310n177
Irlbacker-Fox, Stephanie, 30
Iron Cloud, Paul, 160
iron taconite mining. See Penokee Hills mine and Bad River Ojibwe
Israel, 96, 311n181
It's About the Water, 164
Iverson, Peter, 139

Jackson, Chief Johnny, 70, 71–72, 74, 95
Jackson, Henry, 44
James, Jewell, 174, 196–97
James River Paper Company, 55
Jarbridge Shovel Brigade, 115
Jarding, Lilias Jones, 163–64
Johnston, Tyson, 200, 202
Joint Base Lewis-McChord (JBLM), 58–59
Joseph, Chief, 83–84, 88
Joseph Creek, 85
Julius, Jeremiah "Jay," 195

June, Lyla, 136
jus sanguinis (law of the blood), 228
jus soli (law of the soil), 228

Kammerer, Marvin, 156–57, 164, 165, 290
Kandra, Steve, 93
Kansas, 83, 183
Karuk, 89, 92
Kebec, Philomena (Phoebe), 261–62, 267, 270
Keep the Hills Attractive, 158–59
Keewenaw Bay Indian Community, 258
Kemble, Rebecca, 342n111
Kennecott Copper Corp., 230–34, 258
Keystone XL oil pipeline, 14, 177–87
Kickapoo River dam proposal, 123–24
Kickapoo Valley Reserve, 118, 123
Killsnight, Adriann, 173, 174
Kinder Morgan Trans Mountain pipeline, 193
King, Rodney, 11
Kinley, Eleanor, 197–98
Kinley, Randy, 197
Kirchmeier, Kyle, 192
Klamath, 65, 89, 92
Klamath Basin Restoration Agreement, 92–93
Klamath Hydroelectric Settlement Agreement, 92–93
Klamath Irrigation Act (1905), 89
Klamath Irrigation Project, 93
Klamath River Basin, 88–94, 91, 276, 288
Klamath River Compact, 89
Klamath Settlement Group, 91
Klamath Watershed Partnership, 91
Klauser, James, 221, 229, 232
Kleeb, Jane, 178, 180, 182, 183, 185, 187
Klein, Naomi, 170, 204, 279
Klickitat, 64, 71
Koehn, Frank, 259–60, 262–63
Koenen, Bill, 268–69
Kootenai, 138, 147
Koser-Thoms, Anita, 222, 232, 237
Kosovo, 96, 310n177
Kwel Hoy' Totem Pole Journey, 174, 175

Lac Courte Oreilles Reservation, 210, 211, 215, 222, 264
Lac du Flambeau Reservation, 210, 211, 214–15, 221–23, 234–38, 252–53

LaDuke, Winona, 185, 340n54
Ladysmith copper-gold mine, *211*, 230–34
Lake Michigan, 243
Lake Superior, 207, 257–58, 264, 267
Lakota: Keystone XL pipeline and, 177–79, 185–86; in North Dakota, 137–38, 150; Oglala, 151–52, 174–75; treaty lands map, *151*. *See also* Black Hills and Lakota, South Dakota
Lameman, Crystal, 186
LaMonte, Agnes, 151
Lamphere, Marc, 158–59
landscape as unifying concept, 276
Lane, Chief Phil, Jr., 180–81, 194
LaPointe Iron Company, 259
Lapwai Reservation (Nez Perce), 65, 66, 83–84, 86
Leadership Alliance Against Coal, 195
Leopold, Aldo, 247, 332n22
Leschi, Chief, 39, 298n11
"lightning of the Eighth Fire" prophecies (Anishinaabe), 262
Linebaugh, Peter, 16
Lipsitz, George, 285
Little Rocky Mountains, 146–47
local places, scale of, 95–96
Locke, Waniya, 191
Loomis, Lorraine, 53
Lower Brule, 151, *151*, 187
Lower Elwha Klallam, *38*, 55, 56, 58
Lowman, Bill, 47
Lummi, *38*, 43, 174, 193, 195–98, *196*, 289
Lynne zinc-silver mine proposal, *211*, 234–38
Lyon, Sandy, 231–32, 234
Lyons, Oren, 21

Macedonia, 96, 310n178–311n179
Madison, 122, 125, 213, 219, 241, 247
Mahpiya Luta (Red Cloud), 150
Main, James, Jr., 147, 148, 149, 282
Main, Rose, 149, 282
Makah, *38*, 56, 58, 103
Malcolm X, 30
Mandan, 188, 189
Marcos, subcommander, 285
marginality, shared experiences of, 271, 344n168
Maritime Provinces, 27

Marshall, Carla, 163
Martinez, Ricardo, 52
Martino, Vic, 55
Marx, Karl, 286
Mashel River, *59*
Matusewic, Maureen, 262, 266
Maulson, Tom, 217–18, 219, 221–22, 235–38, 335n79
McAdam, Sylvia, 13
McAllister Springs, 203
McCloud, Janet, 40
McGhee, Heather, 12
McNutt, Debra, 228, 234–38, 246–47, 248, 279
McRae, Clint, 172, 173–74
McRae, Wallace, 142–43, 144, 172, 173–74
Mdewakanton Dakota, 276
Means, Bill, 154–55, 157–58, 165, 276, 281, 282
Medicine Bull, Kenneth, 174
megaloads, 194
Menominee, 241, 243–44, 252–53, 259. *See also* Crandon mine, Nashville, and Mole Lake Ojibwe
Menominee Reservation, *242*, *277*
Menominee Warrior Society, 243–44
Merchant, Carolyn, 16
metallic sulfide mining. *See* mining conflicts, northern Wisconsin
Metcalf, Jack, 44, 56, 299n35
Metcalf, John, 299n35
Mexico, 12, 285
Michigan, 128, 258–59
Mickelson, George, 158
Midwest Treaty Network, 219, 241
Migizi Advocates for Turtle Island, 128–29
military projects and Ho-Chunk, Wisconsin: background, 116–17; Badger Army Ammunition Plant, Sauk Prairie, 124–27, *127*; environmental racism, environmental justice, and, 103–5; flight and bombing ranges, opposition to, 120–22; geographic "shell games" and, 104–5; Hardwood Range expansion proposal, 119–20, 315n115; Kickapoo Valley dam site, 123–24; lessons, 129–31; low-level flights proposal, 117–19; map, *118*; opposition divided by the military, 122; water alliances, 127–29;

whiteness and division of loyalties, 131–34

military projects and Western Shoshone, Nevada: background, 106–9; environmental racism, environmental justice, and, 103–5; geographic "shell games" and, 104–5; map, *108*; MX missile system plan, 109–10; testing ranges, 110–13; whiteness and division of loyalties, 131–34; white ranchers, relations with, 113–15

Milwaukee, 244, 245, 248

Mincey, James, 224

Miners for Safe Energy, 154

mining and shipment. *See* fossil fuel shipping and blocking

mining conflicts, Montana and South Dakota: gold mining at Little Rocky Mountains and Sweetgrass Hills, Montana, 146–50; gold mining near Yellowstone and "coal for gold" deal, 144–45, 149; map, *145*; Powder River Basin coal mines and Northern Cheyenne, Montana, 139–46; sacred lands, sharing, 166–69; uranium, Dewey Burdock site, Black Hills, 163–64

mining conflicts, northern Wisconsin (Ojibwe): Crandon mine, Nashville, and Mole Lake Ojibwe, *211*, 239–57, *242*; Ladysmith mine and Lac Courte Oreilles Ojibwe, 230–34; Lynne mine and Lac du Flambeau Ojibwe, 234–38; map, *211*; Ojibwe treaties, alliances, and metallic sulfide mining, northern Wisconsin, 228–30; Penokee Hills mine and Bad River Ojibwe, *211*, 257–67, *260*

Mining Impact Coalition, 245, 259

Mining Moratorium Law (WI), 263–64

Minneapolis, 20, 139, 152, 158, 262

Minnesota, 3, 150, 162, 192, 210, 276

"minority" status or label, 9, 103, 104

Minthorn, Antone, 81, 82

Mississippi River, 162, 243

Missoula, 194

Missouri River, 28, 164, 188–91, 188–92

Mitchell, Jeff, 92

Moapa Band, Paiute, 313n71

Moccasins on the Ground, 179

Modoc, 89

Moe, Don, 241

Moe, Kristin, 186

Mole Lake Sokaogon Chippewa Community, 210, *211*, 214–15, 221, 230, 240, *242*, 250. *See also* Crandon mine, Nashville, and Mole Lake Ojibwe

Mole Lake Tribal Council, 250–51

Montana. *See* fossil fuel shipping and blocking, Northern Plains; mining conflicts, Montana and South Dakota

Morgan, Lewis Henry, 16, 286

Morgensen, Scott L., 287

Morton, Rogers, 141

Mossett, Kandi, 188

Mother Earth Accord to Oppose Keystone XL, 178

Muck Creek Five trial, 39

Muckleshoot, *38*, 49

Muir, John, 247

Murdock, Bruce, 159

Murdock, Linda, 159

MX missile system, 109–10

Nakota, 138, 150, 179–80

Nashville, WI. *See* Crandon mine, Nashville, and Mole Lake Ojibwe

National Congress of American Indians, 57, 198

National Environmental Justice Advisory Council, 258

nationalism, 23, 284–85

National Native American Vietnam Veterans Memorial, 314n83

National Park Service, 107

"National Sacrifice Areas," 139, *140*, 147

National Wildlife Federation Tribal Lands Partnerships Project, 173

nationhood as preexisting, 21

Native Action, 143

Native Fish Society, 73

Native identities, construction of, 22–24

Native/non-Native alliances: common sense of place as condition, 275–78; common sense of purpose as condition, 278–81; common sense of understanding as condition, 281–83; complexities of, 25–31; conditions combined and applied, 283–84; historical roots of, 17; implications of, 9–15; lessons of, 287–90; levels of

Native/non-Native alliances (*continued*)
conflict and levels of cooperation, 268–
70, 274–75; particularism vs. univer-
salism and, 13, 284–86; place member-
ship strategy and, 96–97. *See also spe-
cific alliances and case studies*
"Native Renaissance," 23
Navajo, 26, 275
Nawtsamaat Alliance, 193–94
Nebraska, 27, 116, 172, 177–91
"negation of the negation," 23, 295n89
Nestlé, 344n1
Nevada. *See* military projects and Western
Shoshone, Nevada
Nevada Cattlemen's Association, 114
Nevada Desert Experience, 112, *112*
New Mexico, 26, 27, 105, 115
New Millennium Agreement (1999), 50
New Zealand, 9, 27
Nez Perce, *65*, 66, 68, 70, 79, 83–88, *86*
Nez Perce Tribal Council, 194
Nez Perce Wallowa Valley Homeland
Project, 86–88
Nicolet Minerals Company, 252, 254–55
Niiwin Tribes, 241, 245, 338n7
Nisqually, *38*, 38–39, 58–60, *59*, 94, 199, 203
Nisqually River, 40, *41*, 58–60
Nisqually River Council, 59–60, 61
Nisqually River watershed, 58–60, *59*, 97
Nisqually State Park (WA), 298n9
Non-Indian Negotiating Group, 299n36
Noranda, 234–38
North Central Idaho Jurisdictional Alli-
ance, 86
North Dakota. *See* fossil fuel shipping and
blocking, Northern Plains
Northern Cheyenne, 138, 139–46, 150, 198
Northern Cheyenne Landowners Associa-
tion, 141
Northern Cheyenne Tribal Council, 176
Northern Paiute, 76
Northern Plains Resource Council (NPRC),
141–45
Northwest Indian Fisheries Commission
(NWIFC), *38*, 42, 48–49, 53, 300n71
Northwest Plateau. *See* water wars, North-
west Plateau
Northwest Power Act (1980), 68
Northwest Power Planning Council, 68, 75

Northwest Renewable Resources Center,
46–48
Northwest Sportfishing Industry Association, 72
Northwood Niijii Enterprise Community,
252–53
Norton, Gale, 90
"not in my backyard" (NIMBY) approach,
104

Oaxaca, 285
Obama, Barack, 11–12, 177, 178, 184, 187
Oceti Sakowin (Seven Council Fires), 150,
188–89
Ogallala Aquifer, 177
Oglala Lakota, 151–52, 174–75
Oglala Sioux Civil Rights Organization
(OSCRO), 152
oil transport and terminals. *See* fossil fuel
shipping and blocking
Ojibwe. *See* Crandon mine, Nashville, and
Mole Lake Ojibwe; mining conflicts,
northern Wisconsin; Penokee Hills
mine and Bad River Ojibwe; spearfish-
ing and Ojibwe treaty rights conflicts,
northern Wisconsin
Ojibwe Eighth Fire prophecy, 31
Oklahoma, 11, 17, 19, 83, 152, 178, 181
Olah, Laura, 126
Olympia, 40, 58, 203
Omaha, 181
Oneida, 302n117, 338n7
One Nation United, 11
Ontario, 27
Operation Northern Lights, 214
Oregon. *See* water wars, Northwest Plateau
Orrick, William, 45
Otter Creek, *289*
Otter Creek Valley and coal mine, 172–77
"outsider" label and status, 226–28, 265,
270–72
Owe Aku / Bring Back the Way, 164, 179

Pacific Coast Federation of Fishermen's
Associations, 70, 90
Pacific Northwest. *See* fish wars, western
Washington; fossil fuel shipping and
blocking, Pacific Northwest
Pacific Salmon Commission, 300n71

Pacific Salmon Treaty (1985), 300n71

Paiute, Northern, 76

Palestine, 62, 96, 169, 311n181

Palm, Sandra, 197

Palumbo, David Liu, 12

Parker, Carolyn, 235, 236, 237, 282

Parker, Steve, 75, 77–78

particularism: nationalism and, 23, 284–85; universalism and, 10–15, 238, 284–86

Patawa, Elwood "Woody," 80, 81

Pavel, Joseph, 49, 55, 61

Pavletich, Jerry, 48

Pawnee, 179, 181

payment in lieu of taxes (PILT), 85, 86

Peaceful Skies Coalition, 115

peacemaking, 96

Pegasus Gold Corp., 147

Peltier, Leonard, 153

Pember, Mary Annette, 186

Pendleton Round-Up, 78–79

Penokee Hills Education Project, 262–63

Penokee Hills mine and Bad River Ojibwe: background, 257–59; eruption of conflict, 259–61; fast-tracked mine proposal, 263–64; future prospects, 266–67; Harvest Educational Learning Project Camp, 264–66; levels of conflict and levels of cooperation, 268–70; maps, 211, 260; outsiders, insiders, and blurring or reconfiguring of boundaries, 270–72; potlucks and fish fries, organizing via, 261–63

Penokee Range Alliance, 259

Perrier, 127–28

Peterson, Larry, 212, 217

Pickerel Lake, 239

Pine Ridge Reservation, 151, 151–53, 160–63, 177, 179

Pinkham, Allen, 74, 86

Pinkham, Jaime, 85

pipelines: Crandon mine, 241–43; Dakota Access Pipeline, 29, 188–92; Keystone XL oil pipeline, 14, 177–87

Pitts, Richard, 249

place membership strategy, 96–97

Point Elliot Treaty (1855), 196

Poler, Sylvester, 251, 253

policies, federal, 18–22, 90. See also specific departments and agencies

political adversaries, common, 279–80

political equalization, 282–83

Ponca, 177–78, 181

Ponca Trail of Tears, 178

Ponca Trail of Tears Spiritual Camp, 181

populism, 5, 12, 25, 28, 115, 213, 229, 247

Portland (OR), 72, 81, 85

Potawatomi, 241, 252, 254. See also Crandon mine, Nashville, and Mole Lake Ojibwe

Potorti, Grace, 111, 112–13

Potter, Aileen, 266

Powder River Basin coal mines, 139–46, 171, 194

Powertech Uranium Corporation, 163

powwows, 24, 79, 86–87, 87, 256

Prairie Island Reservation, 276

Protect Americans' Rights and Resources (PARR), 212–17, 219, 221, 224, 225–26, 229

Protect Our Wolf River (POWR), 245

Protect the Earth Gatherings (WI), 230, 232

Puerto Rico, 133

Puget Sound, 37, 39, 51, 53–54, 58, 67

Puget Sound Anglers, 57

Puget Sound Gillnetters Association, 43, 53

Puget Sound War (1855–56), 38

Puyallup, 38, 38–39, 40–41, 49, 331n191

Puyallup River, 40–41

Puyallup Trilogy decisions, 298n17

Quebec, 27, 199

Quinault, 28, 38, 43, 46, 49–50, 58, 199–202

racial constructions: "cowboys and Indians" stereotype, 9–10; division of loyalties and, 133–34; "minorities," 9, 103, 104; whiteness, 24–25, 132

racism: breaking down the gap, 251; "carrot-and-stick" strategy and, 150, 165–66; disconnection and, 182; Ojibwe spearfishing conflicts and, 215–16, 216, 219, 224; resources used to disguise, 53; team names and mascots, 327n114; territorial boundaries and racialized space, 227

railroads: Burlington Northern Santa Fe
(BNSF), 172–73; Dakota, Minnesota,
and Eastern (DM&E), 162–63; Tongue
River Railroad, 144–46, 172–77; Wis-
consin Central Limited, 258
Rapid City, 157, 163
Rapid River, 84
Rasmussen, Pete, 260
Raven, Allie, 261–62
Reagan, Ronald, 110
Reclamation Act (1902), 79
Red Cliff Reservation, 210, *211*, 215, 267
Red Cloud (Mahpiya Luta), 150
Red Power movement, 20
Reed, Cindy, 158–59
"Reject and Protect" gathering, 184–87, *185*
Republican Party and Northwest fish wars,
44, 56–57, 77, 79–80
reverse racism discourses, 25
RGGS Land and Minerals, 259
"rich Indian" stereotype, 21, 295n73
Rio Algom, 249, 252, 253
Rio Tinto, 258
A River Between Us (film), 92–93
Robinson, Bill, 48–50, 55, 300n62
Robinson, Steve, 49, 51–52
Rock, George, 246, 250, 277
Roediger, David R., 25
Rongstad, Bobbi, 261, 266–67
Rose, Joe, Sr., 257–58, 262, 264–67
Rose, Joe Dan, 258
Rosebud Creek, 141–44
Rosebud Protective Association, 141
Rosebud Reservation, 151, *151*, 161–62, 177
Rosebud Sioux Tribe Spirit Camp, *14*, 187
Rosebud Valley, 174–75
Ross, Gyasi, 13
Rosse, Bill, 111
Rousseau, Jean Jacques, 16
Rural Alliance for Military Accountability,
111
Rusk County Citizens' Action Group, 231
Russo, Pete, 265, 266

Sacred Earth Coalition, 72
sacred lands and places: sharing, 166–69;
spiritual connection to land lived on,
183; Sweetgrass Hills, 147–49; wind
turbines and, 183–84. *See also* Black

Hills and Lakota, South Dakota; burial
grounds; sense of place
Safe Energy Leadership Alliance, 195
Salisbury, Ray, 111
Salish, 17, 138, 147, 193
Salish Sea, 35, 37, 56, 97, 193–98, 273, 276,
288, 297n1
salmon. *See* fish wars, western Washing-
ton; water wars, Northwest Plateau
Salmon Corps, 76, 88
Salmon for All, 70
salmon species, 298n4
Sampson, Donald, 70, 71, 73
Sanchez, Virginia, 112
Sanders, Bernie, 12
Sand Hills, 177, 178
Sandpiper pipeline, 192
Santos, Susana, 72
Satiacum, Robert, 40
Satiacum, Robert, Jr., 187
Sauer, Brad, 176
Sauk Prairie, 124–27
"Save Our Seattle" initiative (1995), 54
Save Our Unique Lands (SOUL), 249
Save the Hills Alliance, 128, 129
Scari, Arlo, 148
Schmidtgall, Melvin "Bud," 82
Schmitz, Bob, 225, 241–43, 246, 248, 282
Schumacker, Joe, 199, 200
Schwarze, Deb, 122
Seamans, Paul, 177, 178–79, 182, 187
Search for Common Ground, 311n179
Sea Shepherd Conservation Society, 56
Seattle, 172, 194
self-determination: extension of concept
of, 20–21; federal policies, unintended
consequences of, 18; Red Power movement and, 20; reframing of, 22; state
citizenship vs., 15; unity vs., 12
sense of place: common, as condition of alliance, 275–78; common, developing,
30–31, 97; Native vs. non-Native, 168;
other conditions and, 283–84; topophilia, 167; Wolf River and, 245. *See
also* sacred lands and places
sense of purpose, common, 278–81, 283–84
sense of understanding, common, 281–84
settler colonialism, history of, 15–18
Sewall, Chris, 113

"Shared Waters, Shared Values" rally, 201, 202

Sharp, Fawn, 200, 201, 202, 204

Shelley, Chris, 76

"shell games," environmental, 104–5, 132, 188

Shell Oil Arctic drilling fleet, 194

Shepherd, Dennis, 254

Shielding the People project, 178

Shoshone. See military projects and Western Shoshone, Nevada

Sierra Club, 103, 154, 200

Simpson, Leanne, 13, 31

Sioux: divisions of, in North Dakota and Montana, 137–38, 150; Oceti Sakowin (Seven Council Fires), 150, 188–89; Sweetgrass Hills and, 147; University of North Dakota "Fighting Sioux," 327n114. See also Black Hills and Lakota, South Dakota

Sioux National Park, 158

Sitting Bull (Tatanka Yotanka), 175

Skagit, 49

Skagit River, 46

Skagit River Valley, 57, 203, 276

Skaleski, Joe, 248

Skokomish, 38, 54–55, 61

Skokomish Watershed Action Team, 55

Sleeter, Chuck, 239, 240–41, 249–52, 253, 256, 340n55

Slipcevic, Milan "Sipa," 197–98

Small, Gail, 142, 143–44, 149, 282

Smith, Claude, Sr., 77

Smith, Susan Lampert, 121, 124

Snake River, 68–69, 88. See also water wars, Northwest Plateau

Snyder, Diane, 85

Sohappy, David, Jr., 68

Sohappy v. Smith, 67

Sokaogon Ojibwe, 240, 254. See also Crandon mine, Nashville, and Mole Lake Ojibwe

Soles, Tom, 244

South Africa, 213, 227, 253, 284

South American indígenas, 27

South Dakota. See Black Hills and Lakota, South Dakota; fossil fuel shipping and blocking, Northern Plains; mining conflicts, Montana and South Dakota

Southern Paiute, 106

South Fork Reservation, 108, 114

sovereignty: concurrent, 27; as exercise thereof, 21, 258; geographic scale and, 95; internal divisions and, 25; Lakota, 150; "minority" status and, 9; movements against, 11, 20; Nez Perce, 86; nuclear waste and, 26; peoplehood and, 15; place membership strategy and, 97; quasi-sovereign status, 21; reframing of, 7; treaty-making and, 18; Trump and, 28; Umatilla memorandum of agreement, 80; universalism and, 13; Western Shoshone, 106

Soverel, Pete, 53

Spain, Glen, 70

spearfishing and Ojibwe treaty rights conflicts, northern Wisconsin: anti-treaty movement, 212–14; background, 209–12; boat landing protests, 214–18, 239, 335n79; decline of anti-treaty movement, 223–26; levels of conflict and levels of cooperation, 268–70; map, 211; mining and, 229; outsiders, insiders, and blurring or reconfiguring of boundaries, 270–72; "outsiders," "insiders," and geographies of exclusion or inclusion, 226–28; pro-treaty movement, 218–19; state role, 220–23

Spears, Patrick, 178–79

Spirit Hill, 240, 256

Spirit of the Salmon (Wy-Kan-Ush-Mi Wa-Kish-Wit) restoration plan, 74

Spotted Eagle, Faith, 179, 180, 182, 183–84, 187, 282

"spotted owl wars," 200

Sprague, Roger, 174

Standing Rock Sioux Reservation, 29, 151, 151, 153, 159, 188–92

state citizenship, 15

St. Croix Reservation, 210, 211, 215

Stearns, Tim, 49, 95

steelhead, 298n4

Steelhead-Salmon Protection Action for Washington Now (S/SPAWN), 47, 53–54

stereotypes: "cowboys and Indians," 9–10, 137; "ecological Indian" image, 23–24; mascots, 327n114; "rich Indian," 21, 295n73

Stevens, Isaac, 35, 37–39

Stockbridge-Munsee (Mohican) Community, 241

Stop Treaty Abuse (STA), 212–17, 219, 221, 224, 225–26, 229

Strawberry Island, 237, 337n160

Strong, Ted, 72, 74

Sturgis Motorcycle Rally, 164

Styczynski, Ted, 232

Sulfide Mining Moratorium Bill (WI), 247–49

Sundown, Jackson, 79

Sundstrom, Linea, 154

Suquamish, 38, 43, 49

Surface Transportation Board, U.S., 163, 173, 176

Sustainable Northwest, 85–86

Swanson, Bea, 232

Sweetgrass Hills, 147–49, 166–67, 275

Sweetgrass Hills Protective Association, 148–49

Swinomish, 38, 53, 57, 193, 202, 203

Swinomish Climate Change Initiative, 203

Swinth, Jim, 49

Tacoma, 40, 54

Tacopina (Sleeter), Joanne, 241, 249, 251

Tall, Joanne, 161

Tamkaliks Celebration, 86–87, 87

Tanderup, Art and Helen, 181

Tashunka Witko (Crazy Horse), 174

Tatanka Yotanka (Sitting Bull), 175

Tayac, Chief Billy Red Wing, 185

Taylor, Joseph E., 44

Te-Moak Band, 106

termination policy, 20, 57, 89, 243

Tesoro oil terminal plan, Vancouver, WA, 199

Texas, 188, 223

Thevik, Larry, 200, 201

Thieltges, Richard, 147–49

Thomas-Muller, Clayton, 186–87

Thompson, E. P., 16

Thompson, Randy, 178, 182

Thompson, Tommy, 212, 215, 221, 222, 231, 246, 249

Thoms, Dorothy, 219, 222

Three Fires Confederacy, 23

Thunder Hawk, Madonna, 156, 162

Tilsen, Mark, 155–56

Timber, Fish, and Wildlife (TFW) process, 46–47

timber industry, 46–47

Timbisha Band, 107

Tongue River Railroad, 144–46, 172–77

Tongue River Valley, 140, 145–46, 288

topophilia, 166

tourism: bison and ecotourism, 126; Black Hills and, 160, 166; casinos and, 253; Chief Joseph Days and, 84, 86; Crandon mine and, 244; Lac du Flambeau and, 233, 237; oil as risk to, 201; Ojibwe spearfishing conflict and, 212, 213, 217, 218, 224–25; Penokees mine, water quality, and, 257, 261; Umatilla and, 82; Warm Springs and, 76

TransCanada, 178, 182, 187

treaties: federal policy and, 18–19; Fort Laramie Treaties (1851 and 1868), 150, 151, 152, 156, 162, 179; in Pacific Northwest, 35–36, 37–39, 38; Point Elliot Treaty (1855), 196; Treaty of La Pointe (1854), 258; Treaty of Medicine Creek (1854), 37; Treaty of Neah Bay (1855), 56; Treaty of Ruby Valley (1863), 106; Treaty of Walla Walla (1855), 66

Treatment as State program: Bad River Ojibwe, 259; impact of, 270, 274; Mole Lake, 251, 255, 276; Northern Cheyenne, 143, 276

treaty rights conflicts and anti-treaty movement. See specific case studies

Tremmel, Germaine, 159

Tribal Canoe Journeys, 50

Tribal Lands Partnerships Project, National Wildlife Federation, 173

tribal legal powers, non-Indian exploitation of, 278–79

Tribble, Fred, 211–12

Tribble, Mike, 211–12

Trout Unlimited (TU), 48–49, 300n62

Trudell, John, 290

Trump, Donald, 28, 187, 192

Trust of Public Lands, 85

Tuan, Yi-Fu, 166, 271

Tucker, Craig, 92

Tulalip, 203

Tutu, Desmond, 213
Two Bulls, Krystal, 176–77
Two Bulls, Lynette, 146
Tygh, 64
Tyler Forks River, 260
Tyra, Dorothy, 240–41, 268, 282
Tyra, Ward, 240–41

Uintah-Ouray, 275
Ukraine, 62
Umatilla, 3, 65, 66, 68, 70, 78–84, 94, 194, 199
Umatilla Basin Project (UBP), 80–81
Umatilla River Basin, 78–83, 288
United Nations Convention on the Prevention and Punishment of the Crime of Genocide (1948), 295n75
United Property Owners of Washington, 47
United Sportspeople Alliance (USA), 216–17
United States v. Dann (1985), 114
United States v. Oregon (1969), 67
United States v. Washington (1974), 42, 45
universalism and particularism, 10–15, 238, 284–86
University of North Dakota mascot, 327n114
Urabeck, Frank, 48, 49
urban relocation policy, 20
usufructuary rights, 19, 37, 39, 210. See also treaties

Vancouver, WA, oil terminal plan, 199
Vanderpuy, Nick, 264
Van Zile, Frances, 208, 245, 247, 250, 251, 256, 272
Van Zile, Robert, 249–50, 262
Van Zile, Tina, 256
Vitek, Mark, 264–65
Vitek, Monica, 264
Voigt decision, 207, 212
Voigt Inter-Tribal Task Force, 212
Voli, Carlo, 194
Voyages of Rediscovery expeditions, 95

Walia, Harsha, 29
Walker, Scott, 128, 259, 263–64
Walker River Reservation, 108, 111

Walker Valley, 111
Walla Walla, 64, 76, 78
Wallowa Salmon Habitat Recovery Plan, 84–85
Wallowa Valley, 83–88, 275
Wandschneider, Rich, 88, 309n139
Wannapum, 64
Ward, Tom, 249, 251, 278–79
Warm Springs, 65, 66, 68, 71, 76–77, 194, 344n1
Wasco, 64, 76
Washington Dungeness Crab Fishermen's Association, 200
Washington State. See fish wars, western Washington; fossil fuel shipping and blocking, Pacific Northwest
Waswagoning traditional village, 237
Wa-Swa-Gon Treaty Association, 221–22, 223, 234–38
Waterkeepers of Wisconsin, 127
watershed councils, 58–61
water wars, Northwest Plateau: background, 64–66; dam breaching movement, 68–69; farmers and ranchers, tribal relations with, 74–76; fishing groups, tribal relations with, 69–74; hydroelectric dams, 66–68; Klamath River Basin, 88–94; map, 65; Nez Perce and Wallowa Valley, 83–88; peacemaking and place membership, 94–97; Umatilla fisheries restoration, 78–83; Warm Springs Reservation, 76–77; Yakima River Basin, 77–78
WaterWatch, 81
Watson, Lilla, 30
Waukau, Hilary "Sparky," 241, 246, 276
Wazijaci (Dwellers among the Pines), 116
Western Shoshone. See military projects and Western Shoshone, Nevada
Western Shoshone Defense Project, 113
Western Shoshone National Council, 106, 110, 111
Western Shoshone Sacred Lands Association, 109, 110
western Washington. See fish wars, western Washington; fossil fuel shipping and blocking, Pacific Northwest
Whalen, Bill, 265
whaling, 56, 103

Whatcom Commercial Fishermen's Association, 197
White Face, Charmaine, 162, 163, 165
Whitehorse, Harry, 314n83
Whiteman, Philip, Jr., 145–46
whiteness, construction of, 24–25, 132
White Pine copper mine, 258
White Plume, Debra, 163, 179
Whitman, Silas, 84–85
Wiggins, Mike, Jr., 208, 257, 260–61, 263, 265–67
Wilcox, Jim, 60
Wilcox Farms, 60
Wildhorse Creek, 82
Wilkinson, Charles, 42
Williams, Pat, 148
Williams, Ted, 47
Williquette, James, 221
Willman, Elaine, 57, 284, 302n117
Willow Flowage, 235–36
Wilson, Dana, 197
Wilson, Richard, 152
wind turbines, 183–84
Winnebago. See military projects and Ho-Chunk, Wisconsin
Winnebago Reservation, 116
Winters Doctrine, 79, 93
Wisconsin. See fishing conflicts, northern Wisconsin (Menominee); military projects and Ho-Chunk, Wisconsin; mining conflicts, northern Wisconsin; spearfishing and Ojibwe treaty rights conflicts, northern Wisconsin
Wisconsin Air National Guard, 117–20, 122, 133, 315n115
Wisconsin Conservation Congress, 230, 266
Wisconsin Department of Natural Resources (DNR): Badger munitions plant and, 125–26; as common adversary, 279; Hardwood weapons range and, 119; mining and, 229, 231, 232, 244, 263; Ojibwe spearfishing and, 211–12, 220–23

Wisconsin Equal Rights Council, 219
Wisconsin Manufacturers and Commerce (WMC), 221, 229
Wisconsin National Guard, 214, 335n79
Wisconsin Resources Protection Council, 229, 236, 246, 248–51
Wise, Jim, 235
Wise, Pam, 235
Witness for Nonviolence (Witnesses), 218–19, 223, 224
Wolfe, Patrick, 21
Wolf River, 207, 239–56, 241, 269, 272, 276, 277. See also Crandon mine, Nashville, and Mole Lake Ojibwe
Wolf River Watershed Alliance, 225
Wolf Watershed Educational Project, 241, 245–47, 254, 256, 280. See also Crandon mine, Nashville, and Mole Lake Ojibwe
Wortman, Pat, 84–85
Wounded Knee massacre (1890), 151
Wounded Knee siege (1973), 152–53, 165
Wreczycki, Sonny, 251, 278, 280
Wy-Kan-Ush-Mi Wa-Kish-Wit (Spirit of the Salmon) restoration plan, 74
Wyoming, 110, 139, 144, 162, 170, 194

Xwe'chi'eXen village, 195

Yakama, 56–57, 65, 66, 68, 71, 77–78, 199
Yakima Basin Integrated Plan, 78
Yakima River, 46
Yakima River Basin, 77–78
Yankton Sioux Reservation, 177, 179–80
Yellowbank, James, 219, 220
Yellow Bird, 145
Yellow Thunder, Dennis, 163
Yellow Thunder Camp, 158
Young, James, 40
Yowell, Raymond, 109, 110, 112, 113–14
Yurok, 65, 89

Zapatistas, 12, 185
Zortman-Landusky mine, 146–47, 148

© Shauna Bittle

ABOUT THE AUTHOR

ZOLTÁN GROSSMAN is professor of geography and Native studies at the Evergreen State College. He is a longtime community organizer and coeditor of *Asserting Native Resilience: Pacific Rim Indigenous Nations Face the Climate Crisis*. Learn more about *Unlikely Alliances* at https://sites.evergreen.edu /unlikelyalliances/.

Indigenous
Confluences

Charlotte Coté and Coll Thrush
Series Editors

Indigenous Confluences publishes innovative works that use decolonizing perspectives and transnational approaches to explore the experiences of Indigenous peoples across North America, with a special emphasis on the Pacific Coast.

A Chemehuevi Song: The Resilience of a Southern Paiute Tribe
by Clifford E. Trafzer

Education at the Edge of Empire: Negotiating Pueblo Identity in New Mexico's Indian Boarding Schools
by John R. Gram

Indian Blood: HIV and Colonial Trauma in San Francisco's Two-Spirit Community
by Andrew J. Jolivette

Native Students at Work: American Indian Labor and Sherman Institute's Outing Program, 1900–1945
by Kevin Whalen

California through Native Eyes: Reclaiming History
by William J. Bauer Jr.

Unlikely Alliances: Native Nations and White Communities Join to Defend Rural Lands
by Zoltán Grossman

Dismembered: Native Disenrollment and the Battle for Human Rights
by David E. Wilkins and Shelly Hulse Wilkins

Network Sovereignty: Building the Internet across Indian Country,
by Marisa Elena Duarte